Psychotherapy

Approaches and Applications

Psychotherapy
Approaches and Applications

Edward Lichtenstein
University of Oregon

Brooks/Cole Publishing Company
Monterey, California
A Division of Wadsworth, Inc.

Consulting Editor: *Edward L. Walker,*
University of Michigan

Printed in the United States of America

10 9 8 7 6 5 4 3 2 1

Library of Congress Cataloging in Publication Data

Lichtenstein, Edward.
    Psychotherapy, approaches and applications.

    Bibliography: p. 347
    Includes index.
    1. Psychotherapy.   I. Title.   [DNLM: 1. Psycho-
therapy.   WM420.3 L699p]
    RC480.L49   616.8'914   79-25036
    ISBN 0-8185-0381-5

Acquisition Editor: *Claire Verduin*
Manuscript Editor: *William Waller*
Production Editor: *Fiorella Ljunggren*
Interior and Cover Design: *Ruth Scott*
Technical Illustrations: *Etc. Graphics*
Typesetting: *Boyer & Brass, Inc., San Diego, California*

Preface

This book's aim is to provide an objective description and analysis of psychotherapy that will reduce the ignorance and confusion surrounding this important social enterprise. A guiding theme throughout the book is the necessity of considering the economic, social, and political factors that impinge on therapists and therapy settings, both community and institutional. Advanced undergraduates considering careers in the fields of mental health or human services and beginning graduate students in counseling or clinical psychology are my primary audiences. But the book is accessible to anyone interested in learning about psychotherapy, both as a social institution and as a helping profession.

The book is divided into four sections. The short first part defines psychotherapy, places it in historical perspective, and describes the participants—both therapists and clients. The second part puts forth a framework for construing and evaluating psychotherapy. The reader is provided with a useful schema for evaluating a broad array of treatments. The third and longest part is the most conventional. The three major approaches to psychotherapy—psychodynamic, humanistic, and behavioral—are described and evaluated using the criteria set forth in Part Two. I have tried to give an objective, sympathetic account of the three approaches while also offering my subjective opinions about their merits.

The final section describes regulatory processes established by government and by the professions, the organization of the delivery system, and how political and economic contingencies affect that system. This material is not usually found in texts on psychotherapy but is of critical importance, I believe, for both aspiring professionals and interested laypersons.

Much of the specific content of the book, especially Parts Two and Three, evolved from undergraduate and graduate courses I teach at the University of Oregon. I have periodically taught a graduate course in "nonbehavioral" psychotherapies, and this led me to read more widely and better organize my thinking concerning psychoanalytic, client-centered, and Gestalt approaches. I originated and taught an undergraduate course entitled Survey of Psychotherapeutic Methods. This course led me to develop a systematic presentation of the role of specific and common factors in therapy and of ways to evaluate the effectiveness of psychotherapeutic methods.

Because I have used material from this book at both the graduate and undergraduate levels, I believe it can be useful in both contexts. It could serve as a primary text in advanced undergraduate courses such as the one I have taught or as an adjunct text for more traditional courses in abnormal psychology, psychology of adjustment, or even personality. Students considering careers in the mental health field should find it useful as a way of learning about the different professions and how the mental health system operates as well as for the descriptions of the major psychotherapeutic methods. The book could also be used in beginning graduate courses in clinical or counseling psychology.

The evolution of my thinking about psychotherapy and human services is reflected in this book. Graduate training at the University of Michigan was an immersion in the psychoanalytic approach to psychotherapy. My focus then was almost exclusively on therapy as a dyadic interaction divorced from the social system, a view consistent with the psychoanalytic emphasis on the uniqueness and privacy of the therapeutic interaction.

My thesis advisor and teacher at Michigan, Edward S. Bordin, introduced me to the conceptual and empirical analysis of psychotherapy. I am indebted to him both for provoking my interest and for imparting a number of key ideas that I still find useful. Although I now think about psychotherapy from a rather different perspective, my respect for many of Bordin's ideas has remained intact over the years.

Since graduate school, I have moved to a behavioral, or social-learning orientation. This was not a dramatic or sudden paradigm shift, but one that unfolded over several years. The behavioral approach seemed more concrete and empirically based and suited my talents and temperament better than did a psychoanalytic frame. But I still find some psychoanalytic ideas compelling and useful. I also learned more about humanistic approaches, especially client-centered therapy. The research literature generated by Carl Rogers and his colleagues was especially compatible with my empirical bent.

I have been most influenced by the writings of Jerome D. Frank, especially the first edition of *Persuasion and Healing*, published in 1961. He was one of the first theorists to place psychotherapy in a sociocultural context and to emphasize the importance of the common features shared by seemingly diverse approaches. Although I have met Jerome Frank only once (and that fairly recently), his ideas have had a profound effect on my view of psychotherapy, and anyone conversant with Frank's writings will see his influence throughout this book, but especially in Chapter Three.

About ten years ago I became interested in the newly developing field of community psychology. The community perspective helped me appreciate that psychotherapy is but one of a number of possible solutions to human misery and deepened my respect for the effects of social settings and social contingencies on both clients and therapists. It is this realization that led to the emphasis on economic and political factors described in the last section of the book.

I am indebted to so many colleagues and students that it is not possible to name them all. My intellectual indebtedness to Bordin and Frank has already been noted. My colleagues and students at the UCLA Center for the Health Sciences, Southern Illinois University, and, especially, the University of Oregon have been invaluable in two major ways. They have taught me much about various psychotherapeutic principles and methods, and they have provided invaluable feedback about my efforts to teach this subject matter in both lecture and written form. The editorial staff at Brooks/Cole and their psychology consultant, Ed Walker, provided much useful reaction and encouragement. I found especially useful the detailed, occasionally biting, but consistently constructive criticism from the reviewers that Brooks/Cole consulted: Hal S. Arkowitz of the University of Arizona, Robert C. Carson of Duke University, Constance T. Fischer of Duquesne University, Donald J. Kiesler of Virginia Commonwealth University, David G. Martin of the University of Manitoba, Frank C. Noble of Arizona State University, and Ronald J. Prinz of the University of South Carolina. Jane Ganter-Neary cheerfully deciphered my handwriting, decoded my dictation, and corrected ungrammatical and sexist language, and Emeline Dale helped to obtain the numerous permissions that were needed.

Edward Lichtenstein

Contents

Part I: The Psychotherapeutic Endeavor and Its Participants   1

Chapter One: Introduction   3
Scope and Limitations of This Book, 4   A Working Definition of
Psychotherapy, 5   Historical Trends, 5   Summary, 10
Suggested Readings, 10

Chapter Two: Psychotherapists and Clients   11
Psychotherapists, 11   The Clients, 28   Compatibility of
Givers and Receivers, 34   Summary, 35   Suggested
Readings, 37

Part II: A Framework for Construing and Evaluating Psychotherapy   39

Chapter Three: Common Processes in Psychotherapy   40
Surface Diversity, 40   Four Kinds of Psychotherapy, 42
The Distinction between Specific and Common Processes, 52
Placebos and Common Processes, 56   Summary, 61
Suggested Readings, 61

Chapter Four: Evaluating Psychotherapeutic Methods   63
Three Evaluative Dimensions, 64   Evaluating Psychotherapeutic

Outcome, 67   Implications for Evaluating Professional and
Popular Literature, 89   Epilogue, 93   Summary, 95
Suggested Readings, 97

Part III: Theory and Clinical Application: Three Approaches to Psychotherapy   99

Chapter Five: Psychoanalytic Psychotherapy   101

Introduction: Assumptions and Distinctions, 101   Theory and
Technique: Basic Concepts, 104   An Illustrative Therapy
Case, 116   Therapy Research: Two Examples, 122
Evaluation of Psychoanalytic Therapy, 129   Summary, 132
Suggested Readings, Films, and Tapes, 134

Chapter Six: Humanistic Psychotherapy   136

Client-Centered Therapy, 138   Gestalt Psychotherapy, 160
Summary, 173   Suggested Readings, Films, and Tapes, 176

Chapter Seven: Behavior Therapy   177

Introduction: Assumptions and Definitions, 177   Treatment
Strategies, 187   An Illustrative Therapy Case, 216
Evaluation of Behavior Therapy, 220   Epilogue: The Three
Approaches Compared and Contrasted, 223   Summary, 231
Suggested Readings and Films, 233

Part IV: Reality: Social, Economic, and Political Influences on Psychotherapy   235

Chapter Eight: Organization and Economics of the Delivery System   237

Community Psychotherapy, 238   Institutional Treatment, 246
Coordination of Institutional and Community Care, 260
Third-Party Payment, 265   Summary, 267
Suggested Readings, 269

Chapter Nine: The Regulation of Psychotherapy   271

Government Regulation of Institutional Treatment, 272
Government Regulation of Community Psychotherapy, 280
Professional Regulation, 285   Consumerism and the Regulation
of Psychotherapy, 296   Choosing a Psychotherapist, 301
Summary, 304   Suggested Readings, 306

**Chapter Ten: The Future of Psychotherapy:
Problems and Prospects   307**

A Boom for Whom? 307   Federal Policy and the Future of
Psychotherapy, 310   Increasing the Supply of Psychotherapy, 316
Reducing Demand: Prevention, 319   Suggestions for
Citizen Inquiry and Involvement, 324   Summary, 327
Suggested Readings, 328

Appendix: Selected Therapeutic Methods   329

Treating Larger Social Systems: Couples, Families, and Groups, 330
Psychoanalytic Therapies, 334   Humanistic Therapies, 339
Directive Therapies, 344

References   347
Name Index   361
Subject Index   365

PART I

The Psychotherapeutic Endeavor and Its Participants

This book is divided into four parts. Part One consists of two chapters. First, a short chapter introduces the reader to the rationale of the book, offers a definition of psychotherapy, and provides an overview of current trends in the light of the historical evolution of the field.

The second chapter considers psychotherapists and their clients. The various paths to becoming a psychotherapist are outlined, and the functions and characteristics of the different psychotherapeutic professions are described. In parallel fashion, the characteristics of clients and some of the paths to becoming a client are described.

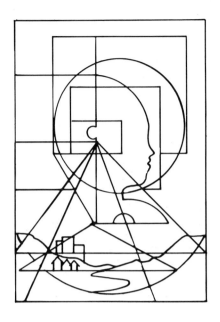

ONE

Introduction

Psychotherapy is a major social enterprise affecting hundreds of thousands of people and consuming millions of dollars in fees and taxes. Yet there is great popular ignorance and confusion about the enterprise and widespread and often vehement disagreement among its practitioners. This book attempts to provide the reader with a reasonably objective description of psychotherapy that will reduce the level of ignorance and confusion. Differences among practitioners will be described and clarified, but reconciliation of the various approaches is beyond the scope of this book and our current state of knowledge.

An understanding of psychotherapy requires a description of *who* the participants are and how they come together, *what* activities the participants engage in, and the settings *where* psychotherapy takes place and the financing of these settings. The characteristics and backgrounds of the participants—clients and therapists—are the focus of Part One.

It is the *what* of psychotherapy that has been given primary attention in texts and scholarly writings, most of which advocate particular theories and techniques. This is an important aspect of the enterprise, and the chapters in Part Three present a description and evaluation of three major approaches—psychoanalytic, humanistic, and behavioral. Today there are also a striking number of other psychotherapeutic and quasi-psychotherapeutic methods competing for our attention and our dollars. The professional and popular literature proclaims the virtues of such diverse methods as primal therapy, body massage, encounter groups, and Zen meditation, not to mention the more traditional therapies and their subvarieties. Part Two offers a framework with which to sort out these many varieties, understand some of the important common processes they share, and evaluate their effectiveness.

But an exclusive emphasis on theory, technique, and method yields a very distorted picture to both professional and layperson. For example, the public erroneously tends to view psychotherapy as typically involving a long series of interviews in which unconscious conflicts are thrashed out or problems of intimacy or existential despair are slowly resolved. Professionals, especially those engaged in research and teaching, tend to ignore the political and economic realities that impinge on psychotherapy. The social realities of the delivery system and the role of government—the *where* of psychotherapy—are the subject of Part Four of this volume.

Scope and Limitations of This Book

Psychotherapy has been the subject of such a tremendous amount of writing that a single volume cannot claim comprehensive coverage. This book is concerned with therapy and counseling carried out by private practitioners and agency personnel in mental health clinics and with treatment in federal, state, and private mental hospitals. The distinction between counseling and psychotherapy is not a clear one, and much of what is said here applies to both. For convenience and brevity, I will primarily use the single term *psychotherapy* rather than *counseling and psychotherapy*. Some of the key differences between clinical and counseling psychologists are described in Chapter Two. The focus is on individual psychotherapy; the special properties of group methods are touched on lightly.

Of those involved in the three major psychotherapeutic professions—psychiatry, psychiatric social work, and clinical or counseling psychology—psychologists are neither the most numerous nor the most influential. Yet because of my training and identity as a clinical psychologist, I will draw most heavily on the writings of psychologists.

The choice of the three theoretical approaches to be considered was based on two major considerations. The three are the most widely practiced and influential approaches on the contemporary scene, and I believe that understanding them well will give the reader an uncluttered overview of the field. This limited selection naturally results in the omission of many therapies, especially those invented by and associated with particular psychotherapists. It is hoped that the principles and framework developed here will permit interested readers to pursue these other therapies with enhanced understanding.

Another important omission is the contribution of chemotherapy. This should not be construed as slighting the importance of drugs in the treatment of behavioral and emotional dysfunction.

A Working Definition of Psychotherapy

Given the numerous and varied theories and techniques it is not surprising that professionals have difficulty in agreeing on a precise definition of psychotherapy. This difficulty is nicely illustrated by the partly tongue-in-cheek definition of psychotherapy as "an unidentified technique applied to unspecified problems with unpredictable outcomes." Such definitional difficulties are not unique to psychotherapy. For example, how would you define "education"? You might despair of reaching consensus on a formal definition and instead point to what goes on in the schools. Similarly, you can think of psychotherapy as consisting of what psychotherapists do. Fortunately, Jerome Frank, utilizing a sociocultural perspective, has offered a definition that is both comprehensive and useful. Frank viewed all psychotherapies as comprising three essential features:

1. A trained, socially sanctioned healer, whose healing powers are accepted by the sufferer and his social group or an important segment of it.
2. A sufferer who seeks relief from the healer.
3. A circumscribed, more or less structured series of contacts between the healer and the sufferer, through which the healer, often with the aid of a group, tries to produce certain changes in the sufferer's emotional state, attitudes, and behavior. . . . Although physical and chemical adjuncts may be used, the healing influence is primarily exercised by words, acts, and rituals in which sufferer, healer, and—if there is one—group participate jointly [Frank, 1973, pp. 2–3].

As we will see in Part Two, these common features of the psychotherapeutic situation have profound implications for understanding the enterprise and the changes it produces. The emphasis on the social aspect of therapy points up the importance of the social, political, and economic factors taken up in Part Four.

Historical Trends

Behavioral and emotional problems are as old as civilization itself, and so are methods to deal with disturbed or disturbing individuals. Treatment methods are heavily determined by the shared beliefs a society has about the nature and causes of disturbance. It follows, then, that treatment methods will differ at different periods in history and in different societies.

As Frank (1973) has noted, current practices evolved from "two historical traditions of healing—the religio-magical and the naturalistic, or scientific" (p. 3). If it is believed that disturbed behavior or suffering is caused by supernatural powers or evil spirits residing within the person, then treatment responsibilities are assigned to priests or shamans and involve rituals and magic. Frank argued persuasively that the religiomagical tradition remains influential and that many of its principles have been incorporated into naturalistic forms of therapy.

If suffering and disturbance are viewed as natural phenomena, treatment is vested with physicians or similarly sanctioned healers. The form of the naturalistic intervention will depend on the particular theory of natural causation held by a given society. Until the late 19th century, naturalistic explanations heavily emphasized organic causes of disturbance. Correspondingly, treatment was the province of physicians and involved physical or medical procedures.

Sigmund Freud pioneered the development of a psychological yet naturalistic explanation of disturbance. He concomitantly originated a purely psychological treatment method, which relied exclusively on words and the doctor/patient relationship. Even before Freud, humane and largely interpersonal treatment of the hospitalized "insane" had been successfully employed in both Europe and the United States (Bockoven, 1972). And, of course, distressed persons throughout history have often benefited from conversations with sympathetic others, be they clergy, physicians, witchdoctors, innkeepers, or friends.

Nevertheless, psychotherapy and counseling as generally recognized methods of treatment and as distinct professions are 20th-century phenomena. Two of the three major psychotherapeutic professions—psychiatric social work and clinical or counseling psychology—were born in the 20th century. (Psychiatry, the third profession, has a much longer history.) The application of psychotherapy to a wide array of maladaptive behaviors—rather than an exclusive concern with the seriously and blatantly disturbed—is also a recent phenomenon. So is the use of psychotherapeutic methods to enhance growth rather than just relieving distress.

The growth and change in psychotherapy as a social institution can be appreciated by viewing developments from before World War II to the present. There have been dramatic changes in *givers, receivers, settings*, and *methods*. The major trends are briefly described in this section; several of these will be elaborated on in later sections of this book.

An oversimplified description of pre–World War II psychotherapy, outpatient variety, would have a medically trained psychiatrist giving long-term, psychoanalytically oriented treatment to an upper-middle-class White female. Psychiatry was clearly the dominant psychotherapeutic profession. Clinical and counseling psychologists were few in number and were clustered in academic settings. And psychiatric social workers tended to participate in therapy in peripheral ways. Psychotherapeutic treatment was available to the very severely disturbed in state hospitals or to those less disturbed and affluent individuals who could afford private care, either in the community or in a private institution.

Changing Givers

There has been considerable *horizontal* and *vertical* expansion in the "giving" of psychotherapy. Horizontal expansion refers to the spread of other professions—clinical and counseling psychology, psychiatric social work—into the field of therapy and the legal and medical recognition of their roles and competencies. Psychiatric social workers have increased greatly in number and in their range of responsibilities. Their traditional function was to provide expertise about the availability of community resources and the contribution of the environment to the client's difficulties. For example, the social worker would interview the designated client's family, perhaps visit the home to "size up" his or her living situation, and feed this information to the psychiatrist, who acted as the primary psychotherapist. Although this role is still often performed in hospital settings, in community settings the psychiatric social worker now frequently carries primary treatment responsibility for clients—individuals, families, and groups—in a way parallel to that of a psychiatrist or psychologist.

The traditional role of the psychologist was that of diagnostician/tester. Using objective and projective measures of intelligence, abilities, and personality, the psychologist would provide comprehensive evaluations to aid the psychiatrist in diagnosing the client's difficulties and formulating a treatment plan. The testing procedure might be repeated at the end of treatment to help evaluate the progress of the client. Now psychologists assume primary responsibility for treatment in most settings and—if they have the necessary training and experience—can be legally certified or licensed for independent private practice in most states. Psychologists and social workers constitute the great majority of the psychotherapists in most public, community settings.

Two qualifications must be added to this brief description of horizontal dispersion. First, the primary responsibility of medically trained persons—physicians and psychiatrists—in many settings must be clearly recognized. There are certain situations—involving medication or involuntary hospitalization, for example—in which medical judgment is legally required. And in hospital settings the medically trained person invariably holds final responsibility for patient care, although a nonmedical person may carry out the treatment program. Second, there is sometimes friction among the primary professions. Boundaries of role and responsibility are quite variable from setting to setting and are also subject to change over time.

Vertical dispersion of therapeutic responsibility refers to the increasing involvement of nonprofessional therapists. The three primary professions—psychiatry, psychology, and social work—require from two to seven years of postgraduate training. The academic, personal, and financial demands of such training programs, as well as the limited number of training places, necessarily restrict the number of professionals in the work force. The perceived need for more therapists—especially to work with the relatively poor less-educated clients—led to experimentation with nonprofessionals. They have been found to be quite satisfactory in many settings with many kinds of clients. The uses, advantages, and limitations of non-professional therapists are being actively debated by both professionals and administrators. There now seems to be no shortage of professionally trained psychotherapists, and other justifications for using nonprofessionals—for example, their willingness to work in rural areas—must be found.

Changing Receivers

There has been a great increase in the number and range of people reached by psychotherapy. Mental health services have followed trends in general medicine toward better reaching the poor and the disadvantaged. Although there are still significant social-class, ethnic, and geographical biases in the distribution of psycho-therapeutic services, these have diminished. There has been a shift away from allocating resources to intensive treatment for the few toward provision of briefer services for the many. "In keeping with the *zeitgeist*, a little, but significant change for a lot of people is seen as preferable to protracted efforts to produce large-scale changes in a few members of the upper social classes" (Bergin & Strupp, 1972, pp. 12–13). As we will see, this greater inclusiveness has presented some difficult problems both for conventional theories of psychotherapy and for the delivery system.

Changing Settings

Concomitant with the trends just mentioned have been shifts in where services are delivered. Two major trends will be noted here and discussed at greater length in Chapter Eight. The most striking shift in setting has been away from the large state hospital toward smaller community settings. Because of the powerful utility of drug therapy, as well as changes in public policy, the hospital populations have been decreasing markedly. With the aid of chemotherapy and improved community services and support, it has been possible to maintain in the community clients who previously required continuing hospitalization.

A second and more recent shift has been toward taking community psychotherapy to the clients rather than expecting clients to travel to centrally located clinics. This trend is closely related to the previously noted efforts to provide psychotherapeutic services to formerly unserved client groups. Urban storefront clinics and mobile mental health teams visiting rural communities are but two examples.

Changing Methods

The changes in givers, receivers, and settings are less dramatic and therefore less visible than changes in theory and technique. Psychoanalytic ideas were accorded an initially favorable reception in the United States and later received much impetus from European scholars and clinicians who immigrated in the 1930s to escape the Nazi movement. Psychoanalytic theory provided the first coherent, comprehensive psychological (that is, nonbiological) framework with which to view maladaptive behavior and its treatment. It is not surprising that, from the late 1930s onward, it came to be the dominant theoretical perspective in psychiatry—and psychiatry, as has been noted, was the dominant psychotherapeutic profession. Theoretical and procedural disputes centered on competing psychoanalytic schools (see Munroe, 1955).

Today, variations among psychoanalytic schools seem trivial compared with the variety and breadth of alternatives to psychoanalysis. There are numerous behavior therapies, several varieties of existential therapy, Gestalt therapy, primal therapy, transactional analysis, and body therapies, to name but a few. Some of these owe much to psychoanalytic thinking; many represent a radical departure.

The public is assailed by claims that the various new therapies produce profound changes in their clients. Testimonials from client participants abound. In one sense the remarkable variety of offerings with their claims of success is very much in the American free enterprise tradition and seems to offer the potential consumer considerable freedom of choice. But because of reality considerations, much of this choice—especially for the less-affluent and less-well-educated client—is illusory. A given community may have only one (or no) tax-supported clinic. And for those able to afford the luxury of choice, on what grounds can they choose? Is the most widely known product the best? Can one choose on the basis of evidence? Cost? What therapies are essentially the same, and which ones are truly different? And what about the choice of therapist, which is perhaps just as important as or more important than the mode of therapy? Are therapists with the most formal education the best? These are hard questions for both the professional and the potential consumer.

There are also hard questions for the taxpayer and for those in policy-making positions. What kinds of psychotherapeutic services should tax dollars support? What sort of accountability is appropriate? To what extent—if at all—should government attempt to regulate psychotherapy in the public or private sectors? There are no

pat or easy answers to these questions, but I believe that a more
informed citizenry is likely to find better solutions.

Summary

Psychotherapy has three essential features: (1) a trained, socially sanctioned healer, (2) a sufferer seeking relief, and (3) a structured series of contacts between healer and sufferer. It has evolved
from two historical healing traditions, religiomagical and naturalistic, and both exert an influence on current practice. Psychotherapy
and counseling as distinct professions are, however, 20th-century
phenomena. Three professional groups now play key roles as psychotherapists—psychiatrists, psychologists, and social workers—
but paraprofessionals are coming to play an increasingly important
role as care providers. There has been a decrease in emphasis on
institutional care and a shift toward making psychotherapy available
to more people.

Although psychoanalytic ideas remain quite influential in guiding therapeutic practice, numerous alternative approaches have been
developed and are being actively disseminated. The many different
kinds of psychotherapy, together with a greatly expanded delivery
system, make it difficult to choose among therapies or therapists.

Suggested Readings

1. Frank, J. D. *Persuasion and healing* (Rev. ed.). Baltimore: Johns
   Hopkins University Press, 1973. A readable and lucid account of
   psychotherapy, emphasizing the importance of the sociocultural
   context.
2. Gross, M. L. *The psychological society*. New York: Random House,
   1978. A critical analysis of psychotherapy by a journalist writing
   for the lay audience. Gross is sometimes savage and excessive but
   also frequently perceptive.

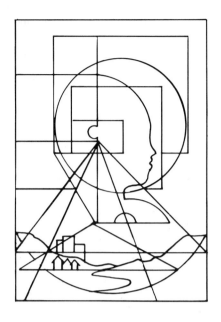

TWO

Psychotherapists and Clients

The first part of this chapter considers the training, characteristics, roles, and competencies of the three professions that dominate the psychotherapeutic scene: psychiatry, psychology, and psychiatric social work. Psychoanalysis, although not a profession in the sense of the other three, is here treated as such because of its great impact on training and practice in psychotherapy (Henry, Sims, & Spray, 1971). The emerging role of paraprofessional therapists is also discussed.

The second section reviews the characteristics of clients and considers why some people with "problems" enter psychotherapy and many do not. A concluding discussion compares the major characteristics of clients and therapists and considers the implications for psychotherapy of the fit between the two sets of participants.

Psychotherapists

There is no single, separate profession labeled "psychotherapy" in our society, although it has been suggested that one be established (Henry et al., 1971). Rather, psychotherapy is an activity or function performed by members of several helping professions.

Psychiatry

Psychiatry has always been the most influential profession in psychotherapy. Historically, mental illness came to be viewed as a natural phenomenon analogous to physical illness and thus came under the aegis of medicine, which was then the only healing profession. Religious healing was a primary contender for clients, but its appeal diminished with the development of rational, naturalistic views of mental illness. Both tradition and the political and legal structure of our institutions continue to invest the physician with primary responsibility for patient care. And the unique characteristic of psychiatric psychotherapists is that they are physicians.

Medical Training

A psychiatrist is a physician who has gone on to specialize in exactly the same way as the internist, obstetrician, or surgeon. With the exception of a few electives in the last two years, medical school is the same for all students irrespective of their plans for specialization. The psychiatrist-to-be, therefore, studies a great deal of basic science and general medicine. The amount of psychiatry or psychology studied in medical school varies considerably but is always subordinate.

At this point in their career, future psychiatrists have put in four years of postbaccalaureate training but have had only scattered and shallow exposure to psychiatry and to the kind of work they will eventually be doing. Some psychiatrists bemoan what they believe to be the irrelevancy of much of their medical training. Observers such as Schofield (1964) have contended that the procedure constitutes an inefficient and expensive way to train people to conduct psychotherapeutic conversations.

Some of the medical training is necessary background for using chemotherapy, diagnosing organically caused disorders, and understanding the effects of psychological stress on bodily processes (such as blood pressure). Equally important is the learning of professional responsibility for patients, which is modeled in medical settings. Psychiatric candidates have to make decisions and take decisive action in life-and-death situations. Later, during their residency training, they engage in similar crisis intervention and quick decision making with severely disturbed psychiatric patients. This kind of experience is unique among the three professional disciplines and is importantly related to psychiatry's dominant role. Society and other mental health professionals turn in emergency situations to psychiatrists.

Residency

After medical school a psychiatrist must complete a four-year residency program in an accredited hospital, which is often, but not necessarily, part of a university medical school. The first six months or so of this residency includes a heavy dose of general medical experience. This experience partially replaces the internship—one year of hospital medical experience—that used to be required before the M.D. was awarded. There are 225 residency programs in the United States approved by the American Medical Association, with an estimated 5000 residents in training (American Medical Association, 1978). While all are officially accredited, unofficially there are perceived to be wide differences in quality, or at least desirability.

University-connected, urban residency programs tend to be sought after; state hospital programs, often in rural settings, tend to be avoided and may often have unfilled places. Such preferences may be based legitimately on the quality of staff and training; or they may at times simply reflect preferences for living environments.

The sought-after residency programs screen and select trainees, often from a large pool of applicants, but there are sufficient residency programs to accommodate almost any physician who wants one. Admission to medical school *is* selective, however, and performance there is carefully evaluated. Psychiatry is not one of the more popular specialties among graduating physicians. Governmental concern about the shortage of psychiatrists has led to the provision of stipends and other inducements to encourage more physicians to take up psychiatry (see Chapter Ten).

Many psychiatric residents are not freshly graduated from U.S. medical schools. There are a goodly number of foreign-trained physicians, especially from non-Western countries. It is estimated that 34% of psychiatric residents are foreign medical graduates (Brown, 1977). These physicians find it easier to compete for psychiatric residencies, especially those viewed as less desirable by their U.S. colleagues, than to compete for specialty training in other areas. This situation is less a reflection on their personal competence than a result of the less-adequate facilities—laboratories, equipment, and so on—in which they received their medical training. Such training deficiencies are less crucial for psychiatric practice, which is less dependent on technology. However, foreign medical graduates also include many Americans who could not get into U.S. medical schools.

Physicians who have practiced general medicine for several years sometimes turn to psychiatry and complete residency requirements. Often, these doctors have been impressed with the pervasive role of emotional and behavioral disorders in general medical practice and want to better equip themselves to cope with it.

The four-year residency programs emphasize supervised practical experience with a wide variety of inpatients and outpatients. Typically, the initial focus is on hospitalized patients, with the new resident having responsibility for a ward or part of a ward. Outpatient treatment of adults and children comes next, and the third or fourth years may be a mix, with the resident permitted some flexibility in choosing activities. There is some required work in neurology and usually some crisis or emergency service work. In addition, the resident participates in a didactic program of lectures and seminars. Especially in university-connected programs, there may be encouragement or even a requirement to conduct clinical research. The resident also gains experience in collaborating with other professionals, such as psychiatric social workers, clinical psychologists, nurses, and occupational therapists. The training is intense and demanding in the usual medical tradition. The resident is frequently on call evenings and weekends and usually carries a heavy case load. There is often a "sink-or-swim" element to the experience, in that there are cases or decisions to be handled that formal training has not prepared the resident to meet.

Residents have regularly scheduled consultation sessions with senior staff members and are frequently called on to present cases for discussion in either clinical team meetings or ward rounds. In these ways they receive comments on their performance and opportunities to compare their work with that of others. But there is usually little, if any, direct observation of their work, except for an occasional tape-recorded interview that may be played for a supervisor. The evaluation of performance tends to be informal and lenient, and very rarely are trainees dropped for poor performance. Because the trainees are already licensed physicians, it is difficult and awkward to impose stringent criteria. As we shall see, the problem of evaluating the clinical performance of trainees is one that plagues all of the psychotherapeutic professions.

The theoretical orientation of residency programs varies from place to place but is primarily psychodynamic. Psychoanalytic concepts are particularly prominent, especially in urban areas. The prestigious senior teaching faculty tend to be those who have undergone formal psychoanalytic training. At the completion of training, a typical psychiatrist is over 30 years of age and is just ready to begin an independent, professional career. As a resident he or she has contributed to the care of the mentally disturbed in public settings. Professional life, however, is likely to be spent primarily in private practice.

Psychology

I will use the term *clinical psychologist* for convenience, but this discussion is also intended to encompass many counseling psychologists. Counseling is sometimes taught in departments of psychology but more often in schools of education. Much of the training is similar to that received by the clinical psychologist, but there is usually less emphasis on research and less exposure to severely disturbed clients. Counseling psychologists and clinical psychologists are interchangeable in many mental health settings.

As an undergraduate, the clinical psychologist was probably a liberal arts student, majoring in psychology. He or she took at least 40 hours of undergraduate work in psychology. Most of the undergraduate work was didactic classroom instruction, although a great many colleges now provide limited opportunities for clinical research or clinical field work.

Doctoral Programs

Gaining admission to a doctoral program in clinical or counseling psychology is a very competitive process. Grades and aptitude as measured by standard tests (usually including the Graduate Record

Examination) are major criteria for selection. Since there are usually a great many applicants who meet the academic criteria, final selections are often based on personal qualities such as motivation and interpersonal skills. These qualities are, however, difficult to assess, and the selectors sometimes fall back on the more quantitative information. Personal qualities are judged through letters of recommendation and sometimes through personal interviews with applicants. Clinical psychology, like the other psychotherapeutic professions, professes a great emphasis on personal qualities in selecting applicants for training but has great difficulty in assessing these qualities in a systematic way.

There are 101 doctoral programs in clinical psychology and 21 in counseling approved by the American Psychological Association (American Psychological Association, 1978). The clinical or counseling doctoral programs ideally require four or five years to complete, but there is much variability, depending on how efficient the student is. Three or four years of the training take place on campus, composed of research, course work in general psychology and clinical subjects (personality, psychopathology, assessment, psychotherapy), and supervised clinical experience. The proportions of the three basic ingredients—research, course work, and practical experience—vary greatly from setting to setting. Some programs include very little on-campus practical experience; others involve their students in clinical work throughout. A basic requirement for clinical training is that the student complete an internship—the equivalent of one full calendar year devoted primarily to supervised clinical experience, usually in a medical or psychiatric setting. This internship accounts for the fourth or fifth year in the training program.

The training, both on campus and during internship, involves a good deal of direct observation and the use of audio (and sometimes video) tapes. Trainees are observed by supervisors and are themselves observers of other trainees and faculty.

The theoretical orientation of clinical and counseling training varies considerably from program to program but is much less likely to be psychoanalytic than is psychiatric training. With its primary base in academic departments, psychology has a greater commitment to empiricism and to theories of psychotherapy based on psychological research. Psychiatry, in contrast, is essentially a clinical science, and its therapies have evolved from clinical practice. Psychologists, therefore, tend to give more weight to evidence from laboratory research. Behavior therapy is a frequent orientation in clinical-psychology programs but is infrequently emphasized in psychiatry.

An important feature of clinical training is that it is largely based in universities where the faculty are most heavily committed to research. Clinical students are trained alongside—and share some courses with—experimental, physiological, developmental, and social psychology students. Research potential is emphasized in selection, and research training and experience are required in all Ph.D. programs. The clinical students, like other psychology graduate students, must take several courses in statistics and research design. And they must complete and write up at least two pieces of research, one of which is the doctoral dissertation. Counseling programs housed in schools of education tend to have less emphasis on research and methodology.

The emphasis on research training—and, to a lesser extent, course work in general psychology—is a matter of controversy parallel to that over the relevance of medical school for psychiatric training. Some think it is superfluous to the functioning of a clinical psychologist, and some think it is essential. Those who think it superfluous believe it leads to an emphasis on inappropriate selection criteria, takes up time that could be better spent on professional training, and detracts from the quality of professional training, because faculty are selected primarily for their research competence (and must publish to climb the academic ladder) rather than their clinical skills. Proponents of this point of view have done more than criticize; they have set up schools of professional psychology whose faculties are primarily practicing clinicians (Dorken & Cummings, 1977). Their impact on the profession of clinical psychology will be considerable—and controversial.

Advocates of research training and course work in general psychology make several points. They insist that such training is needed if psychologists are to maintain their unique role as the "researchers" in clinical settings. Clinical settings, it is argued, provide a unique opportunity for the development of useful clinical knowledge, and it is the psychologist who is trained to capitalize on this chance. At the least, growing pressures for accountability in human services require evaluative research—assessment of a setting's performance and accomplishments—and research skills are needed for this purpose. And even though they may do no research, clinical psychologists need training in order to evaluate and use research done by others. Broad training is also viewed as necessary to avoid professional obsolescence and prepare the psychologist to assimilate new ideas and information. Finally, research training is thought to inculcate an empirical, inquiring attitude—a respect for data—that is critical for responsible professional activity.

The M.A. Psychologist

Psychology has practitioners at two levels of academic attainment—M.A. and Ph.D. (A psychiatrist is by definition a physician [M.D.] with a residency in psychiatry. The social work Ph.D. is primarily held by academics and high-level administrators.) Master's-level psychologists are qualified to practice in nearly all public agencies and institutions and provide much of the service in these settings. Some, however, are engaged in private practice. The selection criteria for the M.A. program are less rigorous, and the program offers an alternative to students with less-successful academic records. It can, at times, be a springboard to gaining entry to a doctoral program. While the training program is shorter than the doctoral program's—usually two years—there is much greater emphasis on practical experience and much less research and theoretical coverage.

Considerable controversy exists over the status and competence of the M.A. psychologist. The policy of the American Psychological Association is that the doctorate is the minimum credential for the practice of professional psychology, and M.A. psychologists are excluded from full membership in the association.

At present there is no evidence that master's-level clinicians provide less-adequate service than Ph.D.'s. Many M.A.-level psychologists have had a great deal of practical experience, and they staff many public agencies that would have difficulty recruiting Ph.D. clinicians. Salary schedules in public agencies reflect differences in academic attainment as well as experience; Ph.D.'s, therefore, command a higher salary and are more expensive for clinics to hire. The question of what level of training is required for which kinds of services and performance remains a vexing one.

Psychiatric Social Work

The psychiatric social worker typically holds a master's degree obtained after two years of work in an accredited school of social work. Undergraduate work can vary widely, but it often includes a major or considerable course work in sociology as well as many courses in psychology and other social sciences. As of 1976 there were 82 accredited master's programs of social work in the United States (Bernard, 1977). There were also 167 accredited baccalaureate programs and 33 doctoral programs. The B.A. programs both prepare students for practice in human-service agencies and serve as preparation for the M.A. programs (Bernard, 1977). It is easier to gain admission to M.A. programs in psychiatric social work than to medical school or graduate work in psychology.

As an undergraduate, the psychiatric social worker has probably pursued a college curriculum emphasizing courses in psychology, sociology, and public health. The undergraduate major may have been sociology or public affairs and have involved study of community organization, family structure, and political and economic aspects of welfare. In graduate school, there is didactic instruction in personality development, psychopathology, community organization, social-welfare programs and agencies, and principles of social casework. A thesis or research project is usually required, but it can often be a collaborative endeavor with other students. Field work or clinical experience begins in the first year, usually in a general community agency (for example, a family and children's service). In the second year, placement is likely in a psychiatric clinic or hospital, where the functions of a psychiatric social worker are observed and then practiced. Social-work programs provide regular and close case-by-case supervision from agency staff or faculty. There is about one year of full-time supervised experience in applied social work. This is a much higher proportion of experiential training than in psychiatry or psychology.

It can be seen from this description that the psychiatric social worker's training has an applied focus and is much more relevant to future on-the-job activity than that of the other two fields discussed. Schofield (1964) noted that the profession uses the term *casework* to describe its interactions with clients. But he commented that this term is used "largely for the purpose of maintaining amicable relationships with [the social worker's] psychiatrist 'overseer.' . . . Attempts to differentiate logically between what should go on in 'casework' and what should transpire in psychotherapy have not yielded either numerous or clear distinctions" (p. 118).

In fact, the working relationships between psychiatric social work and psychiatry tend to be closer and smoother than between either of these professions and clinical psychology. Much of the social workers' experience takes place in psychiatric settings, working collaboratively with psychiatric residents. Social work and psychiatry also share a theoretical bias toward Freudian psychodynamics. The social worker, however, is more likely to favor social action or environmental changes as a means of dealing with client problems. Perhaps because of the emphasis on environmental factors, social work has been relatively open to the contributions of behavior therapy.

In addition to the three disciplines just described, several other professions are involved in psychotherapy, especially in hospital or residential settings. These include occupational therapists, recreational therapists, and psychiatric nurses. These professionals typically work in collaboration with or under the supervision of members of the major psychotherapeutic professions. Psychiatric nurses dispense medication in both hospital and community settings and often participate in or lead ward meetings and group-therapy sessions. In residential settings occupational and recreational therapists, as well as psychiatric nurses, tend to have more contact time with patients than do members of the three primary professions.

Psychoanalysis

Psychoanalysis is not a profession in the sense that the other three are, and analysts are relatively few in number and treat relatively few clients. Yet their influence is profound, and psychoanalysis is especially salient in the public's perception. There are an estimated

4500 analysts or analysts-in-training in the United States and about 30,000 clients receiving psychoanalysis (Gross, 1978). Thus, the direct contribution of analysis is small. But psychoanalysts play a very significant role through their writing and as teachers in psychiatric training. For example, it is estimated that over half of the departments of psychiatry in U.S. medical schools are headed by psychoanalysts (Gross, 1978).

The term *psychoanalyst* refers to a therapist who has completed a formal course of study at a psychoanalytic institute. While a formal certificate (to be hung on the wall alongside one's other diplomas) is awarded, the term *psychoanalyst* is not legally protected in the same way that *psychiatrist* or *psychologist* is. Psychoanalytic institutes are essentially Freudian, but there are theoretical differences between them that can arouse passion among partisans.

Admission to a psychoanalytic institute requires a degree in one of the primary professions. Some institutes exclude nonmedical therapists. Thus, the typical analytic candidate is a psychiatrist who has recently completed his or her residency. In order to support their training, candidates work at their profession and attend the institute part time. Institute training is partly didactic and partly experiential. The didactic part consists of small seminars that probe into the subtleties and complexities of psychoanalytic thought (a general knowledge of psychoanalysis is assumed).

The experiential part is more unpredictable. Each candidate must undergo a personal analysis by an institute-approved analyst. And each candidate must conduct to successful completion an analytic case that is carefully supervised from beginning to end. Inasmuch as a true analysis involves a minimum of two years at four to five sessions a week (with liberal holidays, however), this training is potentially time consuming and expensive; the candidate must pay for the personal analysis, though often at a discount. The length of both the personal analysis and the supervised case is variable. Although the supervised case is carefully chosen, it may not go well. The client may break off treatment, move to another city, or die. Thus, the program has much uncertainty built into it. It does, however, include considerable close supervision, and in addition to the theory seminars there are many case-focused seminars. Analytic candidates thereby become indoctrinated in the particular point of view and also acquire much additional clinical experience. They are in their middle or late 30s on completion and thus have a shorter professional life than that of the 25-year-old social worker.

In U.S. society, the amount and length of required training is highly associated with the prestige (and often salary) of a profession. Perhaps this is an important reason why analysts enjoy great prestige and respect with the public and even among psychotherapists (as well as some envy and derogation). There is also the attraction of acquiring special competence in the use of the all-encompassing

psychoanalytic theory and the increased confidence and self-
knowledge resulting from the personal analysis (although, as we will
see, a great many therapists of all kinds have had personal therapy).

Frank (1973) has written eloquently about analytic training from
the perspective of indoctrination and self-persuasion. He pointed
to such features as the considerable commitment of money, time, and
psychic energy and the effects of an all-inclusive theory that is considered essentially irrefutable. "The analytic institute is a tight little
island in which the candidate comes into continued formal and informal contacts with other trainees and the teaching staff, all of
whom represent a consistent viewpoint" (Frank, 1973, p. 171). In the
personal analysis, he noted, there is an intensive, emotional review of
the candidate's thoughts, feelings, and experiences, which are interpreted in terms of the doctrine. The candidate must internalize and
accept this construction if he or she is to "pass" the analysis. To
disagree is to risk being accused of being resistant.

Frank acknowledged that in their early days the institutes were
crucial for the survival and intellectual productivity of the psychoanalytic movement. But he argued that their negative effects are now
considerable. The institute model has been adopted by many other
therapeutic schools—for example, Gestalt, behavior therapy, and
rational-emotive therapy—testifying to its utility in fostering the
growth of new approaches. An important implication of Frank's
analysis is that these new training institutes may have the very same
negative traits: indoctrination and rejection of external criticism.

There are signs that psychoanalytic training is losing its appeal
among psychiatrists. This may be partly due to growing impatience
with the long, arduous training or to general criticisms of the shortcomings of psychoanalysis. More likely, it is a function of the growth
of more attractive alternatives, such as behavior therapy and Gestalt
therapy.

Professional Differentiation and Overlap

By tradition and training, each profession has a unique role to
play in the treatment of dysfunction. Psychiatrists' medical training
uniquely qualifies them in the important area of chemotherapy and
in dealing with organically caused dysfunctions. In addition, political
and legal precedent gives the psychiatrist ultimate authority and
responsibility in many settings and situations. The psychiatric social
worker possesses knowledge of community organization and community resources and of the impact of the social environment on
behavior. Psychologists' traditional roots and training in assessment
make them the guardians of standardized testing procedures to aid in
clinical decision making and to evaluate treatment outcomes. The
psychologist is also the research expert among the three professions.

Many institutions seek to pool these three sets of expertise for maximum client benefit. One principal means of doing so is the clinical team, comprising at least one representative of each of the professions and often others, such as nurses or occupational therapists. The psychiatrist (or resident) interviews the client, the psychologist administers tests, and the psychiatric social worker interviews the spouse and significant others in the client's social environment. Information and judgments from each are shared, and a treatment plan is developed and implemented by one of the team members. Case conferences in community settings and ward meetings in hospital settings provide opportunities to pool knowledge in the client's behalf. And these mechanisms do work in many settings. Psychiatric or medical time is often scarce and must be devoted to medication and brief evaluation and cannot be spared for psychotherapy.

The problem is that most members of each profession vastly prefer doing psychotherapy themselves to practicing their professional specialties. Schofield (1964) cogently described this situation, and the pace of the trend seems to have quickened. The demand for psychotherapy has kept increasing, and it seemed natural for clinical psychologists and social workers to fill this demand and secure their professional "right" to do psychotherapy with increasing autonomy. Within clinical psychology, testing and assessment activities have become devalued, especially the use of projective tests—for example, the Rorschach inkblot test—which were congruent with an emphasis on psychodynamic therapy. Research has undermined confidence in the reliability and validity of projective tests and also questioned the accuracy of clinical judgment—compared with mechanical procedures—in making decisions or classifying clients (Wiggins, 1973). Behavioral psychologists have raised serious questions about the relevance and utility of clinical testing and assessment, arguing that information about presumed traits (such as defense mechanisms) has little relevance for treatment and questioning whether such information is worth the time and money involved in obtaining it (Mischel, 1968).

Among the medically trained, those who gravitate into psychiatry are usually those who favor psychological rather than chemical treatment strategies; it was the psychological aspect of psychiatry that most attracted them. Within psychiatry the role of psychotherapist is considered more stimulating and prestigious than the role of medication dispenser.

For psychiatric social workers, functioning as a relatively autonomous psychotherapist provides both the inherent gratifications of that activity—helping, satisfaction of curiosity, and the like—and solidifies their professional status as an equal of psychologists and even psychiatrists. No longer need they be seen as an adjunctive resource to treatment; now, especially in community clinics, they can control the course of treatment themselves.

As a function of these forces, role differentiation in many public

community agencies becomes blurred, with members of all professions acting as psychotherapists with the kinds of cases—children,
families, or groups—they are most skilled with. The major exception
is that the psychiatrist still assumes responsibility for medication
and often retains ultimate legal responsibility. This broadening of the
role of psychotherapist can also be seen in the private sector, where
increasing numbers of clinical psychologists and psychiatric social
workers are moving into private practice.

Psychotherapists as People

Thus far I have described the training and roles of members of
the major psychotherapeutic professions. But it is also of interest to
know what sort of people they are, what motivated them to become
psychotherapists, and what kinds of clients they prefer to work with.

In a large survey of metropolitan therapists (in New York,
Chicago, and Los Angeles), the population of therapists was 42%
psychiatrists (18% psychoanalysts), 33% psychologists, and 26%
social workers (Henry et al., 1971). Approximately 70% of the
psychotherapists were male, although a shift toward more women is
occurring. A relatively large number of these metropolitan psychotherapists—34%—were Jewish; 21% were Protestant; 9% were
Catholic; and 36% were either atheistic, agnostic, or reported no religious affiliation. Considering social-class origins, fully 68% were
from either lower or intermediate-middle-class backgrounds. The
data on the origins of psychotherapists have been interpreted to
demonstrate upward social mobility (Howard & Orlinsky, 1972). This
is consistent with the observation that psychotherapy is a relatively
new profession but one that enjoys relatively high status in our society. These class and ethnic trends are likely to be less pronounced in
nonurban areas (Henry, 1977, Note 4, p. 60) and may be less noticeable today than when these data were collected in the middle 1960s.

As might be expected, a strong interest in helping people was an
important motivation for psychotherapists' choice of profession and
is especially emphasized by social workers. Psychologists gave relatively greater emphasis to the importance of achieving an understanding of human behavior. Psychiatrists and psychoanalysts
tended to stress the importance of gaining an identity in their career
choice.

Psychotherapists are also their own best customers. Although
personal psychotherapy is required only of psychoanalysts, the
majority of therapists report that they have received it: 74% of a
metropolitan sample (Henry et al., 1971), and 58% of a national
sample. In the metropolitan sample, 37% had "had therapy" more
than once. In a sample of 855 clinical psychologists, 63% had received
psychotherapy (Garfield & Kurtz, 1977). Even though many training
programs encourage personal therapy, this still suggests that psy-

chotherapists are people with problems and that they have first-hand experience with therapy as a means of personal problem solving.

The three major professions have also been found to be remarkably similar in their conception of the kind of client they prefer to work with. Not surprisingly, the ideal client closely approximates the young, attractive, verbal, intelligent, and successful (YAVIS) client described in Chapter Three, a woman between the ages of 20 and 40 who is married and has had some post-high-school education (Schofield, 1964). Put another way, all psychotherapists prefer to work with intelligent, sophisticated, and motivated clients. However, psychiatrists tend to be most successful in structuring their case load so as to work with the preferred clients, while social workers are least successful (Schofield, 1964). Social workers tend to staff many of the social agencies that deal with the poor and disadvantaged.

In summary, psychotherapists

> emerge from professional training with views and skills highly similar to those of other therapists who have taken different formal routes. Within the complex of each profession, each of these groups of psychotherapists choose highly overlapping experiences and create for themselves highly similar pathways. Finally, it should also be clear that in their post training lives and in their professional maturity, they perform essentially the same resultant activity—psychotherapy [Henry et al., 1971, p. 181].

Based on observations of this sort, Henry and colleagues suggested that there are more efficient ways to train psychotherapists, ways that might capitalize on the similarities of background and interest. They encouraged the emergence of a "fifth profession," *psychotherapy*, as an alternative to current professional specialization.

The similarities in background, orientation, and preferred activities have other implications. I believe that they facilitate cooperation, on a personal and practical level, among the various professions. At the same time, they tend to foster competition and rivalry at the organizational and professional level. Each of the professions tends to regard itself as capable of independent practice and resents any restriction on its autonomy. This rivalry among professional organizations is elaborated on in the last section of this book.

Paraprofessional and "Invisible" Therapists

A great deal of therapeutic-like assistance with personal problems—perhaps the bulk of it—is carried out by people not belonging to any of the professions just described. While this may seem surprising, it is a generalization that has long been recognized by most professional psychotherapists. Much personal assistance is delivered by (1) people who have professional training in fields other than men-

tal health but who are conscripted at times to become psychotherapists or (2) people without formal professional training who are
given some combination of didactic and experiential job training in
carrying out psychotherapeutic functions.

The four most obvious examples of the former category are
clergy, physicians, teachers, and lawyers. Members of these four professions frequently come into contact with troubled individuals, and
a psychotherapeutic type of relationship develops. The troubled person begins to discuss personal problems and is encouraged to explore
them.

Invisible Therapists

Several years ago a large, representative sample of Americans
was interviewed about their mental health problems (Gurin, Veroff,
& Feld, 1960). Of the people who sought help for a personal problem,
42% went to a member of the clergy and 29% to a physician. Several
factors contribute to the frequent functioning of clergy and physicians as informal psychotherapists. There is no clear line between
psychological or behavioral problems and those involving theological
and medical issues. Consider, for example, the psychological reaction
of a mother to the death of a child, the guilt of a husband involved in
an extramarital affair, or a person's developing physical symptoms in
response to prolonged emotional or psychological stress.

Many people are relatively unsophisticated about the role and
availability of psychotherapists and have learned to think about their
problems in medical or moral terms. This makes it quite natural to
seek out a physician or religious counselor in times of stress. Clergy
and physicians are readily available, and many people have an existing and positively valued relationship with a particular minister or
doctor (but rarely with a psychotherapist). Finally, to the extent that
many people attach some stigma or shame to mental illness, it is less
threatening to interpret one's difficulties in physical or spiritual
terms. To visit a physician or member of the clergy involves fewer
barriers than seeking out and making an appointment with a mental
health professional.

Teachers perform similar functions for children and youth.
Schools often provide an opportunity for young people to develop a
relationship with a teacher and discuss matters that they cannot take
up with either parents or other adults. Lawyers often encounter
clients at times of crisis or emotional distress, and this encourages
the confiding of personal information. Divorce is the most obvious
example, but consider that lawyers also deal with death and be-
reavement and various kinds of other emotional reactions associated
with financial or legal conflicts. The line between legal and personal
advice is easily (and frequently) crossed.

For reasons such as this, clergy, physicians, teachers, and

lawyers account for a good deal of the psychotherapy business and have been termed *"invisible" therapists.* Unfortunately, it is difficult to ascertain just how much therapy they do and especially difficult to gauge the effectiveness of their interventions. This is because their work as psychotherapists is rarely scrutinized by peers or research workers. Many professional therapists are skeptical about the adequacy of the services offered by these informal therapists. Their clients do, however, appear to be quite satisfied. Americans rated help received from clergy, doctors, or lawyers equally with or more favorably than help received from mental health professionals (Gurin et al., 1960).

Recognition of the important role of physicians and clergy has practical implications. More attention might be given to providing the clergy with training and skills in pastoral counseling and to recognizing it as a bona fide activity of the ministry. General physicians could be educated to become more competent and confident in dealing with emotional disturbance (but not to encourage them to provide formal psychotherapy). A related effort would be to provide mental health consultation for these professions, to integrate them into the mental health networks in their communities, and to help them learn to make appropriate referrals (President's Commission on Mental Health, 1978). Many professionals will object to labeling the helping activities of clergy, physicians, teachers, and lawyers as "psychotherapy." Admittedly, the encounter between sufferer and healer is not so labeled by either party. But the process, I believe, is fundamentally the same.

Paraprofessional Therapists

Many paraprofessional workers are employed in public agencies and institutions alongside therapists with more credentials (Social Action Research Center, 1978). *Paraprofessional, nonprofessional,* and *lay therapist* are all terms applied to persons who have not gone through a formal academic training program but who are performing the function of psychotherapists. The term *paraprofessional* is used here because it is neutral and seems most descriptive.

The paraprofessional field includes a heterogeneous array of people and roles. Paraprofessionals include hospital volunteers, who may have much formal education but who are virtually without mental health experience; psychiatric aides, with minimal formal education but a good deal of on-the-job mental health experience; the graduates of a two-year associate of arts program operated by a community college, who have been given specific training in certain mental health or psychotherapeutic skills; or the graduates of a four-year bachelor of arts program containing a moderate degree of both didactic studies and field work in mental health settings, including psychotherapeutic activities.

The original impetus for the development and utilization of paraprofessional therapists was economic. An analysis of resources clearly indicated an insufficient supply of therapists from the primary professions (Albee, 1968). Paraprofessionals were also viewed as cheaper to train and employ than persons with advanced degrees and therefore more acceptable to agencies with limited budgets. A second impetus evolved from changes in the traditional mental hospital. Greater participation in therapeutic roles was given to nurses, technicians, and nonmedical members of the staff. Patients in mental hospitals spend much more time with nonprofessional staff members than with doctors or nurses; if such persons are given greater responsibility and training, their therapeutic impact is enhanced.

As experience with paraprofessionals developed, it became apparent that they often bring intrinsic advantages to working with certain kinds of clients. This is especially true of paraprofessionals who come from the same background as their clients and who may even have shared or experienced the same problem. Such persons have been termed *indigenous* paraprofessionals. Because they share a common background, values, orientation, and even language habits with the clients they serve, indigenous paraprofessionals are believed to be particularly effective in relating to certain kinds of non-YAVIS clients who are not reached by conventional, professional mental health services. These non-YAVIS clients are often willing to approach and confide in a person who is seen as sharing their characteristics and values, whereas they distrust and avoid establishment professionals. Some examples are the former heroin addict who now counsels addicts or the former juvenile delinquent who now works with youth groups and street gangs.

Advances in the theory and technology of how behavior change is brought about can provide a rational base for the use of paraprofessionals. There is a great deal of disagreement over the nature of psychotherapy and the essential characteristics of a good therapist. Some approaches emphasize the importance of the therapist's personal characteristics and interpersonal competence. Other approaches emphasize the therapist's mastery of specific techniques and procedures. Recent work in client-centered therapy and behavior therapy have yielded technologies for applying each of these approaches to the training of paraprofessionals.

From the perspective of client-centered therapy, the essence of a good therapist is a set of learnable interpersonal skills: the ability to be genuine or congruent, the ability to be empathic and communicate understanding, and the ability to communicate nonpossessive caring for the client. These key interpersonal skills can be acquired through the process of living or—it is believed by client-centered workers— taught and learned in programs in or outside a professional training setting. Professional psychotherapists have no monopoly on these key skills (Anthony & Carkhuff, 1977). Within this framework, it is possible to select paraprofessionals on the basis of how skillful they are on these three interpersonal dimensions or to provide training that will produce the requisite skills.

Behavior therapy attempts to develop technologies for achieving specific behavior changes and these technologies often are explicit, sequential, and learnable. Within this framework, it is possible to teach paraprofessionals the therapeutic procedures that will be effective with certain kinds of clients, and these can be taught outside formal educational programs. For example, fear-reduction procedures for phobic adults can be standardized and taught to paraprofessionals in a relatively short time. The professional psychotherapist can serve as trainer, consultant, and quality controller of the work of the paraprofessional "technician."

Paraprofessionals, then, are cheaper to train and employ, typically bring enthusiasm and commitment to their work, and are uniquely able to relate to certain kinds of difficult-to-reach clients. A number of studies (Social Action Research Center, 1978) have shown paraprofessionals to be effective counselors. However, the empirical evidence on paraprofessional effectiveness is inconclusive because of both methodological problems and the fact that most of the research has been done with those serving chronic hospital patients.

Paraprofessionals do have their limitations. They may not be as sensitive to ethical or professional issues as those who have gone through professional training programs. Their limited training may blind them to certain aspects of a client's problems. Although they may be competent in *carrying out* a treatment plan, paraprofessionals may lack the skills needed to evaluate clients and *choose* a treatment plan. They may lack the theoretical framework with which to modify treatment plans or react to unexpected events that frequently come up in the course of psychotherapy. Paraprofessionals, therefore, need to have ready access to supervision and monitoring by trained professionals.

The interrelationship of professionals and paraprofessionals is still being thrashed out. Professionals have staked out the territory of private practice while recognizing the appropriateness of using paraprofessionals in institutions or agencies. The relative degree of supervision necessary for paraprofessionals in such settings is still a matter of dispute. Some professionals feel threatened by the fact that persons with much less formal schooling can perform psychotherapeutic services, perhaps as effectively and certainly more cheaply. The emergence of paraprofessionals, however, may serve to make the professionals take more pride in their unique areas of expertise. There certainly seems to be enough psychotherapy business to go around.

Besides serving as supervisor and consultant, the professional will always be valuable as an innovator or developer of new treatment strategies. Once the strategies have been developed, they can usually be turned over to persons with less formal training to carry out.

The Clients

Less systematic information is available about clients than about psychotherapists, so I will have to rely more in this section on estimates and conjectures. For one thing, psychotherapy takes place in so many different settings that it is difficult to collect systematic information. In particular, it is difficult to determine how many people receive psychotherapy-like assistance from invisible therapists such as clergy or physicians. Remember that I am not concerned with describing the various forms of psychological or psychiatric disturbance, but rather with characterizing those clients who do become engaged in some psychotherapeutic process.

Three Categories of Psychotherapy Consumer

Hospital Patients

The easiest group of psychotherapy clients to identify is that group receiving care in mental hospitals (although we must acknowledge that their care includes drug therapy and other medical treatment as well). There are approximately half a million hospitalized mental patients in the United States at any given time, a figure that has remained reasonably stable for several years. These patients represent a major segment of psychotherapy clients: those whose functioning—thinking, judgment, interpersonal relationships—is so impaired that they cannot care for themselves and those who constitute a threat to others.

But severity of disturbance alone does not determine whether a receiver of psychotherapy will be hospitalized. Very important factors are whether the disturbed person's family and friends can or will care for him or her in the community and whether there are adequate community resources to assist in this task. Many disturbed people are able to maintain adequate adjustments in the community because of supportive social networks or suitable community supporting services. The elderly or the "senile" often constitute a significant portion of the hospitalized mentally ill, but many of these people could function adequately in foster homes, nursing homes, or even in the community if there were adequate supporting services available.

Clients Treated in the Community

The great majority of psychotherapy clients are treated in the community, either at publicly sponsored clinics or by private practitioners. In 1973 about 3½ million Americans received services in publicly financed community clinics (U.S. Dept. of Commerce, 1976). This figure includes readmissions—those who stopped therapy and then started again—and so contains some duplication. Many clients come to clinics for only one session in order to get help in a crisis.

Data from the private sector are more difficult to obtain. In a survey conducted in the late 1960s it was concluded that 0.5% of the civilian noninstitutionalized population consulted a psychiatrist during the 12-month period under consideration. Other privately practicing professional therapists are not included in these data. Nor do our estimates include the many students and other young people who receive help at school counseling centers or similar agencies. And, as noted before, it is particularly difficult to estimate the number of people receiving psychological help from physicians, clergy, and other professionals who perform therapeutic services on an occasional basis. Gross (1978) estimates that about 7 million people receive psychotherapeutic intervention annually.

In the last 30 years there has been a dramatic shift from inpatient to outpatient settings. Between 1950 and 1973 the number of mental hospitals remained about the same but the number of resident patients decreased by nearly 60%. Admissions to these hospitals *doubled* during the same period, readmissions increased, but net releases almost *quadrupled* (Ozarin, Redick, & Taube, 1976). Mental hospitals have become more efficient, in the sense that they are returning patients to the community more quickly.

During nearly the same period (1950–1973) publicly supported community services increased markedly. In 1955 inpatient facilities accounted for approximately 77% of patient services and outpatient services for 23%. In 1973 inpatient facilities accounted for only 32% and outpatient facilities for 68%. These trends would be even more pronounced if private practitioners, who do most of their work in the community, were included (Ozarin et al., 1976).

Growth-Seeking Clients

A third and relatively new group of psychotherapy consumers should be noted. A major characteristic of the two groups of clients noted previously is that they are primarily seeking relief from suffering or reduction of symptoms and distress. A growing group of consumers is less concerned about pain relief and instead seeks personal growth, self-actualization, enlightenment, stimulation, or some combination of these. Various group activities—including encounter, T-groups, and est—are often sought in pursuit of these goals. The offerings are frequently given an educational label—workshop, institute, personal growth center, seminar—in order to avoid the legal and ethical constraints on offering and advertising psychotherapy (these issues are considered in Chapter Nine). The "nonpathological" emphasis of these activities serves to make them more attractive and acceptable to many people who do not see themselves as disturbed or who are loath to acknowledge their difficulties publicly by going to a mental health facility.

Differences in Client Characteristics

Social Class

There are well-demonstrated relationships between clients' class, the severity of their disturbances, and the kind of treatment likely to be made available to them. A consistent finding in epidemiological studies is that the highest rate of psychological disorders is found in the lower class. The lower the individual's social class, the more likely he or she is to be given a more serious diagnosis (Bloom, 1975). But the relationship between social status and dysfunction is reversed with regard to the extent to which the severely disturbed receive some kind of treatment (Heller & Monahan, 1977). In a study of psychological disorder among residents of midtown Manhattan, severely disturbed lower-class people were much less likely to receive treatment than were their upper-class counterparts. Thirteen percent of the lower-class respondents displayed "psychotic" behaviors, compared with only 4% of the upper class. Yet only 1% of the seriously disturbed low-status people were receiving treatment, compared with 20% of the seriously disturbed from the upper classes.

Lower-class people are also more likely to be hospitalized in a public institution and are more likely to receive somatic or drug therapy rather than psychotherapy. In a classic study, Hollingshead and Redlich (1958) demonstrated that the relationships between social class and type of treatment were maintained even in a setting where clients were presumably assigned to mode of therapy irrespective of their ability to pay.

Patients in public mental hospitals in Boston were found to be usually poor, lacking in environmental support, and living isolated lives (Ryan, 1969). Twenty percent were diagnosed as suffering from alcoholism. Not surprisingly, they tended to come from sections of the city blighted by poverty, family disorganization, and racial segregation. Clearly, private, paying clients have very different characteristics from those who are seen at public expense.

Age and Sex

There are other striking differences among clients. Hospitalized clients tend to be older and male. Outpatient clients, especially those seen by private practitioners, tend to be younger and female. These relationships are well illustrated by a comprehensive study of the Boston area conducted in the early 1960s (Ryan, 1969). The study focused on clients who were seeing a private psychiatrist and compared these with clients who were being treated in public mental hospitals. The private psychiatric patients covered a relatively narrow age range, half of them falling between 22 and 36. About two-thirds of them were women, and four out of five were attending or had attended college. (A more recent survey of private psychiatric patients also found women in the majority, but to a lesser degree.) Close to half had had previous psychiatric care. Among patients in public mental hospitals, men outnumbered women and patients tended to be in the older age ranges.

As was noted, women constitute the majority of adults in treatment. Women are twice as likely to be treated for depression (Beck & Greenberg, 1974) and four times as likely to display phobias (Marks, 1969). They compose about two-thirds of the case loads carried by private practitioners (Ryan, 1969). Women tend to have more positive attitudes toward seeking help; they more readily define personal problems in mental health terms; and, if they are not employed, they can more easily seek out treatment during business hours. These factors are also related to the observation that male patients tend to be more seriously disturbed than female ones. Men apparently require more serious dysfunction before they can overcome their barriers to seeking or accepting treatment.

In contrast, about two-thirds of child clients are male. Learning disabilities and behavior disorders occur more frequently in boys (Werry & Quay, 1969). And these children, because they manifest their problems in the classroom, account for an important segment of youths in treatment. The bases for these sex differences are not known and can only be speculated on. Howard and Orlinsky (1972) suggested: "This may reflect a cultural pattern which tends to maladapt boys to institutions in which women are the principal authority figures just as the overrepresentation of women among adult patients may reflect the restrictiveness of the traditional feminine role in a male-dominated society" (p. 624).

Three Types of Distressed Citizen

Howard and Orlinsky (1972) sketched out three types of clients, differentiated on demographic and attitudinal characteristics. Type One has the greatest visibility and is most popular among therapists. This type tends to be a young adult in relatively affluent circumstances, generally college educated, and more often a woman than a man. This is the type Schofield (1964) has designated the "YAVIS" client: "youthful, attractive, verbal, intelligent, successful." These clients tend to be less severely disturbed and to positively overvalue psychotherapy as a social institution and means of help. They are overrepresented in private practice and underrepresented in public mental institutions.

The second type of client has received much more attention in recent years, partly as a result of governmental attempts to provide mental health services to previously neglected segments of the population. These clients tend to be distinctly less affluent and are more often older adults. Women still predominate. For the most part these clients do not have more than a high school education, and many have less. This group is less culturally sophisticated and less verbally communicative and tends to be judged as more seriously disturbed. It has more Catholics and non-Whites and in general is less positively oriented toward verbal psychotherapy.

The third type is less well known to the mental health profession, probably because these clients frequently seek help from religious rather than secular sources. This group appears to be middle aged and more variable in social class, but typically middle class. Women again predominate, and they tend to have families. This type of client is less frequently college educated than the Type One client.

This typology is a tentative formulation, and many clients would have mixed characteristics rather than falling neatly into one or another type. The main point is that clients differ greatly in demographic, social, and personal characteristics and that these characteristics affect their willingness to come forth for therapy, the way they're perceived and valued by therapists, and the kind of therapy they receive.

Paths to the Client Role

Clients also differ in their motivation for therapy. Some clients decide for themselves that they want treatment and are willing to pay handsomely for it. Others are involuntary clients receiving psychotherapy because their family or the courts require them to do so. Young children, juveniles who have run afoul of the legal system, and severely disturbed people who are committed to mental hospitals are examples of involuntary clients.

Many clients fall in between these two extremes. An employer may suggest therapy or exert pressure on an employee whose performance appears to be impaired—for example, by excessive drinking. Similarly, a spouse, teacher, or friend may urge treatment on an individual who, although troubled, may be uncertain about making a commitment to therapy. And occasionally, the easy availability of therapy or the possibility of having someone else (for example, the insurance company) pay for it attracts clients who would not otherwise be interested or motivated. The growing role of third-party payment (insurance) is described in Chapter Eight.

It cannot be emphasized too strongly that a relatively small proportion of distressed individuals becomes clients. Psychotherapy is often unavailable or unattractive. Many prefer to try to work things out for themselves or simply to ride out their difficulties. Many individuals seek help from clergy or physicians (Gurin et al., 1960).

Some of the barriers to blue-collar workers' seeking psychotherapy have been described in a recent federal report (Brown, 1976). The United Auto Workers negotiated a contract that paid the entire cost of mental health services (inpatient and outpatient) for about a million workers. Three years of experience revealed that only about 1% of eligible workers used the benefits. One barrier was that, whereas *providers*—therapists—were aware of the mental health benefits, relatively few of the workers or referral agents (shop foremen, union stewards, clergy) were aware of them. Workers and referral agents also tended not to see more subtle kinds of problems—for example, marital conflict—in mental health terms. And the stigma of mental illness also served as a barrier.

In a study of applicants to psychiatric clinics in New York City, Kadushin (1969) identified four stages: (1) realization of a problem, (2) discussion of the problem with laymen, (3) choosing the type of helping profession, and (4) choosing a particular clinic or therapist. The social network of the potential applicants seemed to be particularly important in determining their attitude and approach toward therapy. Kadushin identified an interpersonal network he termed the "friends and supporters of psychotherapy." These are people who tend to have friends who have gone to psychiatrists or psychotherapists, to know others with similar problems, and generally to support the value of psychotherapy as a solution to personal difficulties.

Clients come to therapy with an infinite variety of problems. The chapter headings in a standard abnormal psychology or psychiatry text communicate the more common symptoms or syndromes. Anxiety and depression are the two most common complaints. Frank (1973) theorized that there is a state common to all psychotherapy seekers, *demoralization*. According to the dictionary, to demoralize is to "deprive a person of spirit, courage; to dishearten, bewilder; to throw him into disorder or confusion." Frank maintained that this well describes psychotherapy candidates, who tend to feel powerless, unable to cope, and isolated. He noted that the mere presence of symptoms, even severe ones, does not distinguish those who seek therapy from those who do not. It is the combination of symptoms plus demoralization—the person's attitude toward his or her symptoms—that produces a client. Fortunately, according to Frank, psychotherapy contains several essential features that act to combat demoralization; these will be discussed in Chapter Three.

Once having sought and received psychotherapy, clients apparently find it easier to repeat. A surprisingly high percentage of applicants and clients in clinics have had previous psychotherapy.

Sixty percent of a sample applying to a set of New York City clinics and 60% of a sample of patients in a Chicago clinic had had previous treatment (Howard & Orlinsky, 1972).

Compatibility of Givers and Receivers

In terms of social class, attitude, and ideology, psychotherapists tend to be most similar to the Type One, or YAVIS, client. It is this type they most prefer to work with and most frequently see in private practice. YAVIS clients and their therapists tend to hold similar attitudes and expectations about psychotherapy. Type One clients also tend to be the least seriously disturbed. The non-YAVIS, lower-class client tends to have clearly more negative attitudes toward psychotherapy. Psychotherapists reciprocate by seeing this client as more seriously disturbed and a less suitable candidate for their services.

It is not surprising, therefore, that psychotherapeutic approaches—developed and practiced by YAVIS psychotherapists for YAVIS clients—do not work well with the non-YAVIS group (Goldstein, 1973). Conventional psychotherapy usually requires verbal skills, the ability to observe oneself and describe experiences and emotions, a willingness to endure distress while developing more self-awareness, and an acceptance of a "psychological" perspective toward one's behavior and interpersonal relationships. The majority of non-YAVIS clients has not had opportunity to learn these skills and attitudes.

One of the major challenges in the area of psychotherapy is the problem of developing adequate procedures and services that will be accepted by and effective with non-YAVIS clients. The community mental health movement was a step in this direction, but its critics believe it leaves much to be desired in terms of accomplishments (Holden, 1972). The potential utility of paraprofessional therapists, especially those who share characteristics of non-YAVIS clients, is accented by a compatibility analysis of givers and receivers. Indigenous paraprofessionals share verbal and language styles with non-YAVIS clients. They are more likely to utilize therapeutic strategies and tactics that will be compatible with the world view of the non-YAVIS client.

We are also left with a situation in which the bulk of the efforts of the majority of psychotherapists is devoted to the group of clients least in need of help. Governmental awareness of this imbalance has led to various programs aimed at redressing it—mainly in the form of providing incentives for professionals to work with less-desirable client groups. This problem is discussed in more detail in later chapters. The clients who receive help from clergy and physicians are of considerable interest. It may be that this is a situation that should be left alone. There seems to be no reason to try to educate these clients to seek out already overburdened mental health facilities. A wiser approach may be to improve the capability of clergy, physicians, and other relevant groups to deal more effectively with emotional and behavioral problems.

The supply of publicly financed psychotherapy is no longer expanding. The financial difficulties of federal, state, and local governments have led to a freeze or, sometimes, a reduction in human services, including mental health. Private psychotherapy, however, is booming. Increasing numbers of psychologists and psychiatric social workers are joining psychiatrists in private practice. Increased coverage of psychotherapy by health insurance has been an important contributing factor. These private practitioners, it is safe to assume, primarily service the Type One client.

The private sector also features numerous offerings by "nonprofessionals." *Est* (Erhard Seminars Training) was developed by a man whose formal education ended with high school. Yet many thousands have taken *est* and testify to its effectiveness. The telephone directories of most cities feature psychotherapy or counseling offered by persons with minimal or no credentials in the primary mental health professions. Much of this unorthodox therapy is sought out by the newly emerging group of psychotherapy consumers noted previously, who are seeking growth or enlightenment rather than relief from suffering. Because of the style of these new therapists and the costs involved, they offer little for the non-YAVIS client. Again, it is the least dysfunctional clients who tend to receive treatment.

Summary

Psychotherapy is influenced by the training, values, attitudes, and skills of the therapist, the personal characteristics and attitudes of the client, and the fit between the two parties.

Psychiatry, clinical or counseling psychology, and psychiatric social work are the three major psychotherapeutic professions. Psychiatrists are physicians who first complete medical school and then take a four-year residency, specializing in mental health work. They are the only mental health professionals who can prescribe medication and are also uniquely trained to diagnose and treat biologically caused disorders.

Clinical and counseling psychologists earn a Ph.D. degree in three or four years of university training plus a year's internship in an applied setting. Assessment and research principles and techniques are learned, in addition to psychotherapy and counseling skills. Master's-level psychologists usually have two years of graduate training emphasizing applied skills.

Psychiatric social workers earn an M.S.W. degree with two years of graduate training, including considerable supervised practical experience. Their training emphasizes the importance of the social milieu in the development and treatment of disordered behavior. Although the three professions have very different training programs and each have some unique skills, they share a strong commitment to doing psychotherapy.

Psychoanalysis is not a distinct profession but stands as a specialization available to members of the three major professions, especially psychiatrists, *after* their core training is completed. The training involves didactic seminars, a personal analysis, and supervised clinical work in the use of Freudian theories and techniques. It is usually done part time over a period of years. Psychoanalysts are influential through their writings and their positions as teachers and supervisors in training settings.

Paraprofessional therapists have not completed formal educational programs—that is, have earned less than a master's degree—but have obtained practical training, often on the job. They provide much of the service in public agencies, usually under the supervision of professionals. Invisible therapists are clergy, physicians, lawyers, and teachers who sometimes provide informal psychotherapeutic or counseling services.

There are approximately half a million hospitalized mental patients, many of them labeled "psychotic." Either they are severely dysfunctional or there are no resources to provide them community care. In recent years there has been a dramatic reduction in the number of hospitalized mental patients and a corresponding increase in community care. The great majority of psychotherapy clients is now treated in the community, either at publicly sponsored clinics or by private practitioners. Only a small proportion of distressed individuals becomes clients, either because psychotherapy is unavailable or because it is associated with the stigma of being "crazy." The social network in which the individual functions is an important determiner of whether psychotherapy is sought. A relatively new group of psychotherapy consumers is primarily seeking personal growth or self-actualization rather than relief of distress.

Psychotherapists prefer to work with people who are similar to themselves in social class and attitude. The preferred client has been given the label "YAVIS": young, attractive, verbal, intelligent, successful. Lower-class clients tend to be more disturbed but also to be less attractive to psychotherapists. Lower-class people are more likely to be hospitalized in a public institution and more likely to receive medication or somatic therapy rather than psychotherapy. The partial "mismatch" between clients and therapists often results in inadequate services for disadvantaged people and presents a chronic problem for both policymakers and the psychotherapy profession.

Suggested Readings

1. Frank, J. D. *Persuasion and healing* (Rev. ed.). Baltimore: Johns Hopkins University Press, 1973. Chapter Seven discusses psychotherapists and clients.

2. The following provide information about training and careers in psychology and social work:

   a. Job Opportunities/Career Information Center
      National Association of Social Workers
      600 Southern Building
      15th and H Streets, NW
      Washington, D.C. 20005

   b. American Psychological Association
      1200 17th Street, NW
      Washington, D.C. 20036

PART II
A Framework for Construing and Evaluating Psychotherapy

Part Two has two chapters. Chapter Three discusses the distinction between processes shared by all therapies and the unique features of particular therapies. Four kinds of therapy are illustrated to make this important distinction.

Chapter Four builds on the distinction between common and specific processes and describes a framework for evaluating psychotherapy. It aims to provide the skills to intelligently judge both research reports and more informal "case studies" concerning therapeutic effectiveness. The case examples in Chapter Three are used to illuminate several of the methodological issues.

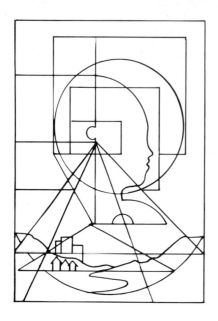

THREE

Common Processes in Psychotherapy

I have defined psychotherapy as a structured series of interactions between a sanctioned healer and a sufferer seeking relief. This chapter presents a framework for construing what goes on during those interactions. Crucial to the discussion is a distinction between common processes that occur in all therapies and components unique to particular kinds of therapy. This distinction is drawn by presenting four examples of psychotherapy and then analyzing both the differences and commonalities among them.

Psychotherapy is an inherently complex process. There is continuous talking back and forth between client and therapist, and each participant's responses are affected by the prior interaction. Sometimes, psychotherapeutic interactions continue for a long period of time and involve a great many sessions; psychoanalytic therapy is an example.

Surface Diversity

What goes on during these interactions? And how can the events best be conceptualized and understood? An obvious reply might be that it depends on what kind of therapy is being conducted with what sort of client. Indeed, a wide variety of events and interactions can occur, and it is easy for an observer to be dazzled by the possible variations. One could find a client reclining on a couch talking intensely about some sexual or interpersonal experience, with the therapist primarily acting as a listener. Or a client might be vigorously pummeling a pillow, perhaps while shouting out his feelings and anger at the person for whom the pillow is serving as a surrogate. A client could be relating a dream to a largely passive therapist. *A therapist* might be relating a dream or fantasy that she has had that included the client. A therapist might be artfully elaborating on some event or situation about which the client is fearful and exaggerating the fearful aspects so that the client becomes maximally aroused. A therapist could be administering a vigorous massage to some portion of the client's anatomy. A therapist and client might be actively role-playing a situation that the client feels inept in dealing with. Or, if we move to the realm of the various group therapies, one could observe numerous kinds of interactions or exercises engaged in by group members individually, in pairs, or in small teams.

Some clients we observe would be encouraged to talk about their past and their fantasies, others about their current behavior, and others about their plans for the future. If we were to engage the therapists in discussion about what they were doing and why, we would hear widely varying views. Each would articulate a plausible and internally consistent defense of his or her own procedures while offering sharp criticisms of the actions and rationales preferred by other therapists.

Surely an obvious conclusion to be drawn from observing therapies and talking with practitioners is that the most striking characteristic of psychotherapy is its variability. Many serious students of both the practice and scientific analysis of psychotherapy have arrived at such a conclusion. For example, Carl Rogers had this to say in 1963, when there was much less variation in psychotherapeutic approaches than there is today:

> It is, I believe, clear that were I to close my paper at this point, a one sentence summary would be, "the field of psychotherapy is in a mess." Therapists are not in agreement as to their goals or aims in therapy. They are in deep disagreement as to the theoretical structure which would contain their work. They cannot agree as to whether a given experience for a client is healing, destructive, growth promoting, or damaging. They are not in agreement as to what constitutes a successful outcome of their work. They cannot agree as to what constitutes failure. They diverge sharply in their views as to the promising directions for the future. It seems as though the field is completely chaotic and divided [Rogers, 1966, p. 6].

Rogers, to be sure, went on to argue that the state of affairs he depicted was a hopeful and exciting one.

Even before Rogers wrote, one author counted 36 different kinds of psychotherapies (Harper, 1959). Today there are undoubtedly many more, the exact number depending on whether one chooses narrow or broad categories. It is also literally true that no two psychotherapists are alike. Each applies his or her particular approach or blend of approaches in a uniquely idiosyncratic way.

It is my conviction that there are important differences among psychotherapies and therapists and that these differences affect both the process and the outcome of the endeavor. But it is all too easy to be dazzled by procedural differences and thereby to overlook what may be equally important similarities.

Selective attention to psychotherapeutic differences is reinforced by the writings and pronouncements of psychotherapists, whose training and professionalization leads them to an almost exclusive focus on the particular theories and procedures in which they were trained (Frank, 1973). Psychotherapists have usually spent considerable time and effort mastering a set of theories and techniques. This training provides them with a conceptual framework for understanding their clients' problems and for planning treatment strategies. The framework also serves to reduce their anxiety and enhance their confidence in what they are doing. Therapists' prestige and "professionalism" is intimately related to how well they can articulate and implement their special brand of therapy.

If a therapist has developed a new theory or variation and some corresponding new procedures, then he or she will be highly motivated to emphasize the uniqueness of the contribution. This will be particularly true if the work has been published or presented to professional audiences at meetings or workshops. Given these considerations, it is not surprising that the great bulk of the professional and popular literature on psychotherapy is composed of descriptions of the different theories, rationales, and techniques.

But if we look beyond the surface variations of psychotherapy, we may find important similarities that will deepen our understanding of the nature of the endeavor. The remainder of this chapter is devoted to such an inquiry.

Four Kinds of Psychotherapy

Paradoxically, it is useful to begin by first describing in some detail four diverse approaches to the psychotherapeutic art. An analysis of the similarities inherent in these four approaches will follow.

Three of the examples—psychoanalytic therapy, an encounter group, and behavior therapy—represent popular approaches in contemporary practice and also reflect the perspectives presented in Part Three. The fourth example was deliberately chosen to be different, in that it takes place in a culture very different from our own. Witch doctors, or shamans, can legitimately be construed as psychotherapeutic practitioners in their cultures, and an example of such practice is presented.

An Example of Psychoanalytic Therapy

Because they typically involve a large number of sessions over a long period of time, psychoanalytic cases are difficult to summarize. The case presented here is best described as intensive, psychoanalytically oriented therapy, rather than psychoanalysis per se. Even though this case was reported in rather succinct fashion (Fine, 1973, pp. 1–33), it was necessary to condense it further for use in this chapter. Do not concern yourself, at this time, with any technical terms you do not understand. They will be discussed in Chapter Five.

> The patient was an unmarried man, age 37, going to school at night. He immediately stated and emphasized that his only problem was vocational. The analyst listened, doing little talking, prompting him with short, open-ended sentences . . . . Although 37 years old, without a job and without a girl, he felt he had no problems. He wanted the analyst to tell him what could be gained by deep analysis. To this the analyst replied that an intellectual discussion would be of little avail, but that in such cases it was customary to have a trial period of two months, at the end of which time Jim would have a better idea of what the analytic experience was. This he finally accepted. He said he could not come more than twice a week for financial reasons. All this occurred in the first interview.
>
> A summary review of his life history revealed that it had been pervaded by aimlessness for many years. He was the second of three children; both others were girls. Soon after reaching adolescence, a severe withdrawal pattern made itself apparent. He went to college in another city, but dropped out before getting his degree. He had then seen no purpose in college for him. During this college period, there was still some contact with his family. Then he moved to the Pacific Coast, where he went to a theological school for a while, supporting himself by odd jobs as cook, dishwasher, and so on. Before leaving home he went steady with a girl for some time, but was too frightened to have any physical contact. In this period at the age of 27 he had one brief homosexual experience, when he was masturbated by an older man.[1]

[The client abandoned his theological studies, was drafted into the army, rebelled against military demands, was threatened with a court-martial, and was hospitalized for a "severe anxiety reaction" for several months. After discharge, he finished college but was still uncertain vocationally. He had his first heterosexual contacts with prostitutes and engaged in two homosexual relationships.]

> The analyst called attention to the discrepancy between the severity of his problems and his reluctance to do anything about them. The patient recognized after a few weeks that his life up to that time had been pretty aimless, and that he really had no idea of how he could go about changing the sense of aimlessness. He also agreed that this aimlessness had been with him for a long time. The unnecessarily long trip to go to college he could now see as a needless detour. When he left college without a degree, it was because there was no purpose to anything. Various enthusiasms had temporarily covered up the feeling of aimlessness. For a while it was a famous professor in college. Later it was Zionism. In the Army he had really let himself go emotionally— particularly in drinking and gambling. After the Army it was homosexuality. That too passed. At the time the analysis began, it was masturbating and movies. Outside of these two pastimes, everything

was frustrating and disappointing, and all the passions of the past had been forgotten.

To trace the meaning of his aimlessness became the central topic in therapy. It did not take long for him to see that his conflicts derived from the lifelong battle with his mother. Jim had very vivid memories of his mother and dwelt on her domineering ways. For quite a while, the complaints poured out in an almost never-ending stream; in milder form they continued until the end of therapy.

[More detail on the mother's domineering behavior is presented; "she bossed the father completely"; was overconcerned about the virtue of her daughters; beat the client when he was a child; and held him, so he thought, in contempt.]

While these initial insights allowed him to make more sense of his life than ever before, they were still highly intellectual and in theory would produce no deep or lasting effect. At this point he had had 16 sessions over a two-month period.

During the two-month exploratory period, which ended quite successfully in that he could see his need for analysis and determined to finish it, a number of transference-resistances emerged and were analyzed. First, he experienced deep resentment toward the analyst, especially when any interpretation was given not to his liking. At other times, he recognized [that] such resentment would have led him to break off the relationship. Here he could see that the resentment toward his mother was being carried over inappropriately, and he changed his reaction accordingly. Bringing this resentment to consciousness helped him for the first time in his life to see the dynamics of his repetitious withdrawal; oral frustration → oral aggression → withdrawal, since the oral aggression toward his mother always had to be inhibited.

After the withdrawal, resentment, and testing, the next manifestation that came to light was the transfer of omnipotence. The analyst became a magical figure who could by a wave of his finger solve all the patient's problems. This first came to light in a dream around the 20th hour: "I go to a dentist, a woman; she drills my tooth." In associations to this dream, the dentist was described as a woman of about 30. To the drilling he associated the analyst. The dentist is made into a woman to facilitate sexual contact. Often, we find that the first dream in analysis combines the core of the neurotic problem with its attempted solution. Here, too, this is the case. He wanted to be drilled by a woman; the tooth is symbolic of his inadequate self and body-image; the drilling makes him a passive recipient of sex. Dentist-analyst-lover are all one, making no demands on him. . . .

Although compulsive masturbation was one of the main complaints in the early part of analysis, he completely denied any connection between masturbation and sexual frustration. The masturbation was free of fantasy; it was a purely mechanical stimulation. The absolute denial of any sexual desire naturally required analysis. No insight dawned upon him, however, until he had relived an experience from earlier days. Several years before, he had been friendly with a group of people in analysis, for whose attachment to their analysts he had nothing but contempt. One of these people was a girl who had a great need to "make" every man she came across. Inevitably the patient, who acted indifferent to her, became a great object of desire. She did everything she could to get him to have sex, even appearing before him in the nude, and going to bed in the next room with another man while he was present and could surmise what was going on. Consciously, Jim felt great contempt for this girl, yet he continued to visit her regularly. He could now see what he was doing. He had derived gratification from being a voyeur and rejecting the eager woman (revenge on mother). Now he could admit that he had some sexual desire for her but this desire could come out now only when he was physically thousands of miles away from her. Consequently, he was able to see that his vehement denial of sexual desire to the analyst was again a transference of feelings called out by mother.

With this memory and transference insight, sexual feelings began to break through. Sexual and aggressive dreams served to mitigate the severity of the superego sufficiently to seek out contacts with women. Characteristically, he sought out Sally, who had been a great admirer of his for many years. He had to be certain that there would be no rejection before he could allow himself to feel more deeply.

When the analysis was in its 14th month, he had his first heterosexual experience with Sally. A general loosening of the personality set in. He became much more relaxed. His job, which had hitherto been an impossible chore, became much more acceptable. The deep dissatisfaction with everything in his life disappeared. He would come into therapy beaming, and often remark on what a wonderful place the world was. His hostility toward his family became less intense. His central problem now was working out of his relationship with Sally. Certain resentments cropped up, especially once when he was sick. But everything could be handled. After some 20 months of analysis, he felt that he had come far enough to marry, and broached the subject of termination. Although there certainly was a strong element of dependency in his feelings about Sally, it seemed to be normal in the circumstances. In the year or so in which he could be observed with her, it seemed to be in every respect an ideal relationship for him. Sally, who was older than Jim, was past the childbearing age, but she had a nine-year-old son to whom Jim became very devoted.

With his marriage the analysis was terminated. It had lasted some 175 hours over a two-year period. The termination left the road open for further treatment if the need should arise, but in the 20 years that have passed since, no such need has arisen.

An Example of Humanistic Psychotherapy

The second example is an excerpt from an encounter group conducted at Esalen, California, and represents a variation of humanistic psychotherapy. Some of the specific procedures are quite similar to the Gestalt techniques discussed in Chapter Six. The material is taken from the last half of the group's first session. There are 11 people in the group. Mike and another man, Alex, have just had an encounter which has led Mike to first hug Alex and then begin to weep.

Ted [the leader] moves swiftly over to the two men [and], as Mike begins to sob more loudly, asks him what he is experiencing. Mike, still crying, says that he is thinking of the gulf and the antagonism that has always existed between him and his father. He feels suddenly in touch with the positive aspects of the relationship that existed between them when he was very young, and he is remembering the longing for affection and comradeship that he felt in relation to his father long ago. Ted, attempting to improvise a spontaneous Psychodrama, asks Mike to talk to Alex as though the latter were his father, and try to express some of these feelings. Mike does so, and finds himself trying to explain to his father why it seemed that they could never get together. Suddenly he lashes out: "It was Mom who didn't want us to be friends—somehow she kept spoiling it." Ted intervenes, and asks "How?" Mike responds: "By speaking about him derogatorily to me, and by tearing him down in front of me—and, you—you shmuck" (here he turns back to Alex) "you let her!"

Ted asks Mike to select from the group the woman who most reminds him of his mother. He picks Mary, a youthful-looking woman in her mid-fifties. Ted tells Mike to begin to express his feelings toward his mother. He instructs Mary to listen, and to begin to respond as she senses Mike's mother might have. Mike begins to upbraid his mother for her behavior toward him and his father; taking his cue, Mary responds in a slightly scared and defensive way. Mike corrects her, and says "No, my mother would counter-attack much more forcefully," and for a moment he takes the mother role, in order to show Mary how he perceived his mother to behave. Mary resumes her role-playing in a more forceful way as Mike struggles to get his anger out; perceiving him as too timid, several members of the group spontaneously, without any direction from Ted, assume alter-ego roles and try to shout down his mother. Mike begins to shout too, but in a few minutes turns to Ted in frustration, saying: "I still can't get it out—I'd like to kill her, the bitch!"

Ted suggests that he go to the couch that is against the wall, that he stand next to it with his feet about a foot apart, and that he begin to beat it as hard as possible, all the while shouting at his mother whatever angry words come to mind. Ted cautions Mike that the activity might seem quite artificial at the beginning, but that he proceed in an attempt to see what feelings emerge. Mike begins; as he proceeds to throw his body more and more into the beating, he starts to pound more savagely, his cries become louder, and his curses against his mother more vehement. After several minutes of this, his pounding gets weaker; he turns to Ted, saying that he feels exhausted and "finished," and Ted suggests that he stop.

The group is silent for a few minutes while Mike continues to lie by the couch, breathing heavily. Doris comments that Mary seems to be in great pain. With some encouragement from Doris, Mary begins to talk about some of the feelings that she experienced during her role-playing with Mike, and about how she was reminded of the guilt that she feels in relation to her daughter, Nancy, who died several months ago at the age of thirty. Mary feels that most of the criticisms that her daughter had begun to direct at her during these past few years had been valid ones; she expresses regret that she had not been a better mother, and that Nancy had probably died without realizing how much Mary had loved her.

Ted now encourages Mary to proceed in a Gestalt therapy exercise in which she places Nancy in the empty chair and speaks to her. She begins by describing for Nancy the loneliness she has felt since her death; as Nancy, she directs angry complaints against her mother. Once again in the role of herself, Mary expresses and is surprised by the anger that Nancy's accusations arouse in her; she defends herself and states her love for Nancy. Returning to the role of Nancy, she expresses great wonderment at the extent of her mother's love, which she (i.e. Nancy) had never permitted herself to fully feel before. At this point, as she plays Nancy in the empty chair, Mary is overwhelmed by her feelings and begins to sob uncontrollably. With some encouragement from Ted, a few of the other participants draw slowly to her side, comforting her and tentatively embracing her. Once Mary has regained some composure, Ted insists that she continue the Gestalt therapy dialogue and say Good-bye to Nancy.

At the end of this exercise Mary is softly weeping. Ted quietly gestures toward the other participants, who slowly gather around her. Performing the "Roll and Rock" exercise, the group lifts Mary to her feet and form a circle around her. Ted instructs her to close her eyes and to let herself go completely limp; as she does so, the other participants gather closely around her and pass her around the circle. After a while, they move her to a horizontal position, and lift her above their heads; holding her in this position, they rock her back and forth for several minutes, while softly singing a lullaby. Then they continue their rocking motion, while they slowly lower Mary to the floor.

By now it is two o'clock in the morning. Nothing is said while Mary continues to lie on the floor with her eyes still shut. Her face appears to be in a peaceful repose, while some participants continue to gently touch her or stay close by her side. Other members are off to the side either singly or in groups of two or three. Most appear to be exhausted; all are silent. Ted says that he is ready to quit for the night, unless anyone has some reaction or feeling that is immediately pressing. Since no one responds, Ted reminds members that they are to reassemble in the same place at ten o'clock that morning, and he bids them good-night.[2]

During the remaining 4½ days, the small group continued to work in this fashion, with each participant having a chance to take "center stage" as Mary and Mike had.

An Example of Behavior Therapy

Our third case represents an example of behavior therapy, an approach described in Chapter Seven. Behavior therapy encompasses a variety of therapeutic strategies and techniques, and several are noted in this case. Systematic desensitization, a major treatment strategy in behavior therapy (Wolpe, 1958), is given greatest emphasis. The procedure involves gradual exposure to a hierarchy of anxiety-eliciting stimuli in the presence of an anxiety antagonist, in this case relaxation. The client is asked to imagine the anxiety-eliciting stimuli. When he can visualize a scene without feeling anxious, the next scene in the hierarchy is presented. Consistent with the behavioral approach, there is relatively little background material about the client. However, there are verbatim passages from one of the therapy sessions that help provide a concrete account of what was done.

The patient, a man of 60, had been chronically depressed for 10 years and had not gone out with his wife for many years. Because his

[2]From *Models of Group Therapy and Sensitivity Training,* by J. B. P. Shaffer and M. D. Galinsky. Copyright 1974 by Prentice–Hall, Inc. Reprinted by permission.

ability to travel was greatly restricted by three phobias—aerophobia, acrophobia and fear of leaving a secure base—he was unable to visit his son (currently living in Japan) or his daughter (currently living in Georgia). "I am unloved and unloving." He had previously been seen by several psychiatrists using non-behavioral techniques, with no apparent improvement.

A behavioral analysis indicated that the patient was exhibiting four major classes of maladaptive behavior: (a) chronic avoidance responses to innocuous stimuli (the phobias noted above); (b) obsessive negative thoughts about himself; (c) inappropriate interpersonal behavior, particularly towards his wife; and (d) repeated suicide attempts.

During the first three interviews, a life history was taken and treatment goals and rationale were discussed with the patient. A battery of objective tests was administered and partially interpreted to him.

The primary mode of intervention was systematic desensitization applied to the three phobic systems (which were all of approximately 14 years duration). These phobias greatly limited the patient's ability to travel, particularly by airplane, and therefore cut him off from many satisfactions that could be powerful positive reinforcers. It was hypothesized that if such reinforcers (e.g., visits to his children) were made available to him, his depressed behavioral repertoire could be greatly altered in a positive direction.

The following is a transcript of the 4th session with this patient, in which systematic desensitization was initiated.

Th: Hi, Mr. H. How did it go this week?

Pt: That tape was quite relaxing and I used it as you suggested. I feel that I can relax practically at will now.

(The client had been given taped relaxation instructions to practice at home.)

Th: Great!

Pt: You know, we found out by a letter we just received that the kids in Japan just had a baby boy. He's small but fine.

Th: There's an incentive to take that trip then.

Pt: That's what bugs me. I cried when I got the letter because I know that I can't even see my grandson. Why do I have this sickness?

Th: To hell with why you have it, Herb! Let's lick it. You remember the bit about hearing that your father died when you got off the airplane in Colorado 14 years ago?

Pt: But I didn't have any fear or anything at that time. I was just angry with my brother-in-law. He. . . .

Th: There is very little evidence that insights about events and feelings in the past causes therapeutic changes in the present. Let's get to work on making you unafraid of airplanes at this point.

Pt: You're the doctor.

Th: OK, let's see you get comfortable on the couch again. Now, in the future I am going to ask you to make up hierarchies in accordance with an instruction sheet. However, there are some hierarchies which are standard for the great majority of people. Airplanes is one of them. Now I want you to lean back and relax. Kick your shoes off. Legs and arms side by side.

At this point, detailed, step by step instructions were given to the patient, to induce complete relaxation. When the patient was completely relaxed, presentation of the hierarchy began.

Th: Now while you're relaxed like that, imagine you are in a movie theatre. You are watching a movie and in the movie there are some people at an airport. They are moving around quickly. They are all in a hurry. Visualize an airport vividly. You can see the runways and the planes in the distance. (Pause 5 sec.) Erase that scene from your mind. If it made you tense move your finger. [Client has been instructed to signal the presence or absence of tension by raising or not raising his fingers.] (No movement.) OK now, I want you to imagine that you are at that very same airport. Perhaps you are in the airport building and you go into the bar and order your favorite drink. (Pause 5 sec.) Erase that scene from your mind. If it made you tense move your finger. (No movement.) Good. Now I want you to imagine that you go to the ticket counter. See the ticket counter. See the sales person in her uniform and buy a ticket to San Diego. Just buy the ticket. You're not flying anywhere. (Pause 5 sec.) Erase that scene from your mind. If it made you nervous move your finger. (Patient moves finger.) OK, erase that scene from your mind and see if you can remain calm and relaxed. Let's relax your body all over again.

[Some conversation and more presentation of scenes have been omitted. We pick up the session further along in the hierarchy.]

Th: Now again I want you to imagine that you are going up the ramp. You're boarding the plane. You meet the pretty stewardess. You hand her the ticket. You start to enter the plane. (Pause 5 sec.) Erase that scene from your mind. If it made you tense move your finger. (Moves finger.) OK, erase that scene from your mind. And now I want you to imagine that it's a different day and you are getting into your car. See yourself sitting down in the car. Now buckle up your seat belt. (Pause 5 sec.) If that scene made you tense, move your finger. (No movement.) Very good. Now let's get back to the airplane. You enter the plane and you sit down in the seat—as if it were the seat of your car. You buckle your seat belt just as if you were in your car. Now vividly see yourself sitting down in the seat buckling up the seat belt. See if you can recapture the same smell of the airliner. (Pause 5 sec.) Erase that scene from your mind. If that scene made you tense, move your finger. (No movement.) Very, very good. Now you are buckled into the seat and let us imagine that you have a window seat. Look down at the runway. The plane is filling up with people and maybe there is some soft music in the background. Simply take a deep breath and relax and look out across the airfield. (Pause 5 sec.) Erase that scene from your mind. If it makes you tense, move your finger. (No movement.) Good.

[After presenting one more scene, the therapist brings the desensitization to a close.]

Th: Well, how did that go?

Pt: (Smiling.) It was amazing how relaxed I was. It really felt good. I really wonder how this works or why it works.

Th: The desensitization part is like how an allergist works. At first small doses—then larger ones until you accommodate, remember. Now this week, I want you to play this tape diligently at least once a day. That way you will benefit from this exposure by repetition. In a sense we're training your nervous system and your muscles to respond in a parasympathetic way to the very things that used to turn on your tension and nervousness.

Pt: Makes sense. I hope it will work for me. Nothing works for me. Is that it for today? (While tape is rewinding.)

Th: Yes. Now there is something else that I want you to do. During the week, as you drive. I want you to imagine, after you buckle into your seatbelt, that you are in an airplane doing the same thing. You think that would make you nervous?

Pt: Oh, I doubt it. After all, I know that I'm really on the ground.

Th: Very good. But every once in a while, let your mind fancy that you are getting into an airplane. Especially the sensation of buckling up. Maybe as you start to drive and as the car starts to move, imagine that you are in a plane and the plane starts to move and is taxiing down the field. After all, that's also on the ground.

Pt: Right. You know, I used to fly a plane. A small private plane, when I was a doctor in San Francisco. Isn't that disgusting?

Th: Amazing! A lot of people develop phobias in the very things they did well in and enjoyed once. Perhaps the fact that you used to enjoy flying is something that you should recall again. It should act in your favor.

[Some further conversation concludes the session.]

[In another part of the therapy,] the patient's obsessive negative thoughts were eliminated by thought-stopping. At the onset of a negative thought sequence (signaled by the patient), the therapist would pair a loud sudden noise with the word "Stop!" After a few training sessions, the patient was able to interrupt quickly any negative thoughts by himself.

In addition to eliminating negative thoughts, attention was given to increasing the frequency of the patient's positive thoughts about himself. The patient was trained to pair positive thoughts with high frequency daily behaviors (e.g., answering the telephone or turning a doorknob). According to the Premack Principle, high frequency behaviors act as reinforcers for any low frequency behavior preceding them. This procedure was successful in increasing the frequency of positive self-evaluative thoughts.

After 23 sessions, the patient is presently able to travel extensively by airplane; indeed, he has traveled completely around the world. He has gone to the tops of tall buildings with no subjective distress. He has visited his son, daughter and grandchildren. Thus, it may be stated that the patient's various maladaptive fears and avoidance behaviors have been eliminated by systematic desensitization.

The patient reports greatly decreased frequency of negative thoughts, and greatly increased frequency of positive self-evaluation. Furthermore, he can now readily interrupt any negative thought sequences that do occur. Thus, the thought-stopping and reinforcement procedures were successful.

After 3 years of occasional follow-up sessions, the patient, the patient's wife and I all agree that his depression has been significantly ameliorated. The range of behaviors he emits has been considerably broadened, as has the range of positive reinforcers available to him. By these criteria, treatment has been unequivocally successful.[3]

[3]Reprinted with permission from *Journal of Behavior Therapy and Experimental Psychiatry*, 1972, *3*, 111–116. Z. W. Wanderer, "Existential Depression Treated by Desensitization of Phobias: Strategies and Transcript." Copyright 1972, Pergamon Press, Ltd.

An Example of Psychotherapy in Borneo

Our last case illustrates the practice of psychotherapy in another culture. It is, however, less detailed, and we must rely on the description of an observer rather than the therapist himself.

The Iban, also known as Sea Dayak, are the original headhunters of Borneo. Now they are industrious, cheerful, and peaceful, making their living by cultivating plots of rice and sago and tapping rubber trees beside the tributaries of the Rejang River.

Therapists among the Iban are called *manangs*. One of the *manangs* whom I visited was Digat Anak Kutak.

As a *manang*, Digat's relationship with his patients is that of a technological expert rather than a father. He has special knowledge about lost souls and how to retrieve them. Other *manangs* have this knowledge too—he is just especially skilled at it. Consequently there is relatively little aura of mystery and charisma about him. He does not have to accept cases that come to him for help but can simply tell them to find another *manang*. Other accounts of Iban *manangs* imply that they are quite selective in the cases that they will undertake. Digat, like most *manangs*, will undertake only one case at a time. The fee charged is usually set before treatment begins and is not dependent upon a successful cure. It varies with the difficulty of the case, the length of the journey necessary to see the patient, and the reputation of the *manang*. It may be paid in cash, goods such as rice, or valued items like Chinese jars.

A typical case for Digat is that of a young widow who complained of generalized weakness and inability to do her work. Fearing that her soul had been lost, her relatives called Digat. He came to her longhouse at dusk and sat down with her relatives in the common corridor that runs the length of the longhouse and connects the twelve separate family dwellings which open onto it.

Digat has decided that this woman is not too sick and only requires a small ceremony. For a more serious case he would use a full-scale ceremony, involving preparations by all the members of the longhouse and lasting sometimes all night.

His first job is to make a positive diagnosis. For this purpose he gets out his private medicine bundle. This bundle is highly valued, and marks him as a *manang* more than any single thing.

The most important item in it is a piece of quartz with the horns of a large beetle attached. This is Digat's "stone of light" which he uses to make a positive diagnosis. By holding it up to the light and looking at the patient Digat can tell whether her soul is missing and, if so, how far it has gone. Other items in the bag include a wild boar's tusk (to help retrieve the soul), large pebbles, roots, and pieces of cotton. The last is to symbolically plug up holes so that the soul will not leave the body again once it has been retrieved.

Having ascertained the location of the lost soul, Digat then begins chanting and goes into a trance. While in a trance he falls to the floor and is covered with a special blanket by his assistant. The blanket is reserved only for special ceremonies like this. It is thought that while Digat is beneath the blanket he goes on a trip to the realm of the spirits to retrieve the lost soul of the patient. His own special guardian spirit guides him on the way.

Retrieval of the lost soul may involve many obstacles and dan-

gers, but he is almost always successful. Some *manangs* in large ceremonies go into an adjoining room and emerge with a bloodied dagger,
proof that they killed the offending spirit who was responsible. Once
the soul is recaptured Digat comes out of the trance and blows it back
into the woman's body through the fontanelle in her skull. Finally,
Digat charges the patient, and often the family or community, with
certain taboos to prevent relapse.

In the above case Digat suggested a redistribution of labor among
the widow's relatives to help her through the prolonged mourning
period.[4]

No information is given as to the success of this particular case,
but there is indirect evidence that this sort of treatment is usually
helpful. The author (Torrey, 1972) noted that he spent time at a
psychiatric hospital interviewing patients. "All eight patients I interviewed had seen a *manang* during the onset of their illness, and seven
of the eight reported improvement from the contact" (p. 108).

The Distinction between Specific
and Common Processes

We return now to the distinction between *specific* and *common*
(or nonspecific) processes in psychotherapeutic interactions. Specific
procedures are based on the theory underlying the therapy, in combination with a particular therapist's idiosyncratic style in implementing the approach. For example, the use of dream interpretation and
free association and even the practice of having clients lie on a couch
out of direct view of the therapist are relatively specific to psychoanalytically oriented therapy and infrequently occur in other varieties. The use of hierarchies in systematic desensitization is specific to
behavior therapy. The specific components account for the many
variations among the psychotherapies and, as we have noted, receive
the great bulk of attention in professional and popular writing.

Common, or nonspecific, processes are found in virtually all
psychotherapeutic or helping situations. The term *common processes*
is preferred here to the more frequently used *nonspecific processes*, to
avoid confusion. The term *nonspecific* was coined to convey the idea
that such processes are not specific to any one form of treatment but
are contained in all of them. Unfortunately, it is sometimes taken to
mean that such processes cannot be specified and measured. This is
no more the case for so-called nonspecific techniques than for
theory-specific ones. The term *common processes* seems better to convey the basic point that such components can be found, indeed are
inherent in, virtually any psychotherapeutic interaction.

[4]From *The Mind Game: Witchdoctors and Psychiatrists*, by E. F. Torrey. Copyright
1972 by Bantam Books. Reprinted by permission.

Specific Components in the Four Examples

Our four clients differed considerably in background and symptoms. The length of training and background of the therapists was also very different, though none was a physician. The time span of the treatment program—two years to two hours—and the number of sessions—1 to 175—varied tremendously. Some therapies tend to take longer than others, but there can be much overlap. A behavior-therapy case could take 100 sessions; a brief case using psychoanalytically oriented therapy might last only five to ten sessions.

The therapies differed in the *rationale*, or conceptual framework, presented to account for the client's difficulty and to justify the intervention procedures. Certainly the sessions were poles apart in content, especially in the techniques used. The psychoanalyst relied on verbal interpretations of the client's defenses and his feelings toward significant people in his life, including the therapist. The encounter therapist used role playing, Gestalt exercises, and group support. The behavior therapist used systematic desensitization as well as homework assignments to reduce avoidance behavior. The *manang* used his medicine bundle and his own trance behavior.

Common Processes in the Four Examples

All the examples satisfied the basic definition of psychotherapy. In all there was a trusting, professional relationship between the sufferer seeking relief and the socially sanctioned healer, and there was a series of structured contacts that both parties expected to be helpful. These basic structural constants yield important common processes that are often sufficient to produce rapid and marked changes in attitude, emotion, and behavior on the part of the sufferer (Frank, 1973).

So far our search for common elements in the four case histories has remained on a rather general level. A more concrete analysis is needed. The discussion that follows draws heavily on Jerome Frank's penetrating analysis (1973, pp. 325–330). Three major common processes can be noted, as well as several other less important ones.

Sympathetic Attention to the Sufferer and the Sufferer's Tale

The three individual therapy encounters started with an information-gathering interview, which included consideration of the clients' complaints as well as their current and past functioning. The therapists differed in emphasis, but all ranged broadly over the clients' life and affairs. Thus, the clients were immediately thrust into an intimate, emotionally arousing review of their problems and functioning in the presence of a sympathetic, nonjudgmental healer.

In the case of the *manang*, the history taking involved the client's relatives as well. In the encounter group, the history taking

focused on Mike's relationship with his father, but it was certainly
emotionally arousing.

Especially in the psychoanalytic and behavior-therapy cases,
the client had an opportunity to confide in—to review his difficulties,
fears, aspirations with—a sympathetic, nonjudgmental, prestigious
person. This is a relatively rare opportunity in modern society and is
usually very gratifying to the sufferer. It can serve to reduce or re-
move fears of being negatively evaluated. In the encounter group,
Mike and Mary drew sympathetic attention from the group as well as
from the therapist (leader). Nearly all of us have experienced the
relief of being able to "talk out" some problem or crisis with a sympathetic listener. Or, as in the case of the young widow, we may have
experienced hope and good feelings when our family and friends
showed concern for us and rallied to our support. Therapy provides a
sanctioned and scheduled opportunity to do this over an agreed-on
period of time.

A Credible Rationale for the Client's Problem and Its Treatment

At the end of the initial information-gathering phase, and sometimes intermittently during treatment, each therapist provided an
"explanation" of the client's problem and how it best could be rem-
edied. Although the content of the respective explanations was very
different, each client received a plausible, apparently authoritative
rationale, or conceptual framework, to account for the problem and
how it could be changed. The therapeutic rationale provided was
congruent with the cultural context. Behavior and emotions that
might have previously been perceived as incomprehensible and in-
dicative of "craziness" could now more comfortably be viewed as
natural, albeit highly troublesome, phenomena.

The encounter group's leader, admittedly, provided little in the
way of a formal rationale. It is apparent, however, that the participants shared a tacit assumption that more direct and spontaneous
expression of feelings would be helpful.

Therapeutic Activities or Healing Rituals Based on the Rationale

Each therapist engaged the client and himself in certain therapeutic procedures or rituals consistent with the explanation of the
problem. These techniques—free association on a couch, relaxing
and imagining situations, pummeling a couch, having the *manang*
blow your spirit back into your body—undoubtedly led the clients to
feel more hopeful, because they were working on their problems. The
specific techniques were, of course, very different, but this should not
hide the important common element: prescribed techniques were
present in each case.

The common processes thus far discussed follow closely from

the structural constants of the therapy situation. Other common processes may also be identified.

Other Common Processes

During the course of the treatment, each client was encouraged to engage in self-observation. For the psychoanalytic client the focus was on observing emotions and thoughts not usually brought to consciousness. He was probably also asked to observe, and perhaps even record, his dreams. The encounter clients observed their feelings and emotional responses. The *manang*'s client observed her behavior in relation to certain natural and supernatural events. The behavior-therapy client was observing his anxiety and the circumstances in which it occurred.

The self-observation process was much more explicit in the behavioral therapy, but this is a difference only in degree. The differences in the content of the self-observation should not obscure the fundamental similarity inherent in all clients' observing themselves within the framework provided by the therapist and thereby becoming further indoctrinated in that framework. The behavior-therapy client learned to appreciate the role of specific stimuli in triggering his anxiety; the psychoanalytic client learned how his anxieties and defenses interacted in shaping his behavior; the *manang*'s client learned about the interplay between her behavior, nature, and the gods; and the encounter-group participant learned to become more aware of emotions and to accept the simultaneous presence of apparently contradictory feelings. This gain in cognitive (and perhaps emotional) understanding is likely to be reinforcing and encourages clients' beliefs that they are progressing.

Most psychotherapy takes place in special settings that are seen as places of healing. These settings contribute to the prestige and authority of the healer and help arouse the client's expectations of help. The only exception to this came in our example of the witch doctor, who went to the client's home. But he took his symbols of healing with him.

All the clients expended considerable effort as well as a certain amount of money to try to relieve their distress. Both the intense review of one's feelings and experiences and the day-to-day monitoring of current behavior are effortful and often emotionally painful. The emotional effort of the encounter participants was self-evident. For the young widow, the coming of the *manang* to her longhouse and the involvement of her relatives called attention to her difficulties and signified the commitment of her primary social group to deal with the problem. The fees differed widely, but the amounts involved probably still mattered to each client. Money has symbolic meanings in our culture; we are accustomed to expect value for money when we pay for goods or services. Thus, even a token payment may strengthen the expectation that change will be forthcoming.

Finally, the "personality" of the therapist/healer constitutes another important common element. The therapist inevitably provides a *model* for the client to emulate and exerts suggestion and persuasion in both explicit and implicit ways. Put another way, the therapist's inherent humanness and charisma may be as important as his or her theory or technique.

In summary, several common processes have been identified in the four examples. These include the presence of a sanctioned healer and a setting containing symbols of healing; the raising of expectations of improvement; an emotionally arousing review of problems and life circumstances; the presentation of an explanation, or rationale, for one's problems; self-observation within the framework provided by the therapist; sympathetic, nonjudgmental listening from a sanctioned healer; and engagement in a set of activities prescribed by the healer. This list is not definitive. Other items might be added, and some workers would define or describe these common processes in different terms. But the presence and importance of common processes is universally recognized. They are important because they lead to client change.

Frank (1973) suggested that the common processes influence clients in several interrelated ways. First, they arouse hope and expectations of relief, and this is believed to be a key factor in both psychological and medical healing. Second, they combat clients' feelings of alienation and demoralization by showing them that their affliction has an understandable cause and that others understand and can help. Third, the therapeutic situation provides opportunities for new learning, at both the cognitive and experiential levels. And, fourth, the provision of successful experiences and acceptance by the therapist and group (if present) enhance the client's sense of competence and self-esteem. Frank summarizes this way:

> In short, when successful, all forms of psychotherapy relieve dysphoric feelings, rekindle the patient's hopes, increase his sense of mastery over himself and his environment, and in general restore his morale. As a result, he becomes able to tackle the problems he had been avoiding and to experiment with new, better ways of handling them. These new capabilities decrease the chance he will become demoralized again and, with good fortune, enable him to make gains after psychotherapy has ended [1973, p. 330].

Placebos and Common Processes

Common processes were known and studied in medical healing before their recognition in psychotherapy. In medical research and practice, common processes have been considered under the concept of *placebos* and *placebo effects*. A placebo is typically defined as any medication or treatment administered for the purpose of bringing about symptomatic change in a client but having no specific action on the symptoms of interest. A pill or capsule containing only sugar is a standard example. A placebo effect is commonly defined as any symptomatic change attributable to such medication or treatment.

Shapiro and Morris (1958) have provided an informative account of the history and role of placebos in medicine and psychotherapy. Because many treatments of the ancients have failed, under modern scrutiny, to show any specific action on the conditions for which they were prescribed, it is not assumed that most of the history of medicine is the history of placebo. Consider that among the common prescriptions patients were urged to ingest in previous days were the blood, dung, feet, fat, urine, eyes, and hair of many animals. The symptom-laden have been "purged, puked, poisoned, cut, cupped, blistered, bled, leeched, frozen, sweated, and shocked" (Shapiro & Morris, 1978, p. 370).

It is deceptively easy to laugh at such procedures, which now seem incomprehensible in view of current knowledge, and to view current medical and psychotherapeutic procedures as qualitatively superior. But it is important to keep in mind that, while often using such treatments, physicians apparently did heal (at least many of) their clients and remained honored members of society. Further, these treatments in their day were "standard procedure" and were believed by both healer and client to be efficacious. Inherent in the context of their administration were nearly all of the common processes described above, and it seems clear that the efficaciousness of the procedures was due to these common processes rather than to their specific effects.

The alert reader may also discern that some of these early treatments (for example, shocking, puking) have their modern counterparts. A disturbing question, which at least deserves to be asked, is whether many of the current psychotherapeutic procedures will be viewed by enlightened citizens of the 21st century much as we view many of the 18th-century prescriptions. Remember that in both cases sanctioned healers were administering treatments for which they believed they had a rational or scientific justification and which their own clinical experience showed were "successful."

The relief of symptoms, especially those involving subjective reactions such as pain, by placebo is a well-established medical phenomenon. Typical reports range from 30% to 60% of studied patients experiencing relief by placebo alone (Lehman, 1964). It should be remembered that subjective or experiential reactions—such as reports of anxiety, depression, or unhappiness—are often the central focus of psychotherapeutic interventions.

Placebo effects are not limited to the relief of subjective symptoms. Placebos have been observed to affect bodily processes. For example, in an early classic study a woman with persistent nausea was given ipecac, a powerful drug that induces vomiting, and was told that it would bring her relief. The result was almost immediate and lasting relief from nausea (Wolf, 1950).

The widest current use of placebos in medicine is as a control, or baseline, against which to evaluate the specific effects of drugs. This is now standard procedure with a wide range of medical pharmaceuticals, including those used by psychiatrists. In a typical experimental arrangement patients are randomly assigned to either a specific drug treatment or a placebo treatment. The therapeutic context, or common processes, remains the same for both, permitting the investigator to detect the specific effect of the drug. In the better research (a double-blind experiment), neither patient nor staff knows whether a given patient has received the specific drug or the placebo, thus ruling out the effects of bias or expectations held by patient or staff. Often, another group of patients receives no drug or treatment but is simply assessed at the same time period.

A typical pattern of results emerges from such experiments. Patients who receive a pill—either drug or placebo—show significantly more improvement than untreated patients. Sometimes the drug group shows more improvement than the placebo group, and the drug may then be said to have specific effects. *An effective drug is one that is superior to a placebo, not one that is merely more effective than no medication (treatment) at all.* However, one must recognize and respect the power of the placebo to produce effects, because patients or clients are often helped by them.

The same reasoning can be applied, by analogy, to psychotherapy. Placebo stands for the common processes inherent in helping situations; the drug stands for the specific techniques employed by a therapist. Both may affect behavior. For a given client or group of clients, both may contribute to therapeutic improvement. If a specific set of procedures is to be accepted as effective, it should lead to more improvement than is produced by the common processes alone.

Attention-Placebo Controls in Evaluating Psychotherapy

What is the psychotherapeutic counterpart of the placebo? That is, how can one evaluate whether a set of specific therapeutic procedures leads to client change beyond that produced by common processes? The problem is solvable, but the complexity of psychotherapy often requires conceptual and practical compromises that lead to less rigorous experiments than those conducted in drug research.

One solution requires finding a dummy procedure—analogous to a placebo pill—against which to compare the effectiveness of the specific treatment. The usual research strategy is to devise a procedure that contains all the major common processes but none of the specific treatment methods under investigation. Such a treatment is often termed an *attention-placebo* control procedure. Thus, clients in the control group receive the same amount of attention as clients receiving the "real" treatment. They engage in therapeutic activities such as discussing their problems with a sympathetic, attentive healer. As a result, they have expectations of success equivalent to those of the "real" clients. As in placebo-drug research, the *form* of the two treatments should be identical, the *substance* completely different. Constructing a plausible attention-placebo treatment often requires great ingenuity.

The following example is taken from a study that evaluated the relative effectiveness of several ways of treating speech anxiety—the fear of talking before an audience (Paul, 1966). First, the innovative treatment devised by the researcher is described for comparison purposes.

The procedure for subjects in one of the treatment conditions was as follows. During the first session, about ten minutes was spent exploring the history and current status of the client's problem to help "break the ice" and establish rapport. Clients were given the rationale that their emotional reactions before an audience were a result of previous experiences with people and situations and were similar to reactions engendered by any stressful situation. The anxiety experience was largely the result of a low tolerance for stress and could be overcome by training to work effectively under stress. The training, or therapy, would involve the taking of a fast-acting tranquilizer and working while under the influence of the drug on a task that was normally very stressful and produced a great deal of anxiety. The drug would prevent the occurrence of anxiety, and with repeated practice the client's mind and body would gradually develop a tolerance for stress. As a result, anxiety would no longer occur in stressful situations such as giving speeches, even without the tranquilizer.

The clients were given a very stressful task, one that had been used in a government project for stress training of astronauts and which consisted of identifying disaster signals from a number of sonar signals presented over headsets from a recorded tape. Clients were told that the usual increase in anxiety experienced by listening to these tapes was due to the combination of noxious sounds and difficult discriminations. After the clients understood the accepted procedure, the drug was administered and the clients were left alone for ten minutes to allow it to take effect. The therapist then checked the clients' pupil response and pulse until they were ready for the procedure. The remainder of this first session was taken up with the clients' listening to the tape and responding "Target" each time a disaster signal was heard. The therapist sat attentively and observed and recorded the clients' responses. A few minutes before the end of the hour, the tape was stopped and the clients' reactions to the session were discussed. The therapist assured them of the progress that was being made, and a check was made to see that the drug effects had now dissipated. There were four subsequent sessions of treatment, primarily spent on working with the tape.

The clients who received this treatment found it credible and as a group displayed considerable improvement, both in objective ratings of their behavior while they were giving speeches before an audience and in their self-reported comfort while giving a speech. The improvement observed with subjects in this treatment was significantly greater than that of comparable clients who received no treatment and was equivalent to the improvement shown by clients who received five sessions of "insight-oriented" counseling.

The treatment just described, however, was an attention-placebo control procedure. The rationale given had no real basis in fact or theory. The "tranquilizer" was actually a placebo, and the "very stressful task" was in fact a very easy task guaranteed to assure that subjects were very successful with it. This attention-placebo control group was constructed to ensure that clients spent their time in structured therapeutic-like activities. Because most of the time was spent listening to the tapes, there was opportunity for little discussion—except for the ten-minute history taking in the first session. This precluded any excursions into insight therapy, which was one of the real treatments under consideration. If you will review the description of this treatment procedure above, you will note that it contains all of the major common processes that have been discussed. But the actual substance consisted of "inert" activities; none of the procedures had any plausible relationship to the target behavior at issue.

Note also that this particular "placebo" worked, in the sense that it led to significantly more improvement than no treatment at all. This result is analogous to the effects of pill placebos in drug research. The example used here is one of the very best in the literature of behavior change. Many attention-placebo control procedures, while useful and valid for their purpose, are not as elegant as the one described here. Some do not provide equivalent levels of treatment time or structured activity.

In viewing and evaluating any psychotherapeutic theory or procedure, it will be useful to keep in mind the distinction between common and specific processes. The ever-present question is whether the results achieved by a given form of psychotherapy are attributable to its specific components or to its common components. Therapists committed to a particular "school" tend to emphasize specific technique; theorists such as Jerome Frank (1973) argue that common processes account for most of the gain attributable to therapy. The position taken here is an intermediate one. Specific techniques are viewed as important, and their development and evaluation should be pursued. Common processes are accorded an equally important role; they need to be more precisely defined and understood. The next chapter, on evaluating psychotherapeutic methods, will return to the issue of determining the effects of common and specific components.

Summary

The content of psychotherapeutic interactions can be divided into two classes of events. *Common* (or *nonspecific*) processes occur in virtually every kind of psychotherapy. *Specific* processes are unique to a particular kind of treatment, such as a Gestalt exercise, a psychoanalytic interpretation, or a behavioral-desensitization procedure. There are a great many specific techniques, or "schools," of psychotherapy, and therapists tend to emphasize their specific methods, which they believe are the most important events in treatment. Common processes, however, may be as important as or even more important than the specific ones.

The bulk of this chapter illustrated the distinction between common and specific elements by describing four very different treatments: psychoanalytic psychotherapy, humanistic therapy, behavior therapy, and psychotherapy in Borneo. Although very different techniques were employed, the four cases were found to have important similarities. All satisfied the basic definition of psychotherapy, in that there was a trusting, professional relationship between a sufferer seeking relief and a socially sanctioned healer. Three other important common processes were noted: (1) sympathetic attention to the sufferer and the sufferer's tale by a prestigious and nonjudgmental healer (and sometimes a group); (2) a credible, scientific rationale for the client's problem and how to treat it; and (3) structured therapeutic activities or healing rituals based on the rationale. Other common processes included self-observation, wherein the clients observed their behavior, emotions, and cognitions within a perspective provided by the therapist. In addition, the four therapies were found to share a special setting that symbolized healing; considerable expenditure of effort, and often money, on the part of the client; and the importance of the personal characteristics of the therapist/healer.

Common processes in psychotherapy are analogous to placebos in medicine. Just as research on the effectiveness of a drug attempts to demonstrate that there are specific effects beyond that produced by a placebo, so psychotherapy researchers attempt to show that a specific technique produces changes beyond those occurring from common processes. The use of an attention-placebo procedure to control for common-process effects was discussed and illustrated.

Suggested Readings

1. Frank, J. D. *Persuasion and healing* (Rev. ed.). Baltimore: Johns Hopkins University Press, 1973. Chapters Six and Twelve are especially relevant to an understanding of common processes.
2. Shapiro, A. K., & Morris, L. A. Placebo effects in medical and psychological therapies. In S. L. Garfield & A. E. Bergin (Eds.),

Handbook of psychotherapy and behavior change (2nd ed.). New York: Wiley, 1978. Pp. 369–410. An analysis of the empirical literature on placebos.

3. Torrey, E. F. *The mind game: Witchdoctors and psychiatrists.* New York: Bantam, 1972. A cross-cultural view of psychotherapy, emphasizing common processes. Written in a lively style for lay readers.

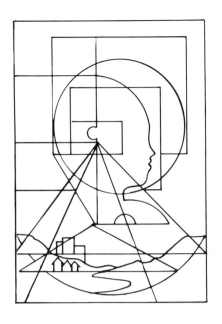

Evaluating Psychotherapeutic Methods

Evaluating psychotherapy will almost certainly be important to you from one or more perspectives during your life. If you aspire to be a mental health professional, you will have to choose which therapeutic approaches to learn and use. You may need psychotherapy for yourself; or a friend or relative may ask for your recommendations. As a potential client you will need to choose both a psychotherapist and a method of psychotherapy. If you do not participate as a therapist or client, you will still be a citizen, voter, and taxpayer. In these roles you will participate in decisions about the use of public funds for psychotherapeutic services. What kind of accountability should be expected from public agencies engaging in psychotherapy? And what kinds of programs should be supported?

This chapter considers what questions can be usefully posed concerning psychotherapy and develops criteria that can be used in evaluating the various methods. It first describes three dimensions to be used in evaluating psychotherapies. The bulk of the chapter then considers in some detail the most important of those dimensions, the *outcome* of psychotherapy. Emphasis is given to the measurement of therapeutic effects, possible rival hypotheses that may account for observed results, and the use of experimental designs to rule out rival hypotheses. The evaluative framework is then applied to professional and popular literature in general and to the Masters and Johnson sex-therapy program in particular.

The framework presented applies the logic of scientific method and experimentation to the evaluation of psychotherapy. Mastery of this framework is well worth the effort, because it has general applicability in evaluating a wide range of interventions in psychotherapy, human services, education, and medicine.

Three Evaluative Dimensions

There are three basic kinds of criteria for making judgments about psychotherapies: theoretical, empirical, and practical. First, one can consider the quality of the theory underlying the method. All psychotherapies include an account of how problematic behavior develops, is maintained, and can be changed. This rationale can be evaluated in terms of (1) how internally consistent the theory is, (2) how reliably and objectively the key concepts can be measured, and (3) how compatible the theory is with available psychological knowledge.

Second, psychotherapies can be evaluated on the basis of their empirical effects, or outcome. This is the most important criterion, and the next section of this chapter will be devoted to a description of how this criterion can be used. It requires the application of the logic of experimentation and of drawing conclusions from data to psychotherapeutic outcomes. The complex nature of psychotherapy requires modification and extension of the basic principles of scientific research.

Third, psychotherapies can be evaluated on the practical basis of their cost-effectiveness. Determining cost-effectiveness involves some measurement of outcome, and often only crude estimates are available. The *costs* of psychotherapy include the amount of professional time the treatment requires, the training requirements for and availability of practitioners, and the applicability of the treatment to various client populations. Costs may also include the effort or suffering involved and the possibility that the client will get worse, rather than better. Cost-effectiveness analysis involves weighting these various factors in order to arrive at some practical decisions.

I will now take up, in this section of the chapter, the two evaluative dimensions of lesser importance, theory and cost-effectiveness.

Quality of Theory

Although therapists expend much energy promoting and defending their particular rationales, for three reasons theory is the *least* useful of the criteria. One reason is that all therapeutic rationales are "weak" with respect to good scientific theory. A strong scientific theory contains concepts or variables that are clearly defined so that they can be reliably and objectively measured. The relationships between concepts are precisely specified, ideally in quantitative terms. The theory generates specific predictions that can be confirmed or rejected. Such rigorous theories are infrequent in psychology but can be found in selected areas of physiological, perception, learning, and cognitive psychology. In the realm of personality and psychotherapy we have cruder theories.

Nevertheless, psychotherapeutic rationales do differ in quality.

Rationales evolved from learning theory or experimental psychology tend to be more internally consistent and to permit more reliable measurement of key constructs than therapies invented by practicing clinicians—for example, bioenergetics (Lowen, 1976) or Gestalt therapy (Perls, 1976). In between stand psychoanalytic and client-centered therapy, to which both clinicians and academicians have contributed. Their therapeutic rationales are relatively internally consistent, and the key concepts have clear conceptual definition. But there is difficulty in achieving objective, reliable measurement of these concepts. Assessment of variables such as client-centered therapy's accurate empathy (Chinsky & Rappaport, 1971) or psychoanalytic therapy's transference (Luborsky, Graff, Pulver, & Curtis, 1973) requires considerable observer inference, making reliability difficult though not impossible. These points will be illustrated in later chapters describing the particular approaches.

The second reason why theories are a weak basis for evaluation is that their crudeness makes it difficult to determine whether they are compatible with available psychological knowledge. All psychotherapies can point to some facts or observations that are consistent with their rationale. Sometimes these observations derive from careful research; sometimes they are clinical observations and their factual status is in dispute. For example, psychoanalytic theory includes a complex set of hypotheses, some of which have empirical support and many of which do not (Fischer & Greenberg, 1977). Proponents and critics of psychoanalytic theory can selectively point to the evidence that best fits their views. Despite the fact that the reliable knowledge that can be cited in support of a given psychotherapeutic rationale may be weak, however, the criterion of compatibility with available psychological knowledge is still important. Is there a consistent body of theory and research findings supporting the rationale, or only isolated findings and informal clinical observations? You should beware of a psychotherapeutic theory that purports to explain all, because such theories are almost certainly vague and imprecise.

This leads to the third reason why quality of theory is a limited criterion. There is no necessary logical connection between the validity of the personality theory underlying a therapy and the clinical effectiveness of its techniques. The theory may have considerable validity, but the therapeutic procedures—which may be suggested by or derived from the theory—may not work.

It is a long way from the psychology laboratory and the theoretician's armchair to the psychology clinic. Because there are unique variables interacting in a clinical setting, procedures that were effective in simple laboratory situations may no longer work. In any case, the applicability of research or theoretically derived therapy procedures to clinical settings must be demonstrated rather than assumed.

Conversely, the personality theory may be invalid but the therapeutic techniques effective. One can dispute Carl Rogers's assumption of inherent self-actualizing tendencies or Freud's emphasis on sexual and aggressive drives, but the clinical effectiveness of client-centered or psychoanalytic therapy in no way depends on the "correctness" of their views. The therapy techniques may work for reasons unrelated to the rationale. In summary, the quality of theory underlying a psychotherapeutic method can be supportive and can direct clinicians and researchers toward promising techniques, but effectiveness must always be considered as a separate issue.

Cost-Effectiveness

The costs of delivering and undergoing a particular kind of psychotherapy can be balanced against the results of the therapy. Some estimate of the outcome of the treatment is clearly required, but this criterion is more helpful in sharpening awareness of differences in cost. A given treatment may be very effective but require large numbers of sessions from a highly trained psychotherapist. For certain people this costly therapy may well be justifiable; for others with different problems a less expensive, even if less powerful, therapy may be preferred.

Four economic costs can be noted. First, there is the length of time or number of sessions required by psychotherapies. The more sessions, the more money a therapy will cost or, if no fees are involved, the more costly it will be in terms of professional time. Second, some psychotherapists, such as psychoanalysts, are more expensive to produce and more limited in availability than others—such as psychiatric social workers. The more training therapists have, the more expensive their therapy is likely to be. A third cost factor is a therapy's applicability to clients and its requirements for their participation. Some therapies require verbal skills and attitudes about behavior and emotions that many clients do not have. Psychotherapies with limited applicability may deserve lesser support. Fourth, the setting and mode of psychotherapy affect the cost. Two obvious examples are that institutional treatment typically costs more than community care and group therapy is cheaper than individual therapy. It would be foolish, however, to base judgments solely on costs. The potential benefits involved often justify more costly treatment—for example, when institutional care is required for a suicidal client.

The *psychological* costs to clients must also be considered. The time and effort involved and the interference with daily routine are one cost. Therapy can be upsetting in the short run, even when it is ultimately quite helpful. There is some risk of getting worse rather than better (Bergin & Lambert, 1978). Any treatment powerful enough to cure can also have negative effects (Frank, 1973). Some clients do seem to become worse after therapy.

Cost-effectiveness analysis has another interesting feature: it requires that value or utility estimates be attached to services and outcomes. Is it more desirable to have a large number of clients receive a few treatment sessions or a small group of clients receive very intensive treatment? Should resources be directed toward the less severely disturbed, who are likely to profit from therapy, or toward the more severely disturbed, who are less likely to improve but who may be expensive to care for if they are not helped? Cost-effectiveness analysis reminds us that there is an important distinction between a therapeutic outcome and the social value we attach to that outcome. Issues of social value and social cost are especially relevant for taxpayers and politicians when decisions about program support and financing are to be made.

Evaluating Psychotherapeutic Outcome

The bulk of this chapter deals with the third criterion—the results of therapy. First, the importance of framing specific questions about therapeutic outcome is noted. Next, the complexities of describing and measuring therapeutic procedures, clients, and—especially—therapy outcomes are discussed. The idea of considering "plausible rival hypotheses" when evaluating therapeutic outcomes is then taken up, followed by a description of different ways to do controlled research. These last two topics are, I believe, the heart of this chapter.

Useful and Nonuseful Questions

What are the proper or useful questions to ask about psychotherapy? As the practice of psychotherapy began to emerge and grow in the 1940s and 1950s, critics raised questions about its overall value or worth. The principal issue became whether psychotherapy, taken as a whole or in its many forms, "worked" in the sense of being more effective than no treatment at all or than simple attention and custodial care (for example, see Eysenck, 1952). Proponents of psychotherapy, and even its critics, soon became aware that this question was too broad to yield a meaningful answer. It was analogous to asking "Does education work?" In fact, the problems in evaluating education are quite similar to those involved in evaluating psychotherapy. Common sense tells us that many educational programs are quite effective but that some are not. We have good schools and bad schools, good teachers and those not so good, and students who profit from education and those who do not. It is necessary to consider particular educational programs aimed at particular goals—for example, vocational education programs in junior colleges. With psychotherapy, too, we need to be more specific. A more precise and useful form of the question of whether psychotherapy works has been stated by Paul (1967): "What treatment by whom is most effective for this individual with that specific problem and under which set of circumstances?" (p. 111).

Stating the question this way also points to some of the important factors that contribute to psychotherapeutic effectiveness or ineffectiveness. The evaluation of psychotherapy needs to consider the contribution of the methods ("what treatment"); the contribution of the therapist ("by whom"); the contribution of clients ("this individual with that specific problem"); and the contribution of situations or environmental factors ("which set of circumstances"). It will be rare for a single experiment to study or measure the effectiveness of all of these factors. However, when investigating just one of them, the researcher must consider the others to avoid confounding the results.

Complexities in Psychotherapy Research

Many of the problems involved in evaluating psychotherapy can be illustrated by comparing it with a typical laboratory experiment in psychology. Guided by a hypothesis, the experimenter selects an *independent variable*, presents it to *subjects* (typically college students), and defines and measures a *dependent variable*—the particular response of the subjects that is of interest. The independent variable is usually a discrete, quantifiable set of stimuli—for example, visual information on a screen. It is presented in a standardized manner to all subjects, often in one session. The individual characteristics of the subjects are usually irrelevant, providing that the subjects do not have any obvious abnormalities or deficits that might interfere with their ability to see or hear or make a response. The dependent variable is also defined precisely—usually in quantitative terms such as reaction time or frequency of error—and the subject is limited to a few choices selected by the experimenter. Another important feature is the inclusion of a *control group* in order to clarify the interpretation of the results.

The complexities involved in describing and measuring these three elements where psychotherapy research is concerned will now be examined.

Describing the Treatment (Independent Variable)

In psychotherapy research the independent variable is the particular form of therapy the investigator is evaluating. Instead of a discrete, quantifiable, and standardized set of stimuli, this independent variable is a series of interactions between therapist and client—and perhaps homework assignments by the client as well. The nature of these conversations is reciprocally influenced by the participants and therefore is never the same for any two therapist/

client pairs. As noted in the previous chapter, there are several *specific* and *common* processes embedded in the interaction. In sum, the independent variable in psychotherapy research is complex, multidimensional, relatively unstandardized, and therefore difficult to measure.

The situation, however, is not hopeless—merely difficult. Precise description of the therapeutic program is the ideal. This description includes the number and spacing of sessions, the rationale given to the client, and the specific procedures used. It is difficult, however, to summarize or quantify the content of a series of interviews. Ratings or coding systems (for example, see Rogers, Gendlin, Kiesler, & Truax, 1967) can be useful for research purposes but are very expensive. Careful clinical description is often the best that can be done. Compare the cases from Chapter Three in terms of the description of their therapeutic procedures. In which one do you have the best understanding of just what was done? The sheer length of the psychoanalytic case impedes description. The use of theoretical constructs in describing the case makes it difficult for those not versed in psychoanalytic theory to understand what happened. The description of the behavior-therapy case is facilitated by its shorter length and more explicit technical procedures.

Describing the Clients (Subjects)

While the characteristics of subjects—including differences in their histories and their current attitudes or motivations—are irrelevant for most laboratory experiments, they are very important in psychotherapy. In naturalistic contexts—for example, a psychological or psychiatric clinic—we can expect considerable variability in the nature of the clients, the kinds of problems they have, and their attitudes toward therapy. While it is possible to generate more-homogeneous groups of subjects by choosing persons having similar problems, such as obesity or specific phobias, there will still be individual variability in the severity of the problem and in motivations. Both common sense and most theories of therapy assume that client characteristics will affect response to treatment, but there is disagreement concerning just what the key client characteristics are and how they can be measured. In sum, there are problems in describing the clients and in identifying key individual differences in personality, attitude, and motivation that are likely to have an important effect on therapeutic behavior and outcome.

Again, the evaluation of psychotherapy will be facilitated the more comprehensive and specific the information provided—whether we are considering a controlled investigation or a clinical case report. The demographic characteristics of the clients; their vocational and family situation; the nature, intensity, and duration of their symptoms and problems; and their motivation and attitudes must be considered. It is preferable that client characteristics be measured in some quantitative way. Careful clinical description can also be very useful, as is demonstrated by the cases presented in Chapter Three. Client characteristics can also be assessed by standardized tests such as the Minnesota Multiphasic Personality Inventory (MMPI). Although such tests may have validity or reliability problems, they do permit comparison of subject populations across different investigations.

Choosing and Measuring Outcome Criteria (Dependent Variable)

In the laboratory experiment the dependent variable is the subject's response to the independent variable, or the experimental task. The subject might, for example, be asked to pull one of two levers, depending on which kind of stimulus he believed had been flashed in front of him. The experimental hypothesis clearly directs both *what the dependent variable will be* and *how it can be measured.*

In evaluating psychotherapy, both of these questions are attended by formidable conceptual and practical problems. First, outcome criteria must be *chosen.* The kinds of changes that a particular therapy is supposed to produce for a particular client must be specified. The choice of outcome criteria depends heavily on the theoretical convictions and interests of the investigator or psychotherapist (Lichtenstein, 1971). The major conceptual issue is whether to emphasize personality or behavioral measures. Personality measures typically focus on covert behavior or internal processes, such as cognition, self-perception, insight, or ego defenses. Behavioral measures typically involve overt responses, which can be given frequency counts or rated in intensity or effectiveness. Psychodynamic and behavioral investigators tend to favor one or the other, but there is increasing agreement that both are important.

A useful starting place is the client's presenting problem (the client's stated major concern) or major symptoms. All psychotherapies agree that symptom relief is an important or necessary goal. But some psychotherapies think symptom relief is sufficient, whereas others believe more should be accomplished.

Problems in choosing outcome criteria are illustrated by the psychoanalytic and behavior-therapy cases described in Chapter Three. In the psychoanalytic (psychodynamic) case the client had no specific symptoms, and considerable psychotherapeutic negotiation was needed before he agreed to work on his "aimlessness." One important criterion of success might then be decreased aimlessness, but this trait is rather vague. Job seeking and work stability as an indicator of a more purposeful life might be a more specific criterion in this case.

In the behavior-therapy case, there was a clear client problem that led directly to one outcome criterion: elimination of his fear of traveling by airplane. There was also concern about other areas of the client's life, notably negative obsessive thoughts and interpersonal problems with his wife, but the outcome criteria remained more specific and behavioral than for the psychodynamic case.

To further complicate matters, one must consider the possibility that changes that are desirable for one client may be undesirable for another. This will present problems if we try to find criteria that apply to groups of clients. The problem involves the distinction previously noted between psychotherapeutic outcomes and the value that one attaches to these outcomes. Marriage counseling may result in one or both partners' deciding to terminate the relationship. For some couples this may be seen as good; for others it may signify failure.

It is hoped that these examples will provide the reader with a "feel" for the complexities involved in choosing outcome criteria in psychotherapy evaluation. These problems arise in part because of variations in therapeutic goals and in part because of the inherent complexity of human behavior.

Thus far we have considered only the *choice* of outcome criteria. Once this choice has been made, the investigator or clinician faces conceptual and practical choices in *measuring* the criteria. Two important issues are *what kind* of information to use in determining outcome and *whom* to obtain the information from. I will take up the second issue first.

Sources of outcome data: Choice of informant. There are three major sources of outcome data: the *client*, the *therapist*, or some *third party*—a family member, friend, or neutral observer ("rater"). It is desirable to include all these sources of information when evaluating psychotherapy. The source of the data imposes certain limitations on outcome measures. Unfortunately, the limitations are greatest for those sources who are most accessible and economical: the client and the therapist (Lichtenstein, 1971).

The clients' data are influenced by their (1) degree of self-awareness and memory distortion, so that they sometimes cannot report behavior or feelings accurately; (2) desire to please or displease the therapist (or experimenter); and (3) tendency to justify, first, the need for treatment and, later, the appropriateness of termination—the "hello/goodbye" effect. Clients first exaggerate their difficulties to justify (be consistent with) their entering therapy. Later they minimize them to justify their commitment of time and money and the appropriateness of termination. Put another way, clients' sensitivity to the demand characteristics of the situation distort their information. Demand characteristics are situational cues that induce subjects or clients to respond in some way—for example, to "look good" if a test is seen to be a measure of adjustment. Demand characteristics are sometimes thought to affect only the more "obvious" self-report measures such as questionnaires, but they can affect any measure where clients know they are being observed with respect to their progress in treatment. There is clear evidence that even the performance measures dear to a behaviorist (such as the snake avoidance procedure) are susceptible to demand characteristics (Bernstein, 1973).

Therapists are biased by their (1) particular theories and assumptions concerning behavior disorder and change; (2) involvement with their clients and with therapy (their own hello/goodbye effect); and (3) limited sample of client behaviors—the one or several hours of verbal report they obtain each week during treatment. For example, behavior therapists give more weight to symptom reduction than psychoanalytically oriented therapists. Thus, a client whose symptoms improved but whose "personality structure" was not believed to have changed would be rated as more successful by a behavior therapist than a psychoanalyst.

For both client and therapist, the more global or inferential the measure used, the greater the opportunity for bias or error to operate. Global ratings of "degree of improvement" or "adjustment" are readily susceptible. If the client is reporting about concrete events in life—grades at school, getting a promotion at work, success on a date—bias or distortion is less likely.

Third-party measures are much preferred in research, because of their relative freedom from the distortions of client and therapist reports and because they can provide information about client behavior in natural settings. For example, family or friends can provide information about the amount of drinking engaged in by a client treated for alcohol abuse, or they can rate the social adjustment of a person recently released from a mental institution.

If the third party is a judge who is uninvolved in the therapy, his or her data can be much more objective and free from bias. Just how objective and reliable will depend on the conditions of the experiment (Johnson & Bolstad, 1973). Third-party data are often expensive to obtain, inhibiting their use in clinical practice. It is possible, however, with the client's written permission to use simple questionnaires or short telephone interviews with significant others in the client's environment.

Kinds of outcome data. There are four basic kinds of information used to measure outcome criteria: (1) client behavior in psychotherapy sessions, (2) behavior on psychological tests, (3) behavior in laboratory or clinic tasks, and (4) behavior in the natural environment.

The client's verbal behavior in therapy is frequently used to index the degree of improvement. This is often done in an informal, clinical manner, as when therapists judge that their clients are manifesting greater insight or awareness or are dealing with some interpersonal problem in a more effective way. Moving toward more

formal evaluation, therapists can complete rating scales of client
improvement. Client therapy behavior can also be subjected to rigorous analysis by means of coding or rating systems. Client-centered
therapy researchers use four-minute samples of interaction to obtain
ratings of client "process," or "experiencing," a key dependent variable (Rogers et al., 1967). Note that therapy behavior is just the
verbal behavior during but one or two atypical hours in the client's
life. The relation of therapy behavior to client changes in the home,
school, or community remains to be demonstrated.

Clients can provide data about themselves by completing numerous written tests and questionnaires. These include global self-
ratings of improvement, symptom checklists, and comprehensive instruments such as the MMPI. Such tests are often convenient and
reliable. But their validity is usually a major issue. Just what they
measure and how well they correlate with or predict important
changes in life-style and behavior remain crucial issues. The validity
and sensitivity to change of tests and questionnaires vary widely.
Standardized tests are also useful in sample description and in
evaluating the comparability of clients or subjects from different
studies.

The client may be interviewed before and after treatment by an
independent interviewer. Or the client's performance in a task
designed to simulate "real life" may be employed. For example, subjects with a snake phobia may be asked to approach and touch a real
snake; they are scored in terms of how closely they approach the
feared stimulus. Married couples may be asked to solve problems or a
parent to interact with a child. The interactions are observed and
coded. These procedures eliminate many of the biases of client and
therapist reports and—in the case of performance tasks—get closer
to meaningful, real-life behavior. They are also relatively expensive.
And, as noted above, there are still situational factors affecting behavior in such tasks. Although the situations are closer to real life,
they are still artificial. The relationship of laboratory or clinic performance to external, community behavior again must be demonstrated rather than assumed.

All therapists agree that the most important information for
measuring outcome criteria involves behavior in everyday life: work,
family, and play. Measuring changes in such behavior often calls for
considerable ingenuity. Two kinds of measures are available: inferred
measures of performance and direct observation.

Inferred measures of client behavior in real life may come from
institutional records or public events such as academic grade-point
average, length of time spent outside a state hospital, police records,
marriage or divorce, or job performance. In research contexts these
must be documented; in clinical contexts the client's report may be
quite acceptable.

Direct observation is a cumbersome and costly procedure. For example, it can involve sending trained observers into a client's home at repeated intervals. Controlled environments such as classrooms or mental hospitals lend themselves more readily to these methods. Though costly, direct observation potentially provides the most objective and meaningful outcome information. Note that it is necessary to specify criteria *before* the observations are made. Direct-observation data also may be distorted by the client's awareness of the observation.

A useful approximation to direct observation is the use of self-monitoring, or client recording of specific information. Clients might record each cigarette they smoke or note each time they behave "assertively," as defined in a specific way. Spouses in marital therapy can observe and record each other's behavior. Or parents can record the frequency of some deviant or desirable behavior exhibited by their child (for example, refusal to comply with parental requests). Self-monitoring is much more convenient and cheaper than direct observation and is used a great deal in both applied and research settings. It is, however, much less objective than direct observation and is potentially vulnerable to all the biases of client self-report.

The criterion (dependent-variable) problem has been discussed at some length because it is so critical for evaluating and comparing psychotherapies. Unless outcomes can be specified and adequately measured, evaluation is impossible.

Considering Plausible Rival Hypotheses

The aim of experimentation is to establish unambiguous relationships between independent variables and their effects on specified responses—the dependent variable. As we have seen, this goal requires specifying and measuring subject characteristics and the independent and dependent variables for any given research problem. A critical issue still remains: identifying and ruling out alternative explanations for the observed outcome. Imagine that we have exposed a carefully described sample of clients to a specified form of psychotherapy and have observed significant changes on our outcome measures. How can we be "sure" that the observed changes were "caused" by psychotherapy. This problem also faces any practitioner who judges that his or her client has improved after receiving therapy and concludes that the therapy produced the improvement. Perhaps the practitioner has more certainty than the researcher. He or she "knows" that the therapy produced a positive outcome, having seen it happen many times. The psychoanalytic and behavior-therapy cases described in Chapter Three seem "obvious" examples of client improvement due to therapy.

Both practitioner and researcher, however, must face the possibility of alternative explanations that may account for the observed changes in their clients. The evaluator's task is to collect information that will rule out the alternative explanations. Campbell and Stanley (1966) coined a useful term to designate these alternative explanations: *"plausible rival hypotheses."*

In psychological research a number of standard rival hypotheses have been identified. They can also be thought of as threats to the internal validity—unambiguous interpretation—of an experiment. We will describe these rival hypotheses as they apply to psychotherapy research and indicate how they can be controlled. It is important to emphasize that the plausibility of any rival hypothesis is dependent on the particular circumstances of the research or clinical situation. A *logically* possible rival hypothesis may be rendered highly implausible by the circumstances. Thus, imperfectly controlled research, a series of case studies, or even a single case study may permit one to rule out one or more rival hypotheses and yield useful information. The investigators' task is to consider the rival hypotheses and evaluate their plausibility with respect to the particular case or research project at issue.

The clinician or investigator would like to conclude that some *specific* psychotherapeutic procedure *caused* a constructive outcome. Before this conclusion can be accepted, the rival hypotheses, or threats to internal validity, must be considered and ruled out. The major plausible rival hypotheses are usefully organized around a series of three basic questions best asked *sequentially.* Each question itself is a general rival hypothesis, with specific ones subsumed under each. Table 4–1 summarizes the basic questions and the rival hypotheses.

Has Change Really Occurred?

The first task of the investigator is to demonstrate that real changes have occurred in the clients and to specify the nature of these changes. The first general rival hypothesis is that no real changes have occurred and that the apparent effects of the psychotherapy are artifactual or illusory. At first, this possibility may seem absurd. If questioned, most clients will assert that they have benefited considerably from their psychotherapy, and psychotherapists will likewise assert that most of their clients profit from treatment. Nevertheless, this is a very plausible rival hypothesis in many psychotherapeutic situations. The three specific rival explanations under this general hypothesis are now examined.

"Change" is illusory because of inadequate measurement. Suppose that the family and friends of our hypothetical clients were asked if these clients had changed. Some would agree with the clients, but some might say that their friends seemed to be the same. A demonstration of change requires a comparison with a prior state of affairs or with another person (or group) who was not subjected to the intervention.

Table 4–1. Plausible Rival Hypotheses in Psychotherapy Evaluation

1. No real change has occurred.
   a. Apparent change is illusory because of *vague, gross measurement;* for example, there is no information on client's status *before* therapy.
   b. Apparent change is an artifact of *bias or error,* such as biased reports by client or therapist (for example, the client hello/goodbye effect).
   c. Apparent change is due to *statistical regression:* the tendency for extreme scores to move toward the mean on retesting.
2. Change has occurred but *has nothing to do with therapy:*
   a. Change is due to *history:* specific (situational) events occurring during the same time as therapy.
   b. Change is due to *maturation:* processes within the client occurring during the time of therapy (such as growing older, more tired, and the like).
   c. Change is due to *reactivity:* the assessment process is a stimulus to change rather than a passive recording procedure.
   d. Differences in change are due to *differential selection:* biases in assignment of clients to groups.
   e. Differences in change are due to *differential attrition:* differential loss of subjects from comparison groups.
3. Change has occurred and is attributable to therapy, but it has nothing to do with specific techniques.
   a. Change is due to common processes (try to identify *which* common processes).
   b. Change is due to therapist, not therapy.
Note: If change is due to the specific treatment components, then the next research question is "Which component or components are efficacious?"

When we speak of someone's having changed, we usually imply that we have knowledge of how he or she was *before,* as compared with their present status. In psychotherapy evaluation an assessment or careful description before intervention (or a nontreated control) is needed to make such a comparison.

Suppose, further, that clients, therapists, and friends were asked to describe specific evidence or examples of the constructive changes that had occurred. Could they do so? We would no longer accept broad therapists' judgments such as "she is dealing with her problems much more realistically" or "his interpersonal relationships are much more mature" without specific information to support them. Similarly, we would be skeptical about client reports of improvement that were vague, such as "I'm much more in touch with my feelings now" or "I've really changed my entire outlook on life." Such statements tell us little about psychotherapeutic outcome, no matter how sincerely they are uttered, unless they are backed up by examples of changed behavior.

"Change" is an artifact of bias or error. The problems encountered in measuring outcome illustrate some of the biases that both client and therapist are likely to exhibit. Both have committed a good deal of

time and energy (and, for the client, money) to their joint enterprise. Cognitive-consistency principles oblige them to perceive positive results from such a commitment. The potential problems with therapist and client reports noted previously must be considered and determined to be implausible before it can be concluded that real change has occurred. Again, the appeal is to specificity and concreteness. If clients describe specific changes in their life, this is more convincing than if they give a general report of improvement. Contrast the client who says "I feel so much better about myself" with the client who reports asking for and receiving a promotion at work, improving his or her grades at school, or engaging in an activity (such as dating) that was previously avoided because of anxiety. It remains possible, of course, that the client is exaggerating or even reporting falsely, and independent corroboration is desirable.

"Change" is due to statistical regression. Changes in test scores are often used to demonstrate changes as a function of psychotherapy, both in clinical practice and in research. Tests may purport to measure specific traits or behavior patterns, such as anxiety or fear, or broader constructs, such as adjustment or dependency. Test changes on such measures are always subject to the possibility of statistical regression. This refers to the tendency for persons with extreme scores on the first occasion of testing to move toward the mean on retesting. The rationale for this tendency is complex and beyond the scope of our discussion here. One process involved is that measurement tends to be less reliable at the extremes. For example, a person who obtains an exceptionally high score on some ability test is likely to have been both good and lucky. On a second testing, the chances are that he or she will be less lucky.

The importance of statistical regression lies in the fact that most people who undertake psychotherapy tend to have extreme scores. And subjects are often selected for research projects precisely because they have extreme scores. Statistical regression, fortunately, is readily ruled out with proper controls. A comparable group tested and retested at the same intervals—and presumably showing no or less change than the treated group—can rule out the plausibility of regression as a rival hypothesis. Statistical regression also becomes less plausible if the outcome measure is known to be highly reliable—for example, if body weight is used as a criterion in the treatment of obesity.

It is hoped that this discussion convincingly demonstrates that the rival hypothesis that no real change has occurred is far from trivial in many situations. Some outcome measures are vulnerable to two or more of the specific rival hypotheses. For example, self-report questionnaires measuring symptoms or distress (such as anxiety) are vulnerable both to client-bias and statistical-regression effects.

Are Client Changes Associated with Therapy?

Assume that you are satisfied, on the basis of the information available, that real client changes have occurred. The next question to consider is whether psychotherapy caused the change. Psychotherapy takes place over days, months, or even years. It is very plausible that events could occur during this passage of time that would produce the observed change. Two important specific rival hypotheses must be considered—*history* and *maturation*—as well as three less important ones.

History. By history is meant situational or environmental events, other than the psychotherapeutic procedures, that might have led to client change. These include such events as changes in economic conditions, changes in employment, changes in the client's social life, or assistance rendered by friends or clergy. There are, in fact, countless occurrences that might occur during the time that the client is in therapy and might cause the observed changes.

Maturation. Maturation refers to the naturally occurring processes within the individual that can lead to changes in behavior. This is a most plausible rival hypothesis with children or adolescents, whose physical development is not complete and who are developing greater knowledge and coping skills as they grow older. It is also possible that some psychological disturbances have a natural course of improvement analogous to certain physical disease processes (for example, the common cold will nearly always get better without treatment). In the case of depression, which has been observed to be a cyclical phenomenon, this hypothesis must be considered.

It cannot be emphasized too strongly that the plausibility of any rival hypothesis depends on the particular circumstances of the psychotherapeutic situation. Both history and maturation become more plausible the longer the duration of treatment. There is more opportunity for them to operate during the course of a two-year psychoanalysis than during a weekend encounter group. Conversely, the longer clients have exhibited their problems, the less likely it is that they will be affected by situational or maturational processes. For example, homosexual conflicts in an adolescent boy may be of relatively recent onset, relatively cyclical or unstable in character, and therefore readily amenable to maturational or situational events. (A warm, accepting girl, for example, might lead the boy toward heterosexuality and away from homosexuality.) A male in his 40s who has been practicing a more or less exclusive homosexual role for over 20 years is less likely to change as a result of maturation or history.

Consider the psychoanalytic case described in Chapter Three. Do you think history or maturation is a plausible rival hypothesis? Maturation is not especially plausible, given the age of the client and his particular problems. But history is quite plausible in this case. There could have been many important events occurring during the 20 months of treatment. The therapist acknowledges the importance of one such event, the relationship with Sally, whom the client later married. It is the therapist's contention that changes because of therapy motivated the client to seek out Sally and enabled him to relate to her. Could the client have found happiness with Sally without having had therapy? Or could the changes noted by the therapist have been due to his satisfactory new relationship? We do not know, nor can we know with respect to this particular case.

The other three specific rival hypotheses—within the general rival hypothesis that change has nothing to do with therapy—are more subtle but still important to consider.

Reactivity. Especially in research projects, but usually in clinical practice as well, an assessment procedure precedes psychotherapy as a means of estimating or even quantifying the client's status on variables of interest. Reactivity occurs when an assessment procedure is a stimulus to change rather than a passive recording procedure. This is to be distinguished from demand characteristics (or the hello/goodbye effect), where the assessment situation pulls for *reported* change. Reactivity refers to *real* changes in clients that are due to the assessment procedure itself, rather than treatment. The plausibility of this rival hypothesis again depends on the particular circumstances.

One standard pretreatment assessment procedure is an interview covering the client's problems, current circumstances, and developmental history. It is possible for such a review of one's life to "trigger" change processes independent of therapy. In certain research projects, trained observers may visit a family at home and code family interactions during a specified time of the day. Such a procedure may sensitize some of the family members to how they interact with one another and lead them to change their behavior.

Differential selection. Observed change may be due to biases in the assignment of clients to the different conditions that are being compared or evaluated. For example, if psychotherapy is being compared with a no-treatment group, it may happen that the "more suitable" cases are assigned to the therapy group and the "less suitable" cases to the waiting-list control group. Some clients may be judged to be in need of immediate treatment and thus switched from the waiting-list group to the therapy group. Or if two or more different kinds of therapy are being compared, the treatment staff may have certain biases about which kinds of clients are most likely to profit from which therapy.

In clinical settings it is more difficult to guard against differential-selection biases than may at first seem apparent. Mere instructions or good intentions are not sufficient. Evaluators often find themselves in an adversary situation with the treatment staff in a particular setting. Staff members may often agree to the principle of random assignment but then find it difficult to follow through in particular cases where the needs of a particular client become paramount. In clinical settings client-care values tend to be stronger than evaluation, or knowledge-seeking, values. Nor does it usually help to argue that there is no good evidence that one treatment is better than another or that receiving therapy is more helpful than going on the waiting list. Staff members' convictions, based on their clinical experience, are very strong. Differential-selection biases are easier to avoid in settings where the researcher has complete control—that is, in laboratory or quasi-analogue research projects.

Differential attrition. Even when clients or subjects are randomly assigned to treatment conditions, there may be a differential loss of subjects from the comparison groups. For example, people on a waiting list may disappear, either because they improve "spontaneously" and no longer need the services of a clinic or because they become so acutely distressed that they seek help elsewhere. In either case, those remaining on the waiting list yield a distorted estimate of the effects of no treatment. Clients who begin treatment may drop out for various reasons. If dropping out is related to treatment, then the therapeutic results may be biased. For example, if treatment is too stressful or if slow progress leads to discontinuing, then counting only those who complete treatment will produce a bias in favor of psychotherapy. Dropouts or attrition should be noted in research reports.

Constructive changes due to history, maturation, or reactivity are sometimes labeled spontaneous remission. Spontaneous remission refers to change or improvement that is not caused by any formal psychotherapy. The rate of spontaneous remission has been a subject of considerable interest—and controversy—sparked by Eysenck's (1952) suggestion that it be used as a benchmark against which to evaluate psychotherapy. Eysenck concluded that about two-thirds of psychoneurotic clients recover without formal therapy within two years of the onset of the illness. Although this conclusion has been convincingly criticized on theoretical grounds and more recent data yield a different picture (Bergin & Lambert, 1978), the myth that two-thirds of therapy clients will spontaneously remit has died hard. Bergin and Lambert convincingly demonstrated that spontaneous remission varies widely across diagnostic groups (that is, different kinds of client problems) but on average is much less than two-thirds. The median rate in the 17 studies analyzed by Bergin and Lambert was 43%, but given the variability across kinds of clients, this figure cannot be used as a general standard.

Spontaneous remission does occur, however, and must be controlled for if possible. Note that "spontaneous" does *not* imply without cause or reason. History, maturation, and reactivity are all possible causes. One variety of "historical" factor is the seeking of help or support from friends or "invisible" therapists, and such help seeking has been well documented (Gurin, Veroff, & Feld, 1960).

Are Changes Due to Common Processes or to the Therapist?

If we can prove that change has occurred and rule out the rival hypotheses discussed above, we can conclude that the observed changes are due to psychotherapy. Now it becomes of critical importance to consider the distinction between common and specific processes described in Chapter Three. The preferred hypothesis, or psychotherapeutic "claim," is that a particular method of therapy has been effective. The plausible rival hypothesis is that the change is due to the common processes inherent in any therapeutic procedure, not the specific methods.

Because specific treatment methods are always embedded in a context of common processes, this is almost always a very plausible rival hypothesis. Consider the case of behavior therapy described in Chapter Three. The client was given a plausible, "scientific" rationale; was put through a series of structured tasks alleged to be necessary for treatment; was praised and supported for any demonstrated improvement; and was given sympathetic attention and encouragement from a sanctioned healer. You may identify still other common processes.

The power of common processes has been sufficiently well discussed in the previous chapter that further elaboration is unnecessary. But there is one component that has not been sufficiently considered and that deserves separate consideration. It is the presence of special characteristics and unique qualities of a particular therapist. The specific rival hypothesis is that change was caused by the *therapist*, not the therapy. A particular therapist may be unusually charismatic, persuasive, understanding, or compassionate. The particular techniques employed may be irrelevant. What is important is the interaction with a helpful human being. Many of us know of such a person in our social network, the person whom others seek out to discuss problems with, confide in, seek advice from. We feel better having talked with him or her, even though we can point to no particular piece of advice, suggestion, or information provided.

Before we can accept the interpretation that a specific therapy produced change, we must rule out the rival hypothesis that it was produced by a particular therapist. In the three cases described in Chapter Three, the possibility that the therapist rather than the particular therapy produced changes is at least reasonably plausible. In fact, in any therapy situation where a few clients have been seen by the same therapist and where no experimental manipulations have been included, therapist effect will be a plausible rival hypothesis.

We may ask *why* it matters whether therapy works because of common or specific processes or whether it was the therapist or the therapy that produced the successful outcome. After all, if you are a client, you want to get better and you probably don't care how or why you are helped. From the client's perspective this is an understandable and defensible position. Indeed, as will be noted later, you may be wise to choose a therapist rather than a particular kind of therapy if you have reason to believe that a particularly good one is available. If you are a therapist, it might be argued that these distinctions make no difference as long as your clients improve. But not all clients do improve, and clients and the problems they present often change from time to time and place to place. The more information you have about which components of your treatment work, the better you will be able to adapt your methods to new situations and to solve problems when they arise. From a theoretical perspective, information obtained about the role of common and specific processes can lead to more valid principles of behavior change. From a practical perspective, we can make our psychotherapeutic technologies more efficient and economical as we learn more about their necessary and unnecessary components.

Ruling Out Rival Hypotheses: Controlled Research

The best way to rule out plausible rival hypotheses is to employ some kind of formal research design. Two kinds of research design are typically applied to psychotherapy evaluation: group designs and single-subject designs. In a group design several subjects receiving psychotherapy are compared with some control group.

Group Designs: Ensuring Equivalence

If proper inferences are to be drawn from comparisons of treated and control subjects, it is necessary that the two groups be truly *equivalent* at the outset of the study. This is a basic principle of experimentation, but it is often difficult to achieve in psychotherapy research.

There are two procedures for achieving equivalent experimental and control groups: random assignment and matching. Matching is sometimes a useful procedure, but it requires knowledge about what crucial dimensions should be used to match subjects and the assurance that one has measured these crucial dimensions reliably. Matching may involve such variables as age, duration of symptoms, or severity of symptoms. It is best to match individuals rather than to match overall group means. The most straightforward way is to find pairs of potential subjects who are equivalent on the relevant dimensions and then to randomly assign one of them to the experimental (or control) group. As noted in the discussion of differential selection, random assignment (with or without matching) often conflicts with clinical values and is compromised.

In psychotherapy research there are two basic control groups: no-treatment groups—in which subjects do not receive any psychotherapy but are assessed at the same time as the psychotherapy subjects—and attention-placebo control groups—in which subjects receive comparable common processes but none of the specific treatment components given to the psychotherapy group.

No-treatment control groups. A no-treatment control group is typically created by randomly assigning potential subjects or clients to a waiting list or informing them that there are insufficient resources to offer them treatment. This is usually done after initial assessment. Then, efforts are made to recall the no-treatment clients for a second assessment at the same time that the clients who have received psychotherapy are assessed after treatment. Where "analogue" subjects, such as college students with small-animal phobias, are being studied or where persons who want to control their smoking or eating are invited to participate in research projects, the creation of a rigorous no-treatment control group presents few difficulties. Subjects can even be paid to motivate them to participate in the second assessment.

In more naturalistic clinical settings, practical problems in establishing no-treatment controls are more vexing. Some of these have already been noted in the discussion of differential selection. Waiting-list subjects may leave the community, seek treatment elsewhere, or refuse to participate in the second assessment. It is also possible that, when persons are told that they are on a waiting list but will receive treatment later, they will take this to mean they should temporarily cease efforts to solve their own problems, thus making spontaneous remission less likely. And there are ethical issues in delaying or withholding treatment. Many settings now require that clients be informed of the research situation and give written permission to be randomly assigned.

These problems notwithstanding, it is still of great value to employ no-treatment controls in order to learn what will happen to clients who do not receive treatment. This is particularly important in the early stages of developing treatment procedures for a given disorder. The first question to be asked of a new treatment method is whether it works better than nothing.

A good no-treatment control group can effectively rule out the first two general rival hypotheses in Table 4–1. If the treated and untreated subjects are given identical assessment procedures at the same time and the group receiving psychotherapy shows significantly greater change, then it can be concluded that the apparent changes are real and were "caused" by psychotherapy. It is important to understand the reasoning behind this conclusion. Statistical regression and error or bias in the assessment of change would be assumed to affect the no-treatment group and the group receiving psychotherapy equally. Yet in our hypothetical example the psychotherapy group displays greater improvement. Similarly, both no-treatment and psychotherapy groups were equally susceptible to the effects of history, maturation, and reactivity, because both were exposed to identical assessment methods and an equivalent passage of time. It is implausible to think that regression, maturation, or situational factors would affect psychotherapy clients and not the equivalent group that received no treatment.

The basic two-group design—treatment and no-treatment—tells us nothing, however, about the possible contribution of common processes and may or may not speak to the issue of therapist effect, depending on how many therapists participated. If the treated clients were all seen by the same therapist, then therapy and therapists are clearly confounded, and therapist effects are very plausible. The more different therapists involved, the less likely it is that the therapist effect is a factor.

Attention-placebo control groups. An attention-placebo group is needed in order to rule out the common-process rival hypotheses. Such a control group is most typically employed in analogue research or studies on recruited or invited populations. A particularly ingenious kind of attention-placebo procedure was described in Chapter Three as part of a study comparing different methods of treating speech anxiety. In clinic settings attention-placebo controls are often not practical or ethical (O'Leary & Borkovec, 1978). However, there are two alternatives that accomplish much the same purpose: a *minimal-treatment control* and an *alternative-treatment control.*

An alternative treatment is any kind of psychotherapy that is customarily used in mental health settings. Behavior therapy might be compared with client-centered therapy or therapy based on psychoanalytic principles. A typical example is to compare some newly developed or novel treatment with an older or more conventional one. This is often the strategy in institutional settings. All clients might receive the basic institutional program—custodial care, group meetings, and medication—but the experimental clients would receive some additional psychotherapeutic procedures.

A minimal-treatment control group typically provides a therapeutic rationale and regularly scheduled—but fewer—therapy sessions. The amount of therapist contact and attention is often less than for the group receiving psychotherapy, thereby reducing the rigor of this control. But it can be argued that sufficient treatment is offered to provide essential common-process components. A good attention-placebo or minimal-treatment control procedure should seem as plausible or credible to the clients as the "real" treatment (O'Leary & Borkovec, 1978). This can be checked by having clients rate how helpful they believe their treatment is likely to be for them.

An attention-placebo or other control can effectively rule out all three general rival hypotheses if the "experimental" treatment proves superior to the attention-placebo or alternative treatment. Both groups have had equal exposure to common processes and thus were equally susceptible to the effects of history, maturation, statistical regression, and so on.

But suppose that the experimental and attention-placebo groups display an equivalent amount of change. Clearly, no specific effect of therapy has been demonstrated. But what of the rival hypothesis that the observed equal changes had nothing to do with therapy? Perhaps *history* or *maturation* equally affected the psychotherapy and the attention-placebo groups. The interpretation of this situation will depend in part on previous knowledge about the problem and also on whether a no-treatment control group was included in the experiment. In the study on speech anxiety (Paul, 1966), partly described in Chapter Three, the attention-placebo group (which experienced success on a supposedly difficult task) showed significantly greater improvement than a no-treatment control group. But a systematic-desensitization group showed significantly greater improvement than the attention-placebo group. This permitted the conclusion that common processes in psychotherapy had produced greater change than no treatment and that the specifics of the systematic-desensitization method had produced change beyond that inherent in the common processes.

An attention-placebo or alternative-treatment control presents a more stringent test of a specific psychotherapy's effectiveness than a no-treatment control. In the early stages of work on a particular therapeutic method it is reasonable to compare psychotherapy with no therapy. But the previous chapter on common processes, as well as a great deal of research evidence, indicates that any kind of therapy usually produces more change than no therapy. Thus, there is usually more information to be obtained in comparing a psychotherapeutic treatment with an attention-placebo procedure or an alternative therapy. A still more complete and safer experiment would include at least three groups—a psychotherapy group, an attention-placebo group, and a no-treatment control. This can permit the investigator to rule out all the rival hypotheses noted in Table 4–1.

Thus far the discussion of control groups has focused on simple one-factor experiments involving but two or three levels of one independent variable—for example, therapy versus no therapy or two kinds of therapy and no therapy. It is often possible and desirable to increase the information yield of an investigation by including other variables in the design. One particularly important variable is the role of the therapist. If we are comparing two different kinds of therapy, and one therapy is administered by one therapist and the other therapy by a second therapist, then there is a confound between

therapy and therapist. That is, if one group showed greater improvement, we would not know whether it was due to the kind of therapy
or the skill of the therapist. It is necessary to "cross" therapists with
therapies, so that a given therapist sees the same number of clients in
the two different therapy groups. It may be difficult to find therapists
who are comfortable in doing two different kinds of treatment. It is
usually easier to train therapists to administer an attention-placebo
or minimal-treatment program.

Client variables such as the severity of the problem, age, or
social class can also be incorporated into the design of an experiment.
Even when therapist and client variables cannot be manipulated or
varied within the design, they can often be measured in order to
permit correlational or after-the-fact analyses of their contribution to
outcome. For a more detailed discussion of complex psychotherapy
research designs, see Paul, 1967.

Single-Case Methodology

An alternative to the use of control groups is the intensive study
of a single case. It has been argued that this method is particularly
appropriate for psychotherapy research, because each case is unique
and the major questions of interest concern what its controlling variables are. Single-case methodology has been widely used in behavior
modification and behavior therapy (Leitenberg, 1973; Hersen & Barlow, 1976).

Basic to the single-case design is the identification of outcome
criteria that can be assessed quantitatively and reliably and expressed in terms of *rate*. By rate is meant the frequency of the criterion behavior with respect to some period of time—for example,
the number of cigarettes smoked per day, the number of temper tantrums per day, or the percentage of time spent in isolation compared
to interaction with peers. This outcome criterion is measured before
intervention in order to establish a stable *baseline* estimate of its rate.
The subject might be a preschooler observed to spend a great deal of
time by herself in a day-care setting. Observers might take daily
half-hour samples of her behavior for one or two weeks and thereby
gauge her typical baseline level of interaction time with her peers.
The establishment of a stable baseline estimate of the target behavior
is a necessary step before intervening.

Two basic designs are employed in single-case research: *reversal*
design and *multiple-baseline* design. Both start with a baseline
assessment.

Reversal design (ABAB). In this arrangement, baseline is considered
the A condition: the client's rate of performance under normal conditions before intervention. Intervention constitutes the B condition
and is intended to change the rate of the target behavior.

In the case of the preschooler who was considered a social isolate, it was observed that the girl spent much more time interacting with adults (such as teachers) than with other children in the nursery school (Allen, Hart, Buell, Harris, & Wolf, 1964). This behavior is shown graphically in the first A phase of Figure 4–1. Her activities and skills—for example, her creative use of paints and clay—drew interest from adults but not from other children. It was hypothesized that adult attention was reinforcing solitary play. The treatment plan was to give her maximum adult attention contingent on play with another child and minimum attention for solitary play or interaction with an adult only. Other nursery school activities and procedures remained constant. This program was carried out for six days. The result, depicted in the first B phase of Figure 4–1, was a sharp increase in the proportion of time spent with peers and a concomitant reduction in time spent interacting with adults.

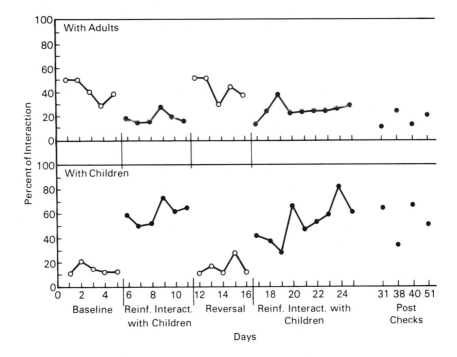

Figure 4–1. Percentage of time spent in social interaction with adults and with children during approximately two hours of each morning session. (From "Effects of Social Reinforcement on Isolate Behavior of a Nursery School Child," by K. E. Allen, B. M. Hart, J. S. Buell, F. Q. Harris, and M. W. Wolf, *Child Development,* 1964, *35,* 511–518. Copyright 1964 by the Society for Research in Child Development, Inc. Reprinted by permission.)

At this point in the case study (AB), what can be concluded about rival hypotheses? Only that real change has occurred (assuming that appropriate precautions about reliable and unbiased observations have been taken). History and maturation remain plausible rival causes of change. Another child might have entered the school and taken a special interest in our target youngster during the two weeks of intervention; some maturational process might have been set off by events at home or in school. Reactivity is less likely in this situation, because the presence of observers did not seem to influence her behavior during the baseline period. But as yet there is no compelling evidence that the intervention caused the observed change in behavior.

Baseline conditions were then reinstated—the contingencies were reversed—so that adult social reinforcement was again dispensed when she was alone and not when she was playing with her peers. This is the second A in the ABA design. Observers continued to take data on her behavior for five days. The results are depicted in Figure 4–1, where it can be seen that her social interaction with other children dropped to baseline level and her adult interaction time increased correspondingly. This additional manipulation rules out history and maturation as plausible rival causes of change. This is so because history and maturation are reasonably assumed to be linear processes; that is, they would tend to operate in one direction. It is implausible that situational events would first lead to an increase in social interaction and then a decrease and that the timing would be coincidental with the therapeutic intervention. Common processes are also well ruled out, because the presence of observers and the overall amount of adult attention and interest have been constant throughout.

This case study is made even more convincing and therapeutic goals are best served when intervention (B) is then reintroduced, as depicted in Figure 4–1. The increase in amount of interaction with children contiguous with the changed contingencies is further evidence in support of the intervention as causal. It is always desirable to conclude a study of this sort at the point where the client is behaving in the desired way. To do otherwise would be unethical.

The basic reversal strategy is widely used, especially in behavior-therapy research, and is a powerful way of demonstrating the effectiveness of intervention procedures. A variation of the reversal design is the withdrawal design. In the third phase (A) the therapeutic procedure is simply discontinued instead of applied to some alternative behavior (Leitenberg, 1973). The use of the withdrawal design in evaluating the effectiveness of a token is presented in Chapter Seven. The intervention—tokens contingent on work—was withdrawn and instead tokens were given whether patients worked or not. Such designs are most useful in institutional settings such as schools, day-care centers or hospitals, where the investigator or clinician can obtain control of the relevant contingencies. One limitation, however, is that there are occasions when the contingencies cannot be altered or reversed or when it is undesirable to do so. Client-care considerations may preclude reversal or it may be impossible to reinstate contingencies, as when a mother may not remember how she once responded to her child.

Multiple-baseline design. The multiple-baseline design is useful for situations where reversal is not feasible and where it is possible to identify two or more problem behaviors, outcome criteria, that are relatively independent (it is, however, usually difficult to find independent problems). Baseline measurements on the problem behaviors are obtained. Then, intervention is introduced selectively for only one of them. After the effect of intervention has stabilized, the same intervention is introduced for the second problem behavior, and its effect is then assessed. The procedure can be repeated on a third problem behavior.

In a study of retardate's eating at mealtime, several problem behaviors were noted: using fingers instead of utensils, stealing food from a neighbor, putting mouth down to food or plate. The effect of removing the retardate from the dining room after undesirable behavior was studied, using the multiple-baseline procedure. A given behavior changed only when the removal-from-dining-room contingency was in effect for that behavior (Barton, Guess, Garcia, & Baer, 1970).

The logic behind the multiple-baseline design is that it is very improbable that history, maturation, or common processes would affect first one problem behavior and then the other in the exact temporal sequence corresponding with the therapeutic intervention. If each problem behavior changes only when contingencies are manipulated, strong evidence exists for contingency causation.

Single-case research is most used in behavior therapy, but it has broader applicability. Client-centered therapy (for example, see Truax, 1966) can also be evaluated with this tool.

Implications for Evaluating Professional and Popular Literature

The material in this chapter is intended to provide a comprehensive framework for evaluating psychotherapeutic claims in both the professional and popular literature. One can judge psychotherapies in terms of how well they perform with respect to the three evaluative criteria: theoretical adequacy, empirical results, and practical efficiency. In judging results, one can consider the thoroughness of descriptions and procedures, the quality of outcome data, and the extent to which plausible rival hypotheses have been considered and ruled out.

While controlled research is the best way to rule out rival hypotheses and establish specific cause-and-effect relationships between psychotherapeutic procedures and outcomes, other kinds of clinical data are valuable, providing some perspective is maintained on the limitations of the information. A well-described case can suggest that a new treatment is worthy of further clinical use or empirical evaluation or that there are problems to be considered in the application of an older treatment. Because clinical technologies are constantly evolving, there will always be a place for the case report in the development of clinical knowledge. The quality of the case report—precision of the outcome data, description of the intervention procedures, and salient characteristics of the client and therapist—remains important in judging the contribution of particular case studies. It must be remembered, however, that for any given case a number of plausible rival hypotheses always exist. Thus, a single case study cannot establish cause-and-effect relationships (unless a reversal or multiple-baseline design is used).

Moving beyond single case studies, the next level of evaluating psychotherapy is a series of cases treated with the same approach. This is termed a *clinical trial* when conducted in a systematic way. For example, the next five or even ten clients who present a particular problem might all be treated with a technique deemed promising on the basis of single case studies. Then the outcome can be carefully evaluated. Clinical trials can be persuasive if the cases are indeed consecutive (unselected) referrals or if they are chosen randomly. These conditions are important, because in both single case reports and clinical trials *differential selection* and *differential attrition* are important rival hypotheses. The client or clients selected for treatment may not be representative or may be chosen because they are likely to improve. Or clients who fail to improve may drop out of therapy and thus not be reported. Selection or attrition bias operates even more clearly in decisions about whether to publish clinical data. The professional journals prefer positive findings; unsuccessful cases have much lower interest value. Therefore, clinicians are much more likely to submit successful cases, and the reader of journals does not know how representative the successful cases are.

Many books on psychotherapy are crude reports of clinical trials. The authors typically describe their theory and technique and include a number of anecdotal reports of successful cases. These accounts are subject to *all* the major rival hypotheses described in this chapter. But if the cases and outcomes are carefully described and selection biases minimized, the plausibility for rival hypotheses lessens as the number of successful cases accumulates. History remains a very plausible rival hypothesis for a single case. But if five cases are successfully handled with a particular therapeutic approach, it becomes much less likely that history or situational events produced the observed changes in all five. And what if ten cases are reported? Or 20? At some point it becomes more plausible to accept the hypothesis that therapy is producing the change rather than invoke situational or maturational events in each case. Of course, if the therapist is the same in all the reported cases, therapy and therapist are confounded and therapist effect remains quite plausible. But what if other clinicians also report successful cases with the same or similar methods? Again, the plausibility of the therapeutic procedure as the causal agent is increased.

I have emphasized the importance of specificity and concreteness in the description of psychotherapy, especially of its results. Reports of satisfaction by clients must be regarded with some skepticism until some of the objections—rival hypotheses—raised in this chapter are met. This is not to argue that client satisfaction is an irrelevant outcome or criterion. The point is that client reports can be influenced by several factors, thus rendering them an imperfect outcome criterion. Much the same point can be made with respect to therapist judgments of therapeutic outcome. Given all of these qualifications, careful clinical descriptions and reports can still lead to the development of reliable, cumulative knowledge. This possibility will be illustrated by discussing an example of an influential clinical study that did not employ either control groups or systematic single-case-study methodology.

The Masters and Johnson Sexual Therapy

In 1970 William Masters and Virginia Johnson published a book describing a rationale and methods of treatment for several kinds of sexual dysfunction, especially male premature ejaculation and female inability to achieve orgasm. A number of cases were described in detail, and figures were presented indexing the percentage of clients that had been successfully treated. It was reported that 83% of women with primary orgasmic dysfunction (had never achieved orgasm during intercourse) were successfully treated; 98% of men with premature ejaculation were successfully treated. This work has had a major impact on the field of the treatment of sexual dysfunction and has inspired numerous programs that essentially followed the Masters and Johnson procedures or introduced modifications and extensions. It is instructive to evaluate the Masters and Johnson work with the framework for considering plausible rival hypotheses.

1. Did change really occur? The data were almost exclusively self-reports by husband or wife concerning orgasmic experience or the duration of intercourse, and self-reports are vulnerable to bias or distortion. But in this case the events reported were fairly discrete, observable behaviors. And husband and wife provided important

checks on each other. The rival hypothesis that no change really occurred seems implausible in this particular situation.

2. Was change due to treatment? Could history, maturation, or reactivity produce the observed changes? Most of the couples were in their
30s or older and had long-standing problems. Maturation, therefore,
seems an unlikely rival hypothesis. Clinical experience indicates that
sexual dysfunction between particular couples does not tend to improve spontaneously and is difficult to treat with conventional
psychotherapy. The success rates reported by Masters and Johnson
are very high. Given the inherent difficulty of treating sexual dysfunctions, the age of the clients, and the duration of their symptoms,
it seems very unlikely that history, maturation, or reactivity caused
the results.

　　　Differential selection needs to be considered, because most cases
were referred by professionals and couples had to be motivated (and
able to bear the expense) to travel to St. Louis for therapy. Whether
the program can be generalized to less affluent couples could be
questioned.

3. Were changes due to common processes or to therapist effect?
Although Masters and Johnson do not make it explicit, several
therapists were apparently involved in their work. This makes a
therapist-effect interpretation less plausible but still possible, because the other therapist pairs were trained by Masters and Johnson
and probably received regular supervision by them.

　　　The common-processes interpretation, however, is worth considering and has some plausibility. Speaking against the common-
process hypothesis is the fact that sexual dysfunctions do not respond
to conventional psychotherapy nearly so dramatically as they did to
the Masters and Johnson program. Because these other diverse
psychotherapies embody common processes as well as specific components, one would have to argue that the common processes in Masters and Johnson's program were unusually potent. There is some
basis for arguing that this was so.

　　　Consider the context of the treatment reported by Masters and
Johnson. Couples were referred by a professional and had to make
appointments some time in advance. These conditions could have
communicated that this kind of treatment was "special" and that it
was a privilege to receive it. More importantly, couples had to arrange to journey to St. Louis and devote two weeks to the intensive
treatment program. This involved considerable expense and a major
disruption in their lives. The therapeutic journey has some rough
similarities to pilgrimages to religious healing shrines and could
have invoked strong expectations of success (Frank, 1973). Most of the
treatment took place in prestigious medical settings. The Masters and
Johnson program may have capitalized on unusually powerful

common processes, which therefore may be a plausible rival cause of the observed change.

Although there is still relatively little controlled research on sexual dysfunction, both subsequent clinical experience with Masters and Johnson's program (or variations of it) and controlled research have been consistently promising over a wide range of settings and therapists (Marks, 1978). Sexual-dysfunction therapists have varied tremendously in age, level of experience, and prestige. Sexual-skills training programs have worked in a variety of settings and with groups as well as individuals. Thus, although the original work was susceptible to the common-process rival hypothesis, subsequent work has tended to make this possibility much less plausible. Client couples have also varied widely in demographic and personality characteristics, making the differential-selection hypothesis less plausible as well.

The Masters and Johnson program illustrates the potential of careful clinical description and accumulation of statistical information on a series of cases. Their work may be considered a careful *clinical-trials* evaluation of the treatment program. More-rigorous research methodology is still needed to clarify the role of common processes and to isolate which elements within the complex treatment are more and less effective.

Epilogue

This chapter has emphasized *outcome research* in psychotherapy and, in so doing, has intentionally neglected other issues. Below, several important issues are briefly discussed to help guide you through the literature of psychotherapy research.

Process Research "versus" Outcome Research

Process studies typically deal with therapist/client interactions or with characteristics of clients or therapists. Is it wiser to demonstrate first that psychotherapy works (its outcome) before examining processes, or must process be understood before outcome can be meaningfully evaluated? My own view is that promising outcome effects should be demonstrated before any expensive search for process variables is undertaken. Process variables are potentially of great importance in understanding how various outcomes come about. It is desirable to obtain process data—as well as "before-and-after" data—in order to determine the relationship between the two. Process and outcome are complementary phenomena rather than adversaries (Kiesler, 1973).

Many process variables have been studied, including various characteristics of therapists and clients believed to be important for therapeutic success (Kiesler, 1973). Important process variables are, to a large extent, determined by the particular therapeutic rationale. The relationship between a therapist's depth of interpretation and a client's resistance is an important issue for psychoanalytically oriented therapy. A study directed at this issue (Speisman, 1959) is described in Chapter Five. A client-centered process issue is the relationship between therapist levels of genuineness, warmth, and empathy, and client levels of experiencing. Studies illustrating this issue are considered in Chapter Six.

A very appealing process issue is the matching of clients and therapists to facilitate communication and, it is hoped, outcome. Researchers have sought matchings in terms of demographic characteristics, personality variables, cognitive structure, and values. Although some of this literature is promising, no strong findings have yet emerged (see Parloff, Waskow, & Wolfe, 1978, pp. 255–273).

Analogue Research "versus" Naturalistic Research

This is another false dichotomy, but the terminology is often useful for description. Naturalistic research involves studying therapy as it normally occurs in clinical settings, and it is often correlational in nature. Clients have sought help for disabling problems, and the therapists are "real" in the sense of doing it for a living. Analogue research involves studying phenomena that are believed to be like therapy in some important way. For example, the way therapists make judgments or decisions could be studied by presenting real therapists with (controlled) artificial information about hypothetical clients. Or analogue research may involve applying therapy techniques to subjects who are recruited—college students with specific phobias—but who are relatively "normal."

Analogue therapy is usually much more standardized in terms of sessions and procedures than real therapy. Analogue studies are typically experimental rather than correlational and often permit more-rigorous control, so that rival hypotheses can be ruled out. They may be criticized as having little relevance for "real psychotherapy." For example, much work on the treatment of phobias has been with college students whose fears are not incapacitating and who are generally well adjusted. The results obtained may not apply to clinical phobics, who are usually incapacitated by their fears and have other serious psychological problems (Kazdin, 1978).

Internal Validity "versus" External Validity

Internal validity involves drawing unambiguous conclusions from a research study by ruling out plausible rival hypotheses. The concern is that the conclusions drawn are valid for the particular circumstances of a given experiment. External validity (Campbell & Stanley, 1966) refers to the confidence we have that the conclusion will apply to groups or situations other than the particular one studied. That is, can the conclusions be *generalized* to other clients or therapists?

Analogue studies may have better internal validity than naturalistic studies, but their findings may not generalize to "natural" settings. A therapeutic procedure that works with "weak" fears of normal persons may be ineffective with strong fears in disturbed individuals. The extent to which research findings can be generalized can be ascertained only by further (research) experience.

Follow-Up and Maintenance of Change

Our discussion of therapy evaluation has focused on changes that immediately follow treatment. This criterion is much too limited. Effective psychotherapy must produce durable, lasting changes, and follow-up assessment is needed to determine whether it has. Therapy clients or subjects should be evaluated after the passage of an appreciable amount of time. Unfortunately, it is expensive and difficult to track down former clients and obtain follow-up data. Note that, in both the psychoanalytic and behavior-therapy cases described in Chapter Three, anecdotal follow-up information was available and added considerably to the credibility of the treatment's effectiveness.

Summary

Quality of theory, cost-effectiveness ratio, and outcome all need to be considered when evaluating psychotherapy. The quality of the theory can be judged in terms of its internal consistency, how reliably and objectively its key concepts can be measured, and its compatibility with available psychological knowledge. Cost-effectiveness analysis balances the cost of delivering and undergoing a particular kind of psychotherapy against the results of the therapy. This dimension provides a useful focus on differences in cost among therapies. Outcome, the most important of the three dimensions, refers to demonstrable constructive changes produced by specific kinds of therapy. Its evaluation involves the application of research methodology to psychotherapy.

The broad question "Does psychotherapy work?" is too vague and must be replaced by more specific questions, such as what treatment works best for what problems and under which set of circumstances. Psychotherapy research is complicated by inherent difficulties in defining and measuring the independent variable—the subjects or clients—and, especially, the dependent variable—treatment outcome. The more specific the description of what was done, to whom, and with what effects, the more useful the experiment or report.

Measuring psychotherapeutic outcomes first involves decisions about the goals of treatment. Both client values and the particular theoretical orientations of psychotherapists enter into such decisions. The measurement of outcome may involve one or more sources of data: the client, the therapist, or some third party such as a significant other, rater, or judge. Data from clients and therapists are the easiest to obtain but are likely to be biased by the interest and commitment of the parties to the treatment. Third-party measures are likely to be more objective but are also more expensive. Information about therapy outcomes can be obtained from the client's behavior in therapy sessions, questionnaires, performance tests or tasks in the clinic, and observations or inferences about the client's behavior in the natural environment. This latter approach is likely to be more meaningful and valid, but it tends to be quite expensive and can often be afforded only by research projects and not by practitioners.

Psychotherapists tend to believe that clients improve in response to their specific techniques. But three major classes of plausible rival hypotheses offer alternative explanations of what occurred and why. The first is that no real client change has occurred and that apparent change is due to inadequate measurement or some kind of bias or artifact. The second is that change has occurred but has nothing to do with therapy. History (situational events) or maturation (naturally occurring processes within the client) are strong rival hypotheses in any therapeutic situation, especially when therapy occurs over a long period of time. Third, change may have occurred due to therapy but have nothing to do with specific techniques. The common processes described in Chapter Three or the specific therapist may have produced them.

Research designs are the most powerful way of ruling out plausible rival hypotheses. In a group design, subjects receiving psychotherapy are compared with a control group. Three major kinds of controls are a nontreated control group, which receives no intervention; an attention-placebo group, which receives the common processes of therapy but no specific treatment that is believed to be effective or relevant; and a group that receives an alternative treatment. Only an attention-placebo procedure or some kind of alternative treatment controls for common processes.

Single-subject designs are another way to rule out rival hypotheses. In this arrangement, baseline measurements are made, intervention is introduced for a time, and then it is withdrawn or the contingencies are reversed. Measurements are taken at baseline, after intervention, and following the removal of the intervention. In the multiple-baseline design, two problem behaviors are measured, and intervention is introduced one behavior at a time. Changes in the designated problem behavior at the time of intervention reflect specific treatment effects.

Case studies, a series of cases, or quasi-research designs can also contribute useful information about psychotherapeutic effectiveness.

An example of an influential but nonexperimental program is the Masters and Johnson treatment for sexual dysfunction. The plausibility of several important rival hypotheses was greatly reduced by careful description of treatment, clients, and outcome.

Outcome evaluation is but one approach to research on psychotherapy. Many investigators focus on process variables believed to be important for outcome. Psychotherapy research also differs in the extent to which it is naturalistic—dealing with real clients or therapists—or uses analogues, wherein elements of the psychotherapeutic situation are simulated. External validity—whether findings can be generalized to situations other than the one directly studied—is an empirical issue that must also be considered in psychotherapy research.

Suggested Readings

1. Cozby, P. C. *Methods in behavioral research*. Palo Alto, Calif.: Mayfield, 1977. A primer on research principles and methods for students not having prior work on the process of scientific inquiry.
2. Campbell, D. T., & Stanley, J. C. *Experimental and quasi-experimental designs for research*. Chicago: Rand McNally, 1966. An influential classic. Describes various research designs and details how they do or do not rule out rival hypotheses.
3. Hersen, M., & Barlow, D. H. *Single case experimental designs*. New York: Pergamon Press, 1976. A comprehensive review of single-subject methodology in psychotherapy and behavior modification.
4. Lichtenstein, E. Techniques for assessing outcomes of psychotherapy. In P. McReynolds (Ed.), *Advances in psychological assessment* (Vol. 2). Palo Alto, Calif.: Science and Behavior Books, 1971. Pp. 178–197. A critical discussion of outcome measures.

PART III

Theory and Clinical Application: Three Approaches to Psychotherapy

The aim of Part Three is to describe and evaluate the major forms of psychotherapy. Because there are so many different kinds of therapies, there is a problem in choosing which to present. One alternative is to present brief, perhaps schematic, descriptions of a large number of psychotherapies. The alternative I have chosen is to concentrate on the three approaches I believe to be most important. To judge "importance" I considered historical impact, current use, and implications for the future. Each of the three chosen approaches contains a number of variations. Although some of these are noted and described, I have mainly attempted to present the "central tendency," or basic core, of each approach. My choices, though defensible, are also arbitrary. For interested readers, Appendix One at the end of the book presents brief descriptions of various additional psychotherapies as they relate to the three major approaches.

The three approaches considered are the psychoanalytic—Freudian-based therapies; the humanistic—notably client-centered and Gestalt therapy; and behavior therapy. These three have distinctive features that illustrate several of the important differences among psychotherapies.

Ideally, if you are to "know" a psychotherapy, information from three sources should be integrated. First, you should consider what therapists *say* about what they do and why they do it; these are the theories and descriptions of psychotherapeutic techniques. Second, you should consider what therapists actually *do* in practice. Theory and practice are different. It is difficult to find out what therapists really do, but your psychology department may have audio tapes or films demonstrating therapeutic procedures. Third, you should consider the empirical source—what information about processes and outcomes is available from clinical or laboratory research.

The chapters in Part Three are organized around these three sources. The basic theory, or rationale, for each approach is described, along with the key concepts and techniques. A case example is then discussed. These case studies, along with the ones presented in Chapter Three, provide some idea of what therapy is like. Each chapter also contains descriptions of representative research studies, as well as some summary statements about empirical information bearing on the therapeutic method.

This book's organization is not meant to imply that all, or even most, therapists use one approach exclusively. In fact, most counselors and therapists view themselves as eclectic, using principles and techniques from many approaches (Garfield & Kurtz, 1977). Yet most therapists do have a primary reference, or position, that can usually be construed as one of the three approaches considered here. This primary orientation serves as a base on which other principles and methods can be added.

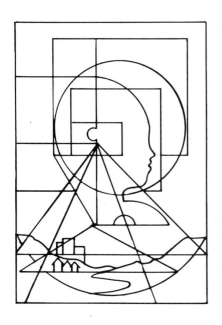

FIVE

Psychoanalytic Psychotherapy

Introduction: Assumptions and Distinctions

Psychoanalytic theory is the most influential one in the field of psychotherapy. This chapter briefly summarizes the basic theory and then describes the key features of therapy. An illustrative case is presented, followed by two examples of research in psychoanalytic therapy. The chapter concludes with a consideration of psychoanalytic psychotherapy in the light of the three evaluative dimensions described in Chapter Four—quality of theory, cost-effectiveness, and outcome.

Childhood Origins of Mental Illness

Psychoanalytic therapy is based on the theories and techniques first developed by Sigmund Freud and later modified by both his followers and those who defected to form rival approaches. Psychoanalysis is a theory of personality, a theory of psychopathology, and a theory and technique of therapy. Psychoanalytic therapy is based on three fundamental assumptions about mental illness (Robbins & Wallerstein, 1959, p. 27):

1. Mental illness derives from otherwise insoluble intrapsychic conflicts. ["Otherwise insoluble" means that symptoms represent partial solutions to conflicts that the person is unable to solve in a more adaptive way.]
2. These intrapsychic conflicts are largely unconscious.
3. The unconscious intrapsychic conflicts are related to early-childhood experiences and represent inadequately resolved infantile conflicts.

Because psychoanalytic therapy is based on these assumptions, it is useful to consider their implications in detail. Psychoanalytic theory emphasizes organismic, or internal, processes as crucial for the development and maintenance of behavior, both normal and deviant. Freud used the terms *id, ego,* and *superego* to describe, in a metaphorical way, the three major sets of processes that underlie behavior. Although some psychoanalytic writing appears to reify these constructs, they are best viewed as processes. The id represents the drives or wishes that energize behavior. The ego represents those processes concerned with mediating the person's relationship to the external world, as developed through repeated interactions. The superego represents the individual's internalization of moral standards imparted by those responsible for early socialization.

Intrapsychic conflicts involve inconsistencies among (or within) these three sets of processes. In psychoanalytic theory, the workings of these processes are largely below the level of awareness; they are unconscious. This is theorized to be especially true for id and superego processes and partly true of ego functions. The less awareness an individual has of ego processes, the less control he or she has and the greater the potential for dysfunctional conflict. Childhood is seen as a fertile learning ground for behavioral and emotional dysfunction, because children's drives or wishes are relatively strong relative to the controlling or modulating capacity of their ego functions.

Both child and adult have the difficult task of satisfying basic drives and wishes within two demanding sets of constraints: (1) the limits imposed by external reality, in the sense both of availability of resources and the need to avoid serious negative consequences; and (2) the constraints of internalized moral standards, which if violated might lead to shame or guilt. It is learned—at an unconscious level—that expression of drives or needs may lead to pain or negative consequences from either the environment—for example, parents— or from internalized moral standards. Therefore, the child experiences anxiety over expressing drives or needs and learns various *defense mechanisms* to help master this anxiety. Defense mechanisms reduce anxiety and partially satisfy drives or needs. Defenses operate primarily at the unconscious level.

Defenses, in psychoanalytic theory, are viewed as normal processes, in that all of us must learn to compromise some of our needs in order to get along both with our environment and our own internalized standards. But problems often develop. There may be inherited or constitutional factors that produce unusually strong drives or inhibit adequate learning from the environment. More frequently, the environment may be unfavorable. The nuclear family is viewed as crucial for the child's development of adequate ego and superego processes. If key family members are insufficiently available, insensitive, inconsistent, harsh, overly indulgent, or some combination of these, the "balance of power" among the three sets of processes will be disrupted. For example, inappropriate moral standards (superego processes) may develop because of the inadequacies of the primary socializing agents. Excessively strict but caring parents might lead the child to adopt overly severe internalized standards; highly inconsistent, rejecting parents might leave the child unable to internalize acceptable standards.

To summarize, psychoanalytic theory believes that neurotic conflicts are primarily learned in childhood through faulty interactions with significant socializing agents. The conflicts are primarily unconscious and lead to characteristic ways of dealing with impulses and significant others that come to create difficulty for individuals or those around them. The job of psychoanalytic therapy is to restore a favorable balance of interaction among the three sets of mental processes. Crucial to this task is the developing of greater ego control, or awareness of the defensive, maladaptive cognitive and interpersonal behaviors and of their origins in childhood. This ego control permits the individual to adjust his or her behavior more appropriately to the current situation, rather than repeating old routines learned in childhood.

Psychoanalysis and Psychoanalytic Psychotherapy

It is important to distinguish between psychoanalysis and psychotherapy based on psychoanalytic principles and techniques. Psychoanalysis is a rather specialized form of psychotherapy and, strictly speaking, may only be carried out by someone who has undergone formal psychoanalytic training as described in Chapter Two. In contrast, numerous therapists of various persuasions utilize psychoanalytic ideas in their work. Psychoanalysis as a form of treatment typically refers to therapy occurring four or more times a week for a minimum of two years. Typically, a couch is employed, with the therapist sitting to the side and in back of a reclining client. Both parties have a long-term commitment to resolve intrapsychic conflicts. Pure psychoanalysis is an infrequently conducted treatment, because it requires a uniquely trained therapist, is time-consuming and expensive for the client, and is not viewed as appropriate for several kinds of problems. In addition, circumstances frequently dictate shorter treatment.

Psychoanalytic psychotherapy varies greatly in structure and format. Some clients might be seen twice a week for as long as two years, and others might be seen once a week for but a few months. Typically, client and therapist are in a face-to-face relationship, and the goals are relief of symptoms or a more limited resolution of intrapsychic conflicts. The number and spacing of sessions varies considerably, and there are also differences in goals or objectives depending on the particular therapists and clients. A unifying theme is the utilization of basic psychoanalytic ideas. Although psychoanalysis is infrequently practiced as a pure treatment approach, psychoanalytic ideas are widely used and remain the most influential body of clinical knowledge and lore in the mental health field. Freudian notions about the importance of childhood experience, unconscious processes, and the role of anxiety and defense mechanisms in the formation and maintenance of deviant behavior are exceedingly influential among practicing psychotherapists.

Theory and Technique: Basic Concepts

Preliminaries

Before psychotherapy of any sort begins, the therapist and prospective client must share information in order to decide whether they should begin therapy together and, if so, under what arrangements or ground rules. This is especially important for psychoanalysis (or any long-term treatment) in which the commitments of time and money involved dictate careful consideration by both parties. The psychoanalytic therapist will want to find out about the client's problems, their origins and history, and the client's current interpersonal and vocational situation and will probably also do a developmental review of the client's life. The client will probably want to know something about the therapist's fees and working arrangements and will want to consider the therapist's treatment recommendations. The information exchange and negotiation may take several sessions before treatment per se begins. The preliminaries are almost always conducted face to face, and, if psychoanalysis is agreed on, then the positioning of the participants changes accordingly.

It is not uncommon to agree on a trial period—say, three to six months—after which the client and therapist will decide whether to continue. This is sometimes done in order to permit the client to have some direct experience with the process of psychoanalysis or psychoanalytic psychotherapy, because verbal descriptions of such a complex process must necessarily be incomplete. The two-month "exploratory" period in the psychoanalytic case study described in Chapter Three illustrates this procedure.

The ground rules of psychoanalytic treatment are especially important. These include fees and billing; the scheduling of appointments; responsibility for cancellation, missed appointments, and lateness; and what kind of behavior is expected from client and therapist. The client must be clearly told about the rules for each of these matters —which may vary somewhat from therapist to therapist—in order to minimize complications that may arise if one or the other party does not follow through.

The Couch

If psychoanalysis is agreed on, the client is asked to recline on a couch or sofa with the therapist out of the patient's line of vision. It is important to remember that *the couch is rarely employed outside of formal psychoanalytic treatment.* Freud admitted that he resorted to the use of the couch because he could not bear to be looked at by patients for hours at a time. Subsequently, it became apparent that such a physical arrangement has certain advantages. Being out of sight, the analyst provides relatively fewer cues about his or her reactions to the client's talk. Clients are thus thrown more on their own, in the sense of having to evaluate their thoughts and feelings without external help. The lessening of cues and response from the analyst also facilitates the development of the all-important transference described below. Because little information about the therapist is available, it is easier for the client to develop fantasies about the therapist.

Free Association

Whether the therapist uses psychoanalysis with the couch or psychoanalytically oriented psychotherapy, the client's principal task is that of free association. This does not mean that the client is expected to emit "word-salad" gibberish or to speak in disconnected sentences. It means that the client is given full responsibility for initiating talk and is instructed not to censor any thoughts or feelings that he or she may have. All thoughts, feelings, or images that come to awareness are to be reported, no matter how trivial, embarrassing, or socially unacceptable. Here is how one therapist stated it to a client:

> I can help you best if you say whatever thoughts and feelings come to your mind, even if they seem irrelevant, immaterial, foolish, embarrassing, upsetting, or if they're about me, even very personally, just as they come, without censoring or editing [Lewin, 1970, p. 67–68].

Free association is a technique for indirectly examining the unconscious processes that are the focus of psychoanalytic treatment. The influence of external or situational factors is minimized, so that the client's talk is primarily determined by internal factors. The psychoanalytic therapist does not expect that free association will lead to unconscious material directly, but rather that it will lead to defenses or resistance and that these will provide clues to basic conflicts. Thus, the patient's difficulties in free associating—blocking or avoidance of topics—are extremely important in and of themselves.

Early in his career, Freud used other techniques for getting at repressed material, including hypnosis and a pressure technique, in which he held or rubbed the patients' heads and commanded them to remember. These techniques were associated with earlier versions of psychoanalytic treatment, which focused on coaxing material into consciousness. As psychoanalysis became more of an ego psychology and focused more on resistance and defense mechanisms, free association became increasingly important.

The content of client talk under the therapist's instructions to free-associate varies, depending on the particular problem. Contrary to popular belief, clients in psychoanalytic therapy are *not* expected to talk *primarily* about their childhoods or their fantasies, although these are important topics. Current reality issues—interpersonal problems with family, friends, or colleagues—are of great importance and are the expected starting place. Clients, after all, seek help for current problems. But it is expected that, over the course of therapy, client talk will include childhood and the analytic (therapeutic) situation as well.

In less-intensive treatment, free association is likely to be modified by the therapist's focusing on certain issues or asking more questions. However, within any given topic or issue, clients are still expected to talk or respond to the best of their ability without censoring.

Resistance

As the client tries to free-associate, the therapist remains a neutral "blank screen" and gives the client's productions "evenly divided attention." That is, the therapist listens in a nonjudgmental but sympathetic manner and permits clients to tell their stories. Inevitably, resistance emerges. Resistance can be defined as a defense operating against the efforts of therapy, or the client's failure to comply with an agreed-on rule of the therapy. In this case the rule is not to censor any ideas or feelings.

Resistance permits the client and therapist to observe the client's characteristic defensive or avoidance behaviors *in situ*—that is, while they are actually occurring. Examples of resistive behavior would be difficulty in free-associating, quarreling about the rules of therapy (for example, scheduling), lateness or absence; abrupt change of topic; or avoiding certain topics. Departures from the client's customary way of talking or describing events or experiences are often a sign of resistance. Examples are silence in a client who usually talks freely or failure to mention a relationship that had previously been the focus of attention.

Why does resistance develop, given the client's apparent commitment to undergo therapy? The client also has a major investment in the status quo. To change, to come to know what has been repressed, may be frightening. Many of us delay or avoid consulting a doctor or dentist because of a similar kind of resistance. Psychoanalytic therapists are not critical of resistances. They view them as inevitable and as informative about defenses and the neurotic conflicts underlying the defenses.

Regression and Frustration

As psychoanalytic psychotherapy proceeds, the client experiences a regression to more childlike ways of thinking, feeling, and acting *while in the therapeutic situation.* This therapeutic regression is facilitated by several factors: the use of a couch and the reclining position (in psychoanalysis), the frequent sessions, the inherent dependency involved in seeking help from another, and the frustration that arises from the unusual and "asymmetric" interpersonal relationship between client and psychoanalytic psychotherapist. The client self-discloses a great deal, but the therapist self-discloses very little and gives relatively little reaction. Not surprisingly, the client experiences irritation and frustration at this "unfavorable balance of trade" (Menninger, 1958).

The therapeutic regression is important and useful, because infantile childhood conflicts and childlike ways of dealing with conflict are assumed to be crucial in the development and maintenance of neurotic behavior. The therapeutic regression permits both client and therapist to observe how much and in what ways the client still relies on immature thinking and behaving. It is important to emphasize that therapeutic regression refers to behavior in the psychotherapeutic situation and not to behavior in the natural environment. Psychoanalytic clinicians try to select clients who have the necessary "ego strength" to maintain stability in their everyday lives while working through a therapeutic regression with their psychotherapist. The less intensive or the briefer the therapy, the less intense the regression.

Transference

In transference, clients feel and behave toward the therapist as they did toward significant figures in their childhood, especially their parents. Transference is one aspect of a therapeutic regression and is viewed as a natural and exceedingly important process in psychoanalytic psychotherapy. Transference reactions are largely unconscious.

The concept of transference often seems strange, and it is occasionally the target of ridicule by critics of psychoanalysis. Psychoanalytic theory assumes that many of our characteristic ways of relating to people were learned early in life from interactions with parent figures. The therapist becomes an important figure in the client's life and becomes the target of these pervasive interpersonal modes of behaving. Why does the therapist become so important and become the target of transference? One reason is the structure of psychoanalytic therapy and the inherent dependency of the client role. In psychoanalysis the two parties may be meeting four or five times a week, and the client is looking to the therapist for wisdom and help. Consider also that the client is in enough psychological pain to have entered treatment and is probably paying hefty fees for therapy. The same previously noted factors that facilitate the therapeutic regression are also relevant. Therapists may be out of sight on a couch, tend to provide relatively little information about themselves, and thus facilitate the development of "unrealistic" fantasies.

Typically, the client develops a positive transference in the early stages of therapy, when there is an expectation of help and the optimism that one usually experiences when starting a course of treatment. This often turns into negative transference, sometimes strongly so, toward the middle of therapy. The client often gets discouraged and develops angry feelings because the therapist is so unresponsive; that is, as part of the therapeutic regression, more-infantile attitudes and feelings emerge. If therapy progresses well, the client typically develops a more realistic and mildly positive attitude toward the therapist toward the end of treatment.

The development of transference may be manifested in a number of ways. Clients may express interest in or curiosity about the therapist's training, opinions, or personal life. The therapy situation and the behavior of the therapist may be compared, by the client, with situations in the client's life. For example, "Unlike you, my wife often doesn't seem to understand what I'm driving at." Criticism about the progress of therapy or the way the therapist is behaving is one way negative transference is indicated. Some examples of transference were noted in the case study presented in Chapter Three.

Transference is given such special importance because it allows the therapist and client to examine the client's interpersonal behavior *in situ*. Clients may talk about their current reality situation or their childhood, but their feelings and behavior in the therapeutic situation are directly felt and are observable by both parties.

> It is undeniable that the subjugation of the transference-manifestations provides the greatest difficulties for the psychoanalyst; but it must not be forgotten that they, and they only, render the invaluable service of making the patient's buried and forgotten love-emotions actual and manifest; for in the last resort no one can be slain *in absentia* or *in effigie* [Freud, 1963, pp. 114–115].

Consideration of transference behaviors, then, is a basic element in psychoanalytic therapy. The more that therapy approximates pure psychoanalysis, the greater the importance of the development and interpretation of transference becomes. "Of all the interpretations made in therapy none carries greater weight in modifying defenses" (Colby, 1951, p. 114).

Interpretation

To summarize thus far, after the taking of the client's history and other preliminaries, a therapeutic contract is arrived at. The client is given responsibility for initiating and maintaining conversation while trying not to censor any thoughts, feelings, or images. As clients talk about themselves and attempt to follow the general rule of free association, resistances or defenses emerge and are occasionally commented on by the therapist. The structure of the therapeutic situation in combination with the clients' neurotic conflicts leads to the development of a therapeutic regression, and clients begin to feel and act toward the therapist as they did toward parental figures.

By what means are changes effected in the clients' defenses, and how does greater insight or ego control develop? In part, clients gain insight or awareness simply by being able to tell their tale in the presence of a sympathetic, nonjudgmental person. But the therapist also helps, by occasionally offering *interpretations* of the material the clients present. Interpretation is the primary specific technique for changing intrapsychic structure in psychoanalytic therapy. It may be defined as any therapist statement that has the intent or function of providing a client with new information. An interpretive statement confronts clients with something in themselves that has not previously been admitted into consciousness.

Using this definition, one can gauge the depth of an interpretive comment in terms of the psychological distance between the client's awareness and the therapist's apparent awareness (Speisman, 1959). For example, a therapist might simply restate or clarify something that the client has been saying; this constitutes a quite shallow interpretation. Alternatively, a therapist might relate what the client has been saying to some unconscious childhood conflict that is completely out of the client's current awareness. This is a "deep" interpretation; it is considered to be very poor psychoanalytic technique.

There is much misunderstanding about the nature of psychoanalytic interpretation, the most common misconception being that deep interpretations are customary and appropriate. Deep interpretations are considered poor technique because, even if they are correct, they are so far removed from the client's current awareness that they are not helpful. The client simply ignores or rejects them. In fact, a general rule in psychoanalytic treatment is to interpret what is already at the surface "and just a little bit more" (Fenichel, 1941). The therapist, in effect, helps the client discover what the client is already groping toward and is on the verge of knowing. Such new information will be acceptable and help facilitate the process of self-discovery. It is important, too, that the client understand interpretive comments, so they should be worded simply and stated in a tentative fashion. The effectiveness of an interpretive comment is judged not so much by the client's direct acceptance or rejection but by the extent to which it leads to further productive exploration by the client.

The principle of focusing interpretations on what is at or near the surface also implies that defense mechanisms or resistance should be interpreted first. Defensive behavior is closer to the surface than the underlying anxiety or drives (wishes) being defended against. A general procedural rule in psychoanalytic therapy is to interpret defenses first and "content" later. The shorter and less intensive the therapy, the greater the emphasis on defense interpretation.

Colby (1951) lucidly described several kinds of interpretive comments and provided some useful examples. As you read them, consider the principles of staying near the surface and focusing on defense mechanisms.

Clarification interpretation. Clarification interpretations are statements by the therapist that focus the client's attention on a particular issue, perhaps selecting out a theme from among several that the client has been discussing. Clarification interpretations may take the form of questions or of simple restatements or reflections of what the client has been saying.

> In each of the first few interviews, a young man has spent most of the time describing the events of several love-affairs. None of them worked out very satisfactorily. Sooner or later there would be an argument or falling-out.
>
> The therapist has been struck by a characteristic of these affairs as yet unmentioned by the patient, namely that, in all but one instance, he was at ease within himself when the affair was platonic, while, when intercourse took place, an inner turmoil developed with insomnia, restlessness, etc. Thus far the therapist's remarks have been confined to interpositions. Now he wishes to point out this theme and send the patient's further thoughts along these lines.
>
> *T:* It seems in these affairs you've described, that when intercourse began is when you began to get upset.
> *C:* Yes, I've thought of that, too. Don't know what it is exactly.
> *T:* And when you began to get upset, then the arguments would start? [pp. 83–84][1]

In effect, the therapist identifies a theme or an issue and invites the client to think and talk about it.

Comparison interpretation. The therapist can place two or more sets of events, thoughts, or feelings side by side and invite the client to consider the relation between them. The therapist may be interested in

[1]From *A Primer for Psychotherapists*, by K. C. Colby. Copyright ©1951 by John Wiley & Sons, Inc. This and all other quotations from this source are reprinted by permission of John Wiley & Sons, Inc.

the client's becoming aware of the similarity or contrast: "Common typical subjects compared are past with present behavior, fantasy with reality, the patient's self with others, childhood with adulthood, and attitude toward parent with attitude toward friend, spouse, or therapist" (Colby, 1951, p. 85).

> Outstanding in this man's life has been his rebellion against his father as a person and as a representative of certain social values. In previous interviews he has given the therapist an extensive roster of traits that he finds repellent in his father.
>
> Today, having not referred to the father for a few interviews, he reports how he enjoys entering a bar where he is well known. The bartenders, the waitresses, and the regular patrons give him the glad hello, and when he moves from table to table chatting and joking he gets the pleasant feeling of being a "big shot." The therapist recalls that one of the patient's complaints is that his father often acts the part of a "big shot" among his friends. The therapist then compares the patient's behavior with that of his father.
>
> T: In a way, isn't that like what your father does?
> C: How so?
> T: You mentioned once that it griped you how your father acted like a big shot. Now you say that you sometimes enjoy being like a big shot.
> [Colby, 1951, p. 85]

Wish/defense interpretation. Sometimes the therapist's statements focus directly on the wish and defense components of a neurotic conflict. "Wish" here is roughly synonymous with drive or impulse. An important procedural rule in psychoanalytic psychotherapy is to first focus on the defensive aspects of neurotic conflicts rather than the wish, or drive, aspects.

> The husband of this patient complains that she is a constant nag and this trait is responsible for his drinking. However, she feels that what he calls nagging is really her motherly concern for his welfare. From evidence gathered in previous interviews, the therapist knows that behind her kind protectiveness lie sadistic impulses toward the husband. But interpretations around this subject are first made in reference to her defense, not her wish-impulse.
>
> T: Do you feel you are overly protective toward him?
> C: Maybe at times. Like if a rainstorm comes up during the day, I worry he might be caught in it. That's silly because there's no reason to think he couldn't be in a dry place.
> T: And he gets annoyed when you fuss over him?
> C: He says it's too much. I mother him, but I don't think it's that bad.
> T: But why do you think your concern is so exaggerated? It's as if you were afraid he's always in danger of something.
> [Colby, 1951, p. 114]

This is a more complicated example. The therapist obviously hopes that if the client is first helped to understand the sources of her "protectiveness"—the defensive aspects of the neurotic conflict—she will later be able to approach and understand her sadistic or angry feelings toward her husband.

Interpretive statements are employed to help the client understand *resistance* and *transference* behaviors. Below is an example of how a therapist deals with one common form of resistance: silence. A transference theme is also present in the client's talk. Can you recognize it?

> Several months of therapy have passed in the case of a hysterical woman suffering from arm and abdominal pains. She begins the hour with a few remarks about her job and then lapses into silence. Her manner and facial expression indicate her feelings of resentment.
>
> *T:* What are you thinking about?
> *C:* [sullenly] Oh, nothing much.
> *T:* You sound angry.
> *C:* I am.
> *T:* What are you mad about?
> *C:* I didn't like your comment last time on my exaggerating things.
>
> In the previous interview she had told of manipulating her boy friend by threatening to kill herself unless he took her to the beach. One of her typical maneuvers is to heavily dramatize situations in order to get her way. The therapist had pointed out her mechanism of exaggerating the importance of her desires as an interpersonal weapon. At the time she agreed to the truth of the interpretation.
>
> *T:* But you agreed with me last time.
> *C:* I know it. But thinking about it later I didn't like it.
> *T:* You felt I was reprimanding you?
> *C:* No, not that. You were accusing me of being a phony. That's something I can't stand. Jerry says the same thing. He accuses me of always acting. Once we were at a party and. . . .
> The silence is broken and the patient continues to produce.
> [Colby, 1951, p. 105]

The transference theme involves her false perception that the therapist is being critical of and reprimanding her. She sees him as behaving the way her boyfriend (Jerry) does. Later, some of the childhood origins of her sensitivity to male judgment and criticism might become the focus of therapy.

Dream Interpretation

Dream interpretation is a relatively exclusive focus of the psychoanalytic approach and is a particularly important part of pure psychoanalysis. Freud termed dreams the "royal road to the unconscious" because they present an excellent opportunity to observe wish/defense conflicts. Clients in psychoanalytic therapy are encouraged to remember and report their dreams, and they quickly develop skill in so doing. A brief review of dream theory is necessary to understand therapeutic dream interpretation. Psychoanalysts distinguish among the *manifest dream content,* which is the consciously remembered dream; the *latent dream content,* which is the unconscious material content that threatened to wake the dreamer; and the *dream work,* the unconscious mental operations that transform the latent dream content into the manifest content.

While dreamers are sleeping, their conflicts strive for expression. This conflictual material is a combination of drives and current reality concerns. The ego's defenses are lessened but not absent. The result is a compromise formation, so that enough energy is discharged to let the dreamer sleep, yet the content is sufficiently disguised to "hide" the conflict. Anxiety dreams—that is, dreams that are subjectively highly distressful—represent the failure of ego defenses. Most dreams are composed of conflict expressions that can be construed as wish fulfillments. (Recall Freud's dictum that all dreams are wish fulfillments in one sense or another.) Because the analyst is most interested in wish/defense systems, the wish-fulfilling nature of dreams makes them of considerable interest.

A first step in dream interpretation is to ask the client for reactions or associations to various elements in the dream. The choice of elements and their order is a matter of clinical judgment and depends on the client and the therapeutic context. The dream material— including associations—is then subjected to the same kind of scrutiny by client and therapist as is any other kind of client talk. The therapist offers interpretations to facilitate client self-understanding of the themes. Psychoanalytic notions about symbolism are also used to help therapist and client decode the dream. For example, basements, downstairs, upstairs, attics, front porches and the like are often considered to symbolize anatomical parts of the body. The degree of detail in dream interpretation depends on the overall intensity of the therapeutic contract—that is, whether psychoanalysis is being used or psychoanalytically oriented psychotherapy. In psychoanalysis, dreams can provide clues to important new material. In less intensive treatment, the therapist is likely to focus on dream content that relates to previously identified issues.

> *C:* I had a dream last night that I can remember clearly. Usually I can't remember them the next day. It was about dogs. I was standing in a large field. Across the field I could see a dog—an Irish Setter— coming through the grass. When he got closer I could see that he, or I guess it must be she, was carrying a little puppy in her mouth. It was a mother dog and her puppy. The puppy was sick I imagined, because his nose was running and he was being carried. Otherwise he could have walked.
>
> *T:* So the dream is about a mother dog and her sick child.
> *C:* Of course it must refer to me and John. We've talked about my being a mother and he a child.
> *T:* And he gets a lot of colds with a running nose?

> *C:* Yes. I wonder why I dreamed about dogs. We don't have a dog. I was thinking of getting one, but there's no one home in the daytime to take care of him. A dog is like a child. Maybe the dream is about that, too. I always wanted to have children, but now I'm not so sure. I'd never try to raise a child with John the way he is now.
>
> *T:* How is it that you haven't become pregnant?
>
> [Colby, 1951, pp. 127–128]

Working Through

Working through can be defined as a process of repeated verbalization by the client and corresponding interpretations by the therapist of central neurotic conflicts. "Over and over, now here in one area and there in another, important defenses and their motivations are brought into the patient's consciousness" (Colby, 1951, p. 119). It is by means of repeated interpretations of defenses and neurotic conflicts, as they are manifested in childhood, dreams, current reality, and the therapeutic situation, that the client gradually achieves insight and is able to change.

Another frequent misconception about psychoanalytic treatment is that the therapist makes a dramatic interpretation that is experienced by the client as a "revelation" and that the insight thus experienced enables the client to view a variety of experiences and interactions in a new light. Instead, the psychoanalytic therapist realizes that insight and change are relatively situational. It is necessary, therefore, for the client to become aware of defenses in many different contexts and situations in order for genuine insight to emerge. Insight in psychoanalytic psychotherapy develops cumulatively and inductively as a product of many small interpretations, rather than the other way around. The need for repeated working through of key conflicts is a major reason for the length of psychoanalytic therapy.

Insight

Insight has been noted as the major goal of psychoanalytic treatment. It refers to the client's achieving greater awareness and understanding of defenses and conflicts, so that behavior becomes more adaptive and productive.

Menninger (1958) offered an eloquent definition of insight that nicely illustrates the ambitious goals that analysts set for themselves and their clients:

> I define insight as the recognition by the patient (1) that this or that aspect of his feelings and attitudes, this or that technique of behavior, this or that role in which he casts other people, is of a *pattern;* (2) that this pattern, like the footprint of a bear which has lost certain toes in a trap, originated long ago and stamps itself on every step of his life

journey; it is present in his contemporary reality and situational relationships, and it is present in his analytic relationships; (3) that this
pattern originated for a reason which was valid at the time, and per-
sisted despite changes in some of the circumstances which originally
determined it; (4) that this pattern contains elements which are offen-
sive and injurious to others as well as expensive and troublesome to the
patient. . . . Insight is the simultaneous identification of the characteristic behavior pattern in all three (childhood, analysis, reality) of
these situations, together with an understanding of why they were and
are used as they were and are [pp. 147–148].[2]

Menninger's definition highlights the emphasis on changes in
awareness or understanding relative to changes in overt behavior as a
goal in psychoanalysis. In fact, psychoanalytic therapists seek *both*
insight and behavioral change.

Applications

The basic principles and techniques of psychoanalysis and
psychoanalytic therapy have now been presented. Remember that
these specific procedures take place in the context of the common
processes described in Chapter Three. In the next section a relatively
short case of psychoanalytic therapy is summarized and discussed as
a means of illustrating the major concepts.

The many possible variations in the use of basic psychoanalytic
concepts and techniques in psychotherapy cannot be emphasized too
strongly. The shorter the treatment, the more limited the goals of
therapy are. Thus, there is a corresponding lessening of the development of regression and transference reactions, a lesser focus on
dream interpretation, and a greater focus on current reality problems. Psychoanalytic therapists use the term *supportive psychotherapy* to describe treatment in which the goal tends to be shoring up
of existing defenses and ways of relating rather than fundamental
reconstruction. In short-term supportive therapy, a psychoanalytic
therapist is sensitive to transference phenomena but tries to develop
and maintain a cooperative attitude and relationship with the client.
By relating in a face-to-face manner and by active involvement, the
therapist avoids the development of strong and, especially, negative
transference feelings. Greater activity on the therapist's part is
another distinguishing feature of short-term psychoanalytic therapy
in contrast to psychoanalysis per se. Brief psychotherapy (for example, see Lewin, 1970), crisis intervention (see Lindemann, 1944), and
even consultation (Caplan, 1970) are readily approached from a
psychoanalytic perspective. The broad applicability of psychoanalytic concepts contributes to their appeal.

[2]From *Theory of Psychoanalytic Technique*, by K. Menninger, M. D. Copyright
1958 by Basic Books, Inc., Publishers. Reprinted by permission.

An Illustrative Therapy Case

Choosing a "typical" psychoanalytic case is made difficult by the many variations and by the length and complexity of much psychoanalytic treatment. Limitations of space preclude presenting one of Freud's classic case studies. The complexity of a psychoanalysis is difficult to capture in a few pages. Therefore, I have chosen a case illustrating psychoanalytic psychotherapy. Chapter Three summarized a fairly lengthy case of this sort: 175 sessions over two years. In contrast, the case chosen here is much shorter.

The psychoanalytic conceptualization and treatment of a phobia provides a nice contrast with the behavior-therapy formulation discussed in Chapter Seven. The therapist is a woman psychiatrist, and the therapy took place in the late 1930s or early 1940s. This may help the reader better understand the sexual attitudes and mores described. The therapeutic approach was greatly influenced by the work of Franz Alexander, who pioneered the application of psychoanalytic principles to short-term and brief psychotherapy (Alexander & French, 1946).

A senior in a coeducational college, an attractive, friendly twenty-one-year-old girl, requested treatment for a severe generalized anxiety and confusion which was most troublesome when she was away from home and particularly acute in the classroom and at dances. This anxiety had recently become so extreme that the patient insisted on staying at home and refused to let her mother leave her side. Excellent results were brought by a treatment which extended over a period of two months (interviews twice a week for the first month and once a week for the second), followed by two interviews a month apart to assure the therapist that the healing process continued.

Although the patient remembered that she had always been anxious and uncomfortable in social situations, these acute manifestations had developed suddenly about six months before, during a Christmas visit to the parents of a male friend. Her distress had increased so greatly that, upon her return from the visit, she ceased going to classes and regularly refused to attend dances or other parties. She had been thrown into acute panic upon several occasions—once in a large class with a male instructor, the other times at college parties.

Sufficient historical material was freely given by the patient in the first interview to furnish a background from which to reconstruct the causes of the conflict responsible for the present symptoms. The patient was an only child. Her mother had been widowed when the patient was two and from the time of her husband's death had devoted most of her life to her child. The mother and daughter had lived with the maternal grandparents who were also very devoted to the patient. She spoke of her grandmother as being very dependent upon her mother, and of her grandfather as a gentle, lovable man who played a very important role in the planning for the family—which was of definite matriarchal organization. She remembered having always been a very obedient child, although she had been told that, when very young, she had indulged in severe temper tantrums which had ceased suddenly at about four years.

At about ten, the patient was taught masturbation by an older girl in the neighborhood and had practiced it occasionally since then, but with a severe sense of guilt. She could remember no childhood curiosity about sex, but she was unusually ignorant of such matters and had felt embarrassed when she heard other children discussing them.

Being an intellectually precocious and musically talented girl, she was pushed in school and was expected to practice her music for long hours. She had planned to be a concert musician, but two years previous to her illness she had taken an aversion to her instrument and became anxious whenever she considered returning to her music. Socially, she had always had a circle of acquaintances, but during her school years her work schedule offered little time for them. Her main recreation as she was growing up was visiting adult friends of her mother, an occasional concert, and moving pictures.

When she went to college, her mother left the grandparents' home and established an apartment for the two of them near the college. Although the patient joined a sorority, she had little social life with the other girls for fear that her mother might be lonely during her absence. When boys visited her, she always included her mother and even took her on all dates other than college dances. Consciously she considered her mother as a "pal," but she admitted that because her mother was gay and good company she had often thought the boys liked her only because of her mother. One boy, however, who had been devoted to her for over a year, insisted upon omitting the mother from their dates. He proposed marriage to the patient and was accepted. Since she considered herself engaged, she had indulged in "necking" with him before the onset of her illness. Although she enjoyed it, she had felt guilty and was sure her mother would disapprove.

Her fiancé had invited her to his home for the Christmas holidays to meet his parents. During this visit, which was the first trip on which she had ever been away from her mother, she developed the severe symptom picture described. It started with insomnia the second night of her visit, after he had given her an engagement ring. She became fearful during the night that something dreadful might happen to her mother, and the next day became so ill that she insisted upon returning home.

It was evident from this history and from the symptom content that the girl had been precipitated, by the realization of the nearness of her approaching marriage, into a conflict between her dependent wish toward her mother and the more adult sexual wish toward her fiancé; this conflict was near the surface but not yet in consciousness. Fear of injury to her mother suggested also a stirring of unconscious hostility toward her mother who had always stood in the way of her interest in sexuality and its coincident independent life, and who might also win away her fiancé as she had taken away the father, the grandfather, and (more recently) the other boys who had been attentive to the patient.

Guilt and anxiety thus played a role in producing the symptoms, the secondary gain of which was to solve the conflict temporarily by renouncing sexuality and an independent life. When she was so ill, she need not consider marriage or independent activity—as classes, dances, companionship and so forth. At the same time, she intensified her dependence upon her mother through her illness. Her mother dared not leave the patient, even in the home, for fear symptoms would develop in her absence.

In the first interview, the patient was given insight into her hostility toward her mother, with an explanation of how it grew from her mother's restriction of her independence and self-expression—a result of her mother's ambitions for her—and from the consequent restrictions of her social life. The therapist discussed with her the fact that all children develop such hostilities toward their parents, and showed the patient how, from fear of losing love, she had formed defenses against her own childhood hostility by exaggerated obedience, shyness, and avoidance of tabooed activity. An explanation was given to her of how the conflict had been intensified into severe symptom formation during her first trip away from home, because she was really deserting her mother in choosing to be with her fiancé and yet was enjoying herself. A hint was also offered her about guilt reactions to any enjoyment because of her training to sacrifice so much for achievement in work. This guilt in turn made her even more dependent upon her mother, the childhood disciplinarian whose presence could protect her from indulging her wishes for pleasure.

These interpretations were followed with a permissive suggestion that she might try to refrain from repressing angry feelings toward her mother when critical thoughts occurred, with an explanation of the naturalness of such feelings in spite of the traditional teaching that one should love one's parents under all circumstances. It was then suggested that some mild self-indulgence such as lunch with her sorority sisters or an after-class drink in the drugstore with them if she felt the inclination might aid in her recovery, and that she go to classes or begin to study again only when she felt comfortable and wished to. But, in order to protect her from losing prohibitions too rapidly, she was urged not to indulge herself beyond her feeling of comfort.

In this first interview, the sexual component in her conflict relative to pleasurable indulgences was not touched upon. Since this element seemed to be much more deeply repressed than her conflict between her dependent and independent wishes, and since it was emotionally charged, it could be handled only after some freedom from the mother had been achieved and the dependent transference to the more permissive therapist had gained strength.

In the second interview, three days later, the patient's manner was less tense and she reported that she had begun to feel that she would recover. She had not been back to classes but had spent her days at the sorority house studying. In the afternoons, she had worried lest her mother be lonely and had returned home early for dinner. She had not seen her fiancé although he had telephoned daily.

Tears came when the patient reviewed in detail memories of deprivation as a child, when she had longed to play with other children and had been made to practice or to visit adults with her mother. Occasional excursions with her grandfather, to the circus and to the zoo in particular, were marred by her mother's criticisms of the grandfather who kept her out too long. On these trips she was happy and felt her grandfather was like Santa Claus, but her pleasure was always tempered by fear of eventual criticism. Sympathy for her deprived childhood was offered by the therapist, and again the hostile feelings of any child toward a parent in such a situation was discussed with her. In order to soften the guilt resulting from the anger which was obviously reaching consciousness, she was helped to recognize the fact that parents, meaning well, often deprive children unwisely in an attempt to do the best they can for their training. Her response expressed relief. "I feel better to think that mother wasn't really mean, and maybe wanted me to have the best of things."

At this point the therapist asked permission to talk with the mother in order to explain the patient's need for freedom and to warn her that her daughter might occasionally be irritable at home during the treatment period. The patient was assured that there would be no discussion of confidential information.

In the resultant interview, the mother proved quite willing to cooperate, both because she was truly distressed by her daughter's symptoms and because she suffered some personal discomfort from the patient's intensified dependence upon her. Not only was the mother able to be tolerant of the girl's whims but, following the therapist's suggestion, she also began to develop a richer social life for herself and to renew old friendships. At the same time, she did not withdraw her "mothering" completely and the patient's dependent satisfactions were not cut off abruptly as she experimented with greater freedom in satisfying her own wishes. That this gradual change of attitude on the part of the mother had a profound influence on the patient's progress could be seen with increasing clarity as the therapy proceeded.

In the third interview, the patient brought the information that she had been sleeping well, had gone to classes, and, although there were sudden moments of anxiety, had not had to leave the classroom. She had lunched daily with friends; and the previous day she had taken a walk along the lake with her fiancé which both had enjoyed, but after about half an hour she had begun to worry about leaving her mother alone and had gone home. A new symptom, however, had developed which was frankly hostile to her mother. She had impulsive wishes to hit her mother when away from her, and when she was with her she heard what her mother said but could not see her clearly. Although these symptoms had not really frightened her, they were startling and convinced her of the intensity of hostility toward her mother.

In this interview, insight was offered in two realms. The transference relationship was discussed in detail and it was suggested that in indulging herself now she was doing it partly to please the therapist, who was momentarily a parent-figure, just as she had always inhibited herself previously to please her mother. And she was shown the split which had occurred in the parent-image—the therapist as the good parent and her own mother as the bad one who could be hated. At this point, an explanation was given of her conscious and unconscious need for dependence, and of her use at the moment of the therapist as the person upon whom she depended. Again she was encouraged to enlarge her social experiences by the use of opportunities as they presented themselves. In giving advice of this kind it is, of course, essential for the therapist to be quite sure not only of the needs of the patient, but of both the external situation and the patient's capacity to act independently without an increase of anxiety. It would be highly traumatic, naturally, to a patient if in trying to be friendly he were met with rejection.

The second point in this interview was her attitude toward sexuality. This subject was introduced easily by the discussion of possible reasons for the precipitation of the anxiety symptoms at a time when she was with her fiancé and away from her mother and girl friends. She was encouraged to talk freely of her fiancé and of her concept of marriage. She revealed fear of sexual intercourse and a puritanical attitude as well, saying that she had thought of it as an evil to be endured because of the "base nature of man." For a person of her generation, her general sexual information was very vague. As is often true of persons brought up by persons with strong sexual taboos, she did not remember ever having been curious about birth, sex differences, and so forth, nor did she remember masturbating as a child. She admitted having indulged in masturbation as an adolescent after she had been taught by an older girl, but she had done this only rarely and with tremendous guilt and fear.

Sex information was therefore given to this patient as part of the treatment procedure, just as one often teaches a child in the course of psychotherapy. As with the child, answering the sex questions of an adult whose information is confused or incorrect has a two-fold therapeutic result. It tends to relieve unconscious guilt connected with sexual curiosity and (through the transference) it tends to bring sexual wishes to consciousness, since the good parent in the form of the therapist does not condemn interest in sex.

At the beginning of the fourth interview, the patient was again tense and cried while she told that her fiancé was begging her for dates and was urging her to go to a dance the following week. She had been preoccupied since the last interview with sexual thoughts, and had felt that marriage would be impossible since the idea of sexual relations with him revolted her. She told a fragment of a dream she had had the previous night: She was running from a large man along a dark street; then she found herself in a small basement room and just as the man was going to grab her she saw that he had no arms. She awoke screaming and trembling.

She offered two enlightening associations to this dream. One was that the fiancé had a slight limp as a result of childhood poliomyelitis, and the second was a memory of seeing a man expose himself in an alley when she was a small child. Her recollection was of seeing an enormous penis and of running home in terror, but of being afraid to tell her mother of the experience.

The patient then confessed that she had recently doubted her love for her fiancé and thought that perhaps she was sorry for him, although his paralysis had not been severe enough to handicap him in athletics or other activities. She wondered if she did not cling to him for fear that other men would not love her if they knew her well. The therapist interpreted only the safety which she felt with the man in the dream when there were no arms, which was similar to her previous feeling of safety with her fiancé when she had thought of him as also injured. It was suggested that her fear arose only after he gave her the ring which might assure marriage and make her face relations with a real man. Her reaction to this was a smiling admission that her fiancé was certainly much more dominating than she had first thought him.

The next three interviews covered details of her doubts about her fiancé, her decision that she really did not love him, her plans to move to the sorority house while her mother visited friends in another city, and questions concerning possibilities of seeing other men. She also reported active classwork and weekly parties.

In the following interview she reported another dream fragment: She was in the woods and started to take hold of a tree trunk when she noticed that she was holding a penis which was attached to herself. In telling the dream she laughed and said it reminded her of the time when as a little girl she tried to urinate standing up and the urine went over the toilet cover. She had no memory of seeing a boy urinate, but admitted that she must have. The therapist told her of penis-envy in little girls and the hostility which sometimes developed toward boys as a result. She admitted then the despair she had always felt in her musical achievement because she believed that men would always be more successful.

Little fresh insight came with further interviews. There was repetition and elaboration of the material of the previous hours, and much of the time was consumed by reports of her activities and requests for detailed suggestions about how to meet certain social situations, such as dates with men other than her fiancé or the correct behavior as bridesmaid at a wedding in which she decided to take part although she had previously refused for fear her old symptoms would reappear. Her menses had been reestablished, and except for some insecurity socially her symptoms had ceased. Plans for the summer were also worked out with her mother so that she could spend half the time with friends and half in a resort with her mother.

Seven months after the termination of treatment, the patient was seen again in a friendly visit, and she appeared as a charming, self-reliant young woman. She had returned to her music; was engaged to be married but to another man, this time with inner conviction of success; and was working temporarily in an office while making plans for her marriage. She had encouraged her mother to return to the grandparents and was living in an apartment with a college chum who was also working. She stated that she saw her mother about once a week and enjoyed her as a companion. She could now feel amused at both her previous dependence on her mother and her hostility toward her.

Three years after the last treatment interview, her marriage of two years' duration was still obviously happy and there had been no symptom return [pp. 234–243].[3]

Discussion

This case illustrates several psychoanalytic principles and methods. There is much emphasis on the client's developmental history and its relationship to her symptoms. The phobic reaction of the young woman was analyzed almost exclusively in terms of internal, or psychodynamic, determinants. The conflict between her dependent wish toward her mother and her sexual feelings toward her fiancé was viewed as the major cause, and remediation of this inner conflict was seen as necessary in order to effect a change in behavior. The evidence presented is persuasive that marked improvement occurred and was maintained over a three-year period. What factors may have operated to produce the observed improvement? The therapist offered several interpretations that apparently increased the client's insight into her sexual and dependent feelings. This is consistent with psychoanalytic thinking that interpretation is the primary specific technique. The use of dream interpretations to help promote insight is also illustrated, as is the importance of repetition, or working through the key conflicts.

The authors of the case report, however, observed that "insight alone was not the curative factor." They suggested that the therapeutic relationship was also critical in providing "the opportunity for a

[3]From *Psychoanalytic Therapy: Principles and Application*, by F. Alexander and T. M. French. Copyright © 1946 by John Wiley & Sons, Inc. This and all other quotations from this source are reprinted by permission of John Wiley & Sons, Inc.

dependent relationship to a mother figure (the therapist) who is neither demanding of love nor ambitious for success and who was permissive of the patient's sexual interest and her wish for pleasure with friends of her own age" (Alexander & French, 1946, p. 243). The therapeutic relationship—with an accepting, nonjudgmental therapist—is one of the *common* elements in psychotherapy, and it was critical in this case. The case may be construed as one in which specific and common therapeutic processes combined to produce a successful outcome.

But there was another important factor in the success of this case: the constructive involvement of the client's mother, who by changing her own attitudes and behaviors permitted the client to experience a corrective mother/daughter relationship that was more satisfying for both parties. Thus, specific and common therapeutic elements and altered environmental circumstances—the mother's attitudes and behaviors—were all critical elements in the client's improvement. These three factors were interrelated. First, the client needed the therapist's support and interpretation to increase her awareness of her relationship with her mother. When the client was prepared to change the mother/daughter relationship, the therapist intervened to help ensure that the mother would support (reinforce) the daughter's new behavior. A less cooperative mother (environment) would have impeded the client's progress. It is quite likely that these three factors—specific techniques, common processes, and changes in the environment that support new attitudes and behavior—need to be present in successful outcomes, no matter what kind of psychotherapy is employed.

Therapy Research: Two Examples

"Quantitative psychoanalytic research remains little known. Rare is the psychoanalyst who knows of any of these studies and even rarer is the psychoanalyst whose practice has been altered by them" (Luborsky & Spence, 1978, p. 331).

These opening sentences from an authoritative and comprehensive review of quantitative research on psychoanalytic therapy communicate the relative lack of emphasis on controlled research by psychoanalytic workers. Several factors have contributed to this state of affairs.

First is an attitude, modeled by Freud, that the psychoanalytic method itself yields reliable observations and valid conclusions about psychotherapeutic phenomena. In the 1930s Freud was asked to comment on some early laboratory investigation of his concept of repression. He replied: "I have examined your experimental studies for the verification of the psychoanalytic assertions with interest. I cannot put much value on these confirmations because the wealth of reliable observations on which these assertions rest make them independent of experimental verification. Still it can do no harm" (reported by Luborsky & Spence, 1978, pp. 356–357).

Most psychologists would dispute Freud's assertion, contending instead that there are inherent biasing factors in the psychoanalytic situation that render the observations unfit for the *verification* of hypotheses. For example, the capacity of the psychotherapist (or interviewer) to bias or influence the content of the client's verbal behavior is well demonstrated (for example, see Truax, 1966). Because the behavior of the psychoanalyst may influence client talk—for example, shaping the client to report certain kinds of dreams—the content of this talk cannot be accepted as independent evidence of the validity of the analyst's theory. Nor can apparent therapeutic successes provide strong evidence for the validity of the psychotherapeutic rationale, because of the several plausible rival hypotheses described in Chapter Four.

A second factor contributing to the lack of emphasis on psychoanalytic research is the nature of the training program for therapists. Training is heavily clinical and rarely involves research experience. In contrast, psychologists involved in client-centered or behavior therapy usually have had considerable research experience during their doctoral studies.

Third, there are some very real practical difficulties. The sheer length of psychoanalytic treatment is a formidable obstacle to quantitative research. Because psychoanalytic treatment often takes three to five years, planning and executing an outcome study is a major life commitment on the part of the researcher. Much research in academic settings is done to meet the requirements of a doctoral dissertation, and few graduate students can await the outcome of psychoanalysis.

In spite of these attitudes and obstacles, there has been a good deal of research on psychoanalytic therapy, probably more than is generally recognized. I have chosen two examples. First is a *process* study, which investigates the relationship between the depth of interpretation offered by a therapist and the subsequent verbal behavior of the client. An important feature of research on psychoanalytic therapy is an emphasis on process rather than outcome (see Chapter Four). My second example, the Menninger Foundation Psychotherapy Research Project, deals with both process and outcome issues. It illustrates some of the formidable practical and conceptual obstacles involved in psychoanalytic therapy research.

A Process Study

Interpretation is the major specific technique in psychoanalytic psychotherapy. Consistent with the tenet about interpretations advanced earlier in this chapter—that the therapist should interpret what is already at the surface and "just a little bit more"—Speisman

(1959) hypothesized that deep interpretations would lead to the most resistance, moderate interpretations would produce the least resistance, and superficial interpretations would have an intermediate effect. To test this hypothesis, it was necessary to develop quantitative measures of depth of interpretation and resistance, obtain tape recordings of therapeutic interviews, and use these data to look at the relationship between therapist talk and client talk. This kind of research is termed *process* research, because it looks at the relationship between two components, or processes, of psychotherapy but is not directly concerned with outcome (which in Speisman's study was not measured). It is assumed that interpretation and resistance are critical to outcome, but this assumption was not directly tested in Speisman's research.

Speisman defined depth of interpretation as "the disparity between the therapist's view of and the patient's awareness of his own emotions and motives" (p. 93). Depth of interpretation was measured by means of a seven-point scale, ranging from superficial interpretation—in which the therapist merely repeats material of which the client is fully aware—through medium interpretations—such as the therapist's reformulating client behavior during the interview in a way not explicitly recognized by the client—to deep interpretations—which are completely beyond the client's conscious grasp. The research group with which Speisman worked had devoted considerable attention to the measurement of depth of interpretation (for example, see Harway, Dittmann, Rausch, Bordin, & Rigler, 1955). Because of this groundwork, the reliability among judges of the depth-of-interpretation index in Speisman's studies proved to be quite satisfactory—about .8.

It was also necessary to define *resistance*. A review of psychoanalytic writings and some preliminary data-analysis work led to the development of two dimensions, exploration and opposition. *Exploration* was defined as the degree to which the patient was actually exploring either new material or material that had been discussed at some previous time. *Opposition* was defined as the degree to which the client's statements contained the qualities of opposition or denial toward the therapist or therapy—for example, "I don't seem to be getting anywhere." The reliabilities for the two resistance measures were also adequate.

Speisman wanted to obtain data from a broad range of cases while at the same time doing an intensive analysis of one case. He analyzed *all* responses in a sequence of five consecutive interviews from a single case and randomly selected 11 successive responses from 21 different cases. The approaches represented by the therapists—both psychologists and psychiatrists—included nondirective, modified psychoanalytic, Adlerian, and eclectic. The judges were either graduate students or faculty members, and all had at least 100 hours or more of supervised experience as psychotherapists. Sophisticated judges sensitive to the psychoanalytic dimensions were believed necessary. Different sets of judges rated the depth of interpretation and resistance categories. The raters of depth of interpretation read both the therapist's interpretation and the patient's subsequent response, because an estimation of patients' awareness is critical to the definition. Resistance judges read only the clients' statements.

Data analysis involved examining what the client said immediately after an interpretive remark by the therapist. This was done separately for the intensive case (five consecutive interviews) and for the 11 successive responses from the 21 cases. For both analyses, a consistent pattern emerged: deep interpretations led to the most opposition and the least exploration; moderate interpretations led to the least opposition and the most exploration; and superficial interpretations fell in between. The magnitude or strength of the relationships, while statistically significant, was not large, indicating that other factors also influenced expression of exploration or opposition.

The study by Speisman, as well as others from the research team with which he worked (Bordin, 1959), was a careful and systematic effort to investigate empirically the key concepts of psychoanalytic psychotherapy. It showed that constructs such as depth of interpretation and resistance can be reliably measured and are related as predicted by the theory. Such research can be difficult and costly. Tape-recorded therapy sessions must be carefully transcribed. Judges must have considerable sophistication in psychoanalytic psychotherapy and require specific training for the rating task. Interjudge agreement on such ratings can fluctuate greatly, and there is always the possibility that the judges are responding to conceptually irrelevant cues that are correlated with the main construct.

Results like those of Speisman do suggest some guidelines for therapist behavior and also provide some theoretical support for psychoanalytic concepts. To merit attention, however, it remains to be demonstrated that moderate levels of therapeutic interpretation and the resulting client self-exploration are related to meaningful changes in client behavior outside of therapy. Process variables must be important for therapeutic outcome.

The Menninger Project

The Menninger Clinic, in Topeka, Kansas, is a large and influential psychiatric training and research center whose programs are heavily influenced by psychoanalytic ideas. It has provided training for hundreds of psychiatrists, psychologists, social workers, and other mental health workers. The foundation also supports an active research program, of which the Psychotherapy Research Project is a part. The size and scope of this psychotherapy project and its spon-

sorship by the prestigious Menninger Clinic mark it as the prototypical psychoanalytic research effort, and it has been the subject of
numerous publications over the 25 years of its existence. This description and analysis focuses on the project's quantitative study of
psychotherapy outcomes and is based on a final report published in
The Bulletin of the Menninger Clinic (Kernberg, Burstein, Coyne, Appelbaum, Horowitz, & Voth, 1972).

The Menninger project, unlike Speisman's study, was not intended to test a specific hypothesis but rather was an exploratory
study to try to determine what changes occurred in clients and how
the changes came about. Toward this end a large number of hypotheses and variables were investigated. A very important consideration
was a decision to maintain the integrity of the naturalistic treatment
situation. Thus, neither clients nor therapists were aware that they
were part of the research project.

The Menninger project sample consisted of 42 adult hospital
patients and outpatients with various diagnoses. It excluded persons
with organic brain damage, mental retardation, or overt psychosis.
The clients ranged in age from 17 to 50 and were equally divided with
respect to sex. The therapists had a wide range of experience, with a
minimum of three years of therapy experience.

Treatment duration averaged three years. The clients were
equally divided between two kinds of treatment. Half the sample
underwent standard psychoanalysis; the other half received face-to-
face, psychoanalytically oriented psychotherapy. Clients were *not*
randomly assigned to these conditions; treatment assignment was
determined by naturally occurring processes of clinical judgment.
The intention was not to compare the outcomes of the two different
kinds of therapy but rather to study change and variables influencing
change *within* the two kinds of treatment.

Data were organized around three factors: the client, the treatment, and the environment. Information relevant to these three factors was collected at three different times: at the beginning of treatment (initial), the end of treatment (termination), and two years after
the end of treatment (follow-up). Much of the information was of the
sort routinely collected in normal clinical activity at the Menninger
Clinic, such as psychological testing before treatment, therapist
progress notes, and reports of social workers. It is important to note
that the raw data were already subjective judgments made by trained
psychoanalytically oriented clinicians. For example, client information included inferences about the client made by the person who
administered and interpreted psychological tests; information about
treatment included the therapist's perceptions as recorded in weekly
progress notes; information about the environment included a social
worker's report on the family situation. This is in contrast to Speisman's study, in which transcriptions of the actual therapeutic interactions were analyzed.

The data were then rated on psychoanalytic variables by sophisticated judges. Examples of some of the variables used are shown in Table 5–1. The table also contains descriptions of a patient variable, a treatment variable, and a situation variable.

Table 5–1. Selected Patient, Treatment, and Situational Variables Studied in the Menninger Psychotherapy Research Project

Patient Variables	Treatment Variables	Situation Variables

A. Anxiety and symptoms
  1. Level of anxiety
  2. Severity of symptoms
B. Ego factors
  1. Insight
  2. Patterning of defenses
  3. Ego strength
C. Motivation
	A. Basic techniques
	  1. Interpretive
	  2. Supportive
	B. Subject matter
	  1. Past life, childhood
	  2. Current life situation
	  3. Transference
	C. Therapist skill
		A. Stress
		
		B. Interpersonal
		   support
		
		C. Material
		   support

Illustrative Definitions

Patient variable—ego strength. It is when the ego can resist disorganization and function adaptively in the face of internal and external pressures that we speak of ego strength. The concept of ego strength embraces those ego resources qualitatively distinguishable as adaptive, integrative and defensive functions whose organization and interplay contribute to the individual's effective dealing with inner and outer realities. Ego strength therefore refers to the general resiliency, resourcefulness, productiveness, and adjustment of the ego [p. 205].

Treatment variable—interpretive technique. This variable refers to the extent interpretive techniques were relied upon. A predominance of interpretation and the use of other techniques only to make effective interpretations possible would constitute the highest level of reliance on interpretive techniques. Lower levels would be represented by a predominance of noninterpretive techniques such as manipulation and suggestion [p. 206].

Situational variable—stress. This variable refers to continuous sources of strain as well as to single traumatic events which are noxious in their own right and, therefore, would have a harmful impact on anyone. Included also in this variable are those sources of strain brought about by the patient's problems and their repercussion in his life situation [p. 208].

The rating procedure was quite different from that of the Speisman study, whose judges rated therapist or client statements on a seven-point scale. Instead, a sophisticated paired-comparison method derived from basic research in psychophysics was used. Judges were presented with descriptions of the concept or variable to be judged. The variables, as illustrated in Table 5–1, were described in abstract, theoretical terms, so that judges would need considerable knowledge of psychoanalytic theory and practice. The judges were then given the available relevant information—for example, psychological test reports or therapist progress notes—for a batch of 12 clients. Judges then took two clients from this batch and simply judged which member of the pair had more or less of the variable being judged. The paired-comparison procedure then continued until each of the 12 clients was compared with all of the others—that is, 66 judgments $(N \times (N - 1))/2$. For example, a judge had to choose which of two clients had more ego strength. A paired-comparison judgment is relatively easier than rating a single client on a seven-point scale. But the method is cumbersome and repetitious. The research team estimated that "an average of one and a half hours was consumed in reading the writeups and making the judgments about one variable for one batch of patients; the 66 judgments made on each batch necessitated reading 66 pairs of paragraphs and to complete the whole task over 30,000 comparisons had to be made" (Kernberg et al., 1972, p. 13).

The paired-comparison ratings generated a rank order of all clients within each general treatment—psychoanalysis proper and psychoanalytically oriented psychotherapy.

A great many hypotheses were examined, consistent with the exploratory nature of the study. Here are some examples:

1. The higher the ego strength before treatment, the higher the global improvement at termination and follow-up. This was confirmed.
2. Clients with low initial ego strength treated with a high degree of interpretive technique will have less global improvement at termination and follow-up than low-ego-strength clients treated with a low degree of interpretive techniques. This was not confirmed.
3. The greater the decrease in (environmental) stress, the higher the global improvement at termination and follow-up. This was confirmed at termination but not at follow-up.

A consistent finding from several analyses was that a high level of initial ego strength was related to successful outcome for all of the different treatments embodied in the research project. This finding may appear to be a confirmation of generally accepted clinical lore, but an empirical verification is nevertheless satisfying. A less "obvious" finding with practical implications was that therapist skill was more critical in psychoanalytic therapy than in classical psychoanalysis.

The scope and complexity of the Menninger project make it difficult to evaluate. Advocates of a psychoanalytic approach will surely take comfort from many of the statistical confirmations of their clinical theory. And the Menninger study is probably known to most practicing psychoanalysts. Critics of psychoanalysis will also find much to focus on. One weakness from a behavioral perspective is the lack of an objective data base; the entire study can be viewed as an analysis of clinical judgment—the impressions of clinicians constituted the raw data—rather than a study of psychotherapy per se. On the plus side, the rating task and subsequent statistical analysis led to clarification of the meaning of many psychoanalytic concepts.

A cost/benefit analysis of such a costly project is surely in order and must, I think, yield a rather pessimistic conclusion. Were the methodological innovations and substantive findings of the Menninger Psychotherapy Research Project worth the enormous expenditure in professional time and money over 25 years? In terms of substantive results, I think not. I doubt that other investigators will have the resources or motivation to pursue the findings. The methodological contributions are probably more significant. One critic observed that many psychoanalysts and psychiatrists "were exposed to formal research as a respected and valuable enterprise" and that the project methods and instruments—especially the Health-Sickness Rating Scale used to measure global outcome—have had considerable impact (May, 1973).

The Menninger project illustrates most of the essential features of psychoanalytic research. These include the reluctance to interfere with natural clinical phenomena; the reliance on the perceptions and judgment of sophisticated clinicians in providing primary data; the use of trained judges to rate complex psychoanalytic variables; and the use of sophisticated statistical data analyses. The project also illustrates the major practical barrier to psychoanalytic research noted above—the duration of psychoanalytic treatment and the complexity of the subject matter.

Evaluation of Psychoanalytic Therapy

This section evaluates psychoanalytic psychotherapy with respect to the three criteria discussed in Chapter Four. These three criteria are the quality of the theory underlying the therapy, the empirical effectiveness of the therapy, and the cost-effectiveness of the therapy.

Quality of Theory

Psychoanalytic theory is a complex set of propositions and hypotheses varying in clarity or testability. Many of the propositions and hypotheses have been subjected to empirical tests; some have not. The methodology employed has varied in quality, and the results, too, have often been quite inconsistent. Such a state of affairs provides evidence for both critics and proponents of psychoanalytic therapy. Critics often assert that it is based on a theory of personality that is either unproven or has been demonstrated to be invalid. This criticism neglects research that has supported some psychoanalytic concepts (Fisher & Greenberg, 1977).

As illustrated in the examples of psychotherapy research, psychoanalytic theory remains rather abstract, and there is often a large gap between conceptual definition and observable behavior. The lack of explicitness or clarity of concepts and definitions remains a problem. For example, transference is a crucial phenomenon in psychoanalytic therapy, but judges—including psychoanalysts—have great difficulty in reaching agreement on its presence and intensity when they rate transcribed therapy interviews (Luborsky, Graff, Pulver, & Curtis, 1973). Many critics continue to find psychoanalytic concepts insufficiently precise to be useful. Quality of theory remains a debatable issue and is not yet a decisive criterion upon which to either accept or reject psychoanalytic psychotherapy.

Empirical Outcome

Robert Knight (1941), an influential psychoanalyst, offered five criteria for evaluating the effectiveness of analytic treatment: (1) symptomatic improvement, (2) increased productiveness, (3) improved adjustment and pleasure in sex, (4) improved interpersonal relations, and (5) ability to handle ordinary psychological conflicts and reasonable reality stress. While these criteria are clinically meaningful, psychoanalytic researchers have infrequently used them in a systematic way. One exception is the previously noted Menninger Health-Sickness Rating Scale, which incorporated these dimensions.

Considering the longevity of psychoanalysis and psychoanalytic therapy and the number of therapists committed to them, there has been relatively little research—especially good research—on their outcome. After reviewing the literature, Luborsky and Spence (1978) found only one controlled study comparing psychoanalysis and another therapy, and this study used but four patients.

There have been six clinical reports summarizing outcome data for various numbers of clients. These may be construed as clinical-trial reports, in that they did not employ control groups. Interpretation of these reports has been controversial. Three different reviewers of the same six surveys (Knight, 1941; Eysenck, 1952; Bergin & Lambert, 1978) have used different criteria for outcome and have reached very different conclusions (Fisher & Greenberg, 1977). For example, one writer computed a 39% improvement rate on a report of cases seen at the Berlin Psychoanalytic Institute during 1920 to 1930, whereas another writer computed a 91% improvement rate from the same report (Bergin & Lambert, 1978). The writers were using different but equally defensible assumptions in organizing the data. How one chooses to count premature dropouts, for example, can markedly alter success rates.

It does appear that reports of psychoanalytic therapy employ rather stringent criteria for outcome. The fact remains that there are no good studies evaluating psychoanalysis or long-term psychoanalytic psychotherapy. The Menninger Psychotherapy Research Project is limited in value on this issue, because it tells us only about the rank order of client improvement rather than about the absolute level of client change. Given these limitations in the quality of research, Fisher and Greenberg (1977) have carefully reviewed the available evidence. They arrived at two general conclusions: "(1) psychoanalysis has been shown to be consistently more effective than no-treatment with chronic neurotic patients, and (2) psychoanalysis has not been shown to be significantly more effective than *other* forms of psychotherapy with any type of patient" (p. 341).

As noted above, the sheer length and complexity of psychoanalytic treatment impose severe practical and conceptual constraints on outcome research. Given this limitation, and given the increasing interest in more specific kinds of research questions and in other kinds of psychotherapy, it appears unlikely that we will ever see a controlled outcome study of psychoanalytic treatment. Short-term treatment based on psychoanalytic principles has, however, been subjected to a more systematic evaluation. The results are equivocal—a state of affairs common to psychotherapy research. For example, in one well-controlled and influential study (Paul, 1966) a behavior therapy—systematic desensitization—was clearly superior to insight (psychodynamic) therapy in the treatment of speech anxiety. Clients in this study, however, were recruited for participation, were all college students, and were generally functioning reasonably well except for their anxiety about giving speeches in front of others. In a similar comparison of behavior therapy and (psychodynamically oriented) psychotherapy with "real" clients representing a variety of disturbances, both psychoanalytic psychotherapy and behavior therapy were highly successful, and behavior therapy was only slightly superior (Sloane, Staples, Cristol, Yorkston, & Whipple, 1975). There is as yet no systematic evidence concerning the effectiveness of briefer psychoanalytically based psychotherapy for specific kinds of behavioral and emotional problems.

Cost-Effectiveness

Cost-effectiveness involves consideration of the time and expense of treatment, the applicability to client populations, and the training requirements for therapists. Psychoanalysis and psychoanalytic therapy often require much time. Psychoanalysis can involve four or five sessions a week for three to five years. Psychoanalytically oriented psychotherapy is much more variable, as is illustrated by the examples in Chapter Three—175 sessions—and in this chapter—only 14 sessions.

A highly trained therapist is needed to administer psychoanalytic therapy. Psychoanalytic training is lengthy and costly (see Chapter Two). Even when paraprofessionals—housewives—learned to provide psychoanalytic psychotherapy, two years of training was necessary (Rioch, 1967). The applicability of psychoanalytic therapy is also somewhat limited by virtue of its requiring a fair amount of verbal skill, an ability to introspect, and an ability to tolerate symptoms while undergoing slower personality change. Non-YAVIS clients are usually ill suited to psychoanalytic therapy.

It is my belief that psychoanalytic therapy is clearly weakest with respect to the cost-effectiveness criterion. This is not because it is demonstrably inferior in effectiveness to the other therapies, but rather because it is clearly more costly. Given its more expensive nature, it is reasonable that we ask more from it. Unfortunately, there is no evidence that psychoanalysis and psychoanalytic therapy can deliver more. In fact, we remain uncertain exactly what it does deliver.

Although the above reasoning suggests that psychoanalysis and psychoanalytic psychotherapy are not the optimal treatments for symptom relief or behavior change, it may and undoubtedly will still be highly valued by some as a means for increased self-understanding. For it is self-understanding—in the sense of increased awareness and insight—that psychoanalytic treatment seeks to enhance. Given the nature of humankind and the current human condition, it is likely that there will always be people willing to pay high prices for such increased understanding. Many of us are curious about what we are and how we came to be that way. For the same reasons that history remains a fascinating subject matter for many, psychoanalysis will retain its appeal.

Summary

Psychoanalytic therapy is based on theories developed by Freud that emphasize the importance of unconscious, intrapsychic conflicts. Psychoanalysis is a specialized form of therapy carried out by graduates of a formal psychoanalytic training institute (see Chapter Two) and entails four or more sessions a week for a minimum of two years. Psychoanalytic psychotherapy varies greatly in number of sessions and goals but is usually much shorter and focused on more-specific objectives. While psychoanalysis is infrequently performed, psychoanalytic psychotherapy is probably the most widely practiced kind of psychotherapy. Freudian notions about the importance of childhood experience, unconscious processes, and the effects of anxiety and defense mechanisms on behavior continue to be very influential.

Psychoanalytic psychotherapy (and psychoanalysis) begins with instructions to the client to engage in *free association:* the client is given responsibility for initiating talk and is told not to censor any thoughts or feelings. *Resistance*—defense mechanisms operating against the efforts of therapy—inevitably emerges as intrapsychic conflicts interfere with the flow and content of the client's talk. The manifestations of resistance enable both therapist and client to observe the client's defensive maneuvers.

Processes of *regression* and *frustration* also occur as treatment proceeds. Regression is the falling back to more childlike ways of thinking, feeling, and acting in the therapeutic situation. It is facilitated by the use of the couch (in psychoanalysis) and the inherent dependency in the client role. *Frustration* arises from the rather unusual interpersonal relationship between client and psychoanalytic therapist, in which the client reveals all and the therapist reveals little. The client comes to feel uncared for and unloved in this situation.

Transference is a phenomenon in which the client feels and behaves toward the therapist as toward significant figures in childhood, especially parents. In effect, clients come to transfer their typical ways of dealing with important others to the therapist. The dependency and frustration noted above facilitate the development of transference. Transference is a crucial psychoanalytic phenomenon, because it permits examination of the client's interpersonal behavior *in situ*—that is, while actually occurring toward the therapist.

Interpretation is the primary specific mechanism by which change is brought about in psychoanalytic psychotherapy. An interpretation is any therapist statement that has the intent or function of providing the client with new information. Contrary to popular myth, psychoanalytic interpretations are not "deep" and do not necessarily relate childhood experiences to the present. Interpretation includes clarifying or identifying a theme or issue for further discussion; placing two or more sets of events, thoughts, or feelings side by side and inviting the client to compare them; and pointing out the defensive or avoidant components of some client behavior.

Dream interpretation is often important in psychoanalytic therapy, because dreams provide an opportunity to observe and understand unconscious material. Dreams are material for client and therapist to examine by means of interpretation and client exploration, much as any other verbal behavior would be worked with. *Working through* is a process of repeated interpretations by the therapist of key neurotic conflicts as they are manifested in various contexts. The concept recognizes the importance of examining client defenses in different situations in order to build up increased *insight,* or awareness. Insight, the major goal of psychoanalytic therapy, refers to the client's achieving greater understanding of defenses and conflicts, including their origins and their current manifestations, so that he or she can choose other ways to behave.

Several of these key principles were illustrated in a case of short-term psychoanalytic psychotherapy for a 21-year-old woman with generalized anxiety and phobias. The psychoanalytic case described in Chapter Three also illustrated some of the basic techniques.

Psychoanalysis and psychoanalytic psychotherapy are difficult to study because of the length and complexity of the treatment. Freud's own attitude toward research and the fact that most analysts are psychiatrists with relatively minimal research training have also contributed to the lack of empirical study of psychoanalytic therapy.

Two examples of research on psychoanalytic treatment were described. The first was a *process* study, a typical psychoanalytic research strategy, in which the depth of interpretation offered by a therapist was related to the client's subsequent behavior. It was found that moderate-level interpretations facilitated more exploration and yielded less resistance than either shallow or deep interpretations. The Menninger Foundation Psychotherapy Research Project was also described, as an example of a large, programmatic research effort. Process and outcome in two groups of clients, one receiving psychoanalysis and another receiving long-term psychoanalytic psychotherapy, were studied.

In terms of the three evaluative dimensions, psychoanalytic treatment is viewed as relatively weakest on cost-effectiveness. This is because it is such a costly procedure in terms of length of treatment and the required skill and training levels of practitioners, rather than because its effectiveness is demonstrably inferior.

Suggested Readings, Films, and Tapes

1. Colby, K. M. *A primer for psychotherapists.* New York: Ronald, 1951. May be hard to get, but still the most lucid account of psychoanalytic psychotherapy.
2. Freud, S. *Therapy and technique.* New York: Collier Books, 1963. Freud's views on technique are readable and informative. Selections 3, 7–9, and 11–13 are recommended.
3. Luborsky, L., & Spence, D. P. Quantitative research on psychoanalytic therapy. In S. L. Garfield & A. E. Bergin (Eds.), *Handbook of psychotherapy and behavior change* (2nd ed.). New York: Wiley, 1978. Pp. 331–368. Survey of empirical research into psychoanalytic psychotherapy.
4. *Psychoanalysis* (Film). Bloomington: Indiana University, 1964. A staged series of interactions that illustrate several basic psychoanalytic processes. I am not aware of any good films depicting psychoanalysis. The procedure is simply too long and subtle to make good cinema.

5. Alexander, F. *Psychoanalytic therapy* (Audio tape). Available from Scott, Foresman, 1900 E. Lake Ave., Glenview, Ill. 60025. One of the few available segments of a psychoanalytic therapy session, with the influential Franz Alexander as therapist. Several basic psychoanalytic processes are nicely illustrated. One of the set *Six Modern Therapies.*

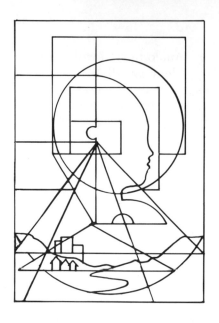

Humanistic Psychotherapy

With psychoanalytic therapy, it was possible to present a modal set of principles and procedures. Humanistic therapies are too diverse to permit this. Given the nature of the subject matter, I will first present some shared philosophical assumptions and perspectives of the humanistic movement. Next, two psychotherapeutic approaches—client-centered and Gestalt—will be described and evaluated. Within each method, the same general outline followed in the discussion of psychoanalytic therapy will be employed: basic theory, key therapy concepts and techniques, typical therapy case, illustrative therapy research, and evaluation.

Although there is no single humanistic psychotherapy, the various approaches share some key attitudes.

Choice and freedom. The humanistic therapies are a reaction to deterministic views of human nature, including both psychoanalysis and behaviorism, which view human action "as determined and constrained, in one case by unconscious instincts and in the other by environmental conditioning" (Korchin, 1976, p. 352). The humanistic approach emphasizes a person's values, options, purpose, and capacity for self-determination and self-actualization.

Uniqueness of the human experience. Both behaviorism and psychoanalysis assume that the methods of natural science can be used to understand neurosis and psychotherapy. The humanistic approach (with the notable exception of some client-centered therapists) rejects this assumption. Clients are not objects to be studied, and the customary scientific methods cannot capture the human experience and the interrelatedness of person and environment. Humans are qualitatively different from animals and machines and cannot be adequately understood with models or concepts derived from them.

Phenomenological emphasis. Personal and subjective experience is critical for understanding people and their behavior. It is the meaning of events for a client, rather than the events themselves, that needs to be understood. The reality or validity of the client's phenomenal world is to be respected.

"Realness" of the therapeutic relationship. An *authentic* interpersonal encounter between therapist and client is viewed as necessary and often sufficient for effective treatment. The authentic encounter is one in which each party respectfully enters, shares, and is affected by the experiential field of the other. The neutral *investigator* in psychoanalysis or the expert *trainer* in behavior therapy is rejected in favor of an *authentic* therapist, who uses intuitive, human reactions to encounter the client (Korchin, 1976). The relationship in psychoanalytic therapy is, by contrast, an artificial one, because the therapist tries to remain a "blank screen" in order to elicit client fantasies or transference.

Emphasis on present experience. Humanism emphasizes current experience rather than historical reconstruction or future expectations. Memories or plans are legitimate concerns of therapy as current acts; that is, the client's *current* experience of a painful memory is valid therapeutic material. Humanistic therapy emphasizes *experiencing* relationships, feelings, and conflicts rather than just talking about them. "To me, nothing exists except the now. Now = experience = awareness = reality. The past is no more and the future not yet. Only the *now* exists" (Perls, 1971, p. 14). Gestalt therapy states this view most forcefully. Other humanistic therapists give more weight to goals and intentions as part of the emphasis on choice and free will.

Health, not sickness. "Therapy is too good to be limited to the sick" (Polster & Polster, 1973). Emphasis is given to the human potential for growth and self-actualization instead of symptom relief and treatment of illness. Notions of "psychopathology" and diagnosis are rejected in favor of positive mental health and growth. Clients do not have to be seriously disturbed or dysfunctional to qualify for services. The humanistic clinician is ready to serve anyone who wants to grow or change. Much humanistic therapy is delivered in an educational context or at "growth centers" and is not labeled as treatment or mental health service.

The two humanistic therapies chosen for presentation illustrate these shared attitudes. They also differ in many respects. Client-centered therapy is one of the oldest humanistic approaches, Gestalt one of the newest. Client-centered workers have sought to validate ideas and methods by research; Gestalt therapists appeal to clinical and subjective experience. Because of such differences, the two complement each other in providing a perspective on humanistic psychotherapy.

Client-Centered Therapy

Like psychoanalysis, client-centered therapy has been heavily identified with a single individual, in this case Carl Rogers. Several books by Rogers and his colleagues present the basic theory and research on client-centered therapy: *Counseling and Psychotherapy* (Rogers, 1942), *Client Centered Therapy* (Rogers, 1951), and *The Therapeutic Relationship and Its Impact* (Rogers, Gendlin, Kiesler, & Truax, 1967). Before the emergence of behavior therapy, client-centered therapy was the main competitor of psychoanalysis. Although it has never been embraced by psychiatry, the client-centered approach has been exceedingly hardy, and it continues to enjoy strong influence in psychology, education, personnel and guidance work, and, more recently, in encounter circles. Rogers himself, in the middle and late 1960s, moved away from doing individual therapy and became primarily involved in working with groups. Theory and research on individual therapy continue to be advanced by many of his former students and associates (Hart & Tomlinson, 1970; Carkhuff & Berenson, 1977).

Client-centered personality theory is very complex, but the theory of psychotherapy is relatively simple. The personality theory is also controversial—more readily criticized. For these reasons I will focus mostly on the theory of psychotherapy.

Rogers has presented a more systematic account of both his personality theory and his psychotherapy theory, including attempts to account for pertinent research literature, than have the other humanistic approaches. This is due to his own training in research as a psychologist and the fact that he developed and applied his therapeutic principles and procedures in academic settings—at Ohio State University, the University of Chicago, and the University of Wisconsin. Like Freudian theory, client-centered theory grew out of clinical interaction—Rogers's efforts to understand his clients' behavior and the processes that led to change during psychotherapy.

Personality Theory

Client-centered theory postulates one motivational force, *self-actualization*: "This is the inherent tendency of the organism to develop all its capacities in ways which serve to maintain or enhance the organism" (Rogers, 1959, p. 196). The person is also endowed with an *organismic valuing process*, which permits the innate evaluating of experiences as positive (consistent with the self-actualizing process) or negative (inconsistent with it).

Through interaction with the environment a portion of the person's experience becomes differentiated as the self-concept. The self-concept is made up of the individual's experiences of his or her own being and functioning and is a fluid concept constantly changing with new experience. The self-system is powerfully influenced by interaction with others, and a universal need for the positive regard of others develops. As Rogers (1959, p. 225) put it, "The infant learns to need love." The individual may experience conflict between the need for positive regard and the organismic valuing process. An experience or feeling may seem "right" or pleasurable to the individual's organismic valuing process but may be negatively regarded by significant others, such as the parents.

From experiences in satisfying or not satisfying the need for positive regard, the individual develops a sense of self-regard or self-evaluation based largely on the perceived evaluations or reactions of others. The sense of self-regard becomes a "pervasive construct" that has a directing effect on the assimilation of new experience. Experiences inconsistent with or threatening to self-regard are denied symbolization or denied awareness. A boy may behave in a way unacceptable to his mother—and now to the boy himself—and then disown the act by some defensive maneuver.

The client-centered view of disordered behavior is essentially a conflict theory similar to the Freudian one: "The fundamental conflict is between the individual's thoughts based on his sensory, visceral, and affective responses, and the evaluative thoughts of other people which he adapts as his own" (Ford & Urban, 1963, p. 414). If many of these internalized standards are inconsistent with the organismic valuing process, the individual may be in a perpetual state of incongruence—an incongruence between, in effect, what her body tells her (experience) and what her internalized standards (self) tell her. This incongruence leads to anxiety, which is—or would be—very unpleasant. Therefore, the individual develops defensive behaviors to avoid the awareness of the incongruence between self and experience. Defensive behaviors include "not only the behaviors customarily regarded as neurotic—rationalization, compensation, fantasy, projection, compulsion, phobias, and the like—but also some of the behaviors customarily regarded as psychotic" (Rogers, 1959, p. 228). The troubled individual has subverted her own self-actualizing tendencies in the interest of attempting to retain love from significant others who are judgmental and so value the individual conditionally.

The therapist must offer the client the requisite conditions for growth—self-actualization—which were apparently not present in the client's environment. "Psychotherapy is the releasing of an already existing capacity in a potentially competent individual, not the expert manipulation of a more or less passive personality" (Rogers, 1959, p. 221).

Theory of Therapy—Basic Concepts

Client-centered therapy has changed considerably over the last 30 years as a function of both clinical experience and research evidence. In its early days it was called *"nondirective" therapy*, a term that emphasized the avoidance of directive therapeutic procedures. The therapist played a relatively passive, or reflective, role. Over the years, client-centered therapy has developed a more active, expressive role for the therapist.

Because Rogers and his colleagues have consistently attempted to develop measures for key concepts and to subject their ideas to empirical testing, the theory of therapy has remained relatively explicit and concise. Client-centered therapy holds that it is necessary and sufficient for the therapist to create a certain kind of interpersonal relationship that permits clients to utilize their own resources. More formally, it is asserted that, *if* the therapist offers sufficiently high levels of certain interpersonal skills, or conditions —*genuineness, unconditional positive regard*, and *accurate empathy*— and if clients are anxious or vulnerable and perceive the therapeutic conditions to at least a minimum degree, *then* the clients will become more *process*—will deepen and broaden their *experiencing*—and this, in turn, will lead to constructive personality change.

The basic "formula" for client-centered therapy is summarized in Figure 6–1. Within the therapeutic interaction the three therapist conditions can be viewed as the independent variables. Process, or experiencing, reflects client change and is the major dependent variable. Constructive personality change—also a dependent variable— refers to improved functioning in everyday life, often indexed by test scores, self-ratings, or therapist ratings.

Therapist Conditions

Three therapist conditions are viewed as necessary and sufficient for client change.

Genuineness/congruence. Genuineness, sometimes termed congruence, is the most important of the three conditions, because it must be present if the other two are to affect the client. The current importance of genuineness reflects the influence of existential thinking on client-centered theory and practice. Humanistic and existential theory emphasize that it is essential for the client to experience a meaningful relationship with an authentic therapist. The therapist "is a real person in an encounter presenting himself without defensive phoniness, without hiding behind a professional facade or other

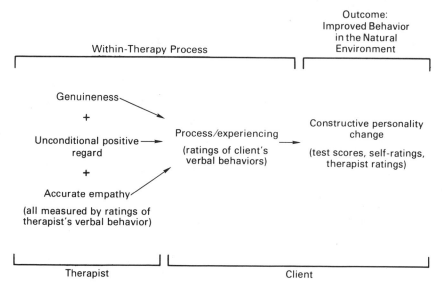

Figure 6–1. Client-centered process of psychotherapy.

role" (Truax & Mitchell, 1971, p. 315). Genuineness is the degree to which the therapist communicates honestly and without artificiality his or her feelings toward the client at the moment of their occurrence in the interaction. This does not imply that therapists constantly unburden their feelings, but rather that they are in touch with their feelings and act congruently with them.

A 5-point rating scale to measure genuineness has been developed and utilized in a number of research projects (Rogers et al., 1967). At low levels of genuineness there should be clear evidence of a discrepancy between the therapist's experiencing of clients and his or her statements or other communication. For example, there may be signs that the therapist is irritated with the client or uncomfortable about the interaction but does not directly acknowledge this. Or the therapist may appear evasive when the expression of some feeling or opinion is either requested by the client or seems called for by the therapeutic interaction. At high levels of genuineness, the therapist communicates feelings and reactions spontaneously and without any trace of defensiveness. Spontaneous expressions of feeling by the therapist indicate high genuineness: "I feel somewhat depressed that this is our last meeting" would be an example.

It has been acknowledged (Truax & Mitchell, 1971) that the genuineness scale primarily measures the *absence* of defensiveness and phoniness. Opportunities for the therapist to communicate genuineness are infrequent and often center on the client's direct or indirect requests for information about the therapist's opinion or feelings. In the absence of specific cues, the rater is instructed to assign a 3, or middle score. It is not surprising, therefore, that genuineness shows the lowest interjudge agreement among the three therapist conditions (Truax & Mitchell, 1971). While theoretically the most important condition, it remains the most difficult one to precisely define and to measure.

Unconditional positive regard. Unconditional positive regard is the conveying of warmth and acceptance of the client without imposing conditions that the client must meet in order to be positively regarded. The term *nonpossessive warmth* is also used to describe this concept. One can discern two aspects of this condition: the communication of warmth and caring, or what Rogers terms "prizing" of the client; and the nonconditional, or nonpossessive, nature of the prizing. A therapist could score low on the "regard" dimension by either not communicating warmth and caring or by doing so but in an evaluative or conditional manner.

The condition of regard does not require that the therapist sanction or approve of behavior and thoughts that are antisocial or inappropriate. Regard, or prizing, is directed at the client rather than at specific behaviors. This is sometimes a difficult distinction to make and to use. The therapist still sets limits on client behavior and would not accept, for example, physical abuse. The therapist, remember, must remain congruent with his or her feelings and behavior. But a therapist can accept socially inappropriate or undesirable behavior as an inevitable consequence of the client's background and experiences. "Thus when the therapist prizes his client, and is searching for the meaning or value of his client's thoughts or behaviors within the client, he does not tend to feel a response of approval or disapproval. He feels an acceptance of what *is*" (Rogers et al., 1967, p. 104).[1]

A 5-point rating scale has been employed to measure unconditional positive regard. At low levels of regard the therapist is actively offering advice or giving clear negative regard. At middle levels of regard the therapist indicates a positive caring, "but it is a semipossessive caring in the sense that it communicates to the client that what the client does or does not do matters to him (Rogers et al., 1967, p. 547)." For example, the therapist may communicate that it is important to him that the client get along at work or with family. At high levels of regard, the therapist communicates deep caring for the person, but it does not matter to him how the client chooses to behave.

Here are two therapeutic interactions that have been rated for unconditional positive regard. As you read them, try to think how you would rate the therapist on a scale of from 1 (lowest) to 5. Example One (the client is in a mental hospital):

[1]From *The Therapeutic Relationship and Its Impact: A Study of Psychotherapy with Schizophrenics*, by C. R. Rogers, E. T. Gendlin, D. J. Kiesler, and C. B. Truax (Eds.). Copyright 1967 by the University of Wisconsin Press. This and all other quotations from this source are reprinted by permission.

C: . . . and I don't, I don't know what sort of a job will be offered me, but—eh—

T: It might not be the best in the world.

C: I'm sure it won't (*T:* and uh.) but—

T: But if you can make up your mind to stomach some of the unpleasantness of things (*C:* M-hm) you have to go through—you'll get *through* it (*C:* Yeah, I know I will.) and, ah, you'll get out of here.

C: I certainly, uh, I just, I just *know* that I have to do it, so I'm going to do it but—it's awfully easy for me, Doctor, to—(sighs) well, more than pull in my shell, I, I just hibernate. I just, uh—well, just don't do a darn—thing.

T: It's your own fault (severely).

[Rogers et al., 1967, p. 570]

Example Two:

T: M-hm. But you say [name] that, that during that time you, you felt as though no one at all cared, as to what (*C:* That's right) what happened to you.

C: And, not only that, but I hated *myself* so that I didn't, I, I felt that I didn't *deserve* to have anyone care for me. I hated myself so that I, I, I not only felt that no one did, but I didn't see any reason why they *should.*

T: I guess that makes some sense to me now. I was wondering why it was that you were shutting other people off. You weren't *letting* anyone else care.

C: I didn't think I was *worth* caring for.

T: So you didn't ev—maybe you not only thought you were—hopeless, but you wouldn't allow people—(Therapist's statement is drowned out by Client.)

C: [interrupting and very loud] I closed the door on everyone. Yeah, I closed the door on everyone because I thought I just wasn't worth *bothering* with. I didn't think it was worthwhile for *you* to bother with me. "Just let me alone and—and let me rot that's all I'm worth."

T: You really avoided people.

C: So that, so that she wouldn't, uh, *talk* with me (*T:* M-hm) and when—the few times that I refused to see you, it was for the same reason. I didn't think I was worth bothering with, so why waste your time—let's just—

T: Let me ask you, ask you something about that. Do you think it would have been, uh, better if I had insisted that, uh, uh, you come and talk with me?

C: No, I don't believe so, Doctor. (They speak simultaneously.)

T: I wondered about that; I wasn't sure (softly).

[Rogers et al., pp. 578–599]

The first example was rated 1, the lowest level of regard. The therapist was clearly concerned about the client but was being directive and seemed to take responsibility for the client. The second example was rated 5, the highest level of regard. The therapist communicated respect and concern for the client's avoidance behavior and was accepting and nonevaluative.

Accurate empathy. The condition of accurate empathy has two components. The therapist must be sensitive to a client's current feelings
and experience and must have the verbal skills to communicate understanding in a way that can be perceived by the client. Empathy
does not imply identification; it is not necessary and is probably
undesirable for the therapist to feel the same emotions the client
feels. Rather, the therapist is to communicate an awareness or understanding of the client's feelings. Accurate empathy is probably the
most influential client-centered construct in its impact on the mental
health profession. It has come to be accepted as one of the key listening or communication skills required of good helpers.

A 9-point scale has been employed to measure accurate empathy. At low levels the therapist is unaware of or ignores client
feelings. At the middle stages the therapist "usually responds accurately to the client's more obvious feelings and occasionally recognizes some that are less apparent." The desire and effort to understand may both be present, but accuracy is low. At higher stages of
empathy, the therapist is sensitive to clients' feelings and "also un-
covers the most deeply shrouded of the clients' feeling areas . . . and
does so with sensitivity and accuracy" (Rogers et al., p. 566).

Below are two examples of therapeutic interactions that have
been rated for empathy. What would your ratings be on the 9-point
scale, where 1 is the lowest?

Example One:

> *T:* The way she wanted me and I was always terribly afraid that she
> wouldn't put up with me, or would put me out, out. (*C:* Yeah.) I
> guess I can get something else there, too. Now I was always afraid
> that she didn't really care.
> *C:* I still think that though. (*T:* M-hm.) 'Cause I don't know for sure.
> *T:* M-hm. And don't really know for sure whether she cares or not.
> *C:* (pause) She's got so many other, uh, littler kids to think about. (*T:*
> M-hm.) That's why—
> *T:* Maybe she likes them better or—
> *C:* No, it's not that, I think she likes us all. (*T:* Mm.) (pause) I think seein'
> that I'm the, I'm not the black sheep but, uh, the only one that
> served time (*T:* M-hm.) and, that—'n' got in the most trouble. (*T:*
> M-hm.) Seein' that I hurt her so much, that's why I think she's
> starting ta—she just don't care for me anymore.
> *T:* You believe, "Maybe because I have hurt her so much, maybe she's
> fed up with me, maybe she's gotten to the point where she just
> doesn't care" (long pause).
> [Rogers et al., p. 567]

Example Two:

> *C:* I'm here, an' uh—I guess that maybe I'll go through with it, and
> (nervous laugh) I'll have to—there's no use—
> *T:* (interrupting) You mean you're here—you mean you're right here—I
> wasn't sure when you said that—(*C:* Well—) whether you meant

you were—I guess you mean you were in—this is your situation
(stumbling).

C: (interrupting) I'm in—I'm in—I'm in the stage of suffering—well,
yes, I'm here too because of that. (Therapist murmurs "M-hm"
after every other word or so.)—An'—uh—(sighs audibly)—but, I
can see where—uh—

T: (filling in) You feel it's—you feel it's a pretty tough situation to be in?
(inquiringly)

C: Sometimes I do, sometimes I don't (casually).

[Rogers et al., p. 559]

The first example was rated 8, or very high in accurate empathy.
The therapist made a mistake (C: "No, it's not that.") but was tentative in expression and seemed to be voicing the client's feelings.

The second example was rated 3, defined as sensitive to the
more obvious feelings, somewhat aware of more hidden feelings, but
uncertain about their meaning. This therapist recognized that something important was going on in the client but had difficulty describing it. Notice that voice tone and style of speech seem to be important
cues about this therapist condition.

At higher levels of empathy, therapist and client are exploring
and pushing back the boundaries of the client's awareness. There is a
similarity here with the psychoanalytic process of interpretation, in
which the guiding principle is to interpret what is already at the
surface and "just a little bit more." Empathic communications and
interpretations are functionally quite similar, and both aim to clarify
the client's feelings and increase awareness.

Client Experiencing (Process)

We have examined what the therapist does in client-centered
therapy. Now we consider the effect of the therapist's behavior on the
client. Rogers (1961) has described the changes in successful clients in
terms of what they move away from and what they move toward.

Clients move away from facades. They begin to sense what they
are "not" and realize that they are frightened and are using a facade.
Clients move away from "oughts"—images or concepts of what they
should be as taught by their parents and internalized by the clients.
Clients also move away from pleasing others. "I finally felt that I
simply had to begin doing what I *wanted* to do, not what I *thought* I
should do, and regardless of what other people feel I should do"
(Rogers, 1961, p. 170) is an example.

What do clients move toward? They move toward "being process." Rogers (1961) provides a client's remark that illustrates process
movement: "Things are sure changing, boy, when I can't even predict
my own behavior in here any more. It was something I was able to do
before. Now I don't know what I'll say next. Man, it's quite a feeling"
(Rogers, 1961, p. 171). Clients also move toward "being complexity":
being better able to experience and tolerate ambivalence and con-

tradiction. Rogers (1961) observed that "this desire to be *all* of one's self in each moment—all the richness and complexity, with nothing hidden from one's self, and nothing feared in one's self—this is a common desire in those who have seemed to show much improvement in therapy" (p. 172). Clients also move toward openness to experience and toward acceptance of others for what they are. Finally, clients move toward trust of self. They learn to value and to rely on their own feelings, perceptions, and reactions. These are changes in the self-system toward a greater reliance on the innate processes of self-actualization and organismic valuing and away from a reliance on the positive regard of others.

Rogers's description of client change is based on countless hours of listening to transcripts of psychotherapy sessions. In an effort to make his ideas more systematic and explicit, he formulated a 7-stage, 7-variable process continuum, which his colleagues later refined into a widely used rating scale (Rogers et al., 1967). The Experiencing Scale measures the degree to which a client is able to clearly express direct experience. The rating scale, used for research purposes, defines experiencing as "the degree to which the client manifests inward reference in his verbalizations. The client is referring inwardly when he is referring to his own feelings and reactions—when he is searching for the meaning of personal events, feelings, and ideas he is reporting" (Rogers et al., p. 589). The scale focuses on the client's ability to express personally relevant, immediately experienced feelings. All therapies expect clients to talk about themselves and their problems in a personal and emotional manner.

At low levels of experiencing, the client narrates events but reveals few if any feelings of a private nature. At middle levels, the client goes beyond the narrative at times to make occasional comments about reactions and responses. The client is more aware of feelings and reactions and is able to express them. At high levels of experiencing, the client actually uses feelings in a struggle for self-exploration. Feelings and self-concepts are examined, and the conclusions are used to take off into further self-exploration.

A great deal of work has been done on measurement of experiencing, because it is the major dependent variable in client-centered therapy. It is rated from four-minute interview segments, which are randomly selected and randomly presented to raters. Raters are asked to judge the average experience level and the peak experience level for each segment.

Below are examples of two different levels of experiencing. Focus only on the client's statements and try to estimate the modal and peak experience levels for each example on a scale of 1 to 7.

Example One:

> *T:* Sort of get the impression you were wondering what to make of this situation here . . .

C: I don't see that it's benefitting me any.

T: Um . . . What good would it do to talk about things?

C: Hum?

T: Sort of asking yourself what good would it do to talk about things. Is that it ah? . . . Huh? . . .

C: I don't know what you talk about.

T: Hm.

C: Depends on what you talked about, I imagine.

T: Guess that is a lot of it then. (pause) Some things are, really worth talking about and some things are just talk . . . (long pause) You sort of looked over at the microphone there. I'm wondering if the tape recorder bothers you very much.

C: Huh?

T: I was just wondering if the tape recorder bothered you. (pause)

C: (coughs) Doesn't bother me.

T: Hm . . . I'm glad you said that.

C: The idea of recording it does, some, I imagine.

T: Does it? This ah tape won't be listened to by anyone here at the hospital.

C: Huh?

T: I said this tape won't be listened to by anyone here at the hospital . . . This is not hospital property, in fact.

C: By whom?

T: I say, the tape itself doesn't belong to the hospital nor does the recorder for that matter.

C: I see. Whose property is it?

T: Well, the university. (cough)

[Klein, Mathieu, Gendlin, & Kiesler, 1970, pp. 102–103]

Example Two:

C: Well, sometimes I do have a feeling of loneliness. Um . . . this, somehow connected with it, and I do think that the times while I'm depressed I feel lonely, but I don't see that, the two things are synonymous. And ah

T: Uh-huh. Uh, I guess like it's hard to put them in quite in relation to each other except to sort of a time sense, but when you are depressed you also sometimes feel lonely.

C: Yah. Well, now I don't know, let me see, if if the trouble is feeling, you know, how you describe feelings or their intensities when you ah, feelings can contradict each other and then you, what are you going to say. This is the algebraic sum of feelings or . . .

T: It's hard to get feelings to really fit into anything.

C: Yah, because ah I know that there is, I have sensed definitely a feeling of loneliness.

T: Uh-huh.

C: But on the other hand, I know that I also have a very strong sense of the opposite of loneliness. Not wanting to be with people and ah and there's all sorts of different qualities of this. There's there's one of this feeling which I think comes as sort of a reaction of when I feel depressed and so forth. I I like to be left alone. I feel that I'd like to do something, and that I don't feel like being disturbed and. Then, then the other sort of anti-loneliness. The sort of ah just the general feeling of ah disgust with people and and ah with the things that being in contact with them bring, and

the waste of time, and meaninglessness of it all, you know. Sound
and fury signifying nothing. And ah, sort of another type—I don't
know if they're both in the same class of emotions either. They
might.

T: It's that you feel all these things at once and as if they seem to be
somewhat

C: Well, I might say that I'm the unity (laugh) which conveys them all.
That's all I can say.

T: Uh-huh. Uh-huh . . . sort of . . . that you can really kind of . . . Feels
like you do want to be away from people in some sense and doing
things on your own—

C: Like, for instance, one of the things I noticed that I do get, I like to
read when I'm . . .[2]

The first example received a modal rating of 1 and a peak rating
of 2, reflecting this client's disengagement from his feelings and from
therapy. The peak of 2 occurred in his reaction to the tape recorder.
The second example was given a modal and peak rating of 5. Stage 5
requires a purposeful exploration of feelings and experiencing, and
here the client developed and then explored a conflict between loneliness and the desire to be alone.

Constructive Personality Change

Thus far, we have dealt with the within-therapy verbal behavior
of the client and therapist. It must be shown that changes in client
process, or experiencing, are related to changes in behavior outside of
therapy and the clinic. For this, client-centered workers have usually
relied on traditional instruments such as the MMPI and Thematic
Apperception Test, self-report measures of adjustment and self-
concept, and the ratings of therapists and judges. Some studies have
also employed such indexes as length of time outside the hospital (for
previously institutionalized clients) or reduction of overt antisocial
behavior. Client-centered workers use these measures as a means of
quantifying changes in personality and adjustment. With the exception of the Q-sort—a self-report measure of perceived-self/ideal-self
discrepancy—they have usually been content to use the best available instruments rather than develop new ones. Successful therapy is
expected to be reflected in changes in personality and adjustment.

Applications

Client-centered therapy takes place in face-to-face interaction,
usually once or twice a week. The length and number of sessions are
highly variable. Much of the early work with less disturbed individuals tended to average about 30 sessions, possibly because it often

[2]From *The Experiencing Scale,* Vol. II, by M. H. Klein, P. L. Mathieu, E. T.
Gendlin, and D. J. Kiesler. Copyright 1970 by the Wisconsin Psychiatric Institute.
Reprinted by permission.

took place in university settings where 30 weeks approximates an academic year. In their work with hospitalized (mostly schizophrenic) mental patients, however, Rogers and his colleagues saw many of the clients twice a week for up to two years. From the beginning, client-centered therapists emphasized the clients' responsibility in choosing therapy and in guiding the content of sessions. This is consistent with the personality theory, which views the individual as inherently competent and responsible. There is usually less formal negotiation or contracting in client-centered work than in psychoanalytic therapy. Therapists emphasize their availability, and clients always retain the option of continuing or halting treatment. For example, the therapist might comment, after an initial session, "Would you like to see me next week and continue our discussion?"

As in psychoanalytic therapy, clients are free to talk about whatever they wish during sessions. But the client-centered therapist tends to be much more active than the psychoanalytic therapist. The therapist's task is to communicate accurate empathy, genuineness, and unconditional positive regard, and so most client comments are specifically followed by the therapist's attempting to communicate his or her understanding of the client's previous message. Therapist comments typically take the form of reflections or paraphrases of what the client has just said and emphasize the affective, or emotional, component of the client's experience. This approach causes client-centered interviews to differ from everyday conversation in one striking way: the therapist rarely asks direct questions about feelings or events. Yet skillful client-centered therapists are remarkably effective in drawing out clients and helping them to speak freely about their experiences.

An Illustrative Therapy Case

Several excerpts from therapy cases have already been presented to illustrate the major concepts in client-centered therapy. As a full case I have chosen a short example in which the therapist provides a "very brief and general overall picture of the client and her therapy as he viewed it from his frame of reference" (Rogers & Dymond, 1954, pp. 261–264). More-extensive examples of client-centered therapy are readily available. Client-centered therapists have been especially open in presenting concrete examples of their work in books [via transcript], film, and tape recordings. Several examples of these are listed at the end of the chapter.

> The presenting situation was that Mrs. Oak was a housewife in her late thirties who was in a deeply discordant relationship with her husband and also much disturbed in her relationship with her adolescent daughter, who had recently been through a serious illness which had been diagnosed as psychosomatic. Mrs. Oak felt she must be to blame for this illness. She herself was a sensitive person, eager to be honest with herself and to search out the causes of her problems. She

was a person with little formal education, though intelligent and widely read.

By the fifth interview any specific concentration on her problems had dropped out and the major focus of therapy had shifted to an experiencing of herself and her emotional reactions. She felt at times that she *should* be "working on my problems" but that she felt drawn to this experiencing, that somehow she wanted to use the therapy hour for what she called her "vaguenesses." This was a good term, since she expressed herself in half-sentences, poetic analogies, and expressions which seemed more like fantasy. Her communications were often hard to follow or understand but obviously involved much deep feeling experienced in the immediate present.

She was unusually sensitive to the process she was experiencing in herself. To use some of her expressions, she was feeling the pieces of a jigsaw puzzle, she was singing a song without words, she was creating a poem, she was learning a new way of experiencing herself which was like learning to read Braille. Therapy was an experiencing of her self, in all its aspects, in a safe relationship. At first it was her guilt and her concern over being responsible for the maladjustments of others. Then it was her hatred and bitterness toward life for having cheated and frustrated her in so many different areas, particularly the sexual, and then it was the experiencing of her own hurt, of the sorrow she felt for herself for having been so wounded. But along with these went the experiencing of self as having a capacity for wholeness, a self which was not possessively loving toward others but was "without hate," a self that cared about others. This last followed what was, for her, one of the deepest experiences in therapy (between interviews Nos. 29 and 30)— the realization that the therapist *cared*, that it really mattered to him how therapy turned out for her, that he really valued her. She experienced the soundness of her own basic directions. She gradually became aware of the fact that, though she had searched in every corner of herself, there was nothing fundamentally bad, but rather, at heart she was positive and sound. She realized that the values she deeply held were such as would set her at variance with her culture, but she accepted this calmly.

I have termed these realizations "experiencings," hoping to convey something of the half-fantasy, half-trance state into which she could let herself go in the deeper aspects of therapy, when the tears, or the joy, or the hatred, or the tenderness which was the immediately present part of herself could be fully and completely experienced.

One of the outstanding characteristics of the interviews was the minimal consideration of her outside behavior. Once an issue was settled in her, the behavioral consequences were mentioned only by chance. After she had "felt" her way through her relationship with her daughter, there was little mention of her behavior toward the daughter until much later when she casually mentioned that the relationship was much better. Likewise, in regard to a job. She had never worked outside the home, and the prospect terrified her, yet she thought it highly important if she were to feel independent of her husband. She finally settled the issue in her feelings to the extent that she said she thought now that she could look for or take a job. She never mentioned it again. Only through a chance outside source did the therapist learn that, at about the end of therapy, she chose an establishment in which she wished to work, applied for a position, ignored the turn-down which she received, and convinced the manager that he should give her a trial. She is still holding the position. It was the same in regard to her marriage. She decided that she could not continue in marriage but that she did not wish to break up the marriage in a battle or with resentment and hurt. Shortly after the conclusion of therapy she achieved this goal of a separation and divorce which was mutually agreed upon.

When she left therapy, it was with the feeling that a process was going on in her which would continue to operate. She felt that the relationship with the therapist had been very meaningful and in a psychological sense would never stop, even though she walked out of the office for good. She felt ready, she thought, to cope with her life, though she realized it would not be easy [pp. 261–264].[3]

Discussion

This short, informal case summary illustrates several key features of client-centered therapy. There is very little historical or background information. The therapist focused heavily on the client's current subjective world and her personal feelings. There was also limited consideration of specific problems or "outside behavior," in contrast with the focus on these issues usually found in behavior therapy. The therapy focused on the client's developing personal insight into her feelings, attitudes, and relationships, and the therapist clearly felt that she was engaged in process, or experiencing, at fairly high levels: "Her communications were often hard to follow or understand but obviously involved much deep feeling experienced in the immediate present." It was assumed that such experiencing, or insight gains, would translate into constructive personality change in the client's life. In the case of Mrs. Oak, this apparently was so. The importance of the relationship and the client's perception that the therapist understood and cared was also viewed as critical in this case. But the increases in awareness, or insight, that occurred came almost entirely from the client, as would be consistent with the client-centered approach. The therapist functioned as a facilitator, but not through interpretations or advice.

The case of Mrs. Oak was part of a research project Rogers and his colleagues conducted. Therefore, the outcome of therapy was measured in a number of different ways: therapist ratings, self-report tests of self-concept, and analyses of the Thematic Apperception Test. The research data strongly supported the therapist's impressions that there was marked improvement in the client.

Therapy Research: Two Examples

Rogers and his colleagues pioneered in psychotherapy research. In the early 1940s they introduced what was at the time a startling innovation: tape recordings of therapy sessions, so that the actual

[3]Reprinted from *Psychotherapy and Personality Change*, by C. R. Rogers and R. F. Dymond, by permission of The University of Chicago Press. Copyright 1954 by The University of Chicago Press.

data of therapy could be subjected to empirical analysis. Impressive features of client-centered therapy have been its consistent research thrust and the reciprocal interaction between theory, research, and practice.

Client-centered research has centered on the key concepts depicted in Figure 6–1. The major questions asked are whether therapist conditions are related to client experiencing and constructive personality change. Client-centered theory predicts that the higher the levels of therapist conditions, the higher the levels of experiencing and the more constructive personality change shown by the client.

Two research strategies have been employed by client-centered workers. One is *naturalistic,* in the sense that real clients and therapists are utilized and the researcher seeks out *correlations* between therapist conditions, client experiencing, and constructive personality change. A second is an *analogue* research strategy, in which therapist conditions or client experiencing are experimentally manipulated. For example, the therapist might intentionally reduce his or her level of accurate empathy, and the effects of this reduction on client experiencing would be observed.

Both kinds of research rely on ratings of samples of client and therapist verbal behavior to provide measures of therapist conditions (independent variable) and client experiencing (dependent variable). A 30-session therapy case contains about 1500 minutes of client/therapist interaction. It would be a practical impossibility for a rater to listen to so much material. Client-centered researchers have found that four-minute samples spread over the sessions can give a representative picture of therapeutic interaction (Kiesler, Mathieu, & Klein, 1964). The samples are presented to judges in random order, so that the judge does not know which client the segment came from or whether it is from the beginning, middle, or end of therapy. The judges are usually unsophisticated with respect to client-centered therapy but are given much training in making the ratings.

I will now give examples of the two types of therapy research, naturalistic and experimental.

Naturalistic Research: The Mendota Project

The ambitious Mendota Project was designed to test whether client-centered therapy is applicable to severely disturbed individuals (Rogers et al., 1967). The subjects were 32 schizophrenics in a large state institution (there was also a normal control group, which will not be discussed here). Half the clients received intensive, individual, client-centered therapy.

The control clients simply received the normal hospital treatment program. Though this care did not include individual therapy, control clients often attended group therapy and therapeutic community meetings. The state hospital was regarded as of good quality.

The study was a stringent test of client-centered therapy, because the control group also received considerable treatment.

Therapist conditions and client experiencing were measured by means of the scales already described, using four-minute segments sampling the therapy sessions. In fact, these rating scales and the procedures for their use (for example, rater training, and sampling from interviews) were developed by the project staff. Measures of constructive personality change included both projective and objective tests, self-report measures of self-concept, ratings by ward personnel and therapists, discharge rate, and amount of time spent in the community after discharge.

Major hypotheses and results. The first hypothesis was that the greater the degree to which the therapist conditions exist in the relationship, the greater will be the evidence of therapeutic process, or experiencing, in the client.

In general, there was no differential amount of process *movement* during therapy in the schizophrenic clients as a function of different levels of therapist conditions. In fact, there was little change over therapy in experiencing for these clients. But clients who saw their therapist as having a high level of genuineness showed higher levels of experiencing *throughout* the course of therapy.

The second hypothesis was that clients receiving therapy will exhibit a greater degree of experiencing and will also show more constructive personality change than matched controls who do not receive therapy. This hypothesis basically compares outcomes for clients who received treatment and their matched controls who did not.

There were no overall differences in experiencing between those who received therapy and those who did not. Both treated clients and controls showed some degree of constructive personality change (for example, lower MMPI scores). Only one criterion index revealed a significant trend in favor of the therapy group—proportion of time spent in the community one year after discharge from the hospital.

A closer analysis revealed an interesting and important pattern in the data. Clients in the control group consistently showed moderate levels of improvement. Among the clients who did receive therapy, those who received high levels of therapist conditions tended to show marked improvement, whereas clients who received low levels of therapist conditions tended to show very little improvement, and some even appeared to get worse.

Discussion. Only a few of the many hypotheses that were tested have been presented. The Mendota Project stands to client-centered therapy and research in much the same way that the Menninger Foundation Psychotherapy Research Project stands to psychoanalysis. The Mendota Project developed a number of measures and procedures subsequently used in a great deal of research. Several of the participants in the project have been major contributors to client-centered theory and research and have trained a new generation of client-centered workers. Some of the substantive findings have been influential. The finding that low levels of therapist conditions were associated with no improvement or worsening in the client was significant. It had been thought that client-centered therapy could do no harm because of its relatively nondirective nature. It was also surprising that initial levels of experiencing considerably influenced the quality of the therapeutic relationship and the subsequent outcome. Unlike the Menninger project, the Mendota study directly examined therapeutic behavior. Like the Menninger project, it was very expensive and also costly in terms of time and effort.

Experimental Research

A limitation of a naturalistic study such as the Mendota Project is that it was essentially correlational. Although therapist conditions, process level, and outcome were all interrelated, it is difficult to draw causal inferences, because no variables were controlled or varied systematically. If one considers only the relationship between therapist conditions and client experiencing, it is possible to apply experimental methods in order to observe the effects of one on the other. This is done by means of the "ABA" within-subjects design described in Chapter Four.

Truax and Carkhuff (1965) studied the effects of manipulating accurate empathy and unconditional positive regard on the self-exploration (a variable quite similar to experiencing) behavior of three chronic hospital patients. Each client was seen for a one-hour therapeutic interview in which the therapist presented himself as a person trying to offer as much help as possible in the time spent together. During the first third of the interview (the A, or baseline, phase of the design) the therapist attempted high levels of therapist conditions. After 20 minutes there was a knock at the door. The therapist left and returned shortly, saying to the person who had knocked "Well, let me know as soon as you find out."

The interruption provided a cover for the therapist to change his behavior. During the next 20 minutes (the B, or intervention, phase) the therapist intentionally offered lower levels of empathy and regard but tried to be as genuine as before. After another 20 minutes there was another knock at the door. The therapist again left and reentered shortly, saying "Well, I'm relieved to hear that." During the final 20 minutes the therapist again tried to present high levels of all conditions. Both therapist conditions and client level of experiencing (self-exploration) were measured by the standard rating procedures.

The logic of the ABA design requires that the independent variable—therapist conditions—and dependent variables—client self-exploration—rise and fall as a function of the experimental manipulation. Reliable ratings established that the experimental conditions were adequately implemented. Figure 6–2 displays the self-exploration data for the three clients. It can be seen that the clients' level of self-exploration dropped noticeably during the middle phase (B) of the interview and then went back up again when baseline levels (A) were restored.

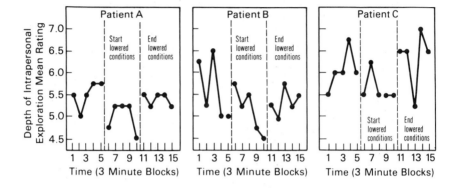

Figure 6–2. Client self-exploration scores as a function of changes in therapist empathy and regard. (From "The Experimental Manipulation of Therapeutic Conditions," by C. B. Truax and R. R. Carkhuff, *Journal of Consulting Psychology*, 1965, 29, 119–124. Copyright 1965 by the American Psychological Association. Reprinted by permission.)

A similar arrangement can be used to study the effects of the client on the therapist. A confederate client is trained to vary experiencing levels during different stages of the interview. Several studies of this sort have been conducted, and one consistent finding is that skillful therapists—those who seem to offer consistently high levels of therapist conditions—are not affected by the client's behavior (for example, see Carkhuff & Alexik, 1967). However, less skillful therapists tend to be considerably affected by the client. When the client's experiencing level drops, the therapist's level of empathic understanding, regard, and genuineness also decrease. In effect, the good therapist seems to lead the client, and the not-so-good therapist's behavior seems to follow the client's lead.

Evaluation of Client-Centered Therapy

Quality of Theory

Much of the criticism directed against the client-centered approach is aimed at the personality theory and is irrelevant to the theory of therapy. I will very briefly review the major criticisms of the personality theory and then consider the theory of therapy in more detail.

Personality theory. Client-centered personality theory is subject to the same criticisms as psychoanalytic theory: that it is overly inferential, vague, and difficult to subject to empirical testing. This is not surprising, because the structural characteristics of the two theories have much in common—both deal with unconscious processes, anxiety, and defensive maneuvers developed to deal with anxiety. Critics are especially uncomfortable with the concept of self-actualization, the master motivation in client-centered theory. Some critics find the notion overly vague and point out that it does not specify how organismic and environmental factors combine to produce learning and change. Others criticize it on the basis of lack of evidence, suggesting that examples chosen to support the notion of self-actualization are highly selected and that Rogers and his colleagues ignore inconsistent evidence (Martin, 1971). I believe that the criticisms of self-actualization have much validity, but I do not see them as a threat to the theory of therapy.

Psychotherapy theory. Relative to other psychodynamic and humanistic therapies, the client-centered theory of psychotherapy deserves high marks for clarity, explicitness, and attention to objective measurement. The basic independent and dependent variables have been made operational by means of the rating-scale procedures already described. Sound principles of measurement and statistical analysis have often been applied. Naive raters—without prior background in psychology or client-centered theory—have been used, much attention has been given to sampling issues, rater bias has usually been controlled for, and reliabilities have often been good. There are, however, problems in rating such complex constructs as accurate empathy, regard, genuineness, and experiencing. At times, the ratings of therapist conditions have not been reliable or interpretable, as was the case with congruence (genuineness) and unconditional positive regard in the Mendota Project (Rogers et al., 1967). Reliabilities for genuineness have often been low.

Accurate empathy has been the most reliably rated therapist condition, and it has also shown predicted relationships with client experiencing and outcome. It has been suggested, however, that the reliabilities of accurate empathy are inflated and, more importantly, that the ratings may reflect a quality other than that defined by the construct (Chinsky & Rappaport, 1971). It has been found, for example, that similar ratings of therapist statements are obtained irrespective of whether the raters are shown the clients' verbalizations, even though the scale definition clearly states that information about client feelings is crucial. It is quite possible that the accurate-empathy scale taps a more global therapist quality, such as the therapist's communicated commitment to the therapy interaction and involvement in the client's problems.

Client-centered theory asserts that therapist conditions are and should be noncontingently dispensed. The therapist's genuineness, empathy, and regard should not depend on what the client says or does. Social-learning theorists (Bandura, 1977), as well as other students of influence processes in psychotherapy (for example, Frank, 1973), contend that a therapist selectively responds to clients in such a way as to shape their talk to be consistent with the therapist's theoretical orientation. Truax (1966) examined therapy transcripts from a case successfully treated by Rogers to determine whether therapist reinforcement processes were at work. Nine separate categories of client behavior were separately and reliably rated. Three therapist behaviors that might function as reinforcers were also measured— empathy, unconditional positive regard, and directiveness.

> If there were no systematic selective use of empathy, warmth, or directiveness, then correlations between these variables and the patient categories would approach zero. The data, however, indicated strong relationships with certain patient behavior classes. The therapist significantly tended to respond selectively with different levels of empathy, warmth, or directiveness to the high and low levels of five of the nine classes of client-patient behavior [Truax & Mitchell, 1971, p. 323].

Truax further reasoned that, if therapist behaviors were functioning as reinforcers, then the client behaviors so being reinforced should increase in frequency over the course of therapy and the four classes of client behavior not reinforced should not show such increases. Analysis of the data confirmed this hypothesis. Thus, evidence from this study, as well as other research (Truax & Mitchell, 1971), suggests that therapist conditions may function as reinforcers. This does not necessarily negate client-centered theory but suggests that some reinterpretation is in order.

Empirical Outcome

Client-centered therapy is the only primarily "talk" therapy that has been subjected to thorough empirical evaluation. There are so many outcome studies, including both individual and group psychotherapy, that it is difficult to summarize them or draw unequivocal conclusions. Further complicating the problem of evaluating client-centered outcome studies are the many different kinds of outcome measures that have been employed. Truax and Mitchell (1971) presented a comprehensive and somewhat optimistic review of earlier work relating therapist conditions to therapy outcome. They found the evidence to be strongly supportive: high levels of therapist conditions were consistently related to favorable therapeutic outcomes. Although many of the studies reviewed by Truax and Mitchell are subject to methodological criticisms—that they were post hoc analyses or treated correlated outcome measures as if they were independent—the weight of the earlier research did seem reasonably supportive of the conclusion that the core conditions are positively associated with outcome.

More-recent evidence, however, is less favorable. And there is now a good deal of evidence indicating that therapist conditions are not associated with favorable therapy outcomes for non-client-centered verbal psychotherapies. Client-centered theory predicts that the relationship between therapist conditions and outcome should hold across all helping, or therapeutic, situations. But the data from a number of studies does not support this contention (summarized by Parloff, Waskow, & Wolfe, 1978).

While noting the generally negative results concerning the client-centered core conditions in non-client-centered therapy, it is important to recognize and commend the application of concepts and measures from one therapy approach to others. Such cross-theory investigation is relatively rare. The fact that client-centered measures have been so broadly applied is a tribute to the influence of client-centered thinking and the impact of client-centered research.

How has client-centered therapy fared when pitted against other therapeutic methods? Relatively little research comparing different therapies has been done. In one pioneering effort, client-centered therapy and Adlerian psychotherapy (the ideas of Alfred Adler) were about equally effective (Shlien, 1964). In the Mendota Project, client-centered therapy was not more effective than normal hospital treatment.

Cost-Effectiveness

Client-centered therapy varies widely in length, or number of sessions, but in general tends to be considerably shorter than psychoanalysis or intensive psychoanalytic therapy. Proponents believe that the principles are applicable in any helping relationship. In practice, the client-centered approach has been applied to a wide variety of client populations, including children, adolescents, and very seriously disturbed individuals. It appears to require some of the same verbal skills—or at least a willingness to talk about one's self and one's problems—as psychoanalytic therapy. This speculation is consistent with some empirical findings that initial levels of experiencing are an important predictor of success in client-centered therapy (Rogers et al., 1967), at least for seriously disturbed people.

Client-centered therapy has some interesting implications for the selection and training of therapists, including paraprofessionals. While non-client-centered therapists tend to doubt that genuineness, regard, and empathy are *sufficient* to produce client change, they do agree that these therapist skills are *necessary* or at least very *important* for psychotherapeutic work. Thus, training programs in the mental health field have often incorporated client-centered principles and have even used client-centered scales to help in teaching the skills.

Client-centered therapy asserts that the therapist conditions are not at all exclusive to trained professional therapists. They may be acquired through the process of living or by means of specific, focused training programs. This point was noted in Chapter Two in the discussion of paraprofessional therapists. Client-centered therapy can be quite economical because it can be administered by someone possessing the necessary therapist skills but with relatively little formal or professional training. Client-centered workers have taught therapist skills to a wide variety of mental health workers, including nurses, psychiatric technicians, and volunteers. The data seem to indicate that such workers are able to learn and use client-centered principles about as effectively as professionals (Truax & Mitchell, 1971). In one provocative finding (Carkhuff, Kratochvil, & Friel, 1968) it was observed that trainees in a clinical-psychology doctoral program showed a decrease in therapist-condition scores as they progressed through their program. Client-centered workers have suggested that traditional training programs, which emphasize conceptual and academic content, may hinder the development of therapist skills.

Client-centered concepts have also had an enormous impact on parent training. Parent Effectiveness Training (PET), developed by a student of Rogers, teaches parents how to use the basic therapist conditions to communicate more effectively with their children (Gordon, 1975). Because PET is widely taught to groups of parents, it represents a very economical application of client-centered concepts.

Client-centered therapy is unique in proposing that a good therapeutic relationship—defined by high levels of therapist conditions—is sufficient for client change. Other therapy approaches contend that a good relationship is necessary but not sufficient; the therapist must then "use" the relationship or add to it in some way, either by means of insight-increasing interpretations—as in psychoanalysis—or by means of specific training procedures—as in behavior therapy. For other therapies, a good relationship is a "common process"; for client-centered therapy, it is also a specific instigator of change.

Client-centered therapy as a distinct therapeutic approach may be dying of natural causes. Third-generation "Rogerians" have been carrying theory and therapy in different directions. On the one hand, some client-centered workers are becoming increasingly experiential and existential (Gendlin, 1979). On the other hand, some workers have developed new scales to measure additional therapist skills (Carkhuff & Berenson, 1977). The basic therapist conditions have been accepted by and assimilated into other therapeutic approaches. But the client-centered approach has left its mark on the therapeutic field by means of its explicit description of the important ingredients in the therapeutic relationship, the development of measurement procedures, and the interplay of empirical research and clinical theory.

Gestalt Psychotherapy

The second humanistic psychotherapy to be considered is Gestalt therapy. Like client-centered and psychoanalytic therapy, it was
developed originally by one man, Fritz Perls (1893–1970), and is now
being extended and modified by numerous disciples. Gestalt therapy
is a relative newcomer on the psychotherapeutic scene and is still
enjoying vigorous growth. Perls was first trained in medicine and
psychoanalysis. Thus, Freudian concepts of mental functioning—for
example, projection—appear in Gestalt theory, but the therapeutic
principles and procedures derive from a combination of Gestalt
psychology and humanistic thought.

Assumptions and Definitions

Gestalt therapy has largely been taught and practiced outside of
academic circles (though that is changing). This nonacademic tendency, the continuing evolution of Gestalt therapy, and Perls's skepticism about formal theory have produced a rather interesting state of
affairs. There is no consensual, systematic Gestalt theory—either of
personality or of therapy. It is necessary to abstract the essential
features of therapy from the primarily clinical writings of Perls and
other Gestalt leaders. Gestalt therapists share the philosophic views
and therapeutic goals of other humanistic approaches. It is technique
that distinguishes Gestalt therapy—the various strategies and tactics
designed to increase client awareness.

Gestalt psychology developed as a theory of perception and was
a reaction to atomistic approaches, which tried to define and measure mental elements or mental content. Gestalt theory emphasized
the role of the perceiver and the naturally occurring patterned, or
organized, nature of perception. Gestalt is a German word that trans-
lates roughly as form or whole. According to Gestalt perceptual
theory, we tend innately to organize our visual field into meaningful
patterns, especially figure/ground relationships.

Perls applied the ideas of Gestalt perception theory to personality (Wallen, 1970). A person's subjective world is organized by
needs. "Needs energize behavior and organize it on the subjective-
perceptual level and on the objective-motor level. The individual
then carries out the necessary activities in order to satisfy the needs"
(Wallen, 1970, p. 9). Before a need is satisfied, need-relevant stimuli in
the environment are salient, or "figure"; after satisfaction they recede into "ground," and new need stimuli are attended to. According
to Gestalt ideas, the mature, well-functioning individual experiences
a smooth, cyclical formation and destruction of "strong" perceptual
and motor Gestalts as needs arise, are recognized, are satisfied, and
subside in favor of new needs. A strong Gestalt in a perceptual sense
means that "figure" is clearly and immediately differentiated from

"ground"; in a motivational sense, a strong Gestalt means that there is a clear and immediate awareness of a need.

Imagine two people finishing breakfast and about to begin the day. One perceives a number of unfinished tasks clamoring for attention. There is tension, an uncertainty about where to begin, a feeling of "I've got to get organized." A task is arbitrarily chosen in order to "get going," but the person has trouble concentrating; it is an effort to continue. The person's attention wanders into daydreams, detracting from his or her performance.

The second person—facing a comparable workload—sorts out all the day's priorities without much conscious thought. Energy and attention are focused on the task at hand and then shifted to the next activity. Although some activities are less enjoyable than others, there is a feeling of closure when a task is completed and a feeling of satisfaction as the work proceeds. We have all had both kinds of experience. It is the aim of Gestalt therapy to produce behavior like the second person's.

For the neurotic, such as the person in the first example, growth has been impeded. The natural processes of Gestalt formation and destruction are short-circuited. Clients may be unaware of their needs because of chronic repression. Or there may be confusion in the hierarchy, with no need emerging as "figure" or with needs competing with one another. Finally, the client may be inhibited or be afraid to express needs.

As with client-centered theory, unacceptable experiences or feelings may be denied or "disowned," and the energy and mechanisms devoted to this defensive work may cause the individual trouble. Gestalt therapy is sensitive to polarities, or conflicts, within the organism, which often arise when a person internalizes "shoulds" from parental figures without conscious awareness of doing so. One of the most important splits, or polarities, dealt with in Gestalt therapy is the top dog/underdog encounter. *Top dog* represents the "I should" part of the personality, the perfectionistic, righteous, demanding part of ourselves. It is similar to transactional analysis's concept of the Parent and to the Freudian superego. *Underdog* is the "I want" part of ourselves, akin to transactional analysis's Child—the bad or rebellious part of ourselves. Top dog and underdog strive for control of the organism in manipulative ways.

The neurotic, then, may be unaware of or afraid to express needs, unaware or unaccepting of polarities within themselves. Clients must learn to be aware and accepting of the totality of themselves, including conflicting needs.

> In therapy, then, we have to re-establish the neurotic's capacity to discriminate. We have to help him to rediscover what is himself and what is not himself; what fulfills him and what thwarts him. We have to guide him towards integration. We have to assist him in finding the

proper balance and boundary between himself and the rest of the world
[Perls, 1973, p. 43].[4]

Gestalt therapy achieves these goals by helping the client toward *awareness*, and awareness is assumed to be necessary and sufficient for client change. Awareness is sufficient for change because of
the client's capacity for self-actualization, another belief shared with
client-centered therapy.

> And I believe that this is the great thing to understand: That awareness
> per se—by and of itself—can be curative. Because with full awareness
> you become aware of this organismic self-regulation. . . . We can rely on
> the wisdom of the organism [Perls, 1969, p. 16].[5]

Awareness is not easily defined. It is similar to high levels of client-
centered experiencing—an integrated sensitivity to both inner feelings (needs) and meanings and to environmental stimuli. But there
is more emphasis on sensory and motor experience in Gestalt
awareness and more emphasis on verbal expression of feeling in
experiencing.

> Awareness is a form of experiencing. It is the process of being in vigilant
> contact with the most important event in the individual/environment
> field with full sensory, motor, emotional, cognitive, and energetic sup-
> port [Yontef, 1976, p. 67].

Therapy Techniques

The presentation of therapy techniques will be divided into
three parts. First, several key *basic strategies* are described and illustrated. Second, five *ground rules* governing client participation are
listed. Third, several illustrative *games and exercises* are outlined. The
ground rules and games and exercises can be construed as tactics for
implementing the basic strategies.

Basic Strategies

Skillful frustration. The therapist behaves so as not to satisfy neurotic
needs or permit neurotic maneuvers in the therapy situation. The
therapist creates situations in which the client experiences what has
been avoided and is unpleasant. Skillful frustration forces clients to
discover their own possibilities and potential—to learn that they can
do for themselves what they are trying to get the therapist (and
others) to do for them. Frustration must be skillfully mixed with

---

[4]From *The Gestalt Approach and Eyewitness to Therapy*, by F. S. Perls. Copyright
1973 by Science and Behavior Books, Inc. This and all other quotations from this source
are reprinted by permission.
[5]From *Gestalt Therapy Verbatim*, by F. S. Perls. Copyright 1969 by Real People
Press. This and all other quotations from this source are reprinted by permission.

empathy and support. This process is analogous to the psychoanalytic therapist's regulating of the therapeutic regression.

Here is Perls's (1973) summary of his use of skillful frustration with a client who had only three months available for therapy:

> The first six weeks of therapy—more than half the available time—were spent in frustrating him in his desperate attempts to manipulate me into telling him what to do. He was by turn plaintive, aggressive, mute, despairing. He tried every trick in the book. He threw the time barrier up to me over and over again, trying to make me responsible for his lack of progress. If I had yielded to his demands, undoubtedly he would have sabotaged my efforts, exasperated me, and remained exactly where he was [p. 109].

Keeping the client in the "now." Staying in the present, tuned to one's experiencing, is difficult, especially for the troubled or neurotic individual. The Gestalt therapist uses several techniques to help keep clients in the present. One is to direct the clients to become aware of who is the target of their thoughts and feelings. If a client is making general complaints about a spouse, the therapist will suggest speaking directly to the spouse. If the client presents a problem or an issue in general terms, the therapist will guide the client toward a concrete current manifestation. For example, a client might complain "I have trouble communicating with people." In a group setting the therapist would ask "Who in this group do you have trouble communicating with?" Once the client names a group member, the therapist can help stage interactions between the two and help the client work on communication issues *in situ.*

Another way of emphasizing the "now" is to ask the client to focus on some aspect of behavior or experience. The therapist may observe some motor behavior or gesture and ask the client either to focus on it or perhaps to exaggerate it. Often this takes the form of one of the basic Gestalt questions, "What are you doing now?" or "How are you feeling now?" If a client is experiencing something unpleasant, such as a painful memory or a feeling of depression, the Gestalt therapist may ask that the client simply "stay with it," or concentrate on the experience and describe the sensations and fantasies involved. This is often difficult and frustrating at first. In Perls's view, the neurotic person "has habitually avoided vigorous contact with a variety of unpleasant and dysphoric experiences. As a result avoidance has become ingrained, a phobic anxiety has been routinized, and major dimensions of experience have never been adequately mastered" (Levitsky & Perls, 1970, p. 149). The stay-with-it procedure, combined with skillful frustration, deals with this neurotic phobic avoidance.

Role playing, or psychodrama. A consistent thrust in Gestalt therapy is to encourage the client to express feelings and attitudes directly, so they can be understood and accepted, or "owned." Psychodrama is a procedure in which the client enacts various roles, usually switching from one to another, so that feelings and behavior can be experienced and examined by client and therapist. Shuttling from one role to another permits clients to experience and integrate different perspectives of their own and others' behavior.

There are two major variations in the use of psychodramatic procedures in Gestalt therapy. One involves the client's role-playing a disowned or inhibited part of himself or herself while interacting with a significant other. Here is an example with Perls (1973, pp. 90–91) as the therapist.

> C: My wife has no consideration for me.
> T: Can you imagine telling this to her face?
> C: No, I can't. She'd interrupt me as soon as I began.
> T: Could you tell her that?
> C: Yes. You never let me talk.
> T: Can you hear your voice?
> C: Yes. Sounds rather weak, doesn't it?
> T: Could you give an order—something starting with the words "you should"?
> C: No, I could not.
> T: What do you feel now?
> C: My heart is beating. I am getting anxious.
> T: Could you tell this to your wife?
> C: No. But I'm getting angry. I feel like saying, "shut up for once."
> T: You just said it to her.
> C: (shouting) Shut up, shut up! SHUT UP!! For heaven's sake, let me get a word in.

A client might also be coached to interact with other clients in a group situation or with the therapist in either a group or individual therapy situation. A client will often be asked to take the role of the other at some point—for example, playing the part of his wife responding to him. This role reversal permits expression of the client's expectations and fantasies about the spouse.

The second variation in the use of role playing might be termed intrapsychic, or within-self, psychodrama. It is used to deal with polarities, or conflicts, within the self. When such a conflict is noted by the therapist, the client is asked to engage in a dialogue between the two parts of the self. This technique can be applied to (1) split roles within the personality, such as masculine versus feminine or top dog versus underdog; or (2) parts of the body, such as head versus stomach. The intent of the procedure is to help the client experience the polarity in the fullest possible intensity, so that all aspects of the self can be owned and eventually integrated. Here is an example with Perls as the therapist and a client who has identified a conflict between her needs to be dependent and assertive or brazen.

F: All right, now let's see whether we can't get these things together. Now have an encounter between your baby dependence and brazenness. /J: O.K./ Those are your two poles.

J: (as brazenness) You really are a punk. You sound just like a punk. You've been around. You've been around for a long time. You've learned a lot of things. You know how to be on your own. What's the matter with you? What are you crying about?

J: (as dependent) Well, I like to be helpless sometimes, Jane, and I know you don't like it. I know you don't put up with it very often. But sometimes it just comes out. Like I can't work with Fritz without it coming out. I can hide it . . . for a long time, but . . . if you don't own up to me I'm gonna really, I'm gonna keep coming out and maybe you'll never grow up.

F: Say this again.

J: I'm gonna keep coming out and maybe you'll never grow up.

F: Say it very spitefully.

J: I'm gonna *keep* coming out and maybe you'll *never* grow up . . .

F: Okeh, be the brazenness again.

J: (sighs) Well I've tried stomping on you and hiding you and shoving you in corners and making everybody believe that you don't exist. What more do you want me to do with you? What do you want from me?

[Perls, 1969, p. 258]

Dream work. Gestalt therapists are particularly interested in recurring dreams, which are assumed to reflect "unfinished business," or parts of the self that have not been fully experienced and accepted. The same techniques are applied to dreams as are applied to any other material. The search for "whys" is avoided. The therapist may ask the client to relate the dream in the present tense. The client is often asked to act out the dream using psychodramatic methods, because the elements in the dream are often assumed to be alienated, or "projected," parts of the person. For example, the client may be asked to role-play various objects in the dream. The therapist, in effect, tries to help the client find clues in the dream.

One woman client reported a dream in which she was 8 years old and was standing on the shore of a beautiful lake.

T: Be a lake and tell me your story.

C: Uh, I'm a round, round lake. I feel, I sort of feel perfect, perfect lake. I, my water is very good and soft to the touch.

T: To whom are you talking?

C: To myself.

T: Now you know the third law in Gestalt therapy. Do unto others what you do unto yourself. Talk to us.

C: Um . . .

T: You're the lake.

C: I'm the lake. You would like to come in me, in my lake, in this lake, because it's very beautiful, and the water feels very . . .

T: The second law in Gestalt therapy—don't say it; say I or you.

[Perls, 1973, p. 188]

Ground Rules

Like all therapies, the Gestalt approach sets forth rules concerning how the client (and therapist) should act. These rules define a way of thinking and talking about oneself during treatment that is consistent with the theoretical framework. They flow from the basic strategies described above.

1. Stay in the "now." The client is asked to express what he or she is experiencing in the here and now. This does not exclude past experience or memories. No content is excluded in advance. Rather, the focus is on how the client is currently feeling about the experience or dealing with it.

2. Communicate directly to your intended audience. The Gestalt therapist wants the client to experience authentic (I and thou) relationships both in and out of therapy. Gestalt therapists often ask "To whom are you saying this?" and then ask the client to restate the message directly to the target. This principle also leads to an exclusion of "gossiping," or talking about other people in the therapy group or even in the client's social environment. If a client complained about another member of a group—for example, "I feel Joan is bored by whatever I say"—the therapist would insist that this be said directly to Joan.

3. Use "I" language rather than "it" language. An important theme in Gestalt therapy is helping the clients become more responsible for themselves and their behavior. If a client were to say "It was a depressing party," the Gestalt therapist would ask that the client restate the thought in the form of "I was depressed by the party." The idea is to get the client to view himself or herself as an active agent who causes things to happen rather than a passive being to whom things are done.

4. Restrict the use of questions. Gestalt therapy perceives client questions as frequently representing passivity or laziness or as hiding an opinion or feeling. It asks that the speaker rephrase the question in the form of a declarative statement.

5. Do not ask "why" questions. Gestalt therapy views "why" questions as intellectualizing, or fruitless searches for reasons. These questions are seen as making it easy for the client to produce rationalizations to justify behavior. The only appropriate questions in Gestalt therapy are "what" or "how" questions. The two prototypical questions used by Gestalt therapists are "What are you doing now?" (or what is your hand, foot, arm, face doing?) and "How are you feeling now?"

Games and Exercises

In addition to the basic strategies and ground rules described, numerous games and exercises are used in both individual and group applications of Gestalt therapy. A few will be illustrated.

Secrets. The leader asks group participants to think of a well-guarded secret—something they would not like to disclose—and then to share with the group their fantasies about what it would be like to reveal the secret. Clients can become aware of the inhibitions and processes that impede intimacy and sharing while at the same time remaining free to disclose or not disclose the specific content of their secret.

Exaggeration game. A client is asked to exaggerate some gesture again and again. This game is used in either individual or group settings to facilitate the understanding of body language. The procedure can also be used with verbal behavior—for example, a phrase or other verbal expression that a client seems to routinely use or overuse. Through repetition, the client is aided in experiencing and becoming more aware of the meaning of the behavior.

I take responsibility. All perceptions are considered to be acts, and the client is asked to describe perceptions and to use the phrase "I take responsibility for it." For example, "My voice is very quiet . . . and I take responsibility for it" or "Now I don't know what to say . . . and I take responsibility for not knowing" (Levitsky & Perls, 1970, p. 46). This game illustrates both staying in the "now" and the accepting of personal responsibility.

Applications

Gestalt principles and methods are applied in widely varying settings and contexts. There may be individual or group application in therapy, where the clients are seeking help for personal problems or distress. Or there may be group or workshop settings in the context of growth or education. A person might register for a weekend workshop out of curiosity, a wish to experience something new or different, or—if he or she is a therapist, to learn new techniques. Weekend-workshop participants may also have some personal problems or issues they want to deal with. It is not uncommon for a client to sample different Gestalt therapists and workshops over a period of time. In effect, one can move in and out of Gestalt therapy in a way that is not feasible in psychoanalytic therapy or behavior therapy.

Individual Gestalt therapy begins with the client's presenting problems. The choice of strategy, game, or exercise depends on the particular client.

Most Gestalt therapists prefer to work with clients in groups. However, Gestalt groups tend to minimize group process or group interaction. Instead, participants take turns in the "hot seat," an empty chair next to the therapist. Members take the chair, signifying that they have a problem or issue that they want to work on. While one member is in the hot seat, the others may participate vicariously or sometimes may be involved in psychodrama. Each member is expected to take a turn in the hot seat during the course of the group.

An Illustrative Therapy Case

There are many examples in the Gestalt literature of episodes from therapy sessions or workshops and illustrations of the application of specific techniques. Both in print and on film, Gestalt therapists have been commendably "out front." The great number of concrete examples contributes to the impact of the Gestalt approach. Interestingly, however, the clinical literature of an approach that emphasizes "wholeness" is made up almost exclusively of fragments of therapeutic interactions. I could not find a case study in which the impact of a course of therapy on a client was described.

Work with dreams constitutes a major part of the clinical literature. I have chosen an example of dream work from a group setting. Perls is again the therapist (Perls, 1969, pp. 162–164). Several Gestalt methods are illustrated. Can you recognize them?

> *C:* In my dream, I'm sitting on a platform, and there's somebody else with me, a man, and maybe another person, and—ah—a couple of rattlesnakes. And one's up on the platform, now, all coiled up, and I'm frightened. And his head's up, but he doesn't seem like he's gonna strike me. He's just sitting there and I'm frightened, and this other person says to me—uh—just, just don't disturb the snake and he won't bother you. And the other snake, the other snake's down below, and there's a dog down there.
>
> *T:* What is there?
>
> *C:* A dog, and the other snake.
>
> *T:* So, up here is one rattlesnake and down below is another rattlesnake and the dog.
>
> *C:* And the dog is sort of sniffing at the rattlesnake. He's—ah—getting very close to the rattlesnake, sort of playing with it, and I wanna stop—stop him from doing that.
>
> *T:* Tell him.
>
> *C:* Dog, stop! /*T:* Louder./
>   *Stop!* /*T:* Louder./
>   (shouts) STOP! /*T:* Louder./
>   (screams) STOP!
>
> *T:* Does the dog stop?
>
> *C:* He's looking at me. Now he's gone back to the snake. Now—now, the snake's sort of coiling up around the dog, and the dog's lying down, and—and the snake's coiling around the dog, and the dog looks very happy.
>
> *T:* Ah! Now have an encounter between the dog and the rattlesnake.
>
> *C:* You want me to play them?
>
> *T:* Both. Sure. This is your dream. Every part is a part of yourself.
>
> *C:* I'm the dog. (hesitantly) Huh. Hello, rattlesnake. It sort of feels good with you wrapped around me.
>
> *T:* Look at the audience. Say this to somebody in the audience.
>
> *C:* (laughs gently) Hello, snake. It feels good to have you wrapped around me.

T: Close your eyes. Enter your body. What do you experience physically?

C: I'm trembling. Tensing.

T: Let this develop. Allow yourself to tremble and get your feelings . . . (her whole body begins to move a little) Yah. Let it happen. Can you dance it? Get up and dance it. Let your eyes open, just so that you stay in touch with your body, with what you want to express physically . . . Yah . . . (she walks, trembling and jerkily, almost staggering) Now dance rattlesnake (she moves slowly and sinuously graceful) . . . How does it feel to be a rattlesnake now? . . .

C: It's—sort of—slowly—quite—quite aware, of anything getting too close.

T: Hm?

C: Quite aware of not letting anything get too close, ready to strike.

T: Say this to us. "If you come too close, I—"

C: If you come too close, I'll strike back!

T: I don't hear you. I don't believe you, yet.

C: If you come too close, I will *strike back!*

T: Say this to each one, here.

C: If you come too close, I will *strike back!*

T: Say this with your whole body.

C: If you come too close, I will *strike back!*

T: How are your legs? I experience you as being somewhat wobbly.

C: Yeah.

T: That you don't really take a stand.

C: Yes. I feel I'm . . . kind of, in between being very strong and—if I let go, they're going to turn to rubber.

T: Okeh, let them turn to rubber. (her knees bend and wobble) Again . . . Now try out how strong they are. Try out—hit the floor. Do anything. (she stamps several times with one foot) Yah, now the other. (stamps her other foot) Now let them turn to rubber again. (she lets knees bend again) More difficult now, isn't it?

C: Yeah.

T: Now say again the sentence, "If you come too close—" . . . (she makes an effort) . . . (laughter)

C: If—if you . . .

T: Okeh, change. Say "Come close." (laughter)

C: Come close.

T: How do you feel now?

C: Warm.

T: You feel somewhat more real?

C: Yeah.

T: Okeh . . . So what we did is we took away some of the fear of being in touch. So, from now on, she'll be a bit more in touch.

You see how you can use *everything* in a dream. If you are pursued by an ogre in a dream, and you *become* the ogre, the nightmare disappears. You re-own the energy that is invested in the demon. Then the power of the ogre is no longer outside, alienated, but inside where you can use it.

Perls used psychodrama several times (playing the dog and the snake). He also had the client focus awareness on bodily feelings: "What do you experience physically?" "How are your legs?" Perls also coaxed her to stay with feelings by having her repeat and exaggerate key statements ("If you come too close"). He also requested her to communicate directly ("Say this to us"). Notice that, although Perls did not supply any interpretation, he was quite active and directive.

Therapy Research

This will be a very short section, because there is no research on Gestalt therapy. It is not surprising to find an absence of controlled outcome research. After all, Gestalt therapy is a relative newcomer on the therapeutic scene; until recently it has been studied and applied outside of academic contexts; and the approach itself is based on an appeal to the validity of subjective experience rather than objective measurement. It is more surprising that there is so little in the way of well-described case studies or clinical trials. The Gestalt literature is rich in clinical example, but practically all of it is in the form of short episodes or fragments from therapy or workshops. Many of these examples depict Gestalt procedures leading to dramatic expressions of feeling and emotion, apparently marked increases in awareness, and the resolution of recurring dreams. But there are few cases that describe a course of treatment and its overall effect on a client's functioning.

As Gestalt therapy becomes more influential, it is certain to attract the attention of research workers and thereby be subjected to empirical evaluation. The major difficulty would be on the dependent-variable side of the therapeutic equation. Research workers and Gestalt therapists will need to collaborate in better defining and measuring awareness and specifying observable behavior changes that follow from Gestalt therapy. It should not be an insurmountable task. Because many Gestalt procedures are relatively specific and can be carried out in a reasonably short period of time, it ought to be possible to evaluate their effects.

Evaluation of Gestalt Therapy

Quality of the Therapeutic Rationale

> Any reasonable approach to psychology not hiding itself behind a professional jargon must be comprehensible to the intelligent layman, and must be grounded in the facts of human behavior. If it is not, there is something basically wrong with it [Perls, 1973, p. 2].

By this standard, something is wrong with Gestalt psychology and Gestalt therapy. In spite of Perls's efforts, the theory underlying Gestalt therapy remains fuzzy to many professional psychologists, not to mention laypersons, and it is only loosely related to the facts of human behavior. The relationship of Gestalt therapy to Gestalt principles of perception is analogical and metaphorical. Gestalt personality theory is subject to the same criticisms made of psychoanalytic and client-centered theories, only more so. This is because Gestalt personality theory has been less systematically described and, especially, because no effort has been made to measure—that is, make explicit—the key variables. Concepts such as contact, awareness, or introjection remain appealing metaphors. They do, however, strike a responsive chord in many of us, and, reading about Gestalt therapy, one can identify with many of the concepts and processes described. But a systematic or scientific approach requires more-formal definition and, especially, operational measurement. Gestalt therapists appeal to subjective experience for verification of their ideas and procedures. Obviously, many clients and therapists feel that the theory and method fit their own behavior and experience.

In contrast with the therapeutic rationale, many therapy techniques are quite specific. Because of this and because of the many verbatim transcripts and films available, the student can readily grasp many of the procedures the Gestalt therapist uses. It is much less clear under what circumstances or in what sequence Gestalt procedures are to be used, because there are few comprehensive case studies.

Empirical Outcome

There are no empirical data on the effectiveness of Gestalt therapy. The only available evidence consists of numerous demonstrations in therapy or in workshops of successful resolutions of dreams, dramatic gains in awareness, and strong expressions of feelings. Lacking, however, is information about how the clients who manifested such changes subsequently behaved and felt after treatment had terminated. Therapists of many persuasions take it on faith that generalization can be made to the real world. This tendency is found especially among Gestalt therapists, who are, after all, committed to the here and now. The following quotation nicely summarizes this position:

> Many people have expressed concern about what, if anything, psychotherapy has to do with a person's life *outside* of therapy. That controversy is a bottomless pit. Good experiences grow beyond their own brief moments of existence just as surely as one moment moves into the next. This is our faith. Individual contact episodes are representatives of styles of contact which exist outside the therapy experience itself and they exert an influence beyond the hours in the therapist's office [Polster & Polster, 1973, p. 184].

The relative contribution of specific and common processes to the outcomes of Gestalt therapy must be considered. I believe that in group and workshop settings, especially the hot seat, common processes are a very plausible explanation for observed changes. All clients know they are expected to take a turn presenting a problem to the leader. The leader is often a charismatic figure whom the clients expect to be insightful and powerful. There is also felt pressure from the group to "perform" as other clients have done, and performing involves playing the Gestalt games and changing. In sum, the hot-seat situation arouses emotionality and the expectation of change, and there is group pressure and support to follow the therapist's directions and change.

Cost-Effectiveness

Any cost-effectiveness analysis of Gestalt therapy must be tentative, because of the lack of information about outcome. Although outcomes remain uncertain, some observations about costs are possible.

Time and expense of treatment. Gestalt therapy is often practiced in groups, thus making it economical. Because of its directive nature, it is often relatively short term, although specific figures are not available. As we have seen, clients come and go as they require. Weekend seminars or workshops allow a group of clients to have a Gestalt experience in an economical way.

Training requirements for therapists. Gestalt therapists come from all of the major mental health professions and from the ranks of para-professionals as well. The primary means of obtaining training in Gestalt therapy is through a training institute similar in structure and function to the psychoanalytic institutes described in Chapter Two. Gestalt institutes are more flexible about admission and will consider persons without formal academic training who are engaged in adequately supervised psychotherapeutic work and have at least one year's experience. In any case, a "trainee" has already acquired basic psychotherapeutic training and focuses on Gestalt principles and techniques. The training could range from a few weekend workshops through three years of part-time study. The more intensive or formal Gestalt training involves personal therapy. In summary, a professional therapist can acquire some Gestalt techniques fairly easily, but intensive training is fairly time consuming and expensive.

Applicability to Client Population

Gestalt therapy requires that the client be able to verbalize experiences and feelings; engage in fantasy, or "as-if" procedures; and feel comfortable in self-disclosing in front of others. It appears to be very much a YAVIS psychotherapy.

> In general, Gestalt therapy is most effective with overly socialized, restrained, constricted individuals—often described as neurotic, phobic, perfectionistic, ineffective, depressed, etc.—whose function is limited or inconsistent, primarily due to their internal restrictions, and whose enjoyment of living is minimal. Most efforts of Gestalt therapy have therefore been directed toward persons with these characteristics [Shepherd, 1970, pp. 234–235].

Although there are millions of such people, they are not the major problem clients for the mental health system. The limitation of Gestalt therapy to verbal but emotionally constricted, neurotic adults is an important one, and it is one shared with most psychoanalytic and humanistic therapies. This limitation must be balanced against the relative economy in delivering Gestalt therapy, especially by means of groups or workshops. It is also uncertain whether Gestalt therapy is applicable to young children.

Gestalt therapy's principles and, especially, its techniques are becoming quite influential. Therapists of many "schools" are borrowing or incorporating Gestalt procedures, which are readily accessible via books, tapes, or films. Workshops offer another way for a therapist to learn about and experience Gestalt (certainly more economically than psychoanalysis can be experienced). Having experienced the effectiveness of Gestalt therapy themselves, therapists are likely to be enthusiastic about learning more and applying it to their clients. As Gestalt therapy receives more attention in departments of psychiatry and psychology, there should be more attempts to clarify the theory and evaluate the effectiveness of treatment.

Summary

There are many humanistic therapies, but they all share several philosophical assumptions and perspectives. People are viewed as possessing choice and freedom as well as such unique properties as consciousness. The study of human beings, therefore, requires methods fundamentally different from those customarily used in natural science. People's personal, or subjective, experience is viewed as critical for understanding their behavior, and current "here-and-now" experiences or events are more important than the past or future. The therapeutic relationship is viewed as a real encounter, and it is critical that the therapist be authentic in this relationship.

Client-centered therapy is based on the assumption of a self-actualizing tendency, the individual's natural capacity to develop and grow, given suitable conditions.

Client-centered therapy holds that, if the therapist offers sufficiently high levels of certain interpersonal conditions—*genuineness*, *unconditional positive regard*, and *accurate empathy*—and these are perceived by clients, then the clients will deepen their *experiencing* and engage in self-exploration, and this will in turn lead to constructive personality change. The three therapist conditions and client experiencing are primarily measured by rating samples of clients' and therapists' verbal behavior. Constructive personality change is indexed by any of the conventional outcome methods described in Chapter Four, such as therapist or third-party ratings, psychological tests, and performance measures.

Genuineness, or congruence, involves communicating honestly with the client without artificiality. Unconditional positive regard is the conveying of warmth and acceptance of the client without imposing conditions that the client must meet in order to be accepted. Accurate empathy involves sensitivity to the client's feelings and experiences and communicating of this understanding in a way that can be perceived by the client. Genuineness is viewed as the most fundamental of these three conditions but has proved to be the most difficult one to rate reliably.

Experiencing refers to a self-exploration in which the client is in touch with and able to verbalize currently experienced feelings and attitudes.

Client-centered therapy takes place in face-to-face interactions, usually once or twice a week, and tends to be shorter than psychoanalysis or psychoanalytically oriented psychotherapy. The client is responsible for initiating talk and steering the content of the sessions. Client-centered therapists ask remarkably few direct questions. But by means of paraphrases, reflections, and communication of empathy, regard, and genuineness they usually manage to draw clients out and help them to speak freely about their experience.

The client-centered approach pioneered objective psychotherapy research. Two major research strategies have been employed. In the *naturalistic* strategy, correlations are sought between therapist conditions, client experiencing, and constructive personality change. In the experimental strategy, usually using analogue situations, therapist conditions or client experiencing are experimentally manipulated, and the effects of this manipulation on other variables are observed. An example of each kind of approach was described and analyzed. The Mendota Project sought to study the effectiveness of client-centered therapy on chronic (schizophrenic) hospital patients. In general, little overall constructive personality change was found in the patients receiving client-centered therapy, compared with controls who received the basic hospital milieu program. There was also little change in experiencing for the patients, but therapists perceived as being high in genuineness had clients who showed higher levels of experiencing throughout therapy.

In an analogue study, a therapist varied his level of therapist conditions in accordance with the ABA design described in Chapter Four. It was found that client self-exploration varied directly as a function of the varying therapist conditions.

While client-centered personality theory with its emphasis on self-actualization is much criticized, the theory of therapy is relatively explicit and amenable to objective measurement. There are, however, some measurement problems, especially concerning the meaning of accurate-empathy scores. Research also indicates that therapist conditions appear to be dispensed more contingently—that is, dependent on particular kinds of client talk—than the theory states. Client-centered theory and research on therapist conditions have been very influential. Therapists of many different persuasions accept the conditions as necessary, although not agreeing with client-centered proponents that they are sufficient.

Gestalt therapists view effective functioning as a series of changing figure/ground relationships. Needs requiring attention or satisfaction are experienced as figure, are attended to, are satisfied, and recede into ground to be replaced by another figure. Interferences with this natural process constitute neurosis. Gestalt therapy aims at increasing *awareness* of such disruptions in order that effective functioning can be restored. Gestalt awareness is similar to client-centered experiencing but with more emphasis on sensory and motor events.

Gestalt therapy uses several basic strategies. In *skillful frustration* the therapist behaves so as not to satisfy a client's neurotic needs. *Keeping the client in the "now"* refers to several tactics designed to help the client become aware of, or "tune into," experience. Role playing, or *psychodrama*, is a way of encouraging clients to express feelings and attitudes directly and to help make them aware of conflicting or ambivalent feelings and attitudes.

Ground rules govern client participation in therapy. The major ones are (1) stay in the "now"; (2) communicate directly to your intended audience; (3) use "I" language rather than "it" language, or take responsibility for whatever you say; (4) restrict the use of questions; and (5) do not ask "why" questions.

Games and exercises are used in both individual and group applications. They include secrets, the exaggeration game, and "I take responsibility."

Gestalt methods are applied in various settings and contexts, but group work is particularly favored. Many Gestalt groups and workshops offer clients the opportunity to participate for a fixed period of time, leave, and then perhaps return to another group or workshop later.

Because of Gestalt therapy's relative newness, the vague character of its theory, and the antiresearch attitudes of its proponents, there is virtually no empirical research on it. The Gestalt approach appears to be weak in the quality or explicitness of its theory. Its empirical effectiveness remains unknown, but it appears to be reasonably cost-effective, because it is practiced in groups and can be used in short-term treatment.

Suggested Readings, Films, and Tapes

1. Rogers, C. R., Gendlin, E. T., Kiesler, D. J., & Truax, C. B. *The therapeutic relationship and its impact.* Madison: University of Wisconsin Press, 1967. The chapters on theory of psychotherapy and some of the case examples are accessible and informative.
2. Perls, F. *The gestalt approach and eyewitness to therapy.* Palo Alto, Calif.: Science and Behavior Books, 1973. Perhaps the most systematic and readable Perls. Lots of clinical examples.
3. *Three approaches to psychotherapy* (Film). Available from Psychological Films, 110 N. Wheeler St., Orange, Calif. 92669. Three famous therapists, Carl Rogers, Fritz Perls, and Albert Ellis, interview the same client, giving a rare opportunity to compare the different approaches. Each film runs about 40 minutes and follows a similar format: the therapist briefly summarizes his basic approach, conducts a 20-minute psychotherapeutic interview, and then debriefs and discusses his work.
4. *In the now* (Film). Available from Film Center, 189 N. Wheeler St., Orange, Calif. 92669. James Simpkins, an influential therapist, illustrates several Gestalt approaches in a group setting.
5. *Madeline's dream* (Film). Available from Films, Inc., 1144 Wilmette St., Wilmette, Ill. 60091. Perls illustrates Gestalt dream interpretation.
6. Rogers, Carl. *Mr. Vac* (Audio tape). American Academy of Psychotherapists Tape Library. An annotated transcript of this case is also available (Rogers et al., 1967, pp. 401–416). This tape presents two consecutive therapy sessions Rogers conducted with a withdrawn and silent chronic mental patient. Nicely illustrates the application of client-centered principles to the chronic client and was one of the cases in the Mendota Project. It is one of the most moving psychotherapeutic episodes I have heard.

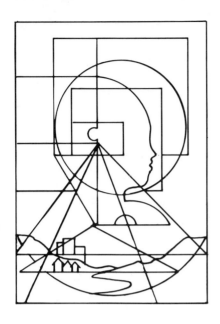

SEVEN

Behavior
Therapy

Introduction: Assumptions and Definitions

This chapter presents the third and final major approach to psychotherapy. Although the chapter organization remains basically the same, you should be alert for two changes. First, the emphasis is more comparative; because this is the last of the three major approaches, it is possible to note similarities and differences. Second, there is no separate section on illustrative research. Because research is such an integral part of behavior therapy, it is more appropriate and convenient to cite research within each major treatment strategy.

Origins

Behavior therapy has markedly different origins from those of the humanistic and psychoanalytic approaches thus far discussed. Those two approaches were rooted in clinical activity and clinical experience. Theory evolved to explain and guide clinical activity, and then research methods—at least with psychoanalysis and client-centered therapy—were applied in an effort to validate clinical theory and methods.

Behavior therapy is rooted in a body of principles and methods developed in psychological laboratories studying the learning process. It began as an attempt to apply these principles and procedures to the clinical situation. Many psychologists believed that psychotherapy was essentially a process of learning and social influence. It seemed plausible that the systematic application of principles of learning and social influence that were derived from research should lead to powerful psychotherapeutic procedures. A few early efforts to apply learning concepts to clinical problems (for example, see Jones, 1924) were promising, but they were not pursued. Efforts to integrate learning principles and psychotherapy then took the form of translating psychoanalytic procedures into the language and concepts of learning (Dollard & Miller, 1950). Such efforts may have increased the academic respectability of clinical methods, but they did not produce new or more effective methods. During the last 20 years the extrapolation of principles of learning and social influence has been successfully accomplished. Behavior therapy is now a vigorous and rapidly expanding approach that has grown beyond its origins in simple conditioning procedures.

Behavior therapy as a distinctive psychological treatment emerged when the psychology of learning was dominated by classical (Pavlovian) and operant (Skinnerian) principles and methods. Early work in behavior therapy, therefore, emphasized applications of classical conditioning principles, most notably the work of Joseph Wolpe (1958) on counterconditioning, and the reinforcement principles put forth by B. F. Skinner (1953).

Classical conditioning is a process whereby a previously neutral stimulus comes to elicit a new response because it is paired (in time) with a stimulus event that naturally elicits this response. In this way, for example, neutral stimuli associated with pain become conditioned elicitors of fear responses. Wolpe's formulation emphasized the critical role of learned fear or anxiety in neurotic behavior. According to Wolpe, fear responses become classically conditioned to stimuli that are present in any situation of high fear arousal. These stimuli, which can include internal events such as thoughts, subsequently lead to anxiety or fear arousal whenever encountered and can become extremely disruptive to the individual. It is necessary, Wolpe contended, to reverse such emotional conditioning for neurosis to be successfully treated.

The *operant* approach emphasizes the importance of reinforcement (or consequences) in developing and maintaining deviant behavior. Skinnerian principles are especially applicable in relatively closed environments—schools or mental institutions—where the antecedents and consequences for appropriate and inappropriate behavior can be readily controlled. In such environments it has been shown that one can readily eliminate or reduce undesirable behavior and increase the frequency of desirable behavior.

But conceptions of learning and behavior change have shifted considerably in the light of new evidence and are continuing to evolve. Three trends are worthy of note. The importance of vicarious, or observational, learning has gained wide acceptance and has been found to have important clinical implications (Bandura, 1969). We learn much by observing others, and modeling is now an important behavior-therapy procedure in helping clients overcome fears or learn new social skills.

A second major development concerns the role of cognitive mediation in the learning process. Early behaviorists were reacting against psychoanalytic theories, which focused on internal processes and were felt to be "mentalistic" in their explanations of behavior. Behaviorists emphasized the importance of the environment—external stimuli—and classical-conditioning and operant processes, which were thought to be free of cognitive mediation. It is now apparent that virtually all human learning involves cognitive or symbolic processes (Bandura, 1977). Humans learn to anticipate stimuli and consequences. Behavior therapists now employ cognitive models, and cognitions are frequently the target of intervention procedures.

A third development is an expansion beyond the psychology of learning. It became apparent to behavior therapists that much research in personality and social psychology had implications for psychotherapy (a notion not at all new to psychoanalytic and humanistic therapists). Behavior therapy is not wedded to learning theory per se but to the application of valid psychological principles. The application of attribution principles, the inferences one makes about the causes of one's own and others' behavior, illustrates the use of social psychological concepts to clinical problems (Kopel & Arkowitz, 1975).

Behavior therapy began as a reaction against psychodynamic theory and techniques, and its early writings emphasized the difference between the two approaches. It is common for new approaches to emphasize their uniqueness and to stake out new territory (London, 1972). For instructional purposes it is convenient to emphasize differences between approaches, but the risk is that one creates stereotypes and oversimplifies issues. Many of the differences between behavioral and psychodynamic approaches have become somewhat blurred as behavior therapy has matured and attempted to encompass a broader array of events and problems. This chapter tries to give a realistic picture of current behavior therapy that retains its unique features while acknowledging some of the similarities it shares with other psychotherapies. The basic theme in what follows is that behavior therapy "is best defined by a rationale and methodology and not by a specified theory or set of principles" (Craighead, Kazdin, & Mahoney, 1976, p. 6).

Orienting Assumptions

Behavior therapy comes in a wide variety of forms. In part this is because, unlike psychoanalysis or the humanistic approaches, it is avowedly *strategic;* the procedures used depend heavily on the nature of the client's problem and the setting (whether in the community or in an institution).

Behavior therapists also differ in their conceptual orientation. Many prefer procedures that follow closely from classical and operant research on learning and try to minimize the importance of cognitive and relationship factors. Others deal much more with subjective or cognitive events, both as targets of therapeutic intervention and in devising treatment procedures. In spite of this diversity, which will be illustrated in later sections on specific procedures, behavior therapists are united by some common assumptions or attitudes that differentiate them from other therapists. One such assumption—that psychological principles derived from laboratory research can be usefully applied in clinical settings—has already been discussed. Three additional distinctive attitudes are described in this section.

Empirical Emphasis

Behavior therapy's empirical emphasis stems from the academic origins and research training of most behavior therapists. It has two components. First, there is an effort to select therapeutic procedures on the basis of the best available evidence, preferably controlled-outcome research. Second, there is a commitment to identify specific problem behaviors and use them to monitor the effects of any psychotherapeutic intervention. This second component is the more fundamental manifestation of the empirical attitude in behavior therapy. That is because the state of the art of controlled research or reliable clinical evidence on the effectiveness of various psychotherapeutic procedures is *relatively* primitive. In part, this is because of the complexities of research on therapy outcome illustrated in Chapter Four. There are, I believe, several disorders—for example, fears and phobias, certain parent/child problems, and sexual dysfunction—for which the research evidence clearly indicates a particular kind of behavioral therapy as the treatment of choice. For the bulk of the clients facing any psychotherapist or agency, however, the choice of treatment must be made on other grounds, usually the therapist's particular skills and attitudes.

Behavior therapists, like other therapists, employ those methods that they know best and value most. What distinguishes behavior therapists, however, is the careful monitoring of therapeutic progress and outcome. In this way, both client and therapist can be aware of progress and problems, can agree to modify or even terminate treatment if necessary, and can agree when treatment is no longer needed.

It would be foolish to imply that nonbehavioral therapists do not track the course of therapy. Any responsible psychotherapist does so within his or her particular framework. But behavior therapy tries to be very explicit and objective in the assessment of therapeutic progress and outcome. The difference, therefore, is essentially a quantitative rather than a qualitative one, but it is an important one nevertheless. The assessment of outcome in behavior therapy is carried out by means of another fundamental common feature.

Specifying Client Goals and Objectives

Behavior therapists work toward defining their clients' goals in ways amenable to objective measurement. Psychoanalytic and humanistic therapies tend to focus on intrapsychic or attitudinal change, and it is often quite difficult to ascertain whether or how much change is occurring. The behavior therapist, by contrast, usually seeks to establish a contract that defines successful outcomes in clear-cut fashion— for example, more frequent and more satisfying sexual relations, reduced feelings of anxiety, elimination of avoidance of previously feared situations, or fewer temper tantrums and greater cooperation from a previously troublesome child.

The specification of goals and objectives in concrete, measurable form is often not easy, especially in more complex interpersonal disorders. Clients often present their difficulties in terms of traits or diffuse feelings of upset. For example, a client might come to a therapist complaining that his life is unsatisfactory because he has no friends and does not know how to relate to people. A behavior therapist would try to clarify whether the client's problem is primarily due to anxiety or lack of communication skills (or both) and what situations (or people) are most troublesome.

Environmental Emphasis

Theories of human behavior and psychotherapy differ in the relative emphasis they give to internal, or organismic, factors and external, or environmental, variables. Psychoanalytic and humanistic approaches tend to emphasize internal events. Psychoanalytic drives and ego defenses, Gestalt needs, and the client-centered self-concept are examples of internal factors. Behavior therapy gives more emphasis to the role of environmental events, especially the individual's social environment. Behavior therapists view behavior as a product of the interaction between personal factors and situations. The importance of situations is often neglected, so the behaviorist thinks, by other therapeutic approaches. For example, a behavior therapist prefers to view unassertiveness not as a general trait but rather as an action tendency much more likely to be elicited by certain situations than others. How people behave in particular situations is the basic issue for the behavior therapist.

Behavior therapists also believe that change can often be more effectively accomplished by altering the environment than by focusing on the individual. This is especially true for controlled environments such as mental hospitals and families. Consider, for example, an adolescent who stays out late at night, does not let her parents know her whereabouts, and often does not do her chores. A behavior therapist would prefer to change the social environment by helping the parents and the adolescent to negotiate mutually acceptable contracts and train the parents to encourage and reinforce good behavior.

Definition of Disorder

Behavior therapy assumes that disordered behavior is acquired through the same learning processes as any other kind of behavior. Behavioral disorders, therefore, are not viewed as manifestations of mental illness or psychopathology. The "goodness" or "badness," "normality" or "abnormality" of behavior are considered labels attached by society on the basis of social norms and judgments about the consequences of behavior. Consistent with the previously mentioned emphasis on the importance of considering the situations in which behavior occurs, behavior therapists note that the same behavior may be considered normal and effective in one situation but abnormal and maladaptive in another. Take, for example, aggressive or even homicidal behavior in wartime and in peacetime.

For the behavior therapist, then, disorder or neurosis is behavior that is situationally inappropriate; that is, it creates problems for the individual or for others. Behavior therapists frequently distinguish two classes of maladaptive behavior: behavioral *excesses* and behavioral *deficits*. This distinction reflects the idea that normal behavioral reactions are either inappropriately exaggerated or insufficiently present.

Two common examples of behavioral excess are phobias and overactivity in children. The phobic individual overreacts—physiologically, cognitively, behaviorally—to a stimulus that is objectively harmless. The fright reaction, however, is physiologically normal and adaptive for really dangerous situations, in that it mobilizes the individual for fight or flight. The overactive child disrupts the home or the classroom, but his or her high rate of behavior may be adaptive on the playground.

Behavioral deficits are problems in which the individual either lacks knowledge or skill about what to do in particular situations or is inhibited in so doing. A child who has not yet learned to control bladder functioning and wets the bed is one example. An adult who has not learned to express needs and assert his or her own rights is another.

In clinical situations behavioral excesses and deficits may occur together. A young man, for example, may experience anxiety in the presence of an attractive woman. His anxiety reaction is a behavioral excess. He may also be deficient in social skills. Treatment may need to involve both anxiety-reducing procedures and skill training to improve communication and interaction with women.

Goals

All psychotherapists hope to change how their clients act and how they feel about themselves—both attitudes *and* behavior. They differ on whether it is most strategic to focus on behavior, on attitudes, or on both. Psychoanalytic and humanistic approaches tend to assume the causal primacy of attitudes and cognitions; they believe that these must be altered before behavior can be changed. Behavior therapists assume a reciprocal interaction between behavior and attitude—that attitude change frequently follows behavioral change and that behavioral change is often easier to accomplish and is therefore a more appropriate focus of therapeutic intervention (Bandura, 1977). Behavior therapists also appeal to a body of literature in social psychology that indicates that people change their attitudes to make them consistent with their behavior (Kopel & Arkowitz, 1975).

Many modern behavior therapists focus heavily on cognitive and symbolic processes and try to change them. But behavior therapists also try to specify some behavioral consequences of the intervention and to monitor whether both cognitions and behavior are changing. Alternatively, the behavior therapist might try to determine what changes in behavior would lead the client to feel or think differently and then try to bring about these changes. Although it is an oversimplification to say that behavior therapy aims at changing behaviors whereas psychodynamic therapy aims at changing attitudes, there is an important difference in relative emphasis.

Behavioral Assessment

The procedures used by the behavior therapist depend heavily on the specific nature of the client's problems. It is important, therefore, to identify these problems as precisely as possible. This is a major reason why assessment is a critical component in behavior therapy. A second reason is that assessment provides a means for monitoring changes in the client's problem behaviors, so that the effectiveness of treatment can be evaluated.

Humanistic psychotherapies deny the importance of assessment. Client-centered theory believes that diagnosis is inherently evaluative and therefore inconsistent with the basic therapist conditions. The humanistic therapist works with whatever the client chooses to share or talk about.

Psychoanalytic therapists are concerned about assessing the nature and intensity of intrapsychic conflicts and ego defenses. This assessment is important for determining whether a client is suitable for more intensive uncovering treatment—for example, formal psychoanalysis—or rather should be guided toward shorter, more focused psychoanalytic psychotherapy. Interview material and, often, psychological tests, especially projective tests such as the Rorschach ink blots or the Thematic Apperception Test, are used to provide *signs,* or indicators, of these internal processes.

Behavioral assessment seeks to measure problematic behavior as it occurs in directly relevant situations. Assessment data are used as a *sample* of the client's behavioral repertoire, rather than construed as providing *signs* of underlying conflicts or disorder.

The behavioral therapist seeks information about the ABCs of the client's problems. This is a handy mnemonic where A = antecedent; B = (problem) behavior; and C = consequence. Starting with the "B" part of ABC, the behavior therapist seeks to identify precisely what the problem behaviors are. This can be deceptively difficult, because the goal is a concrete description that makes occurrences and increases or decreases in them easily recognized. Consider, for example, the difference between "My child is impossible; he's stubborn and willful" and "The child ignores or refuses to obey parental requests and commands."

Antecedents are situations, or cues, that elicit the problem behavior. Does the problem child refuse to obey requests (noncompliance) at home or at school? With both mother and father? In front of other children or other adults? With certain requests but not others? In sum, under what circumstances does the problem behavior occur?

Consequences (reinforcement) include the rewards or punishments that accompany or follow the problem behaviors. They are the effects of the behavior on the social environment, including the client. Consequences determine whether a given behavior will be repeated or not. Does the mother engage in lengthy efforts to reason with or persuade the child to obey? Or is the child permitted to do what he or she wants in order to avoid a scene? Such parental responses can serve to reinforce, or strengthen, the problem behaviors.

Knowledge of the ABCs helps the therapist and client arrive at specific behavioral objectives for intervention. Ways of measuring these objectives can then be devised and used to track the progress of treatment. It is important to realize that antecedents, behavior, and consequences—or some combination of them—can all be cognitive or mediational events as well as overt behaviors. For example, B may be subjective feelings of depression and inadequacy; A may be a self-evaluative judgment that the person has not handled a situation well; and C may be a reduction in activity and verbal behavior as the person withdraws from the situation.

Methods of Behavioral Assessment

The ideal of behavioral assessment is the *direct observation* of problematic behavior in relevant situations. The behavior therapist would like to see how the anxious client responds to a specific, stressful situation—how an unassertive client deals with his demanding boss; how a couple on the brink of divorce interact with each other; or how a noncompliant, demanding child who resorts to temper tantrums interacts with her parents. You might acknowledge the potential usefulness of such voyeurism but would probably question the practicality of it. This is a problem. In research contexts it is often possible to obtain direct observation, because the investigator has considerable resources—for example, observers, equipment, money. In clinical practice, however, a behavior therapist must usually be satisfied with approximations to direct observations. Besides the cost factor, much behavior is intimate or private and not subject to observations by others, as with a couple's problems in their sexual relationship. Beginning with direct observation, several of the most commonly used behavioral assessment procedures will be briefly described.

Direct observation. It is possible, especially in research contexts, to have observers (with permission, of course) enter a home and systematically code interactions among family members. In mental hospitals, staff members can observe whether clients are alone or with others, adequately dressed and groomed, or talking in socially appropriate ways. A clinically feasible example is for a therapist or therapist's assistant to accompany a phobic client into a fearful situation. A client who is afraid of heights might be accompanied as she walked progressively up the flights of a tall building and looked out the windows.

Role playing and simulation. In both research and clinical contexts, the client can be asked to role-play a problem situation so that both client and therapist can observe behavior. The unassertive client who cannot deal with his boss can be asked to recreate a real situation, with the therapist playing the role of the boss. A conflicted married couple can be asked to discuss a problem that is meaningful to them, while the therapist observes. Such interactions can be videotaped for both clinical and research use.

Self-observation. A very popular and practical method is to have clients be their own observers. If the problem behavior—the B in the ABC arrangement—has been reasonably well identified, the client is given the task of counting the frequency with which B occurs and may also be asked to record antecedents and consequences. For example, a client trying to stop smoking is asked to count each time a cigarette is smoked and to note the situation that led to smoking. Self-observation is also very useful in helping clients and therapists zero in on the problem behavior. A client who reports anxiety and tension in social situations might keep a diary in order to get a better idea of just what kind of situation arouses anxiety and how the anxiety manifests itself physiologically and behaviorally. Self-observation is particularly useful for cognitions and feelings that are not observable by others. A chart can record the frequency of obsessive thoughts.

Questionnaires. Most psychotherapists make use of questionnaire data, and behavior therapists are no exception. Questionnaires can be construed as a standardized way for clients to describe themselves and their behavior and therefore is another approximation to direct observation. A distinguishing characteristic of behavioral questionnaires is the focus on situations. Probably the most commonly used behavioral questionnaire is the Fear Survey Schedule (Geer, 1965). A large number of objects or events are listed, and the client reports his or her relative degree of fearfulness for each of them. Behavior therapists working with various kinds of disorders—such as marital conflicts, sexual inadequacy, obesity, or assertiveness—have developed questionnaire instruments pertaining to them. For all psychotherapists, questionnaires are a relatively economical means of assessment, because clients can fill them out on their own time.

Interview. Last, but not least, is the clinical interview. This is the most commonly used method of gaining assessment information. All psychotherapists gain information both from what clients say and how they say it. The content of behavioral interviewing tends to be different from psychoanalytic or humanistic interviewing (but remember that all psychotherapists direct conversation in accordance with their theoretical preconceptions). The behavior therapist is likely to try to be more specific and to try to find out how the client behaves in particular situations. Behavioral assessment is discussed in detail in several recent books—for example, *Handbook for Behavioral Assessment* (Ciminero, Calhoun, & Adams, 1977); and *Behavioral Assessment: A Practical Handbook* (Hersen & Bellak, 1977). I will conclude this section with an example of a behavior-therapy assessment interview (Goldfried & Davison, 1976).

> *C:* I just feel nervous a lot of the time.
> *T:* What is the feeling like?
> *C:* I don't know. It's hard to describe . . . I just feel nervous.
> *T:* So you know what the feeling is like, but it's kind of difficult to describe it in words.
> *C:* Yes, it is. You know, it's just a feeling of uneasiness and apprehension. Like when you know something bad may happen, or at least you're afraid that it might.
> *T:* So emotionally, and perhaps physically, there's a fear that something might happen, although you may not be certain exactly what.
> *C:* Yes.
> *T:* When you're feeling that way, what do you experience physically?
> *C:* Well, my heart starts pounding and I feel myself tense up all over. It's not always that bad; sometimes it's only mild.

T: In other words, depending upon the circumstances, you may feel more or less anxious.

C: Yes.

T: Tell me something about the situations that make you most anxious.

C: Well, it's usually when I deal with other people.

T: I would find it particularly helpful to hear about some typical situations that may upset you.

C: It's hard to come up with something specific.

T: I can understand how it may be hard to come up with specific examples right on the spot. That's not at all uncommon. Let me see if I can help to make it a little easier for you. Let's take the past week or so. Think of what went on either at work, at home, or when you were out socially that might have upset you.

C: O.K. Something just occurred to me. We went out to a party last weekend, and as we were driving to the place where the party was being held, I felt myself starting to panic.

T: Can you tell me more about that situation?

C: Well, the party was at my husband's boss' house, and I always feel uncomfortable about events like that.

T: In what way?

C: Well, I find it difficult for me to be natural in that kind of situation.

T: Do you typically become nervous when you go to social gatherings?

C: Well, a lot depends on the situation.

T: In what way?

C: It depends on how comfortable I feel with the people.

T: O.K., so there are certain situations and certain types of people that make you feel more comfortable, and others that make you more apprehensive.

C: Yes.

T: I think it would be helpful if we focused a little more on the kinds of people and the kinds of situations which upset you to varying degrees.

C: A lot has to do with how loud or how aggressive the people are. I think I get very intimidated when people seem so self-confident.

T: What other kinds of individuals do you find you react negatively to? [pp. 40–42] [1]

The vague way in which this client first described her problem is fairly typical. The therapist sympathizes with her difficulty in describing her anxiety but gently probes for more specific information both about the nature of her anxiety response and the situations that elicit her anxiety.

Treatment Strategies

I have stressed that behavior therapy is essentially strategic, in that treatment and methods vary according to the client's problems. Because of this, there are many behavior-therapy treatment procedures that could be described. My selections are influenced both by historical and current importance and also by a desire to illustrate

[1]From *Clinical Behavior Therapy*, by Marvin R. Goldfried and Gerald C. Davison. Copyright 1976 by Holt, Rinehart and Winston. Reprinted by permission.

how behavior therapy can be applied to complex interpersonal difficulties. The treatment strategies chosen also illustrate the clinical applications of procedures derived from laboratory research. Three methods of anxiety management—systematic desensitization, flooding, and modeling—are described and compared. Next, operant methods in psychotherapy are discussed, with particular emphasis on token economy programs for the treatment of chronic mental patients and strategies for aggressive, noncompliant children. The uses and limitations of aversion therapy are then described. The section on treatment methods concludes with a description of cognitive and self-control strategies.

Methods of Anxiety Management

Anxiety is of central interest to psychotherapists of all theoretical persuasions. Psychoanalytic theory posits that anxiety is at the root of most defensive reactions and neurotic behavior. It is an important symptom for many clients. Some clients experience a diffuse, or "free-floating," anxiety—they feel anxious nearly all the time. Other clients are anxious in response to specific situations or stimuli; these are termed phobics. A fear of snakes is a common, but often not debilitating, phobia; a fear of heights or a fear of driving are phobias that are much more debilitating. Although free-floating anxiety and specific phobias account for only a small percentage of presenting problems, a great many clients present interpersonal difficulties that involve anxiety or avoidance behavior. These include clients who are insufficiently assertive because they are afraid of the reactions of others toward them and clients who have difficulty in heterosexual interactions or with sexual intercourse because they are anxious about their interpersonal or sexual performance. For these reasons, psychotherapists have been eager to find effective procedures for anxiety management.

Within a framework of behavior therapy, classical (respondent) conditioning is viewed as a key mechanism in the development of anxiety reactions. From a classical-conditioning perspective, previously neutral stimuli can become endowed with anxiety-eliciting properties if they are paired with some fear-arousing event. In a classic example, an infant was taught to be fearful of a rabbit by pairing the sight of the rabbit with a sudden loud and very unpleasant noise (Watson & Rayner, 1920). Internal stimuli such as thoughts might also become conditioned to elicit anxiety in this fashion. Some behavior therapists emphasize the role of internal arousal—automatic responses—in this learning process (Wolpe, 1958). Others, especially Bandura (1969, 1977), emphasize cognitive mediation, in which a person learns that certain situations and the experience of pain or upset are correlated.

For the behavior therapist, then, anxiety is a learned response to certain stimuli. Defensive or avoidance behavior is then maintained by its effectiveness in relieving anxiety. For example, a young man has learned to feel acutely anxious in the presence of attractive women. When he terminates or avoids an interaction with such a woman, he reduces his anxiety, and his avoidance behavior is thus reinforced and strengthened.

With a given client, it is often not possible to determine just how the anxiety reaction was learned. But for the behavior therapist it is much more important to determine the nature of the anxiety response and, especially, the situations that now elicit and maintain it—the ABCs of the client's anxiety reaction. The behavioral assessment of an anxiety reaction is illustrated in the clinical excerpt in the previous section. The therapist was attempting to determine how the client manifested her anxiety, what situations elicited these responses, and what the consequences were. Specifying the nature of the anxiety response is important because anxiety has been found to be reflected in three relatively distinct response systems: the cognitive or verbal system—"I feel really scared and shook up"; the physiological response system—automatic reaction such as increased heart rate, sweating, or even, under extreme conditions, a loss of sphincter or bladder control; and the behavioral system, which includes overt avoidance such as running away or more subtle indicators such as trembling or excessive body movement. People tend to vary in how they express their anxiety, and treatment methods may affect the three response systems differently. Thus, it is important to know a client's particular pattern.

Psychoanalytic theory views anxiety reactions or phobias as indicators of unresolved internal conflicts that are proving difficult to manage. Therefore, it focuses on discovering and modifying these unconscious conflicts. The case of the phobic young woman described in Chapter Five illustrates both psychoanalytic reasoning and the resultant therapeutic procedures. Behavior therapy, in contrast, attempts to help the individual unlearn the anxiety response. Systematic desensitization, flooding, and modeling are three treatment strategies for accomplishing this goal.

Systematic Desensitization and Counterconditioning

Systematic desensitization is the most widely used and thoroughly researched behavior-therapy procedure for anxiety reactions. The procedure was developed by Joseph Wolpe, a South African psychiatrist now working in the United States, who is one of the influential figures in the development of behavior therapy. On the basis of his clinical experience and some animal experimentation, Wolpe became convinced that classically conditioned autonomic arousal was central to anxiety reactions. He then sought a way to undo conditioned responses, or neutralize the stimuli that were arousing anxiety. Both his own experiments in alleviating experimental neuroses in cats and a classic experiment by Jones (1924) led him to the principle of reciprocal inhibition. Mary Cover Jones treated a 3-year-old child whose fear of a white rat extended to a rabbit and other furry objects. In one of the procedures the child was given a favorite food while the rabbit was moved closer and closer in small steps. Soon the child could play with the rabbit without fear.

Reciprocal inhibition asserts that the ability of a given stimulus to evoke anxiety will be permanently weakened if a response antagonistic to anxiety can be made to occur in the presence of anxiety-evoking stimuli (Wolpe, 1958). In the case of the 3-year-old child, the rabbit was an anxiety-evoking stimulus, and the pleasure of eating a favorite food was a response antagonistic to anxiety. Wolpe's original theory was based on a physiological model, but it is more parsimonious to describe the process at the psychological level as counterconditioning.

Wolpe then sought a convenient anxiety antagonist, because eating was not always very practical, especially for adults. He hit on the use of deep muscle relaxation, because one cannot be relaxed and anxious at the same time (relaxation is described in more detail below). It proved possible to teach clients to relax reliably and efficiently in the clinic, but it is hard for clients to relax themselves in real-life anxiety situations. Another problem was that it was often impractical or impossible for the therapist to enter into or recreate real anxiety situations with the client and to "control the dosage," or present the anxiety situations in a gradual manner.

In an inventive leap Wolpe tried presenting the anxiety-producing stimuli in *imagination*. In this way, relaxation could be taught and monitored in the clinician's office, and the anxiety stimuli could also be presented under carefully controlled, graduated conditions. It is systematic desensitization using imaginal stimulus presentation that has been most widely used and studied. But desensitization is also done *in vivo*—in real life with the natural phobic stimuli—whenever this is feasible. Wolpe's theory of reciprocal inhibition and the systematic desensitization procedure were described and illustrated in his influential book *Psychotherapy by Reciprocal Inhibition* (1958).

Hierarchy construction. Before desensitization proper can begin, the therapist and client must engage in *hierarchy construction* and *relaxation training.* Hierarchy construction follows from a behavioral assessment in which the major anxiety themes—for example, fear of heights or fear of rejection—and the specific stimuli that arouse anxiety are identified. The client is then asked to rank the situations from least arousing to most arousing. Such a ranking is tentative and subject to change with experience. The items in the hierarchy should ideally be somewhat evenly spaced and should represent the full range of the situations that trouble the client. Table 7–1 presents two hierarchies for an art student whose presenting problem was test anxiety—and who had repeatedly failed examinations—but who was also found to have other debilitating fears. An interesting feature of the test-anxiety hierarchy is that she reported more anxiety on the way to school on the day of the exam than while actually taking the test.

Table 7–1. Hierarchies of Anxiety

A.   Ranking of fears about examinations
    1. On the way to the university on the day of an examination
    2. In the process of answering an examination paper
    3. Before the unopened doors of the examination room
    4. Awaiting the distribution of examination papers
    5. While the examination paper lies face down before her
    6. The night before an examination
    7. On the day before an examination
    8. Two days before an examination
    9. Three days before an examination
   10. Four days before an examination
   11. Five days before an examination
   12. A week before an examination
   13. Two weeks before an examination
   14. A month before an examination

B.   Ranking of fears about being scrutinized
    1. Being watched working (especially drawing) by ten people
    2. Being watched working by six people
    3. Being watched working by three people
    4. Being watched working by one expert in the field (Anxiety begins when the observer is 10 feet away and increases as he draws closer.)
    5. Being watched working by a nonexpert (Anxiety begins at a distance of 4 feet.)

From *Behavior Therapy Techniques*, by J. Wolpe and A. A. Lazarus. Copyright 1966 by Pergamon Press Ltd. Reprinted by permission.

Clinical skill is usually required to trace the major dimensions of the client's fears and to construct the hierarchy. Most clients have several fears, thus requiring more than one hierarchy.

Relaxation training. While hierarchy construction is under way, the client is also taught relaxation, most typically by means of a technique developed by Jacobson (1938). Relaxation training is an important ingredient in imaginal systematic desensitization but is also often taught as a skill in its own right. Many clients experience considerable tension or overarousal, and relaxation training can be a useful skill to help manage their anxiety. Deep-muscle-relaxation procedures involve identifying groups of muscles such as the hand and forearm, tensing the muscle group for 5 to 7 seconds while concentrating on the feelings in the muscle group, and then quickly relaxing the muscles while focusing attention on the contrast between the relaxed state and the tensed state. The therapist at first leads the client through each of the main muscle groups in the body and then encourages the client to practice. Homework is an essential feature in deep muscle relaxation, as it is in many behavior-therapy procedures. Relaxation is presented as a skill the client can master by practicing in a regular and systematic way.

Imaginal desensitization. After the hierarchy has been constructed and the client has achieved some skill in relaxation, desensitization proper begins. First the client is asked to relax as deeply as possible. After a reasonably deep state of relaxation has been achieved, the client is then instructed to imagine the least anxiety-arousing situation in the hierarchy as vividly as possible. Often, some training or practice in imagination is necessary. The client is instructed to signal the therapist (often by some nonverbal means such as raising a finger) whenever any significant increase in anxiety is experienced. Whenever the client signals for an anxious feeling, the therapist instructs him or her to turn off the imagined hierarchy scene and just focus on relaxing.

The counterconditioning paradigm is one where a stimulus—now presented imaginally—typically elicits an anxiety response; but a new response, relaxation, is now being paired with the original stimulus, so that the anxiety response will be "countered," weakened, and extinguished. It is important, from this perspective, that the client not experience any significant anxiety in the presence of the imagined item. When the client has been able to imagine the first scene two or three times for 5 to 10 seconds without signaling anxiety, the therapist then proceeds to the second scene in the hierarchy, and the procedure is repeated. Client and therapist then proceed through the hierarchy, going on to the next scene only when the client is able to tolerate the previous scene without feeling anxiety.

As imaginal desensitization proceeds, the client is encouraged to try out in real life the situations that were successfully mastered in imagination in the clinic. This is a critical aspect of the desensitization procedure. It shows the client and therapist how treatment is proceeding and also helps the client to develop a sense of mastery over anxiety and fear. The client may still experience some subjective or cognitive distress as he or she attempts to deal with situations that have formerly been avoided. The important thing is that the imaginal desensitization reduces anxiety enough so that the client is willing to attempt previously avoided situations under the therapist's gentle prodding. The combination of successful experiences in real situations and the reduction of physiological arousal by imaginal desensitization usually serves to reduce the feelings of anxiety.

Imaginal systematic desensitization has been evaluated in numerous reports, ranging from case studies to elaborate factorial designs. Much of the controlled investigation has been analogue research; the clients were recruited for participation and had relatively circumscribed phobias. Even with this qualification, there is sufficient evidence from both clinical and research sources to validate the effectiveness of imaginal systematic desensitization (Leitenberg, 1976).

One of the most rigorous and influential studies (Paul, 1966) was partly described in Chapter Three. Subjects were college students who had public-speaking anxiety but who were required to pass a speech course in order to complete their college program. Behavioral, physiological, and cognitive measures of speech anxiety were obtained. The behavioral measure was obtained from ratings of the subjects as they gave a speech in front of a small group. Treatment consisted of five individual sessions. *All* (100%) of the subjects receiving imaginal desensitization were rated as improved or "much improved," compared with 47% in both the insight-therapy group and the attention-placebo group described in Chapter Three (Paul, 1966, pp. 39–40). This result was the basis for concluding that psychodynamic therapy, in this particular situation, was no more effective than the common processes inherent in any therapeutic situation. Paul's study also included a no-treatment control group, in which only 17% showed significant improvement on retesting. It is important to note that the improvement shown in the desensitization subjects was largely maintained at a two-year follow-up check.

Variations of systematic desensitization. A number of variations of systematic desensitization have been developed and described in clinical as well as research reports. Many therapists find the variations more effective and efficient than imaginal desensitization in many situations. Two variations will be described here.

The first variation is real-life (*in vivo*) desensitization. Recall that imaginal desensitization was invented because of practical difficulties in gradually engaging the actual feared stimuli and because relaxation could then be used as an incompatible response. However, research has shown that deep muscle relaxation is not an essential component of desensitization (Leitenberg, 1976). Real-life desensitization—where it is feasible—has the advantage of ensuring that treatment effects will generalize to the real world. Many therapists, therefore, prefer real-life desensitization where it is practical and resort to imaginal desensitization only when it is not (Lazarus, 1971).

Hierarchy construction proceeds in much the same manner as for imaginal desensitization. But instead of proceeding through the hierarchy in imagination, the therapist or his assistant accompanies the client to the actual feared situations. Starting with the least-anxiety-producing situations, the client is encouraged to enter and tolerate the situation until discomfort is experienced, at which point the client leaves the situation. The client is guided through the hierarchy much as in the imaginal procedure. The therapist provides reassurance and encouragement throughout the procedure, and this too may weaken the anxiety response.

The second variation involves the employing of real-life desensitization in the treatment of sexual dysfunctions, especially male impotence. Anxiety about sexual performance and sexual response is a major contributor to impotence and frigidity. The male's apprehension that he will lose his erection becomes a self-fulfilling prophecy, in part because of the interrelationship of the autonomic nervous system and the physiology of sexual arousal. Counterconditioning principles can be applied by keeping anxiety at very low levels while sexual stimuli are present. The use of a hierarchy or gradual approach is again employed, and a cooperative sex partner is also crucial.

The therapist instructs the client (and his partner) not to engage in sexual intercourse until advised to do so. This therapist prohibition reduces the client's anxiety, because performance pressure has been removed by the therapist's authority. The client is then instructed to approach the partner and engage in graduated touching, kissing, and fondling activities, only so far as the pleasurable aspects of the experience clearly outweigh any anxiety or apprehension. If the client experiences noticeable anxiety, sex play is interrupted or stopped. The client and partner proceed through the hierarchy, with the client learning to tolerate longer and more arousing sex play without being incapacitated by anxiety. At some point in a program of this sort, for example, the male may be instructed to insert his penis for a few seconds, but not to attempt any thrusting unless he feels completely comfortable. When this step is mastered, the client can then proceed to thrust for a short period of time, again with the understanding that he will stop once anxiety is experienced. Longer periods of active intercourse are developed in this manner.

You may recognize this procedure as essentially similar to some of the techniques employed by Masters and Johnson (1970) in their well-known program for sexual inadequacy.

Systematic desensitization, whether imaginal or real-life, is most readily applied to discrete fears where the stimuli can be readily identified. But the procedure is also adaptable to many interpersonal difficulties. Application to certain sexual dysfunctions has already been illustrated. Interpersonal concerns and inhibitions, such as fear of criticism or fear of rejection, are also amenable to the method.

Flooding and Implosion

The essence of systematic desensitization construed as counterconditioning is that the client approaches the feared situation in small steps so that little or no anxiety is experienced. But research on the acquisition and extinction of fear responses suggests another principle—extinction—for the clinical treatment of fear. While desensitization was influenced by research with cats, "flooding" began with dogs.

A dog is placed in a compartment with an electrified floor. The experimenter sounds a warning buzzer, and ten seconds later the animal receives an intense electric shock through the grid on the floor. The dog barks and jumps about in a frenzy. The only way to escape the shock is to jump over a shoulder-high barrier into an adjoining compartment, where no shock is ever given. Under these conditions a stable, learned avoidance response is quickly acquired, usually in no more than ten trials. The dog avoids the shock by jumping over the barrier soon after the buzzer is sounded. The buzzer has become a conditioned stimulus for the avoidance response (Solomon, Kamin, & Wynne, 1953).

Classically conditioned responses typically extinguish over time when the unconditioned stimulus (the shock) is no longer presented. However, the dogs in the experimental setup continued to jump for hundreds of trials, even though they never received another shock; one dog jumped 511 times and was still going strong when the experiment was terminated. Stupid dogs? Perhaps. But consider that many troubled humans repeatedly avoid or escape situations that are objectively harmless, as with a phobia. The dogs, having been traumatized several times, simply never waited in the gridded compartment long enough to discover that they would no longer be shocked, that the environment had now changed. The experimenters then sought to try to extinguish the learned avoidance response they had created. It turned out to be quite difficult. The only successful method they found was to forcibly restrain the dogs in the gridded compartment, so the animals could experience the fact that they would no longer be shocked there. Naturally, the dogs were very apprehensive at first, but they soon learned that they would not be shocked and stopped jumping the barrier.

Flooding as a psychotherapeutic treatment embodies the basic extinction principle illustrated in the experimental work with dogs. Fearful clients are induced to expose themselves to strong anxiety-arousing situations and remain in these situations until their arousal habituates and decreases. Assessment is necessary to help the therapist get a clear picture of what stimuli and situations arouse intense levels of anxiety. Clients experience directly the fact that there is no reason to be afraid (no unconditioned stimuli), and they are no longer reinforced for avoidance or escape. Although the client experiences some acute temporary distress during the procedure, it is more than compensated for by treatment gains.

Flooding, like desensitization, can be accomplished both in imagination and in real life. Imaginal flooding is sometimes known as *implosion*, a term coined to denote intense, internal experiencing of affect. Implosion and real-life flooding differ in one major way. In implosion the therapist embellishes the feared situation, using psychoanalytic symbolism concerning the feared stimulus (Stampfl & Levis, 1967). Whether by flooding or implosion, the therapist helps the client to imagine as vividly as possible exposure to the most threatening situations and attempts to induce the client to experience high levels of emotional arousal. The therapist uses skill and ingenuity in describing the situation in a way that will help the client to imagine it vividly. Clients may be induced to remain, imaginally, in such a situation 45 minutes or more a session, and the flooding is typically terminated when the client's level of anxiety or arousal has begun to diminish. Below is an example of an implosion story constructed for a 25-year-old woman with a serious agoraphobia (fear of leaving home) and associated fears of violent death, pain, and agony.

> She is walking down the street and noting the color of the lamp poles and the green leaves on the trees. As she steps out into the street, a car runs over her toe. Then she steps back and starts out again and gets knocked down by a bus. This bruises her, and she is feeling some pain and is struggling to get up when her hand is run over by a motorcycle, severing several fingers. A truck crushes her ribs. Her lungs fill with blood. She is dying and people gather around and do not help in any way. They just scoff at her and laugh at the ugly sight. This is one of the things that bothers her—people not helping and criticizing her by saying, That's no loss to the world anyhow. The ambulance comes. People cover her with a white sheet. She dies [Storms, 1976, p. 141].

Real-life flooding consists of the therapist's accompanying the client into the fearful situation and helping him or her remain there for long periods until the anxiety response begins to habituate. English behavior therapists have been the most active in both clinical use and research investigation of flooding (Watson, Gaind, & Marks, 1971). It has been effective in dealing with one of the most debilitating and difficult-to-treat phobias, agoraphobia (Marks, 1978). The agoraphobic is fearful of leaving home and becomes terrified in streets and among large crowds. Severe agoraphobics may be restricted to home or have to rely on others to take them anyplace. Experience has shown this phobia to be quite resistant to most kinds of treatment.

In one study (Hand, Lamontagne, & Marks, 1974) chronic agoraphobics were treated in groups of four or five. The treatment consisted of four continuous hours of flooding (with a lunch break) on three different days in one week. The therapists accompanied a small group of clients into the city (London) to places where they reported that they would be extremely anxious. The therapists also communicated much reassurance and support and discussed the clients' reactions to the procedure with them. Behavioral observations of the

clients conducted before and after treatment indicated markedly reduced avoidance behavior in nearly all of those who were treated.

Modeling

It may seem obvious that we learn a great deal by observing
other people, but it is only in recent years that psychology has seriously taken up the study of observational learning and modeling.
Modeling has a number of therapeutic applications, including helping children to acquire appropriate speech, helping chronic mental
patients learn basic social skills, and helping adults learn appropriate and assertive interpersonal behavior (Rosenthal & Bandura,
1978). For these problems, modeling is usually employed in combination with other psychotherapeutic procedures.

The most systematic clinical and research use of modeling has
been to disinhibit avoidance or fear behavior. A model confronts situations that characteristically produce strong fear and avoidance for
the client, and the client vicariously learns that there are no aversive
consequences. A hierarchy, or graduated-exposure procedure, is frequently used. The model may be real—for example, the therapist—or
be presented symbolically on film or videotape.

Albert Bandura has pioneered the application of modeling procedure to psychotherapy, including a particularly powerful technique
that involves "guided participation" by the client. The therapist first
models one of the hierarchy's items, such as approaching within a few
feet of a (harmless) snake. The client is then encouraged to do the
same. For each item, the client both observes the therapist perform
the behavior without aversive consequences and is then guided in
imitating the therapist's performance.

A widely quoted study compared the effectiveness of two kinds
of modeling with imaginal desensitization in reducing fears (Bandura, Blanchard, & Ritter, 1969). The subjects were adolescents and
adults who suffered from snake phobias that, for most of them, restricted their activities and affected their psychological functioning.
A behavioral-avoidance test was used to measure the strength of their
fear of snakes before and after treatment, and questionnaires were
used to measure the cognitive, or subjective, component of their fear.
One group of subjects received a standard treatment of imaginal systematic desensitization. A second group received a self-administered
symbolic modeling treatment. Clients observed a film depicting
young children, adolescents, and adults engaging in progressively
more threatening interactions with a large king snake. In this treatment the subjects could control the rate of the presentation of the
scenes and so could stop the film whenever a modeled snake interaction made them too anxious. The third group was treated with the
participant modeling procedure described above, including both live
modeling and guided participation. A no-treatment control group

was merely assessed at the same intervals as the treated subjects. Thus the design included both kinds of control groups described in Chapter Four and could rule out all major rival hypotheses.

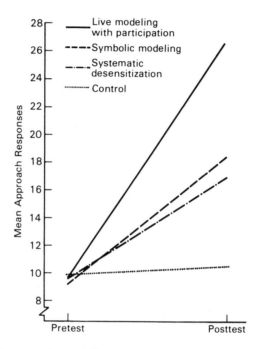

Figure 7–1. Results of different treatments on clients' approaches to snakes. (From "The Relative Efficacy of Desensitization and Modeling Approaches for Inducing Behavioral, Affective, and Attitudinal Changes," by A. Bandura, E. B. Blanchard, and B. Ritter, *Journal of Personality and Social Psychology,* 1969, *13,* 173–199. Copyright 1969 by the American Psychological Association. Reprinted by permission of the author and publisher.)

The results of this experiment are summarized in Figure 7–1. It can be seen that the control subjects remained unchanged in avoidance behavior. Symbolic modeling and imaginal desensitization produced substantial reductions in snake avoidance. But live modeling with guided participation was an exceptionally powerful treatment; fear of snakes was eliminated in 92% of these subjects.

Much work has been done attempting to determine what variables will facilitate or inhibit the influencing effects of a model. The consequences—rewards or punishments—that happen to the model are most critical. It also appears that a model similar in characteristics to the subjects or clients is most effective. For example, a "coping" model—one who initially displays some inhibitions and fear but then engages and copes with the feared stimulus—leads to more behavior change than a "mastery" model—one who appears fearless in engaging the feared stimulus (Rosenthal & Bandura, 1978).

Comparing Desensitization, Flooding, and Modeling

In systematic desensitization the client approaches the feared stimulus in small steps, and the therapist tries to ensure that little or no anxiety is experienced. In flooding the client is exposed to high fear-arousing stimuli, and the therapist attempts to arouse as much anxiety as possible. Modeling also employs graduated exposure to stimuli, but except for participant modeling the client does not make overt responses. All three appear to be effective in research and clinical contexts, and in studies where they are compared the results have often been similar (for example, see Gelder, Bancroft, Gath, Johnston, Matthews, & Shaw, 1973).

On the face of it, however, it is theoretically inconsistent for both graduated exposure (desensitization and modeling), and intense exposure (flooding) to work about equally well. The most plausible hypothesis appears to be that desensitization, flooding, and modeling all provide exposure to the feared stimulus, and this exposure permits extinction of the anxiety response to that stimulus (Leitenberg, 1976). It appears not to matter whether the exposure is gradual or intense but to be essential that it take place in a therapeutic context. Real, imaginal, and vicarious exposure are all effective, but real-life exposure appears to be the most powerful of the three. Real-life desensitization and flooding tend to be more effective than their imaginal counterparts. Live modeling with guided participation (real-life exposure) was more effective than symbolic modeling in the snake-phobia study summarized above (Bandura et al., 1969).

Direct exposure is also a key element in yet another effective procedure for phobias, reinforced practice. Using a hierarchy, the client is encouraged to engage the feared stimuli as much as possible and is given much social reinforcement for success (Leitenberg, 1976). The procedure is similar to guided participation, but there is no therapist modeling.

Behavior therapy has been especially effective with phobias and, to a significant though lesser extent, with other anxiety reactions. Exposure to feared stimuli appears to be the key element in all the treatment strategies described, and real-life exposure seems particularly powerful. As Leitenberg noted, exposure is not a novel therapeutic element, "but the evidence is quite striking that it works, and works better than any other therapeutic approach and better than no therapy at all" (1976, p. 152).

Operant Methods in Psychotherapy

Operant principles and methods were originally developed by B. F. Skinner, generally regarded as the single most influential American psychologist. Skinner's basic research, and that of his colleagues, was performed on animals, primarily pigeons and rats. The principles of reinforcement, stimulus control, shaping, and other processes were evolved almost exclusively by studying a single organism intensively over time, using the ABA paradigm described in Chapter Four.

Operant principles and methods are one of the most striking examples of how basic psychological research can be applied effectively to significant real-world problems. Operant methods have had an enormous impact on education—for example, in teaching machines and programmed instruction—and on mental health. Operant treatment methods have been employed with clinical populations (such as the seriously retarded and the chronic mental patient) who have heretofore been relatively neglected by mental health professionals.

Basic operant principles are relatively simple; but the application of them in clinical contexts and the demonstration of their effectiveness requires a great deal of ingenuity and skill (Azrin, 1977). Workers in the operant tradition have carried out some of the cleverest and most rigorously controlled applied research yet published. Operant methods have been applied to a multitude of behavioral and emotional problems. A partial list would include obesity, alcoholism, nail biting, incontinency, juvenile delinquency, smoking, tics, and intractable pain. A variety of operant principles are used, but altering the reinforcing consequences of behavior is the major tool.

The essence of operant thinking is the notion that behavior is controlled by its consequences. Social (interpersonal) behavior is thus controlled by its effects on others—the reaction of the social environment. Treatment should therefore deal with the social system and try to change the way it reinforces the target client.

Operant principles are most effective in social environments where the antecedents—discriminative stimuli—and consequences —or reinforcers—of problem behavior can be readily identified and controlled by the therapist. This is the most easily accomplished in what I have termed closed environments—settings where the behavior of the client is relatively restricted and is to a significant degree controlled by others. Three major closed environments for the application of operant treatment methods are (1) the family or home, especially with young children who are relatively under the control of their parents; (2) schools and classrooms; and (3) mental hospitals. School and classroom applications will not be considered here; the other two environments will now be examined.

Institutional Treatment for Chronic Mental Patients

Chronic mental patients are a very serious problem for society, because they often require long-term institutional care, which is very expensive. Most of you will not have visited a mental hospital. If you picture a dingy, overcrowded setting with a lot of "crazy" behavior exhibited, such as clients hallucinating or behaving oddly, you are likely to be mistaken (there is great variability across states, however). The physical setting is likely to be neat, clean, and spacious. The most striking feature of a chronic ward is the apathy and inactivity of the patients. They sit. They may watch television, but they usually do little else. One study of the behavior of 100 chronic patients found total immobility during 44% of the waking day; only 2.7% of the patients' time was spent in social interaction (Hunter, Schooler, & Spohn, 1962). A major treatment goal is to increase adaptive behaviors that will enable the patient to function in the community.

The most widely used behavioral strategy for hospitalized mental patients is the *token economy*. Such a program provides patients with tokens—which represent money in that they can be exchanged for goods and services—contingent on the performance of therapeutically desirable behaviors. Implementing a token economy requires (1) specifying therapeutically relevant behaviors that can be reliably observed and recorded; (2) arranging to deliver tokens contingent on performance of the behaviors; (3) finding and controlling backup reinforcers—that is, goods and services; and (4) setting a balance between "wages"—how tokens are earned—and "prices"—what goods and services they can buy (Stahl & Leitenberg, 1976).

A token system is simply a way of rewarding good behavior; the tokens bridge the time gap between performance and reward. Dressing, grooming, eating, and working behaviors are rewarded. For example, tooth brushing at the designated time would earn 1 token; shepherding dishes through an automatic dishwasher—45 minutes of work—would earn 17 tokens (Ayllon & Azrin, 1968). Tokens may be spent for cash, coffee, or cigarettes. Or they may be spent on a privilege such as a nap or a day away from the ward.

It should be obvious that a token economy must be established on a ward basis and requires the cooperation and participation of all ward staff members. Tokens are usually dispensed by psychiatric technicians, occupational therapists, and nurses. Psychiatrists and psychologists participate in the planning and supervision of the program, but it is implemented by the staff members who normally interact with patients. Therefore, the staff must be trained and supervised. This is a major cost of the system. One benefit is that active participation in the treatment program improves staff morale. A second benefit is that, by keeping track of the tokens that clients earn and spend, it is possible to measure the effectiveness of the program.

There is considerable evidence that token systems can dramatically change the behavior of chronic mental patients while they are in the institution (Ayllon & Azrin, 1968). This change can be demonstrated by comparing the behavior of patients before and after entering a token economy. The alert reader may note that there is a strong plausible rival hypothesis for this kind of comparison. Perhaps the increased activity, attention, and novelty involved in the implementation of any new program leads to an increase in prosocial behavior; if so, such change is not specific to the token system. Ayllon and Azrin, however, performed a number of experiments that pretty well rule out this rival hypothesis. A major procedure for doing so is the basic ABA design. After clients have learned to work under a token system, they are given vacation days, or periods of time when token contingencies are removed. Sharp reductions in the activity level and performance of behavior that has been reinforced with tokens are then observed. Reinstatement of token contingencies then leads to a marked increase in activity level (Ayllon & Azrin, 1968, p. 252).

Evaluation of token economies. A proper evaluation of the token-economy approach would compare it with alternative treatments. A rigorous and comprehensive study comparing social-learning treatment with milieu therapy (described in Chapter Eight) and with traditional hospital care has recently been published (Paul & Lentz, 1977). Equated groups of severely debilitated chronic patients received either social-learning (token-economy) therapy, milieu treatment, or traditional hospital care from staff personnel equivalent in number and level of training. Both milieu and social-learning programs were carefully standardized. Both continuous and periodic collection of data verified treatment differences among the three programs and provided outcome results. Exceptionally careful and valid measurements of both institutional functioning and community adjustment were obtained.

The results were clear-cut and impressive. The social-learning program was significantly more effective than either the milieu or traditional hospital program on all three key dimensions: (1) functioning in the institution, (2) institutional release based on the same criteria across all three programs, and (3) community stay. Milieu and social-learning programs were equated in credibility, structure, and specificity for patients and staff. The major difference was the consistent emphasis in the token-economy program on making specific consequences contingent on patients' behavior.

Over 90% of the residents in the social-learning program achieved a significant continuous stay in the community, compared with a little over 70% for the milieu program and less than 50% for the traditional program. Cost-effectiveness analyses found the social-learning program to be the most effective and least expensive. The interested reader is urged to consult the comprehensive report of this project for further details (Paul & Lentz, 1977).

Problems with token economies. Token economies, while permitting more efficient and humane management of patients in the institu-

tion, are not a cure-all. The goal of institutional treatment is to facilitate adjustment in the community. A critical problem for any institutional treatment is that programs that foster adaptive behavior
within the institution may inadvertently be teaching behavior that is
inappropriate for functioning in the community. If the client's behavior depends on smoothly functioning contingencies, it may be
disrupted in the real world. One response to this problem is to try to
phase out token procedures or thin the reinforcement schedule. With
the exception of the work reported by Paul and Lentz, the record of
token economies in improving community adjustment is relatively
equivocal (Stahl & Leitenberg, 1976).

A second problem has to do with finding backup reinforcers that
can legitimately be controlled. The backup reinforcers that have been
employed include meals, choice of special foods, opportunities for
privacy, access to recreational entertainment activities, music, reading materials, writing materials, leave from the ward, social interactions with professional staff, commissary items, access to television,
and the use of a mattress with springs rather than cots (Stahl &
Leitenberg, 1976). A token system is maximally effective if it controls
as many possible sources of reinforcement as can be arranged. This
practice runs afoul of recent court decisions defining the rights of
people confined to institutions, which prohibit withholding access to
most of the items listed above. "The crux of the problem, from the
viewpoint of behavior modification, is that the items and activities
that are emerging as absolute rights are the very same items and
activities that the behavioral psychologist would employ as reinforcers —that is, as 'contingent rights'" (Wexler, 1973). In one landmark
decision, for example, a comfortable bed, a closet or locker for personal belongings, access to exercise and recreation, and many other
rights were declared constitutionally required (*Wyatt* v. *Stickney*,
1972, cited in Wallach, 1976). In sum, there are growing restrictions
on the kinds of reinforcers that can be employed in the service of a
token economy. It then becomes necessary for behavior therapists to
find reinforcers that can be legally and ethically employed and that
will still be meaningful. Such reinforcers often cost money and may
thus prove to be economically unfeasible.

Behavioral Treatment of Children

The second form of closed environment in which operant
techniques can be used is the family. Thus far, my description of the
psychotherapies has focused primarily on adults. It is appropriate
now to consider different approaches to the treatment of children.
There are three ways of treating children: working primarily with the
child, working primarily with the parents, and working with parents
and child together in what is termed family therapy. The three approaches share a belief in the crucial importance of the family en-

vironment, especially the parents, in the development of children's behavior problems. But each approach involves different assumptions about the nature of the problem and how best to treat it.

Child-focused therapy is based on the assumption that child/parent transactions have led to internal conflicts within the child and that these conflicts are the locus of the problem. An aggressive or noncompliant youngster might be diagnosed as conflicted over angry feelings toward parents or siblings and to be acting out these conflicts by means of temper tantrums and noncompliant behavior. Regular sessions would be scheduled with the youngster, sometimes with intermittent conferences with the parents to keep them abreast of developments and to try to coordinate changes in the child with parental behavior and expectations. With relatively young children, therapy sessions often involve a good deal of play interaction, using toys and materials carefully chosen by the therapist. Psychotherapists following psychoanalytic or client-centered approaches to therapy often favor this approach (for example, see Carek, 1972; Axline, 1947).

Family therapy is based on the assumption that a child's behavioral or emotional problem is a symptom of family conflict. Faulty communication patterns among family members or inappropriate role expectations or role behaviors within the family are viewed as locus of the problem. By seeing the family together, the therapist can observe *in situ* how members communicate with one another and can try to intervene to restore family harmony. Resolution of the family conflicts is expected to lead to improvement in the target child (Minuchin, 1974).

The parent-training approach—generally preferred by behavior therapists—assumes that the parents have inadvertently taught the child dysfunctional behavior and are unwittingly continuing to maintain (reinforce) it. The locus of the problem is viewed as lying in the interaction between parents and child. This assumption is similar to the one underlying family therapy. But behavior therapists believe that, because the parents control more resources, they are more amenable to intervention and that it is more economical and effective to deal with the parents alone. Treatment focuses on the contingencies between the parents' behavior and the child's behavior. It is assumed that, if the parents can be taught to ignore or mildly punish inappropriate behavior and reward good behavior, the child will change and become a source of pleasure rather than pain.

Consider a fairly typical child-behavior problem: an 8-year-old boy consistently refuses to obey requests and commands, often makes inappropriate demands on his parents or siblings, and gets angry and has occasional temper tantrums until his requests are granted. The parents scold and resort to punishment when the child does not follow their requests. Parent scolding is partially reinforced—and thereby maintained—by its occasional success in controlling the child. The child's demands and tantrums are reinforced by their occasional success in controlling the parents. Each party is inadvertently training the other to maintain negative—aversive—control strategies.

Behavioral assessment attempts to pinpoint the child's problem behaviors and their antecedents and consequences. Procedures include interviews of parents and child, questionnaires asking about the parents' perception of the child and his or her behavior, parental record keeping of the frequency of problem behaviors, and, if feasible, direct observation of parent/child interactions in the clinic and in the home. Home observations are the most costly assessment procedure but also the most objective and powerful. The results of the assessment and suggestions for intervention are discussed with the parents, and a treatment plan is arrived at.

A common procedure. A popular tactic in dealing with noncompliance and temper tantrums is time out. *Time out* is a shorthand way of expressing the idea of temporary removal from positive reinforcement. It is a form of punishment, but one that does not have the undesirable side effects of most aversive tactics. It is assumed that the child is getting reinforcement from the parents' attention in trying to get him or her to comply. In time out, the child is removed from the (reinforcing) situation and placed in another setting where there is relatively little that is amusing or entertaining. A bathroom or utility room is commonly used in many homes. The child is told to stay in time out for about 2 to 5 minutes. The parent has been coached in how to make requests and follow up if the child does not obey. It is important that the parent not engage in lengthy debate with the youngster. The usual sequence is (a) request; (b) if request is ignored or not complied with, repeat request, adding that time out will follow if it is not complied with; (c) if still no compliance, then order or, if necessary, take child to time out place without further discussion or argument.

There are considerable clinical data attesting to the effectiveness of time out in controlling children's behavior (Wahler, 1976). Most parents find that time out gives them a tool that is efficient and effective.

It is equally important that the parents reinforce appropriate behavior. In situations where parents and child are both using negative control strategies, parents tend to focus on the child's bad behavior and often dispense relatively little reward for good behavior. It is important that the child receive praise, warmth, and attention for good behavior. Often, tangible rewards are used as well, such as candy, a privilege, or an activity.

The principle of contingency is critical to such a program. Rewards are contingent on good behavior; time out is contingent on inappropriate behavior. There is also a graduated principle inherent in the program; the child is not expected to "shape up" at once. Instead, short-term goals are set and rewarded when met. Performing assigned chores for one day might be reinforced with verbal praise; doing them for three days or a week might earn a tangible reward (such as a movie).

Contingent rewards are made possible because the results of the treatment program are being assessed, probably through records kept by the parents. The therapist (or assistant) may telephone to obtain the information and also to encourage the parents. This continuing assessment provides the information on the basis of which the parents can reinforce the child, and the therapist, in turn, can reinforce the parents for conscientiously carrying out the program.

Evaluating outcome. There is considerable clinical and research evidence of the effectiveness of behavior-therapy procedures for a variety of child problems in the home (Wahler, 1976) and classroom (O'Leary & O'Leary, 1976). I believe that working with problem children is one of behavior therapy's strong suits. The work of Patterson and his colleagues (Patterson, 1974; Patterson & Reid, 1973) has been quite influential. A report by Patterson (1974) illustrates both treatment procedures and the careful evaluation involved.

The clients were preadolescent boys referred by community agencies such as the juvenile court because of chronic and serious conduct disorders. Twenty-seven of 35 referrals completed the program. The sample included eight boys from families where the father was absent, and the majority of the sample was from the lower socioeconomic levels. These were non-YAVIS clients with serious problems.

The treatment program was multidimensional and complex, but it was made more economical by working with the parents in groups and using telephone contacts. First, parents were required to study a programmed text on child management based on social learning.

> Then they learned to carefully define, track, and record a series of targeted deviant and/or prosocial child behaviors. They were monitored frequently by telephone during this and all other stages of training. They were then assigned to a parent-training group, where modeling and role-playing procedures were used to illustrate appropriate techniques. They learned to construct contracts that specified contingencies for a list of problem behaviors occurring at home and/or at school. Where necessary, training sessions were conducted in the home with the experimenters modeling the desired parenting skills [Patterson, 1974, p. 473].

In summary, the parents were trained to identify specific problem behaviors and to set up and enforce contingencies relating to these behaviors with their children. For example, if a parent was concerned about a child's staying out late at night and about not knowing the child's whereabouts, the contingency contract would specify a curfew time, would require that the child tell the parent where he or she was going to be, and would indicate the positive and negative consequences for following or not following the contract.

Two measures of outcome were employed. The primary measure involved observation data collected before treatment, during treatment, and at several follow-up intervals. Trained observers entered the home and watched the problem child interacting with family members for a specific period of time. A reliable coding system laboriously developed by Patterson and his colleagues was employed. A second outcome measure was parents' ratings of the frequency of occurrence of the problem behaviors they were concerned about.

At treatment termination both criteria showed significant reductions from baseline, and follow-up data over the course of one year indicated that the treatment effects were maintained. At termination approximately two out of three boys exhibited reductions of 30% or more from their baseline level of problem behavior. Six, however, showed increases. Home observation data for the treatment group as a whole are summarized in Figure 7–2.

The frequency of problem behaviors is expressed in terms of rate per minute and is shown for baseline, intervention, termination, and follow-up. The normal range for the behaviors depicted in Figure 7–2 is based on direct-observation data obtained from families who were

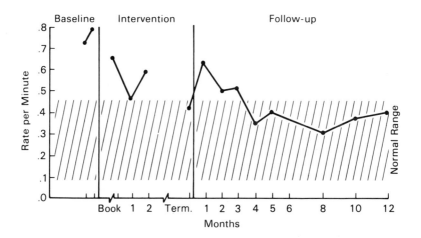

Figure 7–2. Total deviant behavior in the home. (From "Interventions for Boys with Conduct Problems: Multiple Settings, Treatments, and Criteria," by G. R. Patterson, *Journal of Consulting and Clinical Psychology*, 1974, *42*, 471–481. Copyright 1974 by the American Psychological Association. Reprinted by permission of the author and publisher.)

matched for socioeconomic status and other demographic variables but who had not sought treatment. Analogous treatment was provided for classroom-behavior problems of the boys, and it yielded similar results.

It seems clear that intervention had an important effect on the problem behavior of the boys. The effect was obtained at an average cost of 31.5 hours of professional time. Patterson noted that during the month after termination there was an increase in "noxious" behavior for half the families, and many of them received a "booster shot" averaging 1.9 hours. The amount of professional time is rarely reported, but it is very useful in estimating the cost/effectiveness ratio for a given treatment.

As Patterson noted, this report lacks a true control group of comparable families who did not receive treatment. However, he cited other work done in his laboratory that showed that waiting-list control families did not change (Wiltz & Patterson, 1974) and that families receiving an attention-placebo procedure showed no change as determined by direct observation data (Walters & Gilmore, 1973). In this latter study, interestingly, several parents rated their children as improved even though there were no decreases in the rates of the targeted deviant behavior.

Aversion Therapy

Many laypersons think of the use of aversion as synonymous with behavior therapy. And it is true that behavior therapy is the only major psychotherapeutic approach that has systematically used aversive stimuli. However, aversion is used primarily with certain disorders that are relatively infrequent—and not often with these. Aversive procedures tend to be used to reduce or eliminate serious behavioral excesses. These include destructive or self-injurious behavior such as hitting or scratching, sexual deviations such as exhibitionism and transvestism, and addictive problems such as drinking, smoking, or drug abuse. Most of the problem behaviors treated by aversion have a compulsive quality to them, in that the individuals seem unable to control themselves. Most of these behaviors also have serious negative consequences for both the client and the client's social network. And they have been found to be very difficult to treat by conventional means.

Although clinical use of aversion therapy is relatively rare, there is a fairly sizable research literature on it. I believe there are three reasons for the strong research interest. First, aversive treatment procedures can usually be readily quantified and described. For example, if electric shock is the aversive stimulus, the treatment can be described in terms of the number of trials and the intensity and duration of the shocks. Second, aversion techniques are typically applied to specifiable problem behaviors such as drinking, smoking, sexual deviations, or self-injurious behavior. Thus, the dependent variable, or outcome, is also readily measured. Third, those who work with aversive techniques understandably want to evaluate and demonstrate the clinical utility of using pain-producing methods. More justification—that is, outcome data—is required for what are believed to be extreme methods.

Two Aversion-Therapy Paradigms

There are two major kinds of aversive procedures in behavior therapy: aversive counterconditioning and punishment. Aversive counterconditioning follows the classical-conditioning paradigm, in which a previously neutral or attractive stimulus comes to acquire aversive properties by being paired repeatedly with an already aversive event. Consider a client who feels strong sexual attraction to very young boys and has occasionally made overt sexual advances, thereby getting into serious legal and social difficulty. Aversion therapy might consist of presenting slides or pictures of attractive young boys—an attractive stimulus—in conjunction with strong electric shocks—a naturally aversive stimulus. After repeated pairings, the client is expected to experience some of the same pain and fear responses on seeing the slides that he feels in reaction to the shock. This example contains all the elements of classical conditioning. Shock is an unconditioned stimulus; fear and pain are unconditioned responses; the slides of young boys are the conditioned stimulus; and a negative or fearful reaction in reaction to the slides is the conditioned response.

Punishment procedures, evolved from the operant paradigm, focus on the relationship between a response and its consequences. An aversive consequence is delivered contingent on the occurrence of undesirable, problematic behavior. Yelling at or perhaps slapping a child who engages in an undesirable or potentially dangerous act is an example of punishment. The goal of punishment procedures is to decrease the probability of the undesirable response. The goal of aversive counterconditioning is to change the emotional, or affective, qualities of a stimulus from positive to negative, or at least neutral.

Applications of aversive counterconditioning. Aversive counterconditioning has been primarily used with addictive behaviors and sexual deviations. These problem behaviors provide strong, immediate rewards, and the associated stimuli—a tavern or an article of women's clothing—are attractive and arousing. By pairing the arousing stimuli with an aversive event such as strong shock, the therapist hopes to significantly alter the emotional response of the client to these stimuli.

A male transvestite who was greatly aroused by wearing women's clothing was treated by aversive counterconditioning (Marks & Gelder, 1967). In one phase of treatment he was instructed to put on a particular garment, heard a warning signal, and then received random shocks until he took off the garment, at which point the shocks ceased. A penis transducer measured sexual arousal to the garments (the device is attached to the penis and reflects changes in blood volume).

A multiple-baseline design (see Chapter Four) was used to show specific aversion-conditioning effects. One garment was treated (shocked) at a time, and it was found that arousal decreased or ceased only after that particular garment was paired with shock. While treatment was initially successful, the client later relapsed (Marks, 1976). In one sense, relapse is not surprising, because the client surely knew that he would not be shocked again after treatment stopped. The theoretical intent of such treatment is to condition a negative emotional (physiological) response to the previously arousing stimuli. But this rarely occurs (Hallam & Rachman, 1976), even in clients where treatment remains successful. This points up an important puzzle with adversive counterconditioning: there is no satisfactory theoretical explanation of how or why it works, although it sometimes does (Hallam & Rachman, 1976).

Applications of punishment. Punishment involves providing a consequence to some undesirable behavior that will reduce the likelihood of that behavior's occurring. It is crucial that the punishing stimulus be administered right after the undesirable behavior. This is most readily accomplished in institutional settings or families, where a staff member or parent can execute the punishment. (Self-administered punishment is also possible, and it is now used in the context of the self-control strategies described in the next section.) For example, one form of punishment, *response cost*, is often used with token-economy systems of the sort described earlier in this chapter. Patients lose tokens for doing specified undesirable behaviors (that is, they are fined). Another frequently used punishment is the time-out procedure described earlier in the section on children.

Punishment has shown dramatic results with severely disturbed children who have high rates of self-destructive behavior. Such children, often diagnosed psychotic or autistic, may repeatedly bang their heads or strike themselves and will injure themselves seriously if not restrained. Following each such act with a painful electric shock suppresses the self-destructive behavior and makes the children amenable to other therapeutic procedures (Lovaas & Newsom, 1976). It is no casual matter to deliver repeated painful shocks to young children, but it can be preferable to letting them injure themselves or keeping them under constant physical restraint.

Problems with Aversion Therapy

Aversion therapy has several limitations. Below I discuss three of the major issues.

Ethical problems. The use of aversion always requires thorough discussion with the participants, freely given consent, and the freedom to discontinue treatment. The more discomfort or risk involved in a treatment, the more stringent the safeguards. There should be convincing evidence that no nonaversive or safer procedure would be as effective. This requirement can often be met, because many of the problems treated with aversion are very resistant to change. But we can also expect aversion methods to give way gradually to equally or more effective nonaversive methods.

Side effects. Several side effects have been suggested, and some have been demonstrated. Two major ones are noted here. One is the possibility that a negative emotional reaction will be conditioned to the aversion dispenser. Although a client is unlikely to develop such a reaction to a therapist, children may well develop negative reactions to parents, teachers, or other adults who repeatedly dispense punishment.

A second side effect for either aversive counterconditioning or punishment is the negative modeling involved. Inherently, one human being is producing pain for another. Children or adults may get the message that aversive control of other persons is acceptable, a message contrary to most people's value systems.

One-sidedness. Finally, a key inherent limitation of aversion requires emphasis. Aversion methods suppress behavior, or inform people what *not* to do. Other therapeutic methods are necessary to guide clients in developing acceptable adaptive behaviors to replace what they are losing. Aversive methods rarely, if ever, should be used in isolation.

Aversion therapy has been applied to so many different disorders that overall generalizations are very difficult. It has shown modest success with certain sexual deviations (Marks, 1976) and with addictive behaviors such as alcoholism (Nathan, 1976) and smoking (Lichtenstein & Danaher, 1976). Time out has been effective with children (Wahler, 1976). But negative side effects as well as ethical concerns point to the importance of developing nonaversive or minimally aversive alternatives.

Cognitive and Self-Control Strategies

Behavior therapy in its early days emphasized the application of operant and classical-conditioning procedures. Current behavior therapy emphasizes cognitive and self-control strategies (Mahoney,

1977; Meichenbaum, 1977; Thoresen & Mahoney, 1974). These approaches are relatively new and do not yet have the empirical achievements of most of the procedures previously described.

Cognitive behavior therapy is rooted in the growing realization that virtually all learning (even animal learning) involves cognitive or mediational processes (Bandura, 1977). The informational value of reinforcement, for example, is now given greater weight than its power to automatically "stamp in" responses. Treatment strategies that incorporate cognitive processes, therefore, ought to be more effective and efficient. A second impetus for cognitive behavior modification arises from the fact that the problems presented by many clients involve cognitions as much as behavior. Negative self-evaluations, obsessions, or ruminations and self-defeating beliefs or rationalizations are often critical in the dysfunctional behavior of clients.

The emphasis on *self-control strategies* also has more than one facet. In part it is an attempt to counter the criticisms about external control and manipulation that have been leveled against behavior therapists. It is also an attempt to deal with the problems of generalizing behavior change from the clinic to the client's everyday life and the maintenance of therapeutic gains after therapy is over. Clients who respond to contingencies in the clinic or hospital often revert back to dysfunctional ways when externally administered consequences are no longer present.

This section will consider one approach to cognitive behavior therapy and then describe the application of some self-control strategies to obesity.

Rational-Emotive Therapy (RET)

The decision to present rational-emotive therapy as an example of cognitive behavior therapy requires justification. RET was developed and popularized by Albert Ellis (1962). Originally trained in psychoanalysis, Ellis was among the earliest to articulate a cognitive theory of behavior disorder and to describe a practical set of treatment procedures. RET was developed independently of behavior therapy and was later embraced by behaviorists, who correctly perceived it as compatible with a behavioral approach that acknowledged the importance of cognitive or mediational processes. Because RET has had an enormous impact on cognitive behavior and because it is a very important therapeutic approach in its own right, I have chosen it for this section.

A virtue of RET—and one reason it is so influential—is its simplicity. RET posits that dysfunctional or irrational behavior is maintained by the covert sentences that we say to ourselves. It is how we construe reality and what we tell ourselves about it—as taught to us by our parents and other socializing agents—that cause emotional disturbance. Ellis is fond of citing Epictetus, who wrote "Men are not disturbed by things, but by the views which they take of them."

The essentials of Ellis's position have been summarized in his ABCD theory (Ellis, 1976):

A = the activating event—an experience or event that has occurred.
B = your belief system, which relates A to some emotional reaction (C).
C = your emotional reaction, the consequences of the event for you.
D = disputing or challenging the erroneous belief system.

RET asserts that we believe that A causes C when in fact it is B, our belief system, that creates C. Therefore, it is necessary to dispute and change belief systems in order to change our emotional reactions.

Consider the following fairly common example. A young man calls an attractive girl he has casually met and asks her for a date. She responds that she is busy and can't make it. He feels bad about being turned down. Fearing further rejection, he avoids making further overtures to this girl and, perhaps, other girls.

The activating event (A) is the rejection by the girl. The emotional consequences (C) are his feelings of rejection plus his reluctance to extend further social invitations. The young man believes that he feels bad because of the rejection. But RET argues that there must be a mediating belief system (B) that would account for his reacting to this event so strongly. This belief system must be disputed—indeed forcefully attacked—by the therapist in order to avoid repetition of such episodes. Therefore, the therapist would forcefully confront the belief system, attack its irrationality, and later guide the client to think and act constructively. There is a strong pedagogical flavor to RET, in that the therapist carefully explains the rationale behind the procedure and often suggests possible irrational beliefs. In his colorful writings Ellis has listed a number of typical irrational beliefs—for example, the idea that one should be thoroughly competent, adequate, and achieving in all possible respects if one is to consider oneself worthwhile (Ellis, 1962).

In their cogent exposition of behavior therapy, Goldfried and Davison (1976) noted that the irrationality of a client's belief system can be approached at two levels: (1) "the likelihood that the client is correctly interpreting the situation, and (2) the ultimate implications of the way the client has labeled the event" (p. 116). Our rejected and dejected young man probably thinks that the girl refused him because he is unattractive and inadequate. Challenging the likelihood that he is correctly interpreting the situation would involve coaching him to consider other reasons why he might have been turned down. The girl might have liked him but have been busy, might already have a boyfriend, or might herself be shy and insecure.

The second level of approach involves accepting the young man's interpretation of the situation and then considering the ulti-

mate implications. Suppose the girl did think him unattractive and
unlikable. And suppose many women did likewise. This would be
unfortunate, but not catastrophic. One standard irrational belief described by Ellis is "Everybody must love me if I am to be a worthy
person." In our example, it would be easier for the client to deal with
the implications of this particular girl's not liking him than it would
be to consider the possibility that most women find him unattractive.
But the rational-emotive therapist would not shy away from the latter eventuality if circumstances seemed to indicate that it was a
likely possibility.

The rational-emotive therapist also attempts to teach the client
generalized strategies that can be applied to future problem situations. Clients are instructed that, whenever strong, negative
emotional reactions are experienced, they should search out the
underlying belief system, consider whether they are correctly interpreting the situation, and—if they are—evaluate the rationality of
the ultimate implications. Below is an excerpt in which Ellis describes a homework assignment designed to teach a client how to
dispute his irrational beliefs. In his colorful way Ellis combines RET,
self-control, and a bit of reinforcement (1976, pp. 29–30):

> T: Yes, in my group therapy sessions, recently, I have been giving most
>   of the members of the group Disputing assignments and also
>   using operant conditioning—a self-management technique
>   adapted from B. F. Skinner's theories—to help them carry out
>   these ten-minute-a-day disputations.
> C: What do you mean by operant conditioning?
> T: I'll explain in a minute. But first, the point is for you to decide
>   exactly what hypothesis or nutty idea you want to work on for at
>   least ten minutes a day. And, in your case, it would be the idea,
>   again, that it's terrible for you to get rejected by a woman you
>   find attractive. You would take this idea, and ask yourself several
>   basic questions, in order to challenge and dispute it.
> C: What kind of questions?
> T: Usually, four basic questions—though they have all kinds of varia-
>   tions. The first one is, "What am I telling myself?" or, "What silly
>   idea do I want to challenge?" And the answer, in your case, is,
>   "It's terrible if a woman whom I find attractive rejects me." The
>   second question is, "Is this, my hypothesis, true?" And the answer
>   is—?
> C: Uh, well, uh. No, it isn't.
> T: Fine. If you had said it was true, the third question would have been,
>   "Where is the evidence for its being true?" But since you said it
>   isn't true, the third question is, "Where is the evidence that it's
>   not true?" Well—?
> C: Well, uh, it's not true because, as we said before, it may be very
>   inconvenient if an attractive woman rejects me, but it's not more,
>   uh, than that. It's only damned inconvenient![2]

[2]From "Rational-Emotive Therapy," by A. Ellis. In V. Binder, A. Binder, and B.
Rimland (Eds.), *Modern Therapies*. Copyright 1976 by Prentice-Hall, Inc. Reprinted by
permission.

The client was instructed to make a highly desired activity—eating ice cream—contingent on ten minutes of disputation practice.

Although it has had a major influence on behavior therapy, RET per se has not been extensively evaluated. There have been a few studies showing good treatment effects (for example, see Diloreto, 1971). However, two reviewers of the literature concur that the clinical effectiveness of RET has yet to be demonstrated (Mahoney, 1974; Meichenbaum, 1977).

Self-Control: Power to the Person

The heading above—also the title of a book (Mahoney & Thoresen, 1974)—reflects the hope that behavioral self-control will provide a framework and technology for enabling clients to control their own behavior. Although a number of technical definitions of self-control have been proposed, the essential feature is "that it is the person himself who is the agent of his own behavior change" (Thoresen & Mahoney, 1974, p. 11). Procedurally, this implies that clients initiate procedures outside of therapy in order to bring about desired changes.

The concept of self-control also involves the presence of two or more behavioral alternatives, or choices, each with differing consequences: to study or to go drink beer; to smoke or not to smoke; to eat an attractive dessert or not do so. The choice typically pits a pleasurable or reinforcing short-term consequence—enjoying a beer, a smoke, or a rich dessert—against an undesirable but temporally distant consequence—not getting a good grade, developing lung cancer, or gaining weight and looking unattractive. Although the procedural essence of self-control—the client as agent of behavior change—can be applied to pretty nearly any emotional or behavioral disorder, much of the therapeutic application and research have focused on problem drinking, smoking, and obesity. These problems embody the basic choice dilemma—to indulge or not to indulge. Self-control strategies for obesity will be described as an example.

Thoresen and Mahoney (1974) described two basic self-control strategies: (1) environmental planning, in which the client changes the antecedents of the target behavior; and (2) behavioral programming, in which the client self-administers consequences after the occurrence of a target response. It is important that the self-administered contingencies be clearly understood before the choice situation or target behavior is encountered.

For obesity, environmental planning involves changes in the environment that will help the client cut calories and increase energy expenditure. This would include preparing only as much food as one wants to eat, estimating and writing down the caloric value of food before eating it, confining one's eating to specific times and places, and using the stairs instead of the elevator. Obese people often eat or snack on many occasions and in many places. Environmental planning limits eating to only one place—for example, at the kitchen table—and only at certain times—mealtime. In this way, the eliciting stimuli for eating responses are narrowed, making it easier for the person to control his or her behavior.

Behavioral programming consists of prearranging for positive or negative consequences contingent on good or bad eating. Examples could include performing a specified exercise task if stipulated calorie consumption is exceeded; rewarding oneself with a special purchase or activity for a week of appropriate eating; or covert self-rewarding statements after each appropriate meal. In effect, the client makes a contract with himself or herself. The therapist serves as an instructor or guide to the obese client. Self-control strategies are carefully explained, and a manual containing the procedures is often given to the client. The emphasis is on teaching new eating habits that the client can live with indefinitely, so that weight loss will be maintained. Self-monitoring of both weight and food consumption is also a standard part of behavioral treatment.

Behavior-therapy procedures for obesity have been systematically evaluated in a number of studies. There is consistent evidence that they are more practical and effective than alternative procedures (Stunkard & Mahoney, 1976). However, the clients in much of the research have not been particularly representative of the obese population and the weight loss obtained—in terms of absolute number of pounds—has usually not been large. In a classic study emphasizing environmental-planning procedures, eight very obese women lost 26 to 47 pounds in one year (Stuart, 1967). Unfortunately, these spectacular results have never been matched. Treatment programs for the obese have become more complex and multidimensional as the biological and social determinants of obesity become better understood (Stunkard & Mahoney, 1976). But treatment results for this difficult problem are relatively modest.

Illustrative Therapy Case

There are many behavior-therapy cases to choose from, because the emphasis on precise description of treatment methods and outcomes facilitates case presentation. The case summarized here was chosen because it illustrates the application of several basic techniques in a novel manner (Fisher & Winkler, 1975, pp. 912–914).

Client Background

The client was an 18-year-old female who had been raised in a suburb of New York. Previous therapy consisted of contact with two psychiatric social workers during her first and second years at the university. Both of these contacts centered on her social adjustment and sex role identity.

Upon intake, the client complained of severe feelings of deper-sonalization and unreality. According to her report, these feelings were largely caused by several repetitive visual sensations that frightened her, making her afraid that she was going insane. The most regular of these involved flashes of dark colors when she closed her eyes at bed-time, the perception of people and objects as varying in size and dis-tance from her, heads of screaming dogs and cats, a black and white geometric pattern with a spot of light at the center that "comes in and out and flashes around," and the sensation of "tiny white pinpoints moving around like dust" when she looked at the sky in daylight. She reported little control over the occurrence of these sensations with the exception of sometimes being able to stop the variation in size and distance of people and objects by "clearing my head and straightening up" and being able to stop the tiny white pinpoints by looking away from the sky. Prior to intake, the specific sensations had increased in frequency, resulting in increased feelings of depersonalization and desperation and in her becoming convinced that "there's something really wrong with me."

[Treatment]

Therapy commenced with the therapist reflecting and clarifying the client's experiences in order to reduce her anxiety as well as to satisfy both of them that he fully appreciated what she was experienc-ing. After the therapist felt he had gained her trust, conversation within therapy was directed toward the need to establish some control over the upsetting sensations. At this point, the client mentioned that the major source of disturbance was not the sensations themselves but their intrusive quality. The therapist strongly supported this idea, pur-suing its discussion with the suggestion that her therapy might include exercises directed toward gaining control over the intrusiveness of the sensations. The client readily agreed to this. Therefore, part of each of the next four sessions was set aside for these exercises. The rest of these sessions were spent in discussion of the client's feelings and current functioning, still directed toward reassurance and support.

The exercises were conducted with the client seated in a relaxed manner in a lounge chair. Mild relaxation suggestions were given. Addi-tionally, relaxation training of the type used in systematic desensitiza-tion (Wolpe, 1973) was used for the final two exercise sessions in which the sensations being dealt with were not only intrusive but disturbing in content (flashing colors and heads of screaming dogs). For clients with particularly disturbing sensations, use of the present technique in conjunction with more extended relaxation training seems advisable.

Each exercise session consisted of the client practicing the produc-tion and dismissal of the various intrusive sensations. Each exercise trial was commenced with the therapist giving the direction, "Start." After this, the client produced, as fast as she could, a given sensation and signaled success by raising an index finger. Then the therapist repeated several times, "Hold it," and then directed the client to "stop!" after which she dismissed the sensation as rapidly as possible, signaling success by lowering the index finger. The only exception to this procedure was for the flashes of light that the client experienced as instantaneous. For these sensations, the exercise consisted of practicing only the production of the sensations.

The therapist used a stopwatch to time all trials. The "onset la-tency" was the time that elapsed between the therapist's command to produce the sensation and the client's signal that she had succeeded in doing so. The "exposure duration" was the time between her signal that she had produced the sensation and the therapist's direction to dismiss it. The "offset latency" was measured from the therapist's direction to dismiss the sensation to her signal that she had done so. Feedback on the development of control was provided by moving on to the next sensation and by praise, both of which were contingent on decreased onset and offset latencies.

The client initially reported being unable to produce the sensation of screaming dog and cat heads. Since this sensation was upsetting not only because of its intrusive qualities but also because of its disturbing content, an approach hierarchy, similar to that used in desensitization, was used. After unsuccessfully attempting to imagine "a brown dog" for 60 sec., she was directed to imagine walking through a wooded area. In the course of narrating this imagery, the therapist directed her to imagine seeing a boy in a field at the edge of the woods and then to imagine a dog next to him. She was able to do this and in the following session to imagine a dog standing alone. In the third and fourth sessions in which the sensation was addressed, the client was relaxed as for desensitization (Wolpe, 1973), and was able to complete the exercises, progressing through images of pleasant and neutral dog heads, dog heads with bared teeth, and finally heads with the mouth open as if screaming.

The exposure duration varied between 5 and 20 sec. during the course of the exercises. It was found that offset latency was less for shorter exposure durations. If the client had trouble dismissing a sensation, the exposure duration was shortened and, after some improvement, lengthened gradually so that she could work up to quickly dismissing sensations after relatively long exposure durations.

The sensation of flashing colors was practiced in two sessions with a total of 22 trials. The sensation of screaming dog heads was practiced for 25 trials in four sessions. The sensation of people and objects varying in size and distance received 12 trials spread over two sessions, with the client focusing on producing changes in her perception of a table lamp in the interview room. The black and white patterns were given only 2 trials during one session. The sensation of tiny white pinpoints, reported by the client to occur when she looked at the sky, was dealt with by informing her that this was a normal sensation, of no cause for alarm.

In dealing with occurrences of the intrusive experiences or with situations in which their occurrence was likely, the client was encouraged to use the skills being developed through the exercises. However, she was not given instructions to practice the exercises at other times.

Therapy was temporarily terminated at the end of the school semester. The client was seen for six more sessions during summer school. She reported very little disturbance from the sensations at that time so no more exercises were carried out. Therapy continued, however, with attention being given to her general social adjustment and to her vague feelings of depersonalization.

In summary, the client was seen for a total of 12 sessions, 6 during the regular school year (the last 4 of which were devoted to the exercises described above) and 6 sessions during the summer. Follow-up of the effects of the exercises was gathered during the first and last of the 6 sessions during the summer—45 and 85 days after the last session during which the exercises were practiced.

[*Outcome*]

The client reported zero incidence of the flashing colors and screaming animal head sensations 45 days after the last practice session. A further check at 85 days after the last practice session again showed zero incidence. At the 45-day follow-up, she reported that the sensation of people and objects varying in size and distance had not decreased in frequency but had instead become only "a little" upsetting to her. After 85 days, she felt that the sensation was a little less frequent, adding, "I don't pay much attention to it . . . [and] can make it go away more easily." She indicated that she felt she could disperse the sensation by not letting it bother her. The sensation of black and white patterns was said to occur "rarely" after 45 days and "every couple of weeks, maybe" after 85 days. It was also less troublesome in that the only aspect of it that occurred after treatment was the light at the center of the pattern. . . .

The general results of the treatment were positive. The procedure reported here was terminated after the sixth session at the end of the regular school year. At this point, the client's fear that she was going insane was greatly reduced and remained so when she was seen in Session 7 at the start of summer school. By the termination of therapy at the end of summer school, her feelings of depersonalization had abated and she was functioning well. One year after termination, she was still in school and reported doing "fine."[3]

Discussion

A number of common and specific components were present in the treatment of this young woman. The contributions of trust, support, and reassurance — essentially common processes — were acknowledged. The importance of the control exercises was supported by quantitative evidence—omitted here—showing that onset latencies of the intrusive thoughts decreased with practice trials. Other specific treatment components included relaxation, gradual exposure (the hierarchy), feedback, and contingent praise. These are basic components in behavior therapy. In this case, they were applied to some unusual problem behaviors—intrusive thoughts and sensations. These behaviors might have been construed as "psychotic symptoms" by some therapists, who then might have probed for other indications of cognitive disturbance or serious dysfunction. The therapists in this case did not so view them, either because of their theoretical preconceptions or because other data, not reported in the article, indicated that the client was not seriously disturbed.

The basic treatment components were also applied in a self-control framework. The therapist continually emphasized the strengthening of the client's perceived control over her thoughts. The

[3]From "Case Study: Self-Control Over Intrusive Experiences," by E. B. Fisher, Jr., and R. C. Winkler, *Journal of Consulting and Clinical Psychology*, 1975, *43*, 911–916. Copyright 1975 by the American Psychological Association. Reprinted by permission.

follow-up contact indicates that this client was helped considerably by treatment, but we do not know the relative contribution of specific and common processes.

Evaluation of Behavior Therapy

Quality of Theory

There is no single theory underlying the varied methods used in behavior therapy. Instead, there are many therapeutic rationales, one for each of the many treatment strategies. The quality of these rationales varies considerably but is good relative to other psychotherapeutic rationales. (As I noted in Chapter Four, all theories of psychotherapy are "weak" with respect to conventional scientific rigor.) Most behavior-therapy rationales are explicit and internally consistent. The key variables are amenable to precise descriptions and can often be measured reliably and objectively.

The rationale and associated therapy procedures are usually consistent with available psychological knowledge. Admittedly, however, the supporting data are often laboratory research with animals, and it is a large leap from the animal laboratory to the clinical situation. Frequently, especially in clinical contexts, the relationship between basic learning phenomena and treatment procedures is a very loose one. "While borrowing from the laboratory model, the language and techniques frequently used in behavior modification are admittedly metaphorical" (Mahoney, Kazdin, & Lesswing, 1974). But the metaphor has been a useful one. These limitations notwithstanding, I believe that behavior therapy does have superior psychotherapeutic rationales. The advantage is not a large one and, given the limitations of this criterion noted in Chapter Four, would not by itself constitute a sufficient justification to choose behavior therapy over other alternatives.

Cost-Effectiveness

Again, because very different treatment procedures are used for different disorders, it is difficult to make broad generalizations.

Time and Expense of Treatment

Generalizations are especially difficult with respect to the time and expense of behavior therapy, because treatment duration varies considerably. Although behavior therapy tends to be considerably shorter than intensive psychoanalytic therapy, much of it appears to be at least as long, if not longer, than the brief psychoanalytic or humanistic therapies.

Complicating the assessment of time and expense is the fact that behavior therapy often involves relatively little direct professional contact but may require much time from paraprofessional and adjunctive staff. This is particularly true for token-economy programs. In sum, it is unclear whether behavior therapy enjoys any advantage in terms of being shorter or less expensive than alternative treatments.

Training Requirements for Therapists

Because many behavioral procedures are simple and explicit, they can be learned by paraprofessional therapists who have had relatively little formal training. Token-economy programs, once developed by professional staff, can be carried out by usual ward personnel, including nurses, psychiatric aides, and occupational therapists. Parents and teachers can be trained to use contingency-management programs in the classroom and home. The behavioral approach to problem children described earlier makes use of parents as therapeutic assistants. A behavioral consultant can work efficiently with a number of paraprofessionals or "behavior analysts" and thus affect a good many clients (Tharpe & Wetzel, 1969).

Applicability to Client Populations

I believe that behavior therapy requires less verbal and conceptual skill from clients than do either the psychoanalytic or humanistic approaches. Much of behavior therapy is structured and requires action rather than words. For these reasons it is often more acceptable to non-YAVIS clients than the other two therapies. Introspection about feelings, motives, and interpersonal relationships is often not necessary.

It is also clear that behavior therapy has often been applied to non-YAVIS populations that are infrequently and usually ineffectually dealt with by other approaches. Examples here include retarded individuals, chronic mental patients both in institutions (as in token economies) and in the community, and aggressive, acting-out children and adolescents. I see the broad applicability of behavior therapy to such clients as a major advantage.

Empirical Outcome

How effective is behavior therapy? Such a question can be neither asked nor answered in general terms. A more appropriate question concerns whether a particular kind of behavior therapy is effective with a particular kind of behavior disorder. I have tried to consider effectiveness with respect to each of the treatment strategies discussed. A brief summary here may be useful.

Behavioral treatments for phobias and anxiety—desensitization, flooding, or modeling with guided participation—are effective and appear to be superior to nonbehavioral alternatives.

Token-economy programs for institutionalized mental patients produce marked improvement in appropriate behavior within the institution, but the superiority of token procedures in facilitating subsequent community adjustment is not well demonstrated. Growing
legal constraints on the manipulation of backup reinforcers seem
likely to constrain applications of token systems. Parent-training
programs aimed at reducing disruptive home and classroom behavior of young children appear to be clearly effective and efficient.

Aversion therapy is useful with certain sexual and addictive
problems but has limited applicability because of side effects and
ethical concerns. Rational-emotive therapy has not yet been extensively researched. The available data are promising but basically
equivocal. Other cognitive treatment strategies have been more extensively researched but found wanting (Mahoney, 1974). The one
important exception appears to be the work of Meichenbaum (1977),
which has received empirical support, albeit primarily by analogue
studies.

Behavioral self-control strategies have been diverse, and they
have been applied to varying problems with varying success. Applications to cigarette smoking have been relatively less successful
(Lichtenstein & Danaher, 1976); applications to problem drinking
(Nathan, 1976) and to obesity (Stunkard & Mahoney, 1976) have been
relatively more successful.

A subjective box score of this sort can be readily criticized; it is
offered as a tentative guideline. Such generalizations are made possible because of the key cardinal virtue of behavior therapy: the empirical emphasis noted early in this chapter and manifested in the
outpouring of outcome studies on the various treatment strategies.
No other psychological treatment has been so extensively evaluated.
And behavior therapists have frequently been quite self-critical in
evaluating their own work and that of their colleagues.

The relative success of behavior therapy with a number of
specific behavior problems represents a significant achievement in
the field of psychotherapy. Nevertheless, it must be kept in mind that
the bulk of clients presenting themselves to outpatient and institutional settings do not fall readily into these specific categories. Most
clients require treatment programs for which there is no clear empirical validity. Although behavior therapy is frequently applied to such
clients, there is no evidence that it is any more successful than other
treatment approaches (for example, see Sloane, Staples, Cristol,
Yorkston, & Whipple, 1975). It must also be kept in mind that much of
the controlled research in behavior therapy is analogue research: the
subjects or clients were recruited and had no strong concern that
their problems were interfering significantly with their lives.

The contribution of common processes to behavior therapy deserves consideration. Many group design and single-subject studies
include controls for common processes. This is commendable. Often

the attention-placebo group does as well as the "real" treatment group, but at least the issue is faced and tested.

The analysis of common processes presented in Chapter Three implies that they should be especially powerful in behavior therapy. This is so because of the explicit rationale given to the client and, especially, because of the structured activity the client engages in. For example, treatments involving hierarchical or gradual exposure provide the client with structured activity, feedback, and success, which strengthens positive expectations. Practicing behavior therapists tend to emphasize specific techniques but are also capitalizing on common processes.

As I have tried to indicate throughout this chapter, behavior therapy is in a state of flux. It is constantly evolving new methods and trying to deal with more complex problems. Put another way, it is growing away from its original roots in classical and operant conditioning. Many, including myself, applaud this development, seeing it as a necessary progression if behavior therapy is to fully deal with the psychotherapeutic problems of the real world. But, admittedly, there are dangers that it may become too eclectic or stretch its laboratory metaphor too far. As long as new methods and new approaches are subjected to careful evaluation, this is less likely to occur.

Epilogue: The Three Approaches Compared and Contrasted

This chapter has already offered implicit and explicit comparisons of the three approaches. Here I will extend the comparisons. First, the approaches will be compared along theoretical dimensions, and then comparative outcome studies will be reviewed. The effectiveness of psychotherapy compared with no treatment will also be considered.

Korchin's Summary

The theoretical comparison starts with Korchin's (1976) thoughtful analysis of the three approaches. Korchin summarized in tabular form what he believes are the important dimensions of the three approaches. The summary, in modified form, is shown in Table 7–2.

Korchin wrote from an essentially neo-Freudian perspective. I think he overstated behavior therapy's position on the client/therapist relationship, subjective experience, and insight. The behavior therapist as "trainer" seems nicely stated, but trainers or coaches are often quite sensitive to their interpersonal relationships with trainees and are skillful in using the relationship to facilitate learning. So, I believe, is the good behavior therapist. Cognitive behavior therapy, as

Table 7–2. Comparison of Psychoanalytic, Behavioral, and Humanistic-Existential Approaches to Psychotherapy

Issue	Psychoanalysis	Behavior Therapy	Humanistic-Existential Therapy
Nature of psycho-pathol-ogy	Pathology reflects inadequate conflict resolutions and fixations in early development, which leave overly strong impulses or weak controls or both. Symptoms are partial adaptations or substitute gratifications, defense responses to anxiety.	Symptomatic behavior derives from faulty learning of maladaptive behaviors. The symptom is the problem; there is no "underlying disease."	Incongruence exists between the depreciated self and the potential, desired self. The person is overly dependent on others for gratification and self-esteem. There is a sense of purposelessness and meaninglessness.
Goal of therapy	Attainment of psychosexual maturity, strengthened ego functions, and reduced control by unconscious and repressed impulses.	Relieving symptomatic behavior by suppressing or replacing maladaptive behaviors.	Fostering self-determination, authenticity, and integration by releasing human potential and expanding awareness.
Role of therapist	An *investigator*, searching out root conflicts and resistances; detached, neutral, and nondirective, to facilitate transference reactions.	A *trainer*, helping patient unlearn old behaviors and learn new ones. Control of reinforcement is important; interpersonal relation is of minor concern.	An *authentic person* in true encounter with patient, sharing experience. Facilitates patient's growth potential; transference discounted or minimized.
Therapist's qualifica-tions and skills	Highly trained in theory and supervised practice; much technical and professional knowledge. Must have fine self-knowledge to avert dangers of countertransference.	Knowledge of learning principles primary; understanding of personality theory and psychopathology secondary; little concern with self-knowledge. Actual interventions can be done by nonprofessional assistant.	Personal integrity and empathy valued over professional training and formal knowledge.

Issue	Psychoanalysis	Behavior Therapy	Humanistic-Existential Therapy
Time orientation	Oriented to discovering and interpreting past conflicts and repressed feelings and examining them in light of present situation.	Little or no concern with past history or etiology. Present behavior is examined and treated.	Focus on present phenomenal experience, the here and now.
Role of unconscious material	Primary in classical psychoanalysis, less emphasized by neo-Freudians and ego psychologists. To all, of great conceptual importance.	No concern with unconscious processes or, indeed, with subjective experience even in conscious realm. Subjective experience shunned as unscientific.	Though recognized by some, emphasis is on conscious experience.
Psychological realm emphasized	Motives and feelings, fantasies and cognitions. Minimum concern with motor behavior and action outside of therapy.	Behavior and observable feelings and actions. Emphasis on extratherapeutic actions.	Perception, meanings, values. For some, sensory and motor processes.
Role of insight	Central, though conceived not just as coming from intellectual understanding but also as emerging in "corrective emotional experiences."	Irrelevant and unnecessary.	More emphasis on awareness, the "how" and "what" questions rather than the "why."
Research attitude	Goal of research is to verify clinical observations.	Laboratory research valued as suggesting clinical procedures; empirical evaluation of treatment considered crucial.	Skeptical of conventional research paradigms and methods. More value placed on clinicians' personal experience and feelings.

Table 7–2 *(Continued)*

Issue	Psychoanalysis	Behavior Therapy	Humanistic-Existential Therapy
Research strategy	Naturalistic (correlational) research that does not intrude into treatment. Emphasis on *process* rather than outcome and on measuring intrapsychic change.	Controlled experimentation whenever possible. Emphasis on demonstrating outcome effects before process analysis.	Both outcome and process strategies. Focus on effects of therapist attitudes and behavior on client feelings and behavior.

Table 14–2 from *Modern Clinical Psychology: Principles of Intervention in the Clinic and Community*, by Sheldon J. Korchin. © 1976 by Sheldon J. Korchin, Basic Books, Inc., Publishers, New York. Reprinted by permission.

I have tried to show, is quite concerned with subjective experience. The case study presented was primarily concerned with subjective experience. I believe that psychoanalytic and humanistic therapy strive for insight of a different sort from behavior therapy. Insight for the behavior therapist involves the client's understanding the antecedents and consequences that elicit and maintain the troublesome behavior. It is, admittedly, a more cognitive and less emotional sort of insight than that pursued in psychoanalytic and humanistic therapies; but this should not mask the fact that behavior therapy is also concerned with increasing self-knowledge.

Korchin's analysis omitted how the three approaches deal with research. In Table 7–2 I have added comparisons on this important dimension. A major point is that behavior therapy is relatively the most responsive to research findings. Clinical procedures have been generated on the basis of laboratory-derived principles, and research on outcome influences clinical practice. As I noted in Chapter Five, psychoanalytic practice has been influenced virtually not at all by research. It is more difficult to characterize humanistic research attitudes and practice. Client-centered workers have been very active in research, and their findings appear to have influenced practice. But the other, and more numerous, humanistic therapists pretty much disavow the importance of research.

Comparative Outcome Studies: The Box-Score Approach

Another approach to answering questions about comparative psychotherapeutic effectiveness is the "box-score" method. The results from numerous studies are tabulated on the basis of criteria devised by the scorekeeper. For example, one can survey studies in which controlled comparisons were made between a certain kind of therapy and either no-treatment control groups or alternative therapies. Then the scorekeeper counts the number of times behavioral treatment is significantly more effective, no more effective, or less effective than the control group or alternative treatment. The box-score method can be used in an attempt to answer such gross questions as "Does psychotherapy work better than no treatment?" This approach has been used by several investigators and has yielded some interesting information. It is deceptively appealing, in that it appears to offer ready answers to general questions about effectiveness.

There are, however, two major shortcomings of the box-score approach. The first, which the scorekeepers themselves are well aware of, is that the approach glosses over potentially important differences in the quality of individual studies. To continue the baseball metaphor, most hitters will gladly take the infield hit or the pop-fly double that an outfielder loses in the sun because "they all look like line drives in the box score the next day." In similar fashion, the box-score approach to evaluations of psychotherapy equates high-quality studies with ones of inferior methodology. Scorekeepers have attempted to deal with this problem in two ways. First, the methodological adequacy of studies can be judged and incorporated into the box score or at least into the conclusions that are drawn. Second, the investigator can seek to survey a sufficiently large number of reports that unevenness in methodological quality can be considered random error and presumed not to affect the overall conclusions.

A second major problem is inherent in the generality, or grossness, of the questions addressed by the box-score method. As I emphasized in Chapter Four, the evaluation of psychotherapy is most likely to yield meaningful data when such relatively specific questions are asked as "What therapy works best for which kinds of clients?" (while also considering differences in therapists and settings). Although box-score approaches often consider different kinds of therapy, they rarely deal with interactions between various kinds of treatment and various kinds of clients. Further, the treatments compared—the independent variable—are often described in very general terms and mask considerable variability. Given these reservations, I will describe some findings and conclusions from three box-score approaches; you are urged to consult the original articles for more detail than can be given here. A behavioral rebuttal to the conclusions of the box-score tabulators will then be summarized.

The Bergin Review

Bergin (1971) considered 52 reports published between 1962 and 1969 that he felt to be a representative cross-section of outcome studies. He was concerned with the general question "Does psychotherapy work?" According to Bergin's scorecard, 22 studies "are rated as positive, 15 in doubt, and 15 as negative evidence in relation to psychotherapy" (Bergin, 1971, p. 229). Bergin did not specify what he meant by "in doubt" or "negative," but it appears that "negative" means that psychotherapy was clearly not more effective than the control or no-treatment group; "in doubt" seems to indicate that the scorekeeper was uncertain whether psychotherapy was more effective.

Bergin was very much aware of the issue of differences in methodological rigor as well as the possibility that various process variables might affect outcome. He compared outcome among studies differing in adequacy of design and found no differences. The kind of therapy was unrelated to outcome, although Bergin acknowledged the crudeness of this comparison. Only a few behavior-therapy studies were then available for inclusion. Bergin concluded that, taking the various problems into account, "There remains some modest evidence that psychotherapy 'works'" (p. 229).

Bergin reached substantially similar conclusions after reviewing more recent literature (Bergin & Lambert, 1978). It was noted, however, that behavioral methods appear to work best for certain specific problems.

Is It True that "Everybody Has Won and All Must Have Prizes"?

This heading is part of the title of a second box-score analysis. As the authors noted, it implies that many therapists believe that all psychotherapies produce some benefits for some patients (Luborsky, Singer, & Luborsky, 1975). The authors attempted to be comprehensive in their review of the literature but considered only research in which bona fide patients were in bona fide treatment and excluded (analogue) studies using student volunteers. They also graded each study on a scale of methodological adequacy. One of three scores was assigned to each study or each comparison between treatments: "better" if a psychotherapy group was found to be significantly superior to a control or alternative treatment; "tie" when there were no significant differences between the groups compared; and "worse" if the psychotherapy group was found to be significantly worse than the control or comparison. Table 7–3 summarizes the box-score comparisons most relevant to our discussion—namely, client-centered versus other traditional (nonbehavioral) psychotherapies; behavior therapy compared with (nonbehavioral) psychotherapy; psychotherapy versus control groups, where the control groups include no therapy-waiting-list control, and minimal treatment, or routine hospital care.

Although the number of available studies was small, client-centered therapy did not seem to be better than other therapy, and the most common result was a tie. When behavior therapy was compared against other psychotherapy (in 11 different studies), the most

Table 7–3. Box Scores for Comparisons of Psychotherapeutic Outcomes

Client-centered (nondirective) was better	=	0
Tie	=	4
Other traditional (nonbehavioral) psychotherapies were better	=	1
Behavior therapy (usually desensitization) was better	=	6
Tie	=	12
Nonbehavioral psychotherapy was better	=	0
Psychotherapy was better	=	20
Tie	=	13
Control group[1] was better	=	0

[1]Control group includes: no psychotherapy, wait-for-psychotherapy, minimal psychotherapy, and other hospital care.
    From "Comparative Studies of Psychotherapies: Is It True that Everyone Has Won and All Must Have Prizes?" by L. Luborsky, B. Singer, and L. Luborsky, *Archives of General Psychiatry*, 1975, *32*, 995–1008. Copyright 1975, American Medical Association. Reprinted by permission of the author and publisher.

common result was also a tie. But where there was a difference, it was in favor of behavior therapy.

The final box score, psychotherapy versus no treatment, addressed the same question considered by Bergin and with similar results. Luborsky and colleagues concluded that "the control comparative studies indicate that a high percentage of patients who go through any of these psychotherapies gain from them."

Meta-Analysis of Outcome Studies

The most ambitious of the box-score approaches (Smith & Glass, 1977) analyzed 375 reports, including both naturalistic and analogue studies, in which at least one treatment group was compared to a nontreated control group or an alternative therapy. Eight hundred thirty-three comparisons were obtained from the 375 reports.

The major dependent variable was the *effect size*, defined as the mean difference between the treated and control subjects divided by the standard deviation of the control group. The effect size was computed on whatever outcome variable the individual researchers chose to measure. The authors then looked at the effects of various independent variables—such as duration of therapy, type of therapy, and internal validity of the research design—on the magnitude of effect size.

The results were consistent with the other two box-score reports. It was concluded that "on the average the typical therapy client is better off than 75% of untreated individuals" (Smith & Glass, 1977, p. 752). Thus, all three box scores conclude that therapy does work in the sense of producing more change, on the average, than no treatment or minimal treatment. Measurements of fear and anxiety reduction were found to show the largest effect size. Measures of adjustment that "frequently involve indices of hospitalization or incarceration for psychotic, alcoholic, or criminal episodes" (p. 756) had considerably less, but still appreciable, effect sizes.

The authors also compared the effect sizes achieved by various types of therapy. These analyses were complex and involved sophisticated statistical (rather than the obviously impossible experimental) controls. Based on these analyses, the authors concluded that "the behavioral and nonbehavioral therapies show about the same effect" (p. 758). Thus, all three box-score reviews summarized here agree on two major, albeit crude, conclusions: first, that psychotherapy is superior to no or minimal treatment; and second, that in general there do not appear to be any significant differences among different types of therapy.

A very different conclusion was reached in a recent review by two influential behavior-therapy researchers (Kazdin & Wilson, 1978). These authors sharply criticized the box-score approach along the lines noted earlier in this chapter. Their own review of non-analogue outcome studies weights heavily controlled studies with strong internal validity. Kazdin and Wilson concluded that behavioral therapy has been shown to be more effective than alternative approaches for many disorders:

> Behavioral methods are demonstrably more applicable to a much larger range of human problems than verbal psychotherapy, and there is clear evidence of broad-gauged treatment effects across specific target behaviors as well as more general measures of personal, social, and vocational adjustment [1978, p. 103].

A Subjective Comparison

The evaluative criteria set forth in Chapter Four were used in considering the different psychotherapies. In conclusion, I make explicit some comparisons that were implicit in the last three chapters.

Quality of theory does not yield a clear winner. I see a small advantage for behavior therapy and view Gestalt therapy as relatively weak on this dimension.

Cost-effectiveness analysis is a very subjective business. I view psychoanalytic theory as relatively weakest on this dimension because of treatment duration, training requirements for therapists, and limited applicability to client populations. Client-centered, Gestalt, and behavior therapy are shorter and require less formal training. Behavior therapy is best in applicability to diverse and difficult client populations, such as the mentally retarded, who lack the verbal skills needed for the other approaches.

Regarding outcome, behavior therapy has an edge, because it has been shown to be relatively more effective for certain disorders.

But there is no good comparative-outcome data for the majority of clients.

My personal preference for behavior therapy stems largely from its broader applicability and its empirical emphasis. It has the potential to yield cumulative knowledge and to be self-correcting. That is, both givers and receivers can come to know what works best for which problems.

Summary

Behavior therapy attempts to apply principles of learning and social influence derived from laboratory research to the clinical situation. Behavior therapists stress the empirical evaluation of treatment progress and outcome and seek to develop specific therapeutic goals and objectives in order to facilitate the assessment of outcome. The role of environmental—especially social—variables in the maintenance and modification of deviant behavior is stressed.

In behavior therapy the procedures used depend on the specific nature of the client's problem. Therefore, *behavioral assessment* is a key initial process. Behavioral assessment seeks to sample problematic behavior as it occurs in directly relevant situations. Although behavior therapists make use of questionnaires and the clinical interview, as do other therapists, they also use unique procedures such as direct observation, role playing, simulation, and self-monitoring.

Several behavioral strategies have been developed for the treatment of anxiety and phobias. In systematic desensitization, anxiety-eliciting situations are ranked hierarchically by the client. The client is usually taught relaxation, a response incompatible with anxiety. While relaxed, the client is then exposed, in imagination, to gradually increasing anxiety-arousing situations, moving on to the next situation only when the previous one can be tolerated comfortably. *In vivo*, or real-life, desensitization involves gradual exposure to stimuli without relaxation and has been found to be a more powerful procedure than the imaginal variety.

Flooding (or implosion) is a strategy based on the principle of extinction. If a client can be induced to remain in a fearful situation long enough to experience that the unconditioned stimulus, or dreaded consequences, will not actually occur, then anxiety responses will extinguish. Flooding may be accomplished either in real life or in imagination.

In participant modeling, clients observe a model engage the feared stimulus and then are encouraged to engage it themselves, sometimes with direct coaching by the therapist. A considerable amount of research has demonstrated the effectiveness of each of these three procedures. Their relatively equivalent effectiveness suggests the existence of some common underlying process. Exposure to the feared stimulus appears to be the key element, in that exposure—whether gradual, sudden, or imaginal—permits extinction of anxiety responses.

Operant methods have been widely employed in psychotherapeutic settings and are especially useful and powerful in closed environments. A token economy is a way of bringing the principle of reinforcement to bear on the behavior of chronic mental patients. Tokens are generalized reinforcers that can be traded in for specific rewards such as privileges, candy, or whatever the patients want. They are dispensed contingently on performance of certain specified behaviors such as grooming, social interaction, or work. Token economies are demonstrably effective in changing the institutional behavior of chronic mental patients, but it is less certain that they promote better adjustment after patients leave the hospital. The implementation of token systems is constrained by recent judicial decisions concerning the rights of mental patients.

Behavioral treatment of deviant children emphasizes helping parents to consistently reinforce desirable behavior and to ignore or mildly punish unacceptable behavior. Time out, a punishment procedure in which the child is briefly removed to a socially isolated setting where he or she cannot receive any social attention, has been found useful for dealing with unacceptable behaviors such as temper tantrums.

Aversion is another behavior-therapy strategy, but is not so widely practiced as the public tends to believe. It is used primarily to reduce or eliminate serious behavioral excesses such as self-destructive behavior, drinking, smoking, or drug abuse. In aversive counterconditioning, previously attractive stimuli such as the sight of a drink come to acquire aversive properties by being paired repeatedly with an aversive event such as electric shock. In punishment, an aversive stimulus is applied contingently on the performance of some undesirable behavior in order to suppress the behavior. Concerns about possible side effects of punishment as well as humanitarian issues restrict its application and encourage the development of nonaversive treatment alternatives.

Cognitive behavior therapy is an extension of the earlier behavioral paradigm that emphasized overt responses. Mediational or cognitive processes may become the targets of intervention efforts or may be used to implement therapeutic procedures. In the self-control approach, clients administer treatment procedures to themselves in their natural environment, usually under the supervision of a therapist.

A great deal of empirical research has been conducted on the outcomes of various kinds of behavior therapy. Behavior therapy does appear to be demonstrably more effective than other therapies for certain specific problems such as anxieties or phobias, sexual deviation, and children's behavior problems. But the relative effectiveness of behavior therapy for most mental health problems remains unknown. Cost-effectiveness may be the major advantage of behavior therapies, because they require relatively less formal training, tend to be shorter in duration, and seem applicable to a wider variety of client problems.

The epilogue described some broad comparisons of the three major therapeutic approaches. The box-score approach tabulates the results of heterogeneous outcome studies to arrive at an overall relative success figure. This approach suffers from lumping together or equating studies with diverse kinds of clients and different levels of methodological rigor, but it can still yield useful information. Three major box-score analyses converge on the conclusion that psychotherapy in general tends to be more effective than no treatment and that no one kind of psychotherapy appears to be demonstrably superior.

Suggested Readings and Films

1. Bandura, A. *Social learning theory.* Englewood Cliffs, N. J.: Prentice-Hall, 1977. A concise, authoritative description of the theoretical bases of current behavior therapy.
2. Leitenberg, H. (Ed.) *Handbook of behavior modification and behavior therapy.* Englewood Cliffs, N. J.: Prentice-Hall, 1976. Critical analyses of the literature on various methods and issues in behavior therapy.
3. Goldfried, M. R., & Davison, G. C. *Clinical behavior therapy.* New York: Holt, Rinehart & Winston, 1976. A lucid, balanced description of the practice of behavior therapy.

Behavior-therapy methods tend to be structured, explicit, and relatively short. They lend themselves readily to film and tape presentation. Below are two films I have found useful.

1. *Broad spectrum behavior therapy in a group.* Arnold Lazarus, an influential behavior therapist, is featured. Illustrates several basic techniques. East Pennsylvania Psychiatric Institute; available from Pennsylvania State Psyche-Cinema Register, A/V Services, 17 Willard Building, University Park, Penn., 16802.
2. *A social learning approach to family therapy.* Oregon Research Institute. Portrays the treatment program developed by G. R. Patterson that is described in this chapter. Media Guild, P.O. Box 881, Solana Beach, Calif., 92075.

PART IV

Reality: Social, Economic, and Political Influences on Psychotherapy

Our journey is about three-fourths completed. We have examined the participants in psychotherapy, developed a framework for construing and evaluating the enterprise, and discussed in detail several of the major theories and methods. It would be possible to stop here. Viewed from the professional and scientific perspectives, psychotherapy can be analyzed in terms of theory, methods, and results. But psychotherapy is also one of the human services and, as such, is embedded in a sociopolitical context. Psychotherapy as described in textbooks and as practiced in the "real world" are often very different. This difference is due partly to inherent limitations in describing a complex process in print and partly to the variations introduced by individual practitioners. But it is also a function of factors exerted by the sociopolitical environment. Thus, it is vital that potential consumers, future professionals, and citizens be aware of these forces.

Chapter Eight deals with the organization and economics of the delivery system for psychotherapy. The pervasive role of government is noted in order to emphasize the political features of psychotherapy. Economic factors are examined because of their obvious importance to consumers and taxpayers. The effect of economic and status considerations on therapists is also discussed.

Chapter Nine takes up the regulation of psychotherapy. The practice of therapy is affected by the interplay of legal principles, professional standards and guidelines, and, more recently, consumer pressures. Ethical issues are also considered.

The final chapter considers both the limitations and future of psychotherapy. It concludes with some suggestions for how the concepts discussed in this book can be applied to your own community.

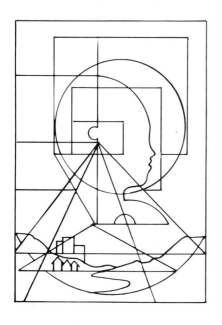

Organization and Economics of the Delivery System

This chapter is concerned with the settings in which psychotherapy takes place and the ways settings influence treatment. Among the factors affected by where psychotherapy takes place are its nature, duration, and cost. The bulk of the chapter describes the important features of public and private psychotherapy, first in community settings and then in institutional ones. Next, the coordination of community and institutional treatment is considered. The role of the National Institute of Mental Health in the psychotherapy delivery system is described. Concluding the chapter is a discussion of the third-party payment (insurance) and interprofessional conflicts.

There are two partially overlapping mental health delivery systems: *public* and *private*. The public system is made up of settings largely supported by taxes. In private settings, services are paid for largely by user fees (or by third-party payments such as health insurance). Public settings are operated by some component of the political system and so are as responsive—or unresponsive—to citizen wishes as any other political institution. Private settings are operated by one or more citizens—sometimes by a corporation or group. Thus, they are in principle less responsive to citizen wishes, but they must be responsive to the supply and demand of the marketplace. Because many essentially private settings receive some public funds and take indigent clients, it is best to think of a *public/private continuum* along which psychotherapy settings are located.

A second useful dimension with which to order therapy settings is the *institutional/community* continuum, corresponding to the inpatient/outpatient distinction in medical practice. The prototypic institutional setting is the mental hospital. The patients spend all their time there, and the institution controls most of their behavior.

Typical community settings are the office of a mental health professional in private practice or a public mental health clinic. The clients appear once or twice a week at the setting and spend the rest of the time in their natural environment. There are various settings that fall in between the two poles. For example, a partial hospitalization program may have the client spending the hours between 9 and 5 in the treatment setting and living at home the rest of the time, including weekends. Or a group home setting might be a residence in the community where clients live while working or going to school.

The two dimensions—public/private and institutional/community—yield a fourfold classification system within which any psychotherapy setting can be placed. This scheme is depicted in Figure 8–1, and some of the major settings are listed. The first section of this chapter is devoted to a description of community settings, first private ones and then public ones. The section concludes with a look at the issue of how much time community treatment requires.

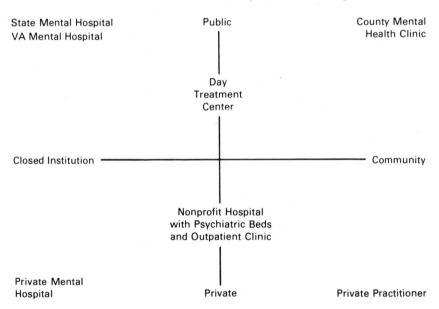

Figure 8–1. Classification system of psychotherapy settings.

Community Psychotherapy

The most common setting in which psychotherapy occurs is the office or consulting room of a mental health professional. The client and therapist schedule meetings at mutually agreed-on times and frequencies. At those times they talk and work on the client's problems. Homework assignments may be used, depending on the situation. Clients are free to terminate the therapeutic relationship at any time. Outside of therapy sessions they pursue their usual daily routine. This is the least restrictive sort of treatment and is usually the preferred mode unless the client is sufficiently disturbed or dangerous to self or others that an institutional setting is required. Office psychotherapy may involve an individual, a family, or a group. The frequency and duration of sessions vary widely, depending on the therapeutic approach, the client's problems, and financial circumstances.

Private Practice

In the private sector, the therapist's income is derived directly from client fees. The "business" model is much like that of the physician, lawyer, barber, or accountant. The fee income must cover the costs of doing business—office rental, secretarial help, liability insurance, and the like—and provide a salary for the practitioner. Fees vary widely, both between and within professions. In general, psychiatrists charge the most and psychiatric social workers the least, with psychologists falling in between. Paraprofessional therapists tend to charge relatively low fees.

These trends are illustrated by a survey of psychotherapists in the Washington, D. C., area in mid-1974. The average fee per hour for psychiatrists was $39; for psychologists, $34; and for psychiatric social workers, $26 (Adams & Orgel, 1975). These figures reflect the current relative differences among the professions but would be higher now because of inflation. Psychiatric time may sell for $50 to $75 a (50-minute) hour, and psychologists may charge from $30 to $60. Fees vary from place to place, tending to correlate with the general cost of living.

Do these fees seem high? Would someone have to be a little crazy to pay $75 for a 50-minute conversation? Many people are jarred by the cost of psychotherapy, but the hourly rates are not high in comparison with those in other professions. The fact is that in our free-enterprise society professional time is very expensive. The rates for physicians, lawyers, accountants, plumbers, and auto mechanics are also high. An office visit to a physician (general practitioner) costs $12 to $16, not counting any medicine or laboratory tests. The next time you consult a physician, time the length of your interaction with the doctor. Office visits usually involve 5 or 10 minutes of the physician's time. Thus, a physician's time costs about $60 to $100 an hour, and most specialists charge even more. A lawyer's time is similarly expensive, and many lawyers charge for telephone conversations and time spent preparing letters and documents and conferring with other attorneys. Psychotherapists generally charge only for direct conversation time. It is only when therapy must involve many hours of treatment that its costliness is accentuated. Psychoanalysis is very expensive, because it involves so many sessions, but remember that an analyst cannot see very many clients.

The private practice of psychotherapy is partly regulated by law, and the issues involved are discussed in Chapter Nine. Psychiatrists are the therapists most frequently found in private practice, followed by psychologists and social workers. Paraprofessionals are also entering the private marketplace by offering programs labeled educational or growth enhancing, thereby avoiding regulatory mechanisms that apply to psychotherapy.

Private practitioners are vulnerable to market economics. They are very much business people and must consider economic issues in their professional activities. Setting up a private practice is a delicate, costly, and risky affair. Most psychotherapists do it gradually, often starting with an agency position, developing a part-time practice, and then taking the plunge on a full-time basis. A junior psychiatrist, or at least one new to a community, often enters as the associate or junior partner of a psychiatrist with an established practice and in this way has the assurance of a case load and supporting services.

Consider the various details to be taken care of in setting up a private practice, especially for someone trained in the major professions. First, one must satisfy state requirements concerning certification or licensing. Suitable office furniture and secretarial services must be arranged. Provision must be made for dealing with emergencies such as the necessity of hospitalizing a suicidal or acutely upset client. Only then can one open the doors, send out cards announcing the opening of a practice, and wait for the clients to start streaming in.

But where will they come from? A professional therapist is constrained from active advertising (probable changes in reducing restrictions on professionals' advertising are discussed in Chapter Nine). Therefore, it is necessary to "make contacts" who refer appropriate clients. Contacts include fellow members of one's immediate profession as well as other psychotherapists who have a similar approach to clients. The new practitioner is also likely to touch base with various public agencies who might refer clients. Most agencies try to refer persons who seem to be able to afford private care to an appropriate practitioner. Depending on the nature of the practice, certain personnel outside the field of mental health may be contacted: school administrators, if the practitioner works with children; attorneys, if one does marriage counseling; or gynecologists if one does sex counseling. Finally, the new practitioner may offer to speak at various meetings of professional and business groups, such as the Rotarians. All of this takes a good deal of time, and a practice may develop slowly. Word-of-mouth recommendations from satisfied clients are a most important way of building a practice.

In contrast with the agency therapist, the private practitioner is directly dependent on clients' remaining in treatment and paying their bills. Judgments about whether psychotherapy is appropriate for a given client and when treatment should be ended may be influenced by this consideration. The practitioner is also understandably concerned about the "competition"—that is, other psychotherapists. Their number, fees, and advertising practices are of direct concern. Physicians have a concept of how many practitioners in any specialty—cardiology, pediatrics, psychiatry—a community can support and may discourage a young psychiatrist from settling. Many established professionals are concerned about the influx of paraprofessionals into private practice. The services of paraprofessionals are often very much like conventional psychotherapy. And they often cost a lot less.

Public Settings

In the public sector the client pays the agency or institution, which in turn pays the psychotherapist a fixed salary. Publicly supported mental health clinics provide psychotherapeutic services for those who cannot afford private fees. The fees at public clinics are based on ability to pay—what is often termed a sliding scale. The range is typically from no fee up to $20 per session. It is assumed that, if clients can pay more than $20, they can find services in the private sector. A typical fee schedule considers gross income and number of financial dependents. For example, a client earning $1,000 a month with three dependents would pay $11 a visit; the same client with no dependents would pay $17.

Because the fees do not support the operation of public clinics, tax monies must also be used. These may come from the city, county, state, or federal government, or from some combination of them. The number, size, and range of services provided by public clinics is determined by the political process. The mental health system competes for public funds with various other governmental services. As funds expand or shrink, so does the availability of psychotherapeutic services.

For example, an agency with a heavy case load and associated waiting list may choose to change some of its policies. It may change selection criteria and devote more resources to initial screening and evaluation to make sure that appropriate clients are referred elsewhere. Or it may require monitoring and review of any clients seen beyond a specified number of sessions to try to discourage prolonged treatment. Programs may be dropped because funds, and therefore staff, are no longer available. Educational and preventive programs are likely to be dropped first in favor of retaining direct services to the seriously disturbed. Although this kind of decision makes sense on humanitarian and political grounds, the long-range effects may be quite unfortunate, in that an opportunity for reducing the flow of mental disorders is lost.

Psychotherapists serving public clinics are the usual "big three," but the mix is different than it is in the private sector. There are relatively fewer psychiatrists and many more psychiatric social workers. There are also likely to be fewer Ph.D.-level psychologists and more staff members with master's degrees in clinical or counseling psychology. Further, some of the staff are likely to be paraprofessionals, in the sense of having had little formal academic training. The reasons for this mix are largely economic. Salaries in public settings are directly proportional to level of education, and psychiatrist time is the most expensive of all. In Chapter Two it was emphasized that mental health professionals all have skills and interest in psychotherapy as well as having unique professional expertise. Psychiatric expertise lies in the use of medication, and so clinics tend to use physicians for this purpose. Because lesser-paid professionals are also skilled in therapeutic conversation, it is economical to use them for this purpose in lieu of higher-priced psychiatrists and Ph.D. psychologists.

Economic and status considerations also operate on the psychotherapists themselves. Psychiatrists and psychologists often prefer the greater professional flexibility and income potential of private practice and so are not attracted to public clinics and hospitals. As noted in Chapter Two, many psychiatrists prefer psychotherapy to chemotherapy and for that reason are not comfortable with the roles often assigned to them in public clinics.

Agency psychotherapists usually earn less than their counterparts in private practice. But the agency setting provides a number of protections and fringe benefits. The agency provides backup coverage for crises or emergencies. It also provides legal protection that a private practitioner must purchase, sometimes at considerable expense. The agency provides an administrative structure and provision for supervision and consultation. Agency therapists continue to receive their paycheck during vacations or when they are sick or attending workshops or meetings. Job security is also fairly good, because local, state, or federal employees usually have a kind of tenure and cannot easily be discharged.

The agency psychotherapist is assured of regular working hours, although occasional evening or weekend time may be expected. An important psychological as well as economic consideration is that the agency therapist receives the same salary whether or not a client keeps or cancels an appointment or pays the bills. Nor does the agency therapist have to "solicit" or arrange for referrals.

There are also, of course, costs connected with being a psychotherapist in an agency support system. Salaries may be low, and there is a ceiling on earning capacity. The psychotherapist must abide by organizational rules and policies and has less freedom in how time is allocated. Organizations often tend to encourage conformity and discourage innovation and change. In sum, the issues are very much those facing people in business or other professions who must choose between salaried organizational positions and independent practice.

Does the fact that public-sector psychotherapists tend to have less formal training than private therapists mean that the quality of treatment is lower for the less affluent? This is a provocative question for which there is no definite answer. Formal training is not demonstrably related to therapeutic effectiveness. Most professionals would give more weight to experience, and many public psychotherapists have accumulated a great deal of it. But it is uncomfortable having two sets of standards for providers of psychotherapeutic services— one for the private sector and one for the public sector. The issue posed is really the same one that confronts all of health care. Critics of the current system believe that there is a difference in standard of care for the rich and the poor. Proposals for national health insurance represent one means of remedying the alleged deficiencies.

There are many kinds of public psychotherapy agencies. Below, the most frequent forms are outlined.

Mental health clinics. Perhaps the most numerous of settings, mental health clinics are usually financed by and politically responsive to local government (though they often receive some federal money as well). The staff is usually composed of psychologists and social workers, with some psychiatric support. Paraprofessional therapists are also usually employed. Because of their public financing and political support, local mental health clinics are obliged to treat all citizens who apply and who cannot otherwise obtain services.

Juvenile department. In most communities, adolescent behavior problems such as vandalism, theft, alcohol and drug abuse, and truancy are handled by a Juvenile Department, which is administratively part of the criminal justice system rather than the mental health system. Some of the work of a juvenile department involves counseling and psychotherapy services for adolescents and their families. The services are usually delivered by M.A.-level staff members trained in psychology, counseling, or social work, often with special emphasis in work with adolescents, family therapy, or corrections.

Public schools. Children and youth—and often their families—may receive therapeutic help from school counselors or psychologists. The focus is on learning or behavioral problems. The school counselor may work indirectly through the classroom teacher, see the child, bring the parents into the helping arena, or use some combination of these tactics. Such services are free and are part of the school's operating budget. School counselors are usually backed by psychiatric or other consultation and often refer families to the mental health system if more intensive intervention seems needed.

College and university counseling services. Campus agencies provide varied counseling services to students and, sometimes, to faculty and supporting staff as well. Although often thought of as settings for only vocational or academic counseling, college counseling centers provide a good deal of personal counseling that is indistinguishable from psychotherapy. They are staffed primarily by psychologists trained in clinical or counseling (with medical consultation as needed), and services are usually free. For those eligible, counseling centers provide about the best psychotherapy bargain available.

University-sponsored training clinics. Many university doctoral programs in clinical and counseling psychology operate clinics open to both students and community people. These clinics are typically staffed by graduate students under the supervision of clinical or counseling faculty members.

Church-sponsored programs. In many communities, churches sponsor counseling services for citizens of any denomination. The counselors/therapists may be clergy or professionals. Such clinics are usually supported by a combination of user fees, charitable donations, and church money.

Special-population clinics. In larger communities there are services for people with particular kinds of problems. For example, there may be treatment services for alcoholics and their families, the obese, handicapped children (both physical and mental) and their families, unmarried mothers, or the aged. Often these programs are staffed by paraprofessionals, especially indigenous paraprofessionals. This is especially likely to be true of programs for alcoholics.

Outpatient clinics associated with hospitals. Medical schools, Veterans Administration hospitals, and state hospitals usually have associated outpatient clinics that provide low-cost service. The clinics serve both patients who have been hospitalized and are returning to the community and those whose problems are not serious enough to require institutional care. Service is provided primarily by professional therapists and trainees in the major professions.

These are but a partial listing of community offerings in psychotherapy. It is important to remember that psychotherapeutic services are not evenly distributed across the nation. Rural areas, smaller communities in the South and Midwest, and even urban ghettos may have few or no programs. But if you live in an urban area, even a small one, a convenient way to survey resources is to "let your fingers do the walking"—that is, consult the yellow pages of your phone book. Look under several headings, including Physicians, Psychologists, Marriage and Family Counseling, Alcohol, and Social Service Organizations. I think you will be surprised at how many listings there are. You should get a good cross-section of the kinds of psychotherapeutic services offered and the professional credentials of the providers.

Length of Treatment

The last issue to be considered for community therapy is the amount of treatment time. This issue is important for both theoretical and practical reasons. Theories of psychotherapy posit some desirable period needed for their treatment to exert its effects. The time period ranges from the 500 or more sessions for formal psychoanalysis to much shorter treatment using other approaches. Humanistic and behavior therapies are not as explicit about treatment length as is psychoanalysis, but inspection of their writings indicates that 10 to 50 sessions is fairly standard. The case examples in Chapters Five through Seven all fall within this range.

From an economic and practical perspective, treatment time is the major cost factor. In the private sector the client may be paying out of pocket for each session, and in public clinics the client and taxpayer are sharing costs. To the extent that psychotherapy services are in short supply, the more time given to Client A, the less time is available for other needy clients. The same principles apply if insurance covers part or all of treatment costs. Taxpayers and consumers are paying either directly or indirectly.

Data are available on the duration of community psychotherapy. As expected, the number of sessions is quite variable. Many clients are seen but once. A crisis or intense problem motivates them to seek help. The one session, perhaps in combination with situational factors, leads to a reduction of the seriousness of the problem, and the client feels no reason to return. Other clients may be seen periodically over many years. For example, some chronic mental patients may check in with their local mental health clinic once or twice a month for several years. The visits may be short and consist of a review of their medication and short, friendly discussion of their social adjustment.

Data are available on the number of sessions of therapy in several settings, though much of it is fairly old. In the early 1960s the median number of visits to a private psychiatrist was 4.7. There was surprisingly little variation as a function of sex—men made 4.6 visits and women, 4.8—or family income—4.1 visits for families making under $2000 a year and 5.4 for families making more than $10,000 (National Center for Health Statistics, 1966). However, patients seen by psychoanalysts tend to have many more sessions. Marmor (1975) reported that patients in psychoanalysis had a median of nearly 150 visits annually, nonanalytic patients of psychoanalysts had a median of nearly 40 sessions a year, and patients of general psychiatrists had a median of about 16 sessions a year. The patients in psychoanalysis tended to occupy professional and high-level managerial positions; those seen by general psychiatrists did not. It appears that psychoanalysts are successful in choosing or attracting patients who are willing and able to pursue extended treatment. The 16 sessions for Marmor's (1975) "generalists" is much higher than the 5 sessions reported in the survey data from the early 1960s. This discrepancy may be due to sample differences or to different criteria for counting cases. Marmor may not have counted one-visit consultations.

In contrast, the data from the public sector indicate that psychotherapy is concluded or ended in relatively few sessions; it is much briefer than would be expected on the basis of clinical theory. Garfield (1978) summarized data from a number of Veterans Administration and other hospital-affiliated clinics between 1948 and 1970. The median number of psychotherapy interviews ranged from 3 to 12 but clustered around 6. I suspect that the values at comparable clinics today would be no higher, and possibly lower. Psychoanalytic thinking is less pervasive today, so there is less impetus for longer treatment. The question arises of how much of standard psychoanalytic, humanistic, or behavioral therapy a practitioner can implement in just five hours. Probably not very much. In nearly all the clinics surveyed by Garfield, brevity was viewed as a problem and was not intentional. In most instances, for example, the client failed to return for a scheduled appointment.

We do not know why so many clients terminate prematurely. It is probably a combination of their attitudes toward therapy and their therapist, their subjective discomfort, and the financial costs. The attitudes and behavior of the therapist undoubtedly play a part. Whatever the reasons, it appears necessary for psychotherapy to adapt to reality. Brief therapy is now often considered a valid form of help by itself rather than a second-best offering or a sign of failure. In brief therapy, time limits are often set in advance, the therapist is more active, and there is a concerted effort to achieve just one or two major treatment goals within the allotted number of sessions (for example, see Butcher & Koss, 1978).

Institutional Treatment

We turn now to hospital treatment, first in public institutions and second in private hospitals. Then, some of the key features of mental hospitals and some controversial issues will be considered.

Public Mental Institutions

There are two major systems of public mental institutions, those operated by individual states and those operated by the Veterans Administration of the federal government. They share many institutional and organizational characteristics but also have some important differences. I will first consider VA hospitals briefly and then focus in more depth on state hospitals.

VA Medical Centers

The Veterans Administration maintains a system of general and psychiatric hospitals and clinics that provides treatment to veterans with both service-connected and non-service-connected illnesses or disabilities. Services are also offered to dependents and orphans of veterans. Family or marital outpatient counseling, which includes the spouse and children of a veteran, can be provided. Any veteran with an honorable discharge is eligible for *free* treatment services at VA hospitals, but veterans with a service-connected problem have priority for hospital beds or outpatient treatment.

There are 172 VA facilities, including inpatient psychiatric facilities and outpatient mental hygiene clinics. The VA employs approximately 1400 doctoral-level psychologists. It is also actively involved in training mental health professionals. There are 132 VA facilities with psychology training programs (Moore, 1979).

The VA is a partly centralized system, with major policy decisions made in Washington and then disseminated to the various hospitals. This makes for more uniformity of facilities, programs, salaries, patient/staff ratios, and quality of care compared with state hospitals, which vary hugely. Each hospital has much operational flexibility, however, especially at the level of ward treatment programs.

The VA programs are financially dependent on Congressional and administration decisions about the federal budget. Because veterans are both numerous and reasonably well organized, they constitute a potent political force, and VA hospitals tend to be reasonably well funded. Hospitals can be compared on how much is spent per patient per day. This is a rough index of the resources allocated. For VA psychiatric facilities the daily cost per patient in 1976 was about $64 (U.S. Veteran's Administration, 1976). For state hospitals, by rough comparison, the average spending in 1974 was about $33 (U.S. Department of Commerce, 1976).

The VA's programs have shifted in recent years to reflect changes in the patient population and new thinking about treatment strategies. Drug abuse, including alcoholism, has become a major problem for veterans since the Vietnam war. Treatment programs for drug disorders now have high priority in VA medical centers. The VA is also moving away from an emphasis on hospital care toward community care. It now serves over 5 million outpatients a year.

The fact that psychiatric treatment is free for veterans makes it very accessible but also subject to abuse. Hospitalization may provide convenient free room and board for someone who is having difficulty getting on in the community.

This problem is aggravated by the fact that many veterans with service-connected psychiatric disorders draw disability benefits from the government; the amount depends on their rated degree of disability. Thus, a hospitalized veteran can receive free care and also draw disability payments of up to $700 a month. Recovery from a psychiatric disorder can mean a reduction in or even elimination of disability payments. Thus, a veteran may be tangibly reinforced for staying in the hospital and remaining "sick." Motivation for constructive change among VA patients continues to be a significant problem.

State Mental Hospitals

State hospitals play a pivotal role in the mental health delivery system, because they interact with local mental health clinics. Community clinics and state hospitals are linked together both functionally and financially. The financial link is that both are funded by the state government. In Oregon, for example, the state and county governments share equally the cost of the community clinics; the state finances the mental hospitals. More importantly, the two are components in a *system*. The specifics of the system vary from state to state, but the goal is to provide continuity of care for citizens as they pass, or sometimes shuttle, from clinic to hospital and back again. The mental health system aims at keeping the individual in the community. If the individual's functioning is severely impaired or the communities' resources are inadequate, however, institutional treatment may be needed. The state hospital may be the only available institution or the one of choice. There may be a private hospital or a public local one available for emergency or short-term care. If lengthy hospitalization proves necessary, then again the state hospital becomes the last resort.

In 1975 there were 313 state and county mental hospitals in the United States, and they cared for about 435,000 patients (U.S. Department of Commerce, 1976). The patients in state mental hospitals tend to be older and less affluent than those in private hospitals (or the general population). State hospitals vary widely in facilities, quality of personnel, and financing. The average cost per day per patient was $33 in 1974, but the range is considerable (U.S. Department of Commerce, 1976).

Contrary to popular belief, state mental hospitals do charge for services if patients, families, or insurance companies can pay. The rates, however, are much less than those in private mental hospitals or in general hospitals with psychiatric beds.

State mental hospitals employ surprisingly few psychiatrists, in large part because American psychiatrists do not prefer this employment setting. Instead, there are many physicians who care for the medical problems of the patients and also perform an array of the duties normally done by psychiatrists, including prescribing psychotropic medication. About 50% of staff physicans in state mental hospitals are foreign medical graduates (Brown, 1977). Many of these doctors are unable to compete for positions elsewhere because of limited English-speaking ability. They are often most comfortable with nontalking therapies.

Private Mental Institutions

Just as public mental hospitals interact with community clinics —and together make up a system—private hospitals interact primarily with the private community sector. Private physicians, especially psychiatrists, serve as the screening and referral agents to private hospitals. A psychiatrist's patient might "decompensate" and require hospital care. Or a family physician might become alarmed at the behavior of a patient and seek a consultation from a psychiatrist colleague; a joint decision to recommend hospitalization might then be made. After leaving the hospital, the patient reverts to the care of the referring physician or psychiatrist.

Why a private mental hospital rather than a public one? This is a complex questio and depends in large part on circumstances that vary greatly. To simplify, the two major considerations are the financial and social status of the patient and the availability of hospital programs. Many communities, especially urban ones, have their own psychiatric beds available in general hospitals for short-term or crisis hospitalization. In fact, such facilities usually accommodate both private and public patients—they are at the very interface between the public and private systems. A private patient pays his or her own bills, sometimes through insurance. A public or indigent patient's bill is paid by the county or state. But some communities do not have *any* hospital beds, and many have medical beds but no psychiatric beds. Further, it may be apparent that longer hospitalization is going to be needed. A private hospital may then be appropriate if a combination of insurance and the patient's own resources can cover the costs. Private hospitals offer more individualized and more intensive treatment and may be preferred for these reasons.

Private mental hospitals do cost more than public ones. This is partly because they provide better facilities and services but mostly because they are not supported by public monies and must be self-supporting. That is, their income must meet their expenses. Part of their income may come from public funds, as when the state or county pays for the treatment of an indigent patient.

Three kinds of private mental hospitals will be noted: psychiatric units in private hospitals, usually located in urban areas; hospitals specializing in psychiatric care only; and "specialty" hospitals, which treat only one or a few disorders. Institutions that treat problems related to alcohol abuse are the most common example of the latter.

Psychiatric beds in general hospitals. In 1973 it was estimated that nearly 700 general hospitals provided some psychiatric services. These hospitals were estimated to have discharged about 467,000 patients (U.S. Department of Commerce, 1976). Mostly, they provide emergency or very short hospitalization for persons in acute distress. Often the general hospital cooperates with the local community clinic or mental health center in providing backup emergency services. Because of the short, emergency nature of the hospitalization, psychotherapeutic interventions are usually minimal. Removal from environmental stresses, medication, and the supportive control of a hospital situation are usually sufficient to alleviate the crisis and make the patient amenable to outpatient treatment or longer hospitalization elsewhere. Costs are high for psychiatric service in a general hospital. Such hospitals have a basic charge for the bed—the same charge as for any medical patient—plus medication and any special nursing or medical care.

Private mental hospitals. In 1974 there were 180 private mental hospitals, and they accounted for nearly 120,000 episodes of patient care (U.S. Department of Commerce, 1976). But the resident population was much smaller, approximately 12,000, indicating a high rate of turnover and relatively short hospital stays. The emphasis in these hospitals is on relieving stresses and working through a patient's problems to the point that community therapy becomes feasible.

A few private hospitals provide fairly long-term psychoanalytic treatment. The Menninger Clinic (whose psychotherapy research project was described in Chapter Five) in Topeka, Kansas; Austin Riggs in Stockbridge, Massachusetts; and Chestnut Lodge in Rockville, Maryland, are three well-known examples. The latter hospital is commonly believed to be the setting for *I Never Promised You a Rose Garden* (Green, 1964), a book describing the intensive treatment of a severely disturbed adolescent girl. Private hospitals often provide better physical facilities and more staff per patient than public hospitals but are usually very much more expensive. They provide another important service that affluent patients are sometimes willing to pay for: they offer more privacy and confidentiality. Patients can arrange for treatment in a private hospital far away from their home community so as to prevent friends and colleagues from knowing of their illness.

Specialty hospitals. Some private institutions deal only with a particular kind of disorder. Treatment facilities for alcoholics or problem drinkers are the most common example. Detoxifying a heavy drinker and then helping the person to renounce and then learn to live without alcohol are viewed as requiring special facilities and personnel. For similar reasons, many public institutions have separate wards and programs for alcoholics. Private hospitals vary greatly in their approach to alcoholics. Some may rely heavily on aversion therapy and medication; others rely strictly on psychological and educational methods. Usually the counselors and many other staff members are themselves former alcoholics or problem drinkers. Personal experience with drug addiction is often argued to be critical for those who want to help addicts, and nonabusers are sometimes disqualified as therapists.

The Social Psychology of the Mental Hospital

My discussion of institutional treatment has thus far emphasized its large-scale political and economic aspects. But the large mental hospital is also a special environment that can have profound effects not only on patients but also on those who work there. Patients are cut off from their usual contacts and sources of support. They are influenced not only by the activities designated as "therapeutic" but also by the entire social structure and routine of the institution. It is appropriate, therefore, to briefly consider the nature, organization, and psychological characteristics of the mental hospital.

Mental hospitals have remained a controversial social institution. Society was first admonished and persuaded to build them on humanitarian grounds (Bockoven, 1972); it is now urged to dismantle them for the same reasons. Both positions were probably correct. In the late 19th century, mental hospitals were probably a more helpful and humane alternative than jails or almshouses. In the middle of the 20th century, considering what mental hospitals have become and the availability of other treatment alternatives, phasing them down if not out seems to be a rational strategy.

Most mental hospitals were located and built when it was believed best to isolate the mentally ill from the normal population. Today, we believe it best to maintain the mental patient's ties with the community. Along with the development of effective psychoactive drugs, this goal has led to a dramatic reduction in the number of patients in state hospitals, but it appears likely that there will continue to be a need for some patients to be hospitalized, perhaps for long periods of time.

Given their existence and the likelihood that they will survive—though in reduced numbers and size—much attention has been given to the organization and management of mental hospitals.

Size and Organization

One simple but important management issue in mental hospitals is their size. Economic considerations helped promote the development of large institutions. Although size saves dollars, it has been found to be less desirable from the standpoint of effective treatment (Ullman, 1967). A system of a few large hospitals, rather than a

number of smaller ones, means that patients will probably be farther
removed from their communities. This separation makes it more difficult for patients to retain contacts with families and friends and
harder for them to coordinate the transition from hospital back to
community. Larger institutions have other undesirable features as
well. They tend to acquire more bureaucratic baggage, to be less
flexible in approach, and to foster dehumanization and alienation
among both patients and staff.

The organization and administration of a mental hospital is a
matter of considerable controversy. The traditional mental hospital
is organized in a way that reflects the view that mental illness is
analogous to medical illness (Ellsworth, 1968; Frank, 1973). The organization is similar to that of a general hospital, with medical staff
at the top of the pyramid, other core mental health professionals in
the middle, and aides or attendants at the bottom. Patients are implicitly assumed to be irresponsible and are expected to comply with
treatment regimes determined by professional staff members. Communication with the staff is minimal and well controlled. Aides and
attendants, who have the most contact with patients, have little perceived or real responsibility in treatment and tend to perform their
duties in a perfunctory fashion. This description still applies to many
large mental hospitals today.

There is certain efficiency in this arrangement, in large part
because it is the way most professionals have been trained to operate.
But it tends to foster passivity and helplessness in patients. Together
with the restricting effects of a closed environment, it tends to promote apathy and the expectation of failure. In those hospitals where
lower-ranking staff have little status and role in treatment planning
or implementation, they tend to avoid patient contact. In either case,
staff members respond to the more attractive newly admitted patients, who seem likely to benefit from treatment, and tend to ignore
the more chronic, less attractive ones.

Alternatives to Traditional Mental Hospital Methods

Viewing mental illness as a "social breakdown" in response to
stress and therefore as curable or at least treatable by psychosocial
means (and this does not preclude an important role for medication)
can lead to a different organization. There are several variations. The
therapeutic community has been defined as the "extensive use of
groups of patients, patients and staff, and staff alone, to create
therapeutic group standards and to provide therapeutic experiences
for the patients as individuals" (Frank, 1973, p. 301). The group meetings open up communication patterns and also diffuse responsibility
for decision making among all levels of staff as well as the patients
themselves. Under such an arrangement, for example, a decision
about whether a particular patient is ready for a weekend pass may

rest with the patient group on the ward, with a staff member serving as consultant.

Milieu therapy is another term to describe a similar approach to the hospital care of the mental patient. Milieu therapy is not clearly defined but is "characterized by increased social interaction and group activities, expectancies and group pressure directed toward normal functioning, more informal patient status, goal-directed communication, freedom of movement, and treatment of patients as responsible people rather than custodial 'cases'" (Paul & Lentz, 1977, p. 7).

Essential to the therapeutic-community and milieu approaches is the shift in focus of treatment away from drugs or specific therapeutic conversations with professionals to the overall psychosocial environment created in the hospital. The basic conception is plausible and appears to be effective in many settings (Bockoven, 1972). It can also be abused or used as a rationalization for whatever activities a hospital happens to have going. Consider a more cynical description of milieu therapy offered by a sharp critic of mental hospitals:

> Technically, milieu therapy means "the making of definite and usually substantial changes in the person's immediate environment or life circumstances." In practice this "substantial change" is effected by clapping the patient in a mental hospital. The everyday ward routine is then defined as a "therapeutic environment" and poof! one need not treat the patient at all! The *milieu* treats him! If he does not seem better, just wait; treatment goes on day and night. What might appear to the lay person to be a vegetative existence is, in fact, a treatment. The same is true of unpaid labor. Anything that happens to the patient is, of course, a part of his milieu and is thus defined as treatment [Reinehr, 1975, p. 59].

Similar assumptions of patient responsibility and democratic organizational structure obtain when a token-economy program, as described in Chapter Seven, is employed. Token systems need active cooperation from all levels of staff, thus requiring a good deal of communication and interdependence.

What Happens in Mental Hospitals?

The foregoing discussion brings us to an issue that you have no doubt been puzzling over: what is the nature of treatment in the typical mental hospital? There are some important common treatment practices in most mental hospitals, whether state or federally financed or privately run. In Chapter Seven it was noted that there is little overt "crazy" behavior in evidence and that a major problem is patient apathy and inertia. One observer described a mental hospital ward thusly: "One absorbs the heavy atmosphere of hundreds of people doing nothing and showing interest in nothing. Endless lines of people sit on benches along the walls" (Bockoven, 1972, p 2). An important reason for this inactivity is that most patients are receiving some form of medication, often one of the phenothiazines, which are used for seriously disturbed persons. The drugs suppress psychotic symptoms, help keep patients in touch with reality, and let them interact rationally with one another and with the staff. But a side effect of many drugs is that they have a sedating effect and reduce activity level.

Besides the prevalence of drugs, another common feature is the relative absence of individual psychotherapy. In fact, institutional psychotherapy is probably a misnomer. Most of the public's ideas about mental hospitals come from books (*I Never Promised You a Rose Garden*, Green, 1964) and movies (*One Flew over the Cuckoo's Nest*). *Rose Garden* describes intensive individual therapy taking place against a context of hospital routine. The heroine received long-term psychoanalytic therapy while hospitalized. It is important to realize that, while fairly accurate, the *Rose Garden* situation is highly unusual and characteristic of only a very few private hospitals. It has been estimated that the treatment described in *Rose Garden* would now cost over $100,000 (Park & Shapiro, 1976). In most public mental hospitals there is little, if any, individual therapy; in fact, there is very little one-to-one conversation with professional staff members.

What does treatment consist of, then, in the mental hospital? There is a large common-process component, as discussed in Chapter Four. A hospital is the essence of a treatment setting, and sanctioned healers are everywhere to be seen (although difficult to talk with). There are therapeutic rituals and routines, in that nearly all that goes on is defined as therapeutic. The hospital also offers removal and relief from the stresses of life, and this often has important short-term effects (Frank, 1973).

As was noted, medication is one important feature. Group therapy or group meetings are another widely used method. Groups may focus on the individual problems of the members or ward management issues—such as when the television should be on and how passes can be obtained—or some combination of both. There is sometimes occupational or recreational activity that has some therapeutic intent. That is, these activities provide the patients with an opportunity to learn job or leisure skills and learn to interact with others in doing cooperative or interdependent tasks. The density of planned activities varies greatly and is partly dependent on the size of the institution and the resources allocated for staff and facilities. In many hospitals the patients may spend a good deal of time wandering around, watching television, talking, playing cards, or just sitting.

Some mental hospitals employ token economies (described in Chapter Seven) or related programs, in which privileges and movement toward discharge are contingent on satisfactory behavior on the ward and at occupational and social tasks. Such programs are also based on the ability of patients to assume responsibility and on the likelihood of their recovery.

The Psychological Climate of Mental Hospitals

Thus far, the focus has been on the physical description of the mental hospital. What of the psychological climate, especially as perceived by the patient? There may be marked differences between a hospital's stated program and the way it is carried out. Institutionalization, even when sought voluntarily, involves considerable reduction of personal freedom and choice. There are set times to go to bed, to get up, to eat meals, to take medicine, to attend various programs and activities. Even though most mental hospitals are "open" in the sense that doors and gates are not locked, there is still restriction of movement and activity. Such regimentation often combines with the structure of the hospital and the attitudes and behavior of staff to produce strong feelings of powerlessness and depersonalization in patients (Rosenhan, 1973). Powerlessness arises from the restriction of freedom noted above. Depersonalization derives from being treated as different from a normal person and from staff members reacting to patients in a stereotypical way rather than as individuals. These issues have been the subject of much study. Below, I present two influential reports. One is a participant-observation study by Rosenhan (1973); the second is a quantitative approach to the problem by Moos (1974) and his colleagues.

The Rosenhan study. The essence of the Rosenhan (1973) paper and most of the controversy it engendered concerned the nature of sanity and the ability of professionals to distinguish the sane from the insane. However, the report also contained much fascinating material on what happens between patients and staff in mental hospitals, and these data illuminate the workings of mental hospitals. In Rosenhan's study eight sane (normal) persons gained secret admission—posing as patients—to 12 different mental hospitals. A representative sample of institutions was sought. They were located in five different states on the East and West coasts, and they varied in age and staff/patient ratios. Only one was a strictly private hospital, the rest being supported by state or federal funds or, in one instance, by university funds. The pseudopatients were hospitalized from 7 to 52 days, with an average of 19 days. While in the hospital they took careful notes on their experiences, and it is these that form the basis of Rosenhan's study (he was also one of the pseudopatients).

The pseudopatients were given nearly 2100 pills, an average of about 9 pills per patient per day, attesting to the heavy use of medication. The pseudopatients did not take theirs but instead dumped them in the toilet. Rosenhan wrote that other patients also did this frequently, but his observers kept no systematic records on this behavior.

Much information was collected on the activities of staff members and on patient/staff interaction. First, it is useful to get a picture of the way in which a mental hospital ward is set up.

> Staff and patients are strictly segregated. Staff have their own living space, including their dining facilities, bathrooms, and assembly places. The glassed quarters that contain the professional staff, which the pseudopatients came to call "the cage," sit out on every dayroom. The staff emerge primarily for caretaking purposes—to give medication, to conduct a therapy or group meeting, to instruct or reprimand a patient [Rosenhan, 1973, p. 254].

So striking was this pattern that Rosenhan used "time out of the staff cage" as the operational measure of staff/patient interaction. Attendants (aides) averaged 11.3% of their time out of the cage, including direct supervision of patient activity. "It was the relatively rare attendants who spent time talking with patients or playing games with them." Because nurses spent so little time out of the cage, the observers simply counted the frequency of emergence: an average of 11.5 instances per shift for day-shift nurses, less for other shifts. Physicians, especially psychiatrists, were even less available, and it was difficult to get reliable data on them. It was estimated that physicians emerged on the ward an average of 6.7 times per day. Psychologists and social workers are not mentioned in Rosenhan's report, indicating that they were not a significant presence for the patients of these institutions.

Rosenhan's pseudopatients also conducted a study of staff response to reasonable patient-initiated contact. In four hospitals a staff member was approached in the following standardized way: "Pardon me, Mr. (or Dr. or Ms.) X, could you tell me when I will be eligible for grounds privileges?" or with some equivalent, appropriate request. It was always a courteous and relevant request for information. The reaction of the staff member was then recorded and later coded. The results for physicians and for nurses and attendants were quite similar and consistent: either no response at all or a brief response while on the move, with head averted and with no eye contact. Over 75% of the questions were met with this kind of avoidant response:

> The encounter frequently took the following bizarre form: (Pseudopatient) "Pardon me, Dr. X, could you tell me when I am eligible for grounds privileges?" (Physician) "Good morning, Dave. How are you today?" (moves off without waiting for a response) [p. 225].

Rosenhan believes that interpersonal encounters of this sort contribute to feelings of depersonalization in patients, who come to learn that they are not treated as individuals.

The Moos studies. Moos (1974) has sought to quantify the social climates of mental hospital wards as perceived both by patients and staff. Both patients and staff were asked to respond true or false to a series of statements about ward activities. Some examples: this is a lively ward; nurses have very little time to encourage patients; patients here are encouraged to be independent; there is very little emphasis on what patients will be doing after they leave (Moos, 1974, Appendix A). Such items form the Ward Atmosphere Scale (WAS), which has 10 subscales. The scales are listed and briefly described in Table 8–1.

The relationship dimensions assess the involvement of patients in ward programs, the perceived supportiveness of patients and staff members toward one another, and the extent to which openness and spontaneity are encouraged. Treatment-program dimensions focus on issues that are believed to be important for rehabilitation and that will reflect differences in program goals. For example, some programs such as a token economy emphasize practical problem-solving skills. Others may focus on personal problems and insight development. System-maintenance dimensions focus on keeping a ward functioning in an organized and consistent manner.

A WAS profile for a large, male ward in a VA hospital is shown in Figure 8–2. The ward profiled was large and not particularly well staffed. It was appropriate, therefore, to emphasize administrative matters—system maintenance—to keep the ward functioning adequately. Staff members and patients both perceived this emphasis (80% or better agreement on items such as "Patients' activities are carefully planned" and "Ward rules are understood by the patients"). But there was also emphasis on relationship issues (involvement and support) and on some treatment-program dimensions (autonomy and practical orientation). Moos (1974) interpreted this profile as demonstrating that an understaffed ward can still achieve clear expectations and a coherent milieu program.

A critical question is whether social climate affects treatment outcome. The answer appears to be a tentative yes (Moos, 1974). Outcome evaluation is, as we have seen, complex. Institutional programs can be evaluated in terms of dropout rates, premature departures from the hospital, release rates, planned discharges, and the time that patients stay in the community before requiring a return to the hospital. Moos summarized his research on the relationship between social climate and outcome thusly:

> In terms of our tripartite categorization of Relationship, Treatment Program and System Maintenance dimensions, programs with high dropout rates have little emphasis in either the Relationship or the System Maintenance area. Programs with high release rates are relatively strong in System Maintenance and in the Treatment program of Practical Orientation. In addition, they are perceived as having moderate emphasis on the Relationship area of Involvement. Programs that

Table 8-1. Ward Atmosphere Scale Subscale Definitions

Relationship Dimensions	Treatment-Program Dimensions	System-Maintenance Dimensions
Involvement measures how active and energetic patients are in the day-to-day social functioning of the ward, both as members of the ward as a unit and as individuals interacting with other patients. Patient attitudes such as pride in the ward, feelings of group spirit, and general enthusiasm are also assessed.	*Autonomy* assesses how self-sufficient and independent patients are encouraged to be in their personal affairs and in their relationships with the staff, how much responsibility and self-direction patients are encouraged to exercise, and the influence on the staff of patient suggestions, criticism, and other initiatives.	*Order and organization* measures the importance of order on the ward in terms of patients (how they look), staff members (what they do to encourage order), and the ward itself (how well it is kept). It also measures organization, again in terms of patients (Do they follow a regular schedule? Do they have carefully planned activities?) and staff members (Do they keep appointments? Do they help patients follow schedules?).
Support measures how helpful and supportive patients are toward other patients, how well the staff understands patient needs and is willing to help and encourage patients, and how encouraging and considerate doctors are toward patients.	*Practical orientation* assesses the extent to which the patients' environment orients them toward preparing themselves for release from the hospital and for the future. Training for new kinds of jobs, looking to the future, and setting and working toward practical goals are among the matters considered.	*Program clarity* measures the extent to which the patient knows what to expect in the day-to-day routine of the ward and how explicit the ward rules and procedures are.
Spontaneity measures the extent to which the environment encourages patients to act openly and to express freely their feelings toward other patients and the staff.	*Personal-problem orientation* measures the extent to which patients are encouraged to be concerned with their feelings and problems and to seek to understand them through openly talking to other patients and staff members about themselves and their past.	*Staff control* measures the necessity for the staff to restrict patients—that is, the strictness of rules and schedules, regulations governing relationships between patient and the staff, and measures taken to keep patients under effective controls.
	Anger and aggression measures the extent to which a patient is allowed and encouraged to argue with other patients and staff members and to display expressions of anger.	

From *Evaluating Treatment Environments*, by R. H. Moos. Copyright ©1974 by John Wiley & Sons, Inc. Reprinted by permission of John Wiley & Sons, Inc.

keep patients out of the hospital longest place a high degree of emphasis in the Relationship and System Maintenance dimensions and also in the Treatment Program dimensions, particularly Autonomy and Practical Orientation [1974, p. 197].

Moos' work demonstrates that it is possible to conceptualize and measure important features of institutional treatment and to relate these to treatment outcome.

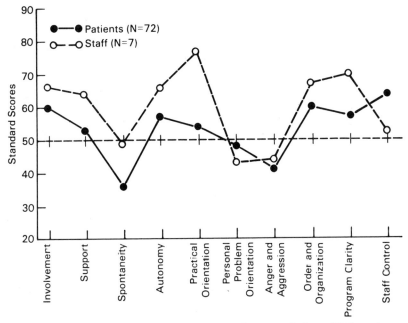

Figure 8–2. Scores on the Ward Atmosphere Scale for a VA hospital ward. (From *Evaluating Treatment Environments*, by R. H. Moos. Copyright © 1974 by John Wiley & Sons, Inc. Reprinted by permission of John Wiley & Sons, Inc.)

Despite the problems afflicting large mental institutions, they have become more humane and efficient in recent years. More human treatment is partly a function of improved legal protection for patients, and these protections are described in Chapter Nine. But institutionalization inevitably exerts its effects on both patients and staff, as Rosenhan's observations so graphically demonstrate.

State mental hospitals have become more efficient, in that the average length of stay has shortened. But it has been observed that admission and discharge statistics mask the fact that each hospital "has actually become 'two hospitals'—one an acute, short-term, rapid-turnover facility, and the other a large, custodial facility with a static population" (Paul & Lentz, 1977, p. 1). Efforts to arrange treatment in the community whenever possible have reduced this static population but have also apparently led to a rise in readmission rates (Paul & Lentz, 1977). The chronic mental patient, whether hospitalized or in the community, remains a significant problem for the mental health community and for society.

Coordination of Institutional and Community Care

Thus far, I have discussed the characteristics of various settings, giving only passing consideration to the interaction between and among settings. But many clients and patients pass from one setting to another and perhaps back again. Or they may require services from a number of different agencies. In recent years much attention has been focused on the "systems" aspect of psychotherapeutic services. How can they best be organized? How best to achieve coordination between agencies and especially between community and institutional services? Two major interrelated efforts in this direction will be considered—state-sponsored efforts to develop a system and federally initiated community mental health centers.

The State Mental Health System

Community clinics serve as a screen or funnel in selecting or directing clients to the state hospitals. Although it is possible for someone to go directly to a state hospital and seek admission, it is more common for the referral or commitment to be mediated by a local agency or professional. (The police and courts also play a role in involuntary commitment.) A community-clinic therapist may judge that a client is too disturbed to function in the community. Such a decision is almost always made by more than one person; that is, it is usually a staff decision. The client and perhaps the spouse or family are then advised of this judgment, and a recommendation is made to go to the state hospital. If the recommendation is accepted, then the local agency contacts the hospital and makes the arrangements.

Involuntary-commitment proceedings are also initiated in the local community. These procedures are discussed in Chapter Nine, with particular emphasis on the legal safeguards for the individual. The important fact here is that the decision about whether the client requires hospital treatment originates in the community.

The hospital is the primary decision maker regarding when a patient is ready to return to the community, especially for involuntarily committed patients. Patients admitted voluntarily can choose when to leave, and the hospital can discharge them with its approval or "against medical advice." In either case the hospital renders a judgment about the person's competence to function in the community that is analogous to the community's original judgment about the need to enter the hospital.

Cooperation between hospital and community is again important at the time of discharge; in fact, it is even more so. The problem is now one of providing patients with an optimum chance of successfully readjusting to the community. This involves the local mental health clinic plus a number of community services and agencies. The hospitalized person's usual living pattern has been sharply disrupted, and the longer the hospitalization, the greater the disruption. The newly discharged patient may need to find a place to live, find a job, and arrange for necessary funds to exist during job seeking. It may be psychologically important to arrange for social and recreational opportunities. Supportive counseling and continued taking of medication are almost always desirable. These needs of the hospital patient returning to the community require the cooperation of several community services. These may include:

1. The community mental health clinic—provides supportive therapy and continued medication. A clinic staff member is likely to be responsible for coordinating the use of other local resources.
2. Public welfare—arranges support if the patient is indigent and eligible for funds.
3. Department of vocational rehabilitation—arranges for needed job training or education.
4. State employment office: assists the patient in finding a job.

All patients do not need such a range of services. Many have spouses or families that can take care of their needs, and many can return to their old jobs. But many returning patients have no community-support network. They are the chronic patients briefly described in Chapter Seven and possess very limited vocational or social skills. Supporting community services are essential to give them a chance to function and stay out of the hospital. Therefore, state mental health systems must make some effort to coordinate community treatment and community services with the state mental hospital's programs. The hospital social worker may be responsible for guiding the patient to make the necessary arrangements for community living and may consult with the patient's family in so doing. But the social worker is based at the hospital; the patient's community is often many miles away, and no hospital-based worker can know the workings of many distant communities.

A better arrangement, in my view, is for representatives from the community to make regular consulting visits to the state hospital. Many state hospitals are now organized by geographical area in order to facilitate such coordination. The patients from a particular county or catchment area are housed together on a ward. Visiting staff from the community clinic then meet with groups of patients nearing discharge and help make the necessary community arrangements. The availability of community supports for chronic mental patients is especially important in the light of efforts to hospitalize fewer clients and treat more of them in the community.

In the previous section we examined the role of government in establishing and financing settings for the delivery of psychotherapy. This is perhaps the most visible or tangible role that government plays: it builds mental hospitals and clinics and pays therapists and other staff members to run them. Decisions about where to place a facility and the services to be offered are political. They reflect the political decision makers' perceptions of citizen wants and needs as well as pragmatic, or "pork barrel," issues. For example, a new hospital has an important economic impact on a community.

Thus far, the discussion has stressed the role of state and local government. Now I will emphasize the federal government's influence, which is more indirect but at the same time more profound. The federal government influences the training of psychotherapists and the delivery system, two issues of primary concern to this book. Federal support of research on the understanding and treatment of mental illness will not be considered, though it involves a great deal of money and has had considerable impact.

Outside of the Veterans Administration, the federal contribution to training, service, and delivery (and research) has been administered by the National Institute of Mental Health (NIMH). A brief history and description of the NIMH is essential, therefore, to our story. This discussion draws heavily on Bloom's (1975) analysis, especially Chapters Three through Five.

The Federal Role in Mental Health

Federal support of mental health services is largely a post-World War II phenomenon and coincides with the expansion of psychotherapeutic services and personnel noted in Chapter One. The NIMH was created by the National Mental Health Act approved by Congress in 1946. A major impetus was the public's concern for the psychiatric casualties of World War II and the realization that existing mental health facilities and personnel were inadequate for the country's needs. "During the ten years following its establishment, NIMH became both the intellectual and the financial source for much that was innovative in American mental health training, research and practice" [Bloom, 1975, p. 22].

Community Mental Health Centers

The delivery system, especially the state hospitals, was little affected by the NIMH during its early years. In 1955, however, Congress passed legislation permitting the agency to provide grant support to assist state mental hospitals in upgrading their treatment programs. And also in 1955, Congress enacted the Mental Health Study Act to provide for an objective analysis and reevaluation of the human and economic problems of mental illness. This study, undertaken by the Joint Commission on Mental Illness and Health, was completed in 1961. Entitled *Action For Mental Health,* it has had an enduring effect on mental health policies and programs. The study recommended more funds for basic and applied research and for training. It also recommended expanded services to the mentally ill [Bloom, 1975, p. 25].

> With regard to these expanded services, the commission suggested (1) immediate and intensive care for acutely disturbed mental patients in outpatient community-mental-health clinics created at the rate of one clinic per 50,000 population, inpatient psychiatric units located in every general hospital with 100 or more beds, and intensive-psychi-atric-treatment centers of no more than 1000 beds each (to be de-veloped by converting existing state mental hospitals), (2) improved care of chronic mental patients in other converted state mental hospi-tals, again involving no more than 1000 beds, (3) improved and ex-panded aftercare, partial hospitalization (hospitalization for less than 24 hours a day), and rehabilitation services, and (4) expanded mental-health education to inform the public about psychological disorders and to reduce the public's tendency to reject the mentally ill. To meet the cost of improved mental-health services, the commission recom-mended, public expenditures (state and federal) should be doubled in five years and tripled in ten, with the bulk of the expense of the ex-panded services to be borne by the federal government.[1]

The joint commission's report was reviewed with great interest by President John Kennedy. The Kennedy administration prepared a set of recommendations based on *Action for Mental Health,* and the president submitted a special message to Congress on mental health and mental retardation. The eventual product of the president's re-commendations and substantial congressional deliberation was the Community Mental Health Centers Act of 1963. This act implemented the basic ideas contained in the joint commission's report and Presi-dent Kennedy's recommendations. The central theme was compre-hensive care based in the community and greatly reduced reliance on large state hospitals. The federal government would provide grants to the states for the construction of comprehensive community mental health centers. These centers would bring mental health services within the reach and cost of all Americans. The states or local com-munities would have to provide matching funds, and although the centers would need to meet federal guidelines, there was provision for local control and variability to meet differing local needs.

The Mental Health Centers Act was politically controversial. There was strong agreement over the nature of the problem—the prevalence of mental disorders, the limited knowledge base, too few trained service providers, and an inadequate delivery system. But

[1]From *Community Mental Health: A General Introduction,* by B. L. Bloom. Copyright © 1975 by Wadsworth, Inc. This and all other quotations from this source are reprinted by permission of the publisher, Brooks/Cole Publishing Company, Monterey, California.

many questioned whether the federal government ought to take on the responsibility for services that were traditionally managed by state and local government. The original legislation compromised on the issue by authorizing funds only for building but not for staffing. Congress rejected a proposal that would have provided matching funds for staffing for a 4-year period, after which local government would have had to pay the bills. There was concern that, once communities relied on federal funds, the federal role would not easily be terminated. In 1965, however, amendments authorizing staffing grants were passed (Bloom, 1975).

Bloom provided a succinct description of basic features of the Community Mental Health Centers Act:

> The community-mental-health-center construction and staffing legislation appropriated funds that could be combined with nonfederal funds for the construction and staffing of the mental-health centers to be built in each catchment area. The federal share of construction costs ranged from one-third to two-thirds of the total cost (depending on the affluence of each state); as for staffing costs, the federal share was to start at 75% and decrease by 15% each year until it reached 30%, after which time nonfederal funds entirely were to be used. Some 1500 catchment areas were created in the United States, and the hope was that in the coming decade each such area would be served by one of these centers [1975, p. 31].

Each center had to provide five basic services: inpatient care, outpatient care, emergency services, partial hospitalization, and consultation and education. Later amendments added other services to be provided (for example, diagnostic services, research and evaluation, and aftercare for former hospital patients) and also expanded the role of mental health centers to include drug addictions (including alcoholism) and children's mental health services. In 1970 the period of federally subsidized staffing grants was increased to eight years. As had been feared, local governments were having difficulties replacing federal support, and many centers were faced with the prospect of reducing services unless more federal aid was provided.

Two basic principles of center functioning deserve highlighting. First, a center is responsible to all citizens in its catchment area regardless of ability to pay. Second, it is responsible for *continuity of care*. It must assure smooth passage through the components of a system—for example, from outpatient treatment to brief hospitalization to outpatient treatment again.

Current Status

There are 675 centers receiving federal funds. When fully operational, they would make services potentially available to about 93 million people, or 43% of the U.S. population. There are considerably more urban (55%) and inner city (12%) centers than ones in rural areas (17%). In 1976 the average center staff was composed of 4.7% psychiatrists, 9.4% psychologists, 13.9% social workers, 9.5% registered nurses, 21.8% paraprofessionals, 13.7% other staff, and 26.4% administrative and maintenance personnel. The high proportion of paraprofessionals is interesting. The centers and their staffs, in 1975, served 1.6 million people, providing nearly 2 million episodes of care, or 29% of the total episodes of inpatient and outpatient care provided by mental health facilities. Outpatient treatment accounted for 81% of patient-care episodes. This is consistent with the centers' emphasis on community care (President's Commission on Mental Health, 1978, Vol. 2, p. 319).

In summary, community mental health centers are jointly financed by federal and local government (fees, including insurance and Medicaid, also contribute). They are available to about 43% of the population and provide a significant proportion of existing public community care. Paraprofessionals are major service providers. Children, minorities, and the elderly appear to be underserved. Without continued federal support there would probably be a sharp cutback in services.

The community mental health centers have been politically controversial. Consistent with their opposition to federal support of mental health training, the administrations of Presidents Richard Nixon and Gerald Ford were opposed to continuing federal support of local mental health services. Again Congress disagreed and acted to retain support for the centers. A Presidential Commission on Mental Health, appointed by President Jimmy Carter and chaired by his wife, Rosalynn, reviewed the federal role in mental health, including the status of community mental health centers. Its report was generally supportive of continuing the program but suggested that more flexibility be introduced to take account of regional differences (President's Commission on Mental Health, 1978).

Third-Party Payment

I have discussed costs and fees throughout these discussions of the delivery system. Third-party payment is an increasingly important issue deserving separate consideration.

Much health care is now paid for by some third party—an insurance company, employer, or the government (as in Medicare). This practice is becoming more prevalent in the area of mental health and psychotherapy as well. Third-party payments tend to cover hospital costs more than community care. In the early 1970s it was estimated that 38% of citizens had coverage for community (outpatient) psychotherapy (Park & Shapiro, 1976). Not all health insurance policies include psychotherapy under their coverage, and, of those that do, many cover only institutional care. "The thrust of insurance policies, thus, is to encourage the most expensive forms of treatment, to put people into hospitals, whether or not they could be treated as well or better as outpatients in their own communities" (Park & Shapiro, 1976, pp. 309–310).

Health insurance seldom covers the entire cost of treatment. Most policies set a limit on how much will be paid for a visit and may also limit the number of visits eligible for reimbursement or the absolute dollar amount that could be paid for a particular illness or in a calendar year.

Health insurance tends to cover *psychiatric* care—that is, medical care. One of the major political issues in mental health concerns extending coverage to include nonmedical providers of psychotherapy. A client may have to see a psychiatrist in order to get reimbursement from the insurance company. Or a physician may have to assume responsibility for a case if treatment is to be given by a nonphysician. In this situation the physician usually participates in treatment and receives some compensation. Psychologists believe that such arrangements both reduce the consumer's freedom of choice and raise costs. Choice is restricted because a client must choose a member of a particular profession. Costs are raised because medical psychotherapists tend to charge more and, if a nonmedical therapist works under a physician supervisor, the supervisor's fees must be added to the total cost. For example, a policy might require an initial evaluation and diagnosis by a physician, after which treatment could be carried out by a psychologist or social worker. The physician might then be required to review the case at termination and also to sign the insurance claim. The physician's fees for these services add to the treatment cost.

Psychologists, primarily through their state associations, have been lobbying actively for "freedom-of-choice" legislation. These laws "entitle health insurance subscribers to freedom of choice and direct access to qualified psychologist practitioners for covered benefits without the need for referral or supervision by another profession" (Dorken, 1976, p. 46). Note that the term *"qualified psychologist"* implies some mechanism for determining who is qualified. Holding a license from a state is one way of qualifying. The National Registry of qualified psychological providers described in Chapter Nine is also aimed at this goal. Over half of the states have now passed some kind of freedom-of-choice legislation.

Third-party payment is likely to increase and thus become a source of even more interprofessional conflict. There is the future likelihood of some kind of national health insurance that would include coverage for "mental illness." Psychotherapists have been active in two ways in the discussion over national insurance. First, they are marshaling evidence that inclusion of psychotherapy would not be unduly expensive and might well be economical (Cummings, 1977). Second, they are debating who should be included as qualified providers.

Interprofessional Conflict

The conflict between psychiatry and psychology over direct third-party reimbursement is part of a more general war between these two disciplines. The basic issue is psychology's wish to achieve parity with psychiatry as an independent mental health profession. It is understandable that psychiatry should see the public's interest best served by preserving medical supervision and control and that psychology should see the public best served by providing it with easier access to a professional discipline with unique skills. Besides freedom-of-choice legislation, other battle grounds are state licensing regulations (discussed in the next chapter) and policy formulation and budget apportionment in the National Institute of Mental Health. The war, mostly cold but occasionally hot, has been going on for some time, and the prospects for a permanent peace treaty do not seem bright.

Psychology, in fact, must wage war on two fronts: seeking parity with psychiatry but denying it to members of its own profession with master's degrees as well as to paraprofessional therapists. There is justification for both fronts in the position that competence is *the* important criterion and that master's-level training is not sufficiently intensive or extensive to develop the competency attained by Ph.D. psychologists and psychiatrists. But this position is weak with respect to the contribution of personal qualities and experience to competency. Decisions about financing of program proposals and hiring of staff are influenced significantly by guild self-interest as well as by genuine concern with public welfare. And there are conflicts both within professions—for example, psychiatrists versus general medicine and clinical versus academic psychologist—and between professions. In my view, interprofessional conflicts remain primarily fueled by guild self-interest rather than genuine concern about public welfare.

Summary

The settings in which treatment occurs and the social and economic contingencies affecting these settings are important influences on the practice of psychotherapy. In the United States there are two partially overlapping mental health delivery systems. The public system is composed of settings that are largely supported by public funds. User fees tend to be low and based on ability to pay, with government subsidies making up the costs. Private settings are largely financed by user fees. Third parties, including both insurance companies and government, significantly underwrite private-sector costs.

Psychotherapy settings may also be ordered along an institutional/community dimension. Institutional settings such as mental hospitals are closed environments in which patients spend all their

time. In community settings clients attend occasional sessions—
usually once a week—spending the rest of the time in their natural
environment. The two dimensions, public/private and institutional/
community, yield a fourfold scheme in which all psychotherapy settings can be placed.

In private community settings the therapist's income is derived
directly from client fees or third-party payments. Thus, the therapist
is essentially a "small businessperson" facing the basic problem of
insuring a steady flow of paying customers. Private psychotherapy
may cost as much as $75 for a 50-minute hour, but this level must be
viewed against that of other professional fees, such as the $16 per
10-minute office visit charged by many general practitioners.

The nature of services provided public clinics is determined by
the political process, and mental health agencies compete for funds
with other government services. There are fewer psychiatrists and
doctoral-level psychologists and more psychiatric social workers and
paraprofessional therapists in public agencies than there are in the
private sector. This difference is due both to the employment preferences of the more-credentialed therapists and to the fact that less-
credentialed therapists and paraprofessionals earn considerably
lower salaries, which permits agencies to hire more personnel with
limited funds. Mental health clinics, juvenile departments, public
schools, college and university counseling centers, university-sponsored training clinics, church-sponsored clinics, special-population
clinics such as those for alcoholics, and outpatient clinics associated
with hospitals are major examples of public community agencies.

Public mental institutions provide the bulk of the hospital care
for seriously disturbed people, especially for those requiring extended treatment. State hospitals play a pivotal role in the mental
health delivery system, because they interact with local mental
health clinics. The Veterans Administration also operates a large
number of hospitals. Private mental hospitals tend to provide short-
term or crisis care, interact more with the private community sector,
and rely heavily on third-party payments as well as user fees.

A large mental hospital is a special environment that can exert
profound effects on both patients and staff. Patient apathy and inactivity are major problems in the mental hospital. Drug therapy is
widely used, and there is very little individual therapy. Group treatment, including ward meetings, is a major focus. Various kinds of
activities, including both work and recreation, are frequently employed with therapeutic intent.

The "traditional" mental hospital is organized in a way that
reflects the view that mental illness is similar to medical illness.
There is a hierarchical administration with medical staff at the top;
patients are implicitly viewed as irresponsible; and the aides who
have most patient contact have little responsibility for treatment. It
is believed that such an organization fosters passivity and helpless-

ness in patients. The therapeutic community and milieu approaches are one alternative to the traditional approach and emphasize shared decision making, patient responsibility, increased social interaction between patients and staff members and among patients, and the communication of expectations for normal functioning.

Two studies that illuminate the psychological climate of mental hospitals were described. In one, the investigators played pseudo-patients and arranged to have themselves hospitalized in a number of settings. They observed that patients and staff were strictly seg-regated, there was little interaction between patients and the professional staff, and staff members tended to treat the patients impersonally when they did interact. The investigators emphasized the powerlessness and depersonalization that the hospital experience appeared to engender in the patients.

The second research approach developed rating scales to quan-tify ward atmosphere dimensions as perceived by staff members and patients. The scales assessed relationship, treatment-program, and system-maintenance aspects of hospital settings. The ward atmo-sphere dimensions appear to be related to treatment outcome.

Most states have striven to develop a *system* to provide optimal interaction between community and institutional services. A well-functioning system can smooth the path to hospitalization for some-one in the community requiring it and can also facilitate the return of patients to the community by providing them the necessary support services.

Federal community mental health centers also aim at producing an integrated delivery system. The Federal Mental Health Centers Act provides matching funds for agencies that meet certain federal guidelines. Guidelines emphasize the coordination of the delivery system and providing services to those who need them most. The mental health centers are subject to the federal political process, and their future remains uncertain.

As with health care in general, much mental health service is now paid for by third parties—insurance companies, employers, or the government, as in the case of Medicare. Insurance plans have tended to reimburse only medical or psychiatric psychotherapy, but this practice is changing as psychologists lobby actively for freedom of choice for the consumer. The possibility of a national health insur-ance plan that would include mental health has important implica-tions for psychotherapy and for its major professionals.

Suggested Readings

1. Bloom, B. L. *Community mental health: A general introduction.* Monterey, Calif.: Brooks/Cole, 1975. A good description of com-munity mental health centers and the interaction of federal and local governments with respect to the delivery system.

2. Reinehr, R.C. *The machine that oils itself.* Chicago: Nelson Hall, 1975. A caustic analysis of the mental health system. An informative, though exaggerated, account.

3. Rosenhan, D. L. On being sane in insane places. *Science,* 1973, *179,* 250–258. Focus on the description of patient/staff interaction and patient behavior.

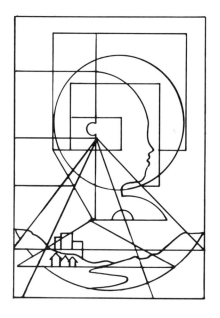

NINE

The Regulation of Psychotherapy

Society has an important stake in psychotherapy. In part this follows from the adage "He who pays the piper calls the tune." And we have seen that society does have a large financial stake in the enterprise. Furthermore, psychotherapists work with very troubled, occasionally dangerous, clients. They are the recipients of sensitive information about their clients. The intimate nature of the therapeutic situation—the common processes described in Chapter Three—makes the client amenable to the therapist's influence, and such influence can be positive or negative. There are documented "deterioration" effects in psychotherapy (Bergin & Lambert, 1978). Therapists occasionally behave unethically with clients, including having sexual relationships (Taylor & Wagner, 1976). It is most reasonable, therefore, that society be concerned that psychotherapists operate competently and within acceptable moral, ethical, and legal boundaries. There is also concern about protecting the rights and safety of therapists, clients, and even, at times, relevant third parties.

Psychotherapists as well as society have a major stake in the enterprise. They desire credibility and public acceptance, and to gain these they must provide assurances of competence and responsibility. The need for some manner of regulation, therefore, is obvious and relatively noncontroversial. The "how" and "who" of regulation is not so obvious, and there is considerable difference of opinion.

Consider the issue of who should be regulated and who should do the regulation. Individual therapists want considerable freedom and autonomy in choosing whom they will treat and in deciding—in partnership with the client—the nature of the treatment. Therapist and client together should be free to make decisions and work together in the client's best interest. Individual therapists recognize the importance of guidelines regarding standards of competence and appropriate and ethical practice, but they often believe that these should come primarily from their professional society or organization. This argument invariably includes the notion that the issues are sufficiently complex that only professionals are capable of making sound judgments about good and bad practice or about good and bad practitioners. For example, can a layperson evaluate whether a hysterectomy is really necessary or whether any other particular course of medical treatment is the most appropriate one? Or can the public decide whether a particular physician or surgeon is qualified to practice? Judgments about psychotherapeutic competence and quality are viewed as no less complex and technical and, therefore, as requiring professional judgment.

The essence of the counterargument is that psychotherapists are asking to let the fox guard the henhouse. More politely put, it is argued that professions, or "guilds," are formed and function primarily to protect the self-interest of their members rather than to protect the public. Although protection of the public is readily construed as consistent with, or even crucial for, the interests of the profession, when the two conflict, the public may well be the loser. Good intentions—and codes of ethics—notwithstanding, professionals have difficulty applying sanctions to their peers. This difficulty may involve traditional reservations about "squealing" and a variation of the maxim "Judge not, that ye be not judged." Whatever the reasons, the evidence indicates that the primary professions rarely sanction their members. Therefore, it is argued, regulation should be accomplished by a group or institution broader than the profession and capable of representing the public interest.

There is merit in both positions, and as a result both are represented in the regulatory process. In fact, the professions and government often work together in developing and implementing regulatory procedures. For convenience of presentation, I will consider governmental and professional regulation separately, but the interrelationships will be noted.

Governmental regulation of institutional treatment will be considered first. The rest of the chapter will deal with community treatment, where the interplay of governmental and professional regulatory processes is more apparent. Governmental licensing procedures will be examined first, followed by a description of several mechanisms of professional regulation. Consumerism as a newly developing "third force" in regulation will then be considered briefly. The chapter will conclude with some guidelines for choosing a therapist, based on the material presented.

Government Regulation of Institutional Treatment

The treatment and care of the severely disturbed mental patient has long been a problem for society. What circumstances require hospitalization, and how is the determination to be made? If a person is hospitalized involuntarily, what are his or her rights and privileges? What responsibilities does the institution have? A set of judicial and statutory principles pertaining to these questions have evolved. (Judicial principles are those established by court decisions; statutory principles are those established by enacted laws.) The courts, in response to legal actions initiated by patients or other interested parties, have been quite active in defining the rights and privileges of the mental patient. The consistent trend of both legislation and court decisions has been toward extending civil and due-process protections to mental patients.

There are two fundamental issues. One centers on the individual's right to refuse treatment and on procedures for involuntary hospitalization. The second centers on the involuntary patient's rights to adequate care and treatment.

The Right to Refuse Treatment

One can enter a mental hospital voluntarily or involuntarily. In voluntary admission a patient signs into the hospital for a specified period of time, usually between 3 and 20 days (Park & Shapiro, 1976). Ideally, the specified period is clearly understood by the patient. But in practice, hospital employees may be careless in explaining the procedure or patients may be so distraught that they are not aware of the implications of their actions. The purpose of the minimum period is to permit adequate time for observation and treatment and to protect the hospital against impulsive entering and leaving. Although voluntary patients have signed a kind of contract on admission, most institutions will discharge them if they and their relatives insist, irrespective of the specified time period.

Involuntary commitment takes place when the patient does not accept the need for hospitalization but "others"—relatives, mental health professionals, the police, or a judge—decide that it is necessary. There are three issues to consider concerning involuntary commitment: the standards, or criteria, for commitment; the procedure, or process; and the commitment alternatives and follow-up. All vary considerably from state to state, and you would be well advised to inform yourself about your own state's laws and procedures. Such information is useful both to professionals and to citizens, who may need to protect their rights or those of a relative or friend. A useful summary of each state's laws is contained in *The Rights of Mental Patients* (Ennis & Siegel, 1973).

Standards for Commitment

Criteria for committing a patient vary considerably but reflect two basic justifications: the state's police power to maintain public order and welfare and the "parental" power to protect those who need it.

Some states, like Delaware and Kentucky, have required only that a person be found to have a mental illness, defect, or disorder. Others, like Idaho, have required that a person be mentally ill and *also* in need of "supervision, treatment, care or restraint." Others, like Ohio, specify that the mental illness must impair self-control and judgment so as to hinder the conduct of the ill person's affairs. Massachusetts' 1970 statute reaffirms the old common-law criterion: a person cannot be confined unless he is found to present a "substantial risk" of physical danger to himself or others, and this is a very common criterion. (Montana and New Jersey include danger to property.) Massachusetts will also commit if there is a "very substantial" physical risk to the person himself because of impaired judgment. Many states combine these criteria in one way or another: someone may be hospitalized if mentally ill *and* dangerous *or* in need of care and treatment. Twelve states require in addition that the mentally ill person lack the capacity to make a responsible decision regarding his own condition and treatment [Park & Shapiro, 1976].

Recent actions by both state legislatures and federal courts have tended to narrow the basis for commitment. The U.S. Supreme Court in *O'Connor* vs. *Donaldson* (1975) held that a finding of "mental illness" alone was not a sufficient basis for the state to deprive people of liberty by locking them up against their will. The decision clearly implied that there is no constitutional basis for confining people involuntarily if they are not dangerous to themselves or others and can live safely in freedom. State statutes are tending to emphasize dangerousness and capability of self-care as commitment criteria. While terms such as *dangerous* or *capable of self-care* are still not easy to define, their use reflects legislative intent that commitment be used more cautiously.

Who is dangerous? This is a critical issue for the public and for the law. The public fears mental patients because of what they might do in the way of physical harm. Such fears are fed by occasional episodes of unprovoked violent acts by patients. "In California, one released mental patient murdered his wife and three of his children before killing himself" (Park & Shapiro, 1976, p. 266). Because such acts often receive much publicity, we weight them heavily in our thinking and conclude that the mentally ill, in general, are more dangerous than "we normals." In fact, there is no evidence for this conclusion. A study of 5,000 patients discharged from New York state mental hospitals over a 5-year period found that, among the patients with no prior arrests, there was a strikingly low record of arrest after release. The overall arrest rate for this group was 8% of that of the general population and was even lower for more serious crimes (cited in Park & Shapiro, 1976, p. 271). In effect, mental patients who have not previously engaged in criminal behavior are, as a group, very unlikely to do so after release from the hospital.

It is very difficult to predict who will commit dangerous or violent acts. Psychiatrists and other mental health professionals tend to greatly overpredict antisocial behavior (Shah, 1978). Thus, if the mental health professional's advice were routinely followed, many "innocent" persons would be incarcerated along with the very few who are truly dangerous. Yet there remains a legitimate concern for the public's safety.

Commitment Procedures

Major advances have been made in protecting the patient's right to refuse treatment. The courts have recognized that involuntary commitment to a mental hospital is a loss of liberty akin to imprisonment and that the mental patient should have due-process protections similar to those enjoyed by a defendant in a criminal proceeding. Watchdog civil-liberty organizations, especially the American Civil Liberties Union, have played a key role as advocates of patients' rights and have initiated or supported the legal actions that gave rise to court rulings.

There are two kinds of involuntary commitment: emergency and long term. Emergency-detention laws limit the period of commitment to five days or less in most states. These laws are a necessary means of dealing with unexpected or crisis situations and often involve the police. For example, a young man is running around the streets naked. Although he does not appear to be dangerous, he is incoherent and confused. One alternative is jail, because he is violating ordinances concerning public nudity. In fact, many emergency mental detentions present the responsible public official with a choice between recommending jail or a mental institution.

In this example, the young man may have been taking drugs or may have been exposed to severe trauma or stress. The criminal aspects of the episode seem less salient than the mental health issues and the potential need for treatment. Therefore, it is more likely that the man will be taken to the local psychiatric emergency room. Detention may be for as little as a few hours. But depending on his response in the emergency room and on whether there are family or friends available to take care of him, he may be detained as a mental patient for a few days for further observation and disposition.

At this point a court hearing is required, and we pass into the realm of long-term commitment. There is a parallel with the criminal-justice system, in which a suspect can be picked up on the basis of probable cause but cannot be held beyond a short time without formal charges' being presented to a court. In most states long-term commitment is only by court order after a judicial hearing (Park & Shapiro, 1976). Thus, the judgment of a doctor or mental health professional is subject to judicial review. The emergency room attendants who observed the disturbed young man may have concluded that he was seriously ill and unable to care for himself, but they will have to convince a judge (or, in some states, a jury) of this.

A nonemergency-commitment hearing is usually initiated by petition. The petition may need to be signed by one or more persons, by a physician, by a magistrate, or by some combination of these. The degree and nature of due process depend on the state. Some states permit the patient to waive judicial review either orally or in writing. Some states require that the patient have an attorney and will supply one if the patient cannot afford it, as is done in the criminal-justice system. Because the potential loss of liberty is as great as for the criminal defendant, there is reason for arguing that the civil protections should be as strong. The Oregon system is one of the more liberal and is summarized as an example of fairly rigorous protection of the mental patient's right to refuse treatment.

Oregon law requires a prehearing investigation to "avoid subjecting a person to the stress and trauma of a commitment hearing unless there is sufficient evidence to believe the person is commitable within the new statutory definition of a mentally ill person" (Kirkpatrick, 1974, pp. 248–249). The investigation is conducted by the community mental health director or his designee; in practice, this means that a staff member of the local mental health clinic is assigned to the task. In one county a precommitment screening program greatly reduced the number of formal hearings. Of the cases that reached the stage of formal commitment proceedings, about 60% were committed.

In Oregon, when an allegedly mentally ill person comes before the court, he or she must be advised of the nature of the proceedings, the possible results, the right to counsel, and the right to subpoena witnesses. The attorney is obliged to review the court file on the client and to advocate the client's position to the best of his or her ability. Oregon law requires that two examining experts be present at the hearing. One must be a physician, but not necessarily a psychiatrist. The other expert may be any qualified mental health professional approved by the state Mental Health Division. In this domain clinical psychologists, psychiatric social workers, and other mental health professionals have achieved parity with licensed physicians (not necessarily psychiatrists), who were previously the only professionals authorized for this task. The "defendant's" attorney has the right to request a third examining expert.

The hearing is more informal than a criminal proceeding. The examining experts testify on the basis of their interviews with the allegedly mentally ill person and their review of the record. Witnesses such as friends or relatives may be called and cross-examined by the patient's attorney or by an attorney for the state. The patient usually appears as a witness and is questioned by one or both attorneys and by the judge.

The Oregon statute now requires that a person be proven to be mentally ill beyond a reasonable doubt, the same standard of proof used in criminal trials. Given the difficulties in diagnosis of mental illness and predicting dangerousness, this can be a complex and difficult question.

Commitment Alternatives and Follow-Up

If the patient is judged to be mentally ill (and either dangerous or unable to care for basic needs) within the law, there may be alternatives to hospitalization. "Full exploration of alternatives is required not only by statute; there is developing authority that the constitution requires a state to use the *least restrictive alternative* required to treat an allegedly mentally ill person" (Kirkpatrick, 1974, p. 268). The Oregon statute provides for two such alternatives: release for treatment in a community facility or conditional release to a friend or relative. In these circumstances the patient is remanded to the custody of the county mental health program.

If the patient is ordered hospitalized, it can be for no longer than 180 days. If the Mental Health Division wants to extend that period, it must petition the court to do so, and the patient has the right to request a lawyer and contest the extension. A review procedure must be repeated at 180-day intervals. The intent is clearly to prevent reoccurrences of the old horror stories in which a committed patient is forgotten in the back ward and remains there indefinitely even though no longer mentally ill.

The overall effect of federal court decisions, changes in statutes, and increased advocacy of patient rights has been to decrease the number of involuntary commitments. As with the criminal-justice system, there are huge variations from state to state and from judge to judge. The role of the attorney is often crucial. It has been estimated (Park & Shapiro, 1976) that the presence of one at a commitment hearing triples the probability that the patient will not be committed. It is likely that a lawyer who is paid by an affluent patient will be more zealous than a court-appointed and court-paid attorney.

What of the right of a person who has been committed to refuse specific forms of treatment? The general answer seems to be that it is greatly restricted. Psychosurgery—a radical and largely irreversible procedure—may be done only after consent is obtained and stringent criteria met, including approval by an independent review board. But the committed mental patient usually has no right to refuse other conventional treatments, including drugs and electric-shock therapy. In fact, the major issue for the committed patient is whether any treatment or "adequate" care will be available.

The Right to Treatment

A committed patient's rights and privileges are defined by both statute and recent court decisions. Table 9–1 presents selected provisions from the Oregon law.

A copy of these rights must be given to each patient on admission and must also be posted prominently at each institution. Several

Table 9–1. Oregon Legal Provisions on the Rights of Confined Patients

Every mentally ill person committed to the division shall have the right to:
- (a) Communicate freely in person, by sending and receiving sealed mail, and by reasonable access to telephones;
- (b) Wear his own clothing;
- (c) Keep his personal possessions, including toilet articles;
- (d) Religious freedom;
- (e) A private storage area with free access thereto;
- (f) Be furnished with a reasonable supply of writing materials and stamps;
- (g) A written treatment plan, kept current with his progress;
- (h) Be represented by counsel whenever his substantial rights may be affected;
- (i) Petition for writ of habeas corpus;
- (j) Not be required to perform routine labor tasks of the facility except those essential for his treatment;
- (k) Be given reasonable compensation for all work performed other than personal housekeeping duties;
- (l) Such other rights as may be specified by regulation; and
- (m) Exercise all civil rights in the same manner and with the same effect as one not admitted to the facility, including, but not limited to, the right to dispose of property, execute instruments, make purchases, enter contractual relationships, and vote, unless he has been adjudicated incompetent and has not been restored to legal capacity.

of the stated rights have important implications for treatment, thus illustrating again the interface between the law and psychotherapy.

In the first place, the right to personal possessions, clothing, and the like constrains using these items as backup reinforcers in a token economy. Personal amenities may be withheld if the deprivation is part of an individualized treatment plan that is consistent with the least-restrictive-alternative principle.

The clause requiring that patients cannot be used for routine hospital maintenance without reasonable—that is, minimum-wage—compensation affects the institution in two ways. It will probably drive up hospital operating costs. And the use of work in the service of treatment, whether it is labeled "occupational therapy" or is available to earn tokens, is also constrained.

More than custodial care is required by statute. Indeed, the courts have already established the principle that the state *must* provide adequate treatment to justify the loss of liberty inherent in involuntary commitment. Several recent court decisions have affirmed the right to treatment.

The most important and widely known case has been *Wyatt* vs. *Stickney* (1972), which concerned the right to treatment of the residents of two mental institutions in Alabama. Interestingly, this case began as a class-action suit contesting the firing—because of budget problems—of a number of employees of the institutions. The employees argued that their firing would threaten the quality of care and deny the patients their constitutional right to treatment. Eventually, the residents and their guardians joined the suit, and the employees withdrew. The judge ruled that the institutions' programs were below minimal standards and thus deprived the residents of their constitutional rights.

> The court reasoned that persons involuntarily committed in a noncriminal proceeding have a right to receive adequate treatment, because without such treatment the confinement becomes indefinite punishment and violates the fundamentals of due process [Wallach, 1976, p. 456].

In a later ruling Judge Frank Johnson declared the treatment programs to be inadequate because they "failed to provide: (a) a humane psychological and physical environment, (b) qualified staff in sufficient numbers to administer adequate treatment, and (c) individualized treatment plans" (*Wyatt* vs. *Stickney*, 1972, p. 375; quoted in Wallach, 1976, p. 456). The court ordered a formal hearing to determine constitutionally acceptable standards and invited expert testimony from various groups, including the American Civil Liberties Union and American Psychological Association. On the basis of testimony, the court later set forth a series of minimum standards and ordered the state to comply. The right of the courts to define standards of acceptable treatment and the essential findings and recommendations of Judge Johnson were subsequently upheld by higher courts.

> The principal focus of the standards set down by the court was to create a humane psychological and physical environment with a sufficient number of qualified staff and individual treatment plans ... [and] guaranteed basic patient rights to privacy, presumption of competency, communication with outsiders, compensation for labor, freedom from unnecessary medication or restraint, and freedom from experimental treatment without informed consent or the consent of a guardian after legal consultation. The right of each resident to the least restrictive setting necessary for treatment was also recognized [Wallach, 1976, p. 456].

Implications of Legal Intervention

Court and legislative interventions into institutional care can be viewed as mixed blessings. They have focused attention on the institutions and forced states to direct increased resources to patient care. But judicial establishment of treatment standards carries with it some problems. The judiciary must seek advice and may have to choose among conflicting arguments by the different mental health disciplines. Stressing a qualified staff may overemphasize the importance of professional degrees and reinforce a medical model that includes autocratic decision making. Such a stress is also inconsistent with trends toward greater use of paraprofessionals and the greater sharing of decision making among all institutional personnel. An emphasis on greater numbers of professional staff does not by itself ensure increased quality of care.

Government Regulation of Community Psychotherapy

State laws affect community psychotherapy in two ways. States *license* or *certify* certain psychotherapists, which determines their right to practice, especially in the private sector. Second, laws affect certain aspects of the therapeutic relationship such as confidentiality.

Licensing and Certification

The next time you see a psychotherapist, examine the diplomas and certificates on the wall. They will inform you of the basic educational attainments of the therapist as described in Chapter Two. Many psychotherapists have acquired additional training and credentials. A credential is some documentation (certificate, diploma) attesting to completion of training or attainment of competence. Keep in mind that mental health professionals have other competencies—for example, assessment or consultation—besides psychotherapy. The state may bestow a license or certificate or the profession may do so. This section considers governmental credentialing.

Variations in the Professions

Psychiatry. For the psychiatrist there is no further governmental licensing beyond the basic license to practice medicine—obtained before specialty training in psychiatry. In fact, licensed physicians can perform psychotherapy within the framework of their practices as long as they do not call themselves psychiatrists. If they do, they will invoke the wrath of the medical profession. A medical license is granted by individual states to a graduate of any accredited medical school. The license is needed to practice in either a public or private setting. As noted in Chapter Two, the term *psychiatrist* is applied only to physicians who have successfully completed formal residency training.

Psychiatric social work. The practice of social work is directly regulated by law in only a few states. The major purpose of the laws is to provide a definition of who may practice social work, in order to assure quality of service. However, several states also license "marriage, family, and child counselors," and a master's degree in social work is sufficient educational background for such a license. In fact, a license as a marriage, family, and child counselor is a convenient vehicle for mental health professionals with a master's degree to obtain legal sanction for private practice. The California law defines the practice as "service performed with individuals, couples, or groups wherein interpersonal relationships between spouses or members of a family are examined for the purpose of achieving more adequate, satisfying, and productive marriage and family adjustments" (California Business and Professions Code, 1978). This definition would cover most psychotherapeutic situations.

Psychology. The recent and rapid professionalization of psychology is illustrated by the fact that Connecticut passed the first *certification* law in 1945, but by 1978 all 50 states had passed either licensing or certification legislation. There is an important distinction between licensing and certification.

> A licensing law is intended to define the practice of psychology and to restrict such function to qualified persons, who may be psychologists or members of other professions using psychological techniques. By contrast a certification law limits the use of the title *psychologist* to qualified persons and may or may not include a definition of practice [Dorken, 1976, p. 39].

The practice of medicine is licensed: only a physician may prescribe medication, perform surgery, or conduct other medical activities. But psychotherapy is much more difficult to describe or define than is "medical practice." In order to avoid definitional difficulties, many states choose certification, which defines a psychologist but not psychotherapy and other psychological services. Licensing laws always include a clause stating that the law does not restrict the activities of other established professionals.

Licensing or certification laws typically apply only to the independent private practice of psychology—that is, offering services to the public for a fee. Clinical psychologists (or social workers) employed in the public sector—by agencies or institutions—usually are not required to be licensed or certified. But in all states the psychologist listed in the yellow pages of the telephone book has passed some kind of screening or evaluation procedure administered by the state government. Your state licenses a large number of educational (nursery schools), business (plumbers and beauticians) and health-related (chiropractors) activities and professions. The same administrative mechanisms are involved in licensing or certifying psychologists—as well as the marriage and family counselors discussed above. A law sets forth basic definitions and guidelines, and administrative rules for examining applicants and enforcing the law are constructed. The examining panel is appointed, usually by the governor, and is composed of practitioners in the profession and often a consumer representative. Applicants pay a fee to take the examination and a yearly fee to maintain their accreditation. These fees are intended to cover the administrative costs of the licensing operation.

In discussing licensing I will draw heavily on Oregon's procedures, but I believe them to be representative. There are three stages. First, the academic and professional record of the applicant is inspected to determine whether basic educational and experiential requirements have been met. Most states, for example, require some amount of post-Ph.D. experience before one can apply for licensing; Oregon requires two years. The statute may also specify a minimum number of courses or credit hours in psychology. Applicants trained in fields outside of but related to psychology—for example, guidance or education—may run afoul of these requirements. One university has a doctoral program in *counseling* psychology that has been approved by the accrediting mechanism of the American Psychological Association. The program emphasizes professional courses and field experience, and its students may not have been psychology majors as undergraduates. Some graduates of this program have had difficulty with the licensing procedure, because their transcripts do not show the number of credits in psychology courses required by the statute. This is a case in which the aspiring professional is caught between two sets of standards: those of the professional association that accredits the program and those of the state.

The second stage in the evaluation is a written examination, usually a standardized, objective, multiple-choice test. (Some states use essay exams; some use both kinds of test.) Many states, including Oregon, use a nationally standardized test developed by the American Board of State Psychological Associations. The exam tests general knowledge of psychology—statistics, learning, neurophysiology—as well as knowledge about abnormal behavior and intervention methods. Because the licensing procedure applies to organizational and industrial psychologists as well, there is a set of items pertaining to these areas. Many applicants question the relevance of the exam—especially the items regarding general psychology—for professional practice. The rationale is that the licensed psychologist is a psychologist first and a professional second and should have basic knowledge of general psychology. Each state sets its own passing score. In Oregon it is the median score for all those taking the exam across the country on a given occasion. Those who fail can retake it after a six-month waiting period.

The third and final stage is an oral exam, in which the applicant meets with members of the licensing board or their representatives. In Oregon, it would be much too burdensome for the board—which serves voluntarily without salary—to conduct all oral examinations. Therefore, it calls on already licensed persons to serve on an ad hoc basis, with a board member serving as chair. There are usually five examiners, and they meet with the candidate for about an hour. The focus is very much on applied, professional issues, including ethics and interprofessional relations. The candidates are urged to state their approach to practice and to set the boundaries of their competence. For example, a candidate may state a competence in working with adults with various problems but would not treat children or adolescents. The administrative rules specify that the oral examination should cover the following issues:

   a. Areas in which candidates consider themselves competent to offer psychological services.
   b. Methods by which candidates anticipate preparing themselves to provide services in new areas.
   c. Plans candidates have for updating their skills.
   d. Candidates' knowledge and awareness of ethical issues and problems in their own practice and for psychologists in general.
   e. Candidates' awareness of current laws regulating the practice of psychology.

The examining committee takes a vote after its discussion with the candidate. The vote and a summary of each examiner's views are then transmitted to the full Board of Psychological Examiners, which makes the final decision. A candidate may appeal a negative decision, and the oral examination is tape recorded so that the full board can review the proceedings if an appeal is lodged. Finally, the candidate may simply retake the examination.

Obviously, there is much subjectivity involved, both in the way the oral exam is conducted and in how the candidate's performance is evaluated. Candidates find it an anxiety-arousing situation. They are concerned about who will be on their examining committee as well as who is on the full board. I hope that you are also curious about this, because the members can exercise much power in determining entry into private practice. Besides the psychological costs involved in failing an examination, the candidate may suffer economic hardship. But because it is very difficult to "unlicense" anyone, what of the negative consequences of unleashing an incompetent practitioner upon the public? Clearly the decision to pass or fail a candidate for licensure is a heavy one.

In effect, then, licensing as a regulatory mechanism is a complex partnership between the profession—whose members constitute the majority of the board—and the public, whose elected representatives passed the guiding legislation, whose governor appoints the board, and who have representation on the board itself. And to further elaborate the interaction, although the legislature passes licensing laws, the initiation of such legislation and the content of the law come from the profession. Licensing, thus, illustrates the interaction of professional interests and standards and the public interest.

Privileged Communication

Both government and the professions recognize the importance of the confidentiality of client/therapist communication. Precedent established by court decisions does protect communication between patients and their physicians, thereby protecting the clients of psychiatrists. In many states this privilege also extends to other psychotherapists and their clients. Privileged communication is given to the client, not to the psychotherapist. If a therapist is subpoenaed to testify in court and the client privilege is waived, the therapist may face a contempt citation by refusing to divulge information. For example, privilege is waived if a client raises his or her own mental condition (for example, insanity) as an element in the defense (Swoboda, Elwork, Sales, & Levine, 1978).

A psychotherapist often has a legal obligation to break confidentiality under certain circumstances. For example, if a client seems likely to commit suicide or harm someone else or has abused a child, the therapist may legally be obliged to intervene and notify family or police (Swoboda et al., 1978). A therapist can be held liable for malpractice or damages for failure to break confidentiality. In one case, a client threatened to kill his girlfriend. The therapist notified the police, who questioned the client but then released him. The man subsequently murdered his girlfriend, and her family was awarded damages because the therapist *failed to warn the potential victim* (*Tarasoff* vs. *Regents of University of California*, 1974). The implications of this case are not yet clear, but many psychotherapists are concerned that an obligation to warn possible "victims" would undermine confidentiality.

Professional codes of ethics are also concerned about the confidentiality of information exchanged between client and therapist. They oblige the therapist to maintain confidentiality except under extreme or unusual conditions.

> A physician may not reveal the confidences entrusted to him in the course of medical attendance, or the deficiencies he may observe in the character of patients, unless he is required to do so by law or it becomes necessary in order to protect the welfare of the individual or of the community [American Medical Association, 1973, Section 9].

The same basic points are contained in the ethical codes of psychology and social work. The basic notion is that it is essential that the client feel comfortable in talking about private matters without worrying about what will be done with the information. A therapist will not divulge any information about a client unless the client first gives permission (usually in writing).

The degree of confidentiality varies according to the setting. In public clinics, therapists feel free to discuss cases with colleagues both informally and formally, as in a staff meeting. This is also true in settings where training takes place such as medical schools or university clinics. In private practice, the range of persons who have access to information is much narrower—often it is only the therapist. There are advantages to having one's case discussed, because that brings to bear other therapists' ideas about the client's problems that may prove helpful.

Professional Regulation

A profession has power over its members by selecting its trainees and setting standards for admission and expulsion (Ellsworth, 1968). I have described the selection and socialization of trainees in Chapter Two. The present section deals with the setting and enforcing of standards and the earning of credentials *after* completion of the basic training program.

Professionalism in mental health is highly valued. Clinical psychology, social work, and nursing have all attempted to upgrade the quality of service by raising educational standards and seeking licensure. Such efforts also serve to enhance the status of the profession (Ellsworth, 1968). Membership in a profession is highly valued because, among other benefits, it legitimizes performance of the activities and functions that society has granted to the profession and implies a basic level of competence. This obliges the profession to maintain standards, but, as I have noted, it is difficult for the professions to impose negative sanctions on their members.

The nature of psychotherapy contributes another obstacle to setting up and applying standards. The role requirements for the psychotherapist are vague with respect to the importance of personal qualities versus training prerequisites. As we have seen in Chapters Five, Six, and Seven, the major therapeutic approaches differ considerably on this issue, ranging from behavior therapy's emphasis on mastery of technical skill to the humanistic emphasis on personal qualities. In spite of these difficulties, all the major mental health professions attempt to regulate in the sense of setting standards and assuring quality.

Professional regulation begins with the selection of trainees. Decisions are made on the basis of both technical competence—judged by grades and test scores—and personal qualities—judged from accomplishments, letters of recommendation, and perhaps personal interviews. We have seen that technical competence is usually weighted more heavily, in part because it is more easily measured. Second, training programs are monitored by each profession to assure that they meet basic standards. Psychiatry, psychology, and social work all have mechanisms for evaluating and accrediting training programs. Criteria typically include the quality and quantity of faculty, adequacy of facilities, and the breadth and coherence of the program's academic and experiential courses. Third, the progress of trainees through the program is evaluated in an effort to ensure that they are developing the necessary technical and personal skills required for effective professional performance. It is difficult to assess the interpersonal skills required for professional activity; therefore, it becomes a sticky matter to disqualify a trainee on these grounds—and it is seldom done.

Such problems notwithstanding, professional training programs do ensure that a graduate (1) has met reasonably high admission standards, (2) was exposed to an approved academic and experiential curriculum, and (3) possessed the necessary skills and motivation to complete a demanding program in acceptable fashion.

But professional regulation does not stop at graduation. There are four additional regulatory mechanisms that professions use in a continuing effort to maintain quality control. One is to establish higher *standards of competence* that members may choose to attain and to provide some kind of certificate or diploma as evidence of such attainment. Second, the profession may encourage or even require *continuing education*, so that members can maintain and improve skills. Third, the profession sets forth *codes of ethical and professional conduct* along with mechanisms for enforcement. And fourth, the professions may establish formal or informal procedures for *peer review* of professional activity. Each of these will now be considered.

Certifying Professional Competence

Government licensing sets basic standards for practice. Professions may want to establish more rigorous standards and mechanisms for determining whether members meet these standards. Psychiatry, psychology, and social work all have such procedures.

Psychology

The American Board of Professional Psychology (ABPP) was founded in 1947 on the assumption that a university degree does not prove professional competence. Four years of full-time post-Ph.D. experience is required before a psychologist is eligible for the ABPP exam. The ABPP now certifies in four fields: clinical, counseling, industrial and organizational, and school psychology. It issues a certificate and periodically publishes and distributes a directory to inform the public of those psychologists who have met its standards (Korchin, 1976).

The ABPP procedure includes an oral examination and the evaluation of a work sample submitted by the candidate. The candidate defines his or her areas of special competence—for example, psychoanalytic therapy, neuropsychological assessment, or family therapy—and the work sample is intended to illustrate his or her usual clinical practice. The sample may include written material, such as diagnostic evaluation or case notes, or an audio tape or even videotape. Part of the examination consists of evaluating the candidate as he or she demonstrates work with a real client. The examining panel tries to assess knowledge of theory and research as well as awareness of professional and ethical issues. The examination usually lasts an entire day, and there is a healthy fee required in order to defray the considerable administrative costs. The candidate may also have to travel to a distant location to take the exam. The examiners donate their time but may be reimbursed for expenses. For the candidate it is a costly procedure in terms of money, time, and the inherent apprehension involved in being closely scrutinized by one's peers.

Relatively few clinical psychologists elect to try the ABPP examination. It is estimated that there are about 2400 ABPP diplomates, about 1600 of them in clinical psychology (Korchin, 1976). The costs involved, noted above, are certainly a barrier. The benefits of attaining the certificate may not be viewed as sufficient compensation.

Psychology has taken another move in the direction of certifying competence. It has established the National Register of Health Service Providers in Psychology, which as of 1978 listed over 11,000 psychologists. Criteria for registration are a doctoral degree from an accredited institution, a current license or certificate from a state board for independent practice, and two years of supervised experience in health service, of which at least one year must be postdoctoral. The purpose of the register is to provide consumers and insurance carriers with a list of legitimate providers. More specifically, Blue Cross/Blue Shield will accept an insurance claim from a registered provider—assuming the policy covers treatment by psychologists. The insurance company is spared the expense and bother of determining whether a particular psychologist is a bona fide provider. The criteria, however, do not extend much beyond the requirements for licensure in most states. The registry serves economic and political needs of psychologists more than it provides useful quality control for consumers.

Psychiatry

A psychiatrist needs two years of documented experience to be eligible for examination by the American Board of Psychiatry and Neurology. A "boarded" psychiatrist is one who has successfully completed such an exam. The procedure is voluntary, and it is estimated that about 40% of U.S. psychiatrists have successfully completed it. The examination is composed of written, oral, and field components. The field portion consists of the candidate's interviewing a selected patient and formulating a diagnosis. There is much similarity between psychiatry "boards" and the psychology ABPP exam.

Psychiatric Social Work

The Academy for Certification of Social Workers (ACSW) is an accrediting agency. Two years of experience after completing a master's degree and passage of a written examination administered by the ACSW are required for certification.

In summary, an ABPP diploma, psychiatric boards, and the ACSW certificate are ways in which professional psychotherapists can document their competence.

Continuing Education

Another way that professions promote standards is by sponsoring continuing-education programs and by encouraging or even requiring members to participate. Obsolescence is a serious problem for any professional, from auto mechanic to psychotherapist. In most fields knowledge and technology are growing and changing at a rapid pace. A psychotherapist's professional degree and license indicate sound training and basic competence at the time they were earned. But you may reasonably wonder whether they have kept up with the field. Psychiatry has more formal continuing-education requirements than do the other professions; the requirements are established by state medical societies and so vary from place to place. All three major psychotherapy professions, however, promote continuing education and urge members to participate. Programs are offered before, after, and, often, during just about every national, regional, and state convention. In addition, professional interest groups and universities sponsor seminars, workshops, and other activities throughout the year. Often the program issues a certificate of completion. Consumers would be wise to inquire about their prospective psychotherapist's recent continuing education.

Monitoring Continuing Education

The difficult issues for continuing education concern what should be taught and what is learned. The question of what should be taught is identical with the old problem of which psychotherapeutic methods are effective and useful. Understandably, many practitioners are especially interested in the new and often exotic methods. But these usually have not been well evaluated. Is new better?

The question of what is learned is similar to evaluating psychotherapy outcome. There are a variety of ways to meet continuing-education requirements, and it is difficult or impossible to determine whether the practitioner (1) has learned anything new, (2) is making use of the new knowledge, and (3) is more effective because of this new knowledge. "Persons who have examined the continuing education requirements of various professions generally agree that these provide only the structure for learning and cannot guarantee content. A requirement that psychologists show evidence of various kinds of continuing education cannot guarantee that new knowledge and improved competence results" (Albee & Kessler, 1977, p. 511).

Given this qualification, it is important to note that the great majority of psychotherapists in both the public and private sectors actively engages in continuing education. This includes reading the professional literature and attending professional meetings where ideas and techniques are discussed and exchanged (admittedly there is also a strong social component to such gatherings). Many therapists pursue more-structured activities. Three mechanisms for providing continuing education are worthy of note.

In-Service Training

Most public and private agencies and institutions set aside some staff time and support funds for in-service training. Frequently there are speakers from outside the setting who may discuss new procedures or new developments in areas relevant to the institution's mission. For example, a Juvenile Department may invite a clinician with experience in family counseling to present her rationale and procedures to the counselors. Agency personnel may be responsible for presenting new information on some topic of interest to their peers. In-service training sessions may be a "one-shot" affair or involve a series of presentations over many weeks or months.

In some settings the entire staff of the agency may go off to a different place for a one-day (or weekend) in-service program. The Oregon Division of Mental Health sponsors such programs four times a year for the professional staffs of the local mental health clinics, whose financial support is shared by county and state. In this way many professionals from a number of different clinics can attend a program involving guest experts. The opportunity to "retreat" to a new setting—for example, at the beach or in the mountains—is a welcome change from the demands of daily routine. Especially in public agencies, where caseloads are heavy and salaries often low, such in-service programs are important for staff morale.

Workshops

A workshop can be defined as an intensive training program, given by someone recognized to be expert in the subject matter, that is partly or largely experiential in format. Workshops range in time from half a day to a week, but one-day and weekend programs are the most common. Workshops usually focus on a particular therapeutic approach, sometimes in combination with a particular client population or kind of problem. They provide a means for professionals to learn new skills or to improve on old ones. Their experiential component may involve role playing or simulations, working with clients provided by the trainers, or using the behavior of the participants of the training group. For example, participants in a Gestalt-therapy workshop would be expected to "work" on their own dreams or reactions to other group members as a way of experiencing Gestalt phenomena. Workshops are offered by individual practitioners or, sometimes, by organizations. A perusal of the bulletin board in my university psychology clinic yielded the following examples:

1. Mind/Body: An integrated approach in Gestalt/neo-Reichian and psychosynthesis. A two-day workshop offered by a psychiatrist. The fee is $70.
2. Family and School Workshop: Designed to teach participants effective family-intervention skills for changing child behavior in home and school environments. There are five-day and eight-day options; fees are $300 and $450. These workshops are jointly sponsored by a nonprofit research institute and a university-based research center, and the trainers are Ph.D.-level psychologists.
3. The Structure of Psychotherapeutic Magic: A weekend workshop; fee is $50. *"This is not a new therapy* but instead provides a set of techniques and strategies which greatly increases effectiveness of a therapist of any theoretical orientation." The trainer is a social worker and a licensed marriage and family counselor.

These examples indicate the range of workshop offerings, their sponsorship, and the background of the trainers.

Workshops illustrate the interplay of scientific, professional, and economic forces as they affect psychotherapy. They present intellectual and technological advances in the field. Their popularity reflects the growing "technical eclecticism" of many therapists—the willingness or eagerness to consider and embrace ideas and techniques from widely varying approaches. For the givers, workshops are usually good business and highly reinforcing. The income generated is sometimes considerable—up to $500 a day for highly visible clinicians—and workshops frequently lead to participants' seeking out further training or treatment from the leader. Chapter Two noted that psychotherapists are their own best customers, and this phenomenon carries over to the workshop realm, where professionals alternate between the roles of givers and receivers. This process not only leads to useful intellectual and experiential interchanges but is also good business. The workshop leader also receives much emotional reinforcement from working with a motivated and responsive group of fellow professionals, who are paying good money to experience the leaders "doing their thing."

Workshops are a convenient mechanism for continuing professional education and growth. But there are also dangers, and I briefly mention two: faddishness and superficiality. The novel or exotic workshop often has considerable appeal, but the ideas and techniques expounded may have little or no scientific validity. Workshops may thus disseminate insufficiently tested or validated methods. The problem of superficiality arises in two ways. A one-time workshop, be it for a day or a weekend, may have little real impact on the participants, who subsequently return to their old environments (agencies) and continue in their old ways of doing things. That is, workshops may be an ineffective means of changing a professional's methods. Alternatively, workshops may foster the illusion of competence in participants who then may try out new techniques—on their clients—without adequate preparation in when and how to use them. Most workshop givers are aware of these issues and often address them during the workshop, but they have little real control of them.

Institutes

An institute is a more formal and stable organization devoted to the development and dissemination of a particular therapeutic approach. Unlike workshops, which are often one-person operations, an institute, or "center," usually involves a group of persons with similar interests who have joined to share ideas, help one another develop professionally, and offer training to newcomers. Whereas in-service training and workshops are often one-time affairs, institutes offer systematic, sequential courses of study that can lead to certified competence in a particular therapeutic approach. We have already encountered the prototype, the psychoanalytic institute, in Chapter Two; certification as a psychoanalyst may take five or more years. Bioenergetics training also may take five years, but other institutes generally provide shorter training programs. Many are arranged so that an interested professional can sample as little or as much as desired. Certification, or some written evidence of completion of a program or a part of a program, is informal credentialing, because it does not have any legal status. However, institute study can be used to satisfy more-formal continuing-education requirements established by law (such as licensing) or by the profession itself, as in the case of medicine. Below are listed several institutes and ceners, along with some brief descriptive material taken from their brochures.

1. Center for Rational Behavior Training, Office of Continuing Education, University of Kentucky College of Medicine. Offers one-week or two-week intensive training, including supervised work with patients. Graduates of the program receive "the appropriate Certificate of Completion from the University of Kentucky College of Medicine." This program is a blend of Albert Ellis's rational-emotive therapy and cognitive behavior therapy as described in Chapter Seven.
2. Gestalt Institute of San Francisco. Open to professionals or to student professionals with at least one year of graduate study. There are three phases of training, each taking about one year of part-time work and including lectures, supervised experience, and personal therapy. A certificate of completion is given. Tuition is $325 per quarter plus payment for individual therapy sessions.

3. Behavior Therapy Professional Training Center of New York. "Introductory seminars, Advanced seminars, Treatment supervision, Certificates granted, Registration now open."

This is only a sample of the institutes now operating. They include nearly every therapeutic approach that you have heard about
as well as many that most of you have not. Like workshops, they also
meet important economic and psychological needs of the faculty, who
are practicing professionals contributing part of their time to instruction. Their financial compensation may be an important source of
income, but there are also psychological rewards. The didactic and
supervisory duties are usually a welcome change from the direct delivery of services that occupies most of their professional time. Most
professionals enjoy passing on their accumulated wisdom to others.
Faculty membership also carries with it some degree of prestige and
status.

Ethical Standards

Each of the major psychotherapy professions has set forth ethical standards to guide the behavior of its members. Ethical standards
are mutually agreed-on rules of behavior; they represent a profession's consensus about proper conduct. Violations of the standards
may result in a member's being reprimanded, suspended from membership for a specific period of time, or expelled from the association.
However, a quasi-judicial process—including filing of the complaint,
investigation, and appeal—is necessary before disciplinary action
can be taken. That is, the upholding of a complaint of unethical behavior is a serious matter. Many complaints are handled informally
and relatively quickly; sometimes the complainant is misinformed,
and sometimes practitioners are unaware of the ethical implications
of their activities. But formal disciplinary actions are relatively few.

Ethical standards do help make a professional accountable to
the public. A citizen or client can lodge a complaint with the ethics
committee of the appropriate professional organization. Ethics
committees also serve an advisory and educatory function. Professionals can seek an opinion about a matter or some planned activity
in order to avoid problems. Primarily, ethical standards are
guidelines for professional conduct that are voluntarily adhered to.
Informal peer pressure is probably the most important factor in
compliance.

Psychiatrists are bound by the Principles of Medical Ethics, an
AMA code that governs the activity of all physicians. The American
Psychiatric Association (1973) approved a set of "annotations" to the
basic ethical code that attempts to apply the principles to psychiatric
practice. Below is an example of such a principle and its annotation:

> A physician should not dispose of his services under terms or conditions which tend to interfere with or impair the free and complete exercise of his medical judgment and skill or tend to cause a deterioration of the quality of medical care [p. 2].[1]

This principle is annotated in some detail, including the following:

> In relationships between psychiatrists and practicing licensed psychologists, the physician should not delegate to the psychologist or, in fact, to any nonmedical person any matter requiring the exercise of professional medical judgment. . . .
> When the psychiatrist assumes a collaborative or supervisory role with another mental health worker, he must expend sufficient time to assure that proper care is given. It is contrary to the interests of the patient and to patient care if he allows himself to be used as a figurehead [p. 5].

This principle was chosen because it deals with interprofessional relationships and sets forth the basis for possible professional disagreement. For example, what "matter" does or does not require medical judgment?

Whereas medical ethics are painted in fairly bold strokes, ethical standards of psychologists are more detailed and extensive. This does *not* reflect any greater ethical sensitivity on the part of psychologists but rather seems due to a wish to cover in a single document the varied therapeutic, assessment, teaching, and research activities that psychologists may be engaged in. Below are some examples that focus on psychotherapy (American Psychological Association, 1977):

> Psychologists recognize the boundaries of their competence and the limitations of their techniques and only provide services, use techniques or offer opinions as professionals that meet professional standards. Psychologists maintain knowledge of current scientific and professional information related to the services they offer [p. 2].
> In announcing the availability of psychological services or products, psychologists do not display any affiliations with an organization in a manner that falsely implies the sponsorship or certification of that organization. . . .
> Announcements of "personal growth groups" give a clear statement of the purpose and the nature of the experiences to be provided. The education, training, and experience of the psychologists are appropriately specified [p. 3].[2]

[1]From "The Principles of Medical Ethics: With Annotations Especially Applicable to Psychiatry," American Psychiatric Association, 1973. Copyright 1973 by the American Psychiatric Association. This and all other quotations from this source are reprinted by permission.

[2]From "Standards for Providers of Psychological Services," *American Psychologist*, 1977, *32*, 495–505. Copyright 1977 by the American Psychological Association. This and all other quotations from this source are reprinted by permission.

Psychiatry has been less needful of elaborate ethical codes and written ethical standards, largely because of its secure place in medicine, where it partakes of medical tradition and status. Standards of medical care and responsibility have evolved over many years, and medical practitioners are well known to consumers and third-party payers such as insurance companies. Psychology and other organized groups of psychotherapists have had to establish themselves as credible and responsible service providers. Legal or statutory definitions as embodied in certification and licensing legislation are one means of so doing. But licensing legislation speaks only to the private practice of psychology. The American Psychological Association sought a single set of standards that would govern services offered by psychologists regardless of setting.

> There is no justification for maintaining the double standard presently embedded in most state legislation whereby providers of private fee-based psychological services are subject to statutory regulations, while those providing similar psychological services under governmental auspices are usually exempt from such regulations. This circumstance tends to afford greater protection under the law for those receiving privately delivered psychological services. On the other hand, those receiving privately delivered psychological services currently lack many of the safeguards that are available in governmental settings; these include peer review, consultation, record review, and staff supervision [American Psychological Association, 1977, p. 496].

Culminating a long deliberative process, the American Psychological Association (1977) published "Standards for Providers of Psychological Services." The document illustrates several of the issues we have discussed. It defines a professional psychologist as a person holding a doctoral degree and requires that others who offer psychological services should be supervised by a professional psychologist. The standards also emphasize accountability: "There shall be periodic, systematic, and effective evaluations of psychological services" (p. 502). And the standards include a declaration of professional independence: "Psychologists shall pursue their activities as members of an independent, autonomous profession" (p. 501). The interpretation of this principle includes the recommendation that psychologists seek to "eliminate discriminatory practices instituted for self-serving purposes that are not in the interest of the user (e.g., arbitrary requirements for referral and supervision by another profession)" (p. 501). Medicine, of course, is this unnamed "other profession."

You should compare this assertion with the passage quoted from the medical ethics code: "The physician should not delegate to the psychologist . . . any matter requiring the exercise of professional medical judgment" (American Psychiatric Association, 1973, p. 5). Suppose, for example, a psychologist and a psychiatrist disagree in their judgments of the desirability of recommending hospitalization of a particular client. Might not they both take comfort in their respective professional guidelines for sticking steadfastly to their positions?

Ethical codes and standards serve several functions. They provide guidelines for professional activity and help make professionals accountable to their clients. In these ways they serve to protect the public. They are also means by which professions stake out their territory and define their boundaries relative to other professions and to government. By providing information to insurance companies and to government, they also help to legitimize the profession and its members as providers who are worthy of reimbursement. Psychiatry, as a medical subspecialty, has had no problem on this score, but other mental health professions, especially psychology, are quite concerned about qualifying for third-party payments.

Formal Peer Review

Professional Standards Review Organizations

The same forces pushing for continuing-education requirements are also working toward peer review of psychotherapeutic services, especially for the private practitioner. As professional services become supported by insurance and government, there is pressure for quality control and accountability by those who are paying the bills. For example, Medicare and Medicaid services must be monitored by Professional Standards Review Organizations (PSROs). A federal law requiring the establishment of PSROs was passed in 1972 over the opposition of the American Medical Association. Although at present PSROs are tied legally only to Medicare and Medicaid, it is suggested that "the operational aspects and experience gained from these programs will most likely serve as the base for any national health program" (Bent, 1976, p. 239). Peer review attempts to consider the appropriateness of a treatment plan before it is implemented in order both to control costs and to assure effective care. PSROs can also serve a consultative or mediator role if a client, therapist, or insurance company feels that services or payments are inappropriate.

Informal Peer Review

Although formal peer review in the form of PSROs is in its infancy, informal peer review among psychotherapists is well established, though quite variable. Agencies and institutions, both public and private, have structural mechanisms that involve informal peer review in the form of supervision and staff meetings. Junior staff and trainees are typically supervised by senior or more experienced staff members. Staff meetings typically include presentations of cases for review and discussion. Senior staff members, while not receiving regular supervision, are usually encouraged to discuss problems with their peers. And because most therapists enjoy discussing or brainstorming about cases, informal peer review in the coffee room or hallways is fairly common. These processes generally provide staff members with reactions about some of their clients, but there is usually not time for thorough discussions of all clients seen by each staff person.

Peer review is less likely in community private-practice settings, especially when a therapist works alone. In group practices there is usually formal or informal peer review—that is, either regularly scheduled meetings or conversations over coffee. Some therapists arrange for consultation or peer review of one another's cases. But many psychotherapists work largely alone and do not have any convenient colleagues to consult with.

Consumerism and the Regulation of Psychotherapy

Thus far we have considered governmental and professional regulation of psychotherapy, with special emphasis on the interactions between these two sets of forces. The impression may have been created that clients or consumers are passive and naive—and, of course, troubled—and therefore unable to protect their own interests. More realistically, the consumer is a third force exerting a controlling effect on psychotherapy in concert with government and professional associations. Mental health care, as a part of health care more generally, is a service to consumers, whose willingness to use and pay importantly affects the product. Psychotherapists have to earn a living and thus must be paid by employers or by the fees they charge their clients. We have seen that many actions of the psychotherapy professions as well as of individual practitioners are strongly influenced by economic issues. Psychotherapists, then, like all other professionals, can be viewed as "sellers" of services and their clients as "buyers." Sellers and buyers have certain obligations toward each other as well as possessing some control over each other's behavior.

The relationship between client and therapist has usually not been viewed as having buyer/seller characteristics. The professional "knew best" and theoretically had the client's welfare in mind in all dealings. It was the professional's responsibility to assess the problem and determine a course of action. The professional's greater knowledge, in combination with the client's vulnerability, does tend to produce an asymmetrical relationship. Nevertheless, the client needs to maintain a buyer's perspective, and an intelligent buyer's greatest need is for reliable information about the services being offered—their cost, the qualifications of the provider, and available options. Professional and governmental regulatory mechanisms are basically means for providing consumers with some of the needed information. How to use this information and how to obtain additional needed information remains a problem for the consumer. "The combination of not knowing what to ask and a sense of awe or respect for the professional that makes the potential client feel that s/he is risking offense to the 'doctor' by asking such questions retards the consumer's access to information" (Koocher, 1977, pp. 155–156).

Consumerism as a social movement has gained impetus during recent years. The aim is to heighten awareness of buyer/seller rights and obligations and help consumers obtain needed information, sometimes by acting collectively. Although early consumerism efforts were directed toward manufacturers and retailers, health-care (and other) professionals have also come under scrutiny. I will describe two recent developments in consumerism as it applies to psychotherapy and then conclude with a summary of the implications of this chapter for selecting a psychotherapist.

Consumer Guide to Psychotherapy

The Public Citizen Health Research Group is a Ralph Nader organization financed by citizen contributions that has sought to compile consumer directories of health-care providers such as doctors and dentists. The work was made difficult by strong resistance from the local and state professional societies. The authors of the group's report believe that professional societies "feel obligated to resist any efforts to crack the veneer of uniformity they give to the public about their members—namely the assumption that anyone who is licensed to practice medicine or dentistry is as good for all purposes as anyone else" (Adams & Orgel, 1975, pp. ii–iii). The group then turned its attention to psychotherapy and sought to construct a directory of therapy for the Washington, D.C., area. Their effort was described in a thoughtful and provocative document, *Through the Mental Health Maze: A Consumer's Guide to Finding a Psychotherapist, Including a Sample Consumer/Therapist Contract* (Adams & Orgel, 1975).

With the aid of professional consultants, a questionnaire was constructed and mailed to all professional therapists who could be located. Information was sought from 719 psychiatrists, 940 psychologists, and 331 psychiatric social workers. The return rate for these three professions was 16%, 26% and 40%, respectively. The time and effort involved in completing the 41-item questionnaire was undoubtedly a deterrent, but it is likely that suspiciousness and resistance were important factors in the low return rate. The local psychiatric organization suggested that members refuse to answer the questionnaire.

The questionnaire sought information that would be useful to

consumers in selecting a therapist. Besides seeking data on credentials and professional experience, it also sought information on
therapeutic approach and policies. Table 9–2 lists several of the
items.

Table 9–2. Selected Items from the Public Citizen Health Research Group
Questionnaire for Psychotherapists

---

  1. Of which type(s) of therapy does your practice mostly consist? (List in
      order of decreasing importance: 1, 2, and 3.)
      _____ behavior modification   _____ marital counseling
      _____ drug therapy   _____ psychoanalysis
      _____ family and/or couples therapy_____ psychotherapy (individual)
      _____ group psychotherapy   _____ other (specify: _____)
  2. Of which type(s) of clientele does your practice mostly consist (give ap-
      proximate percentages)?
      _____ adult _____ adolescent _____ child _____ other (groups, etc.:
      _____)
  3. Do you accept Medicare? yes _____ no _____
      Do you accept Medicaid? yes _____ no _____
  4. a. What is the length of a typical individual therapy session?
      b. What is the usual fee?
      c. What is your minimum fee for a person with limited financial
         resources?
  5. Is there a type of problem or patient with which you especially do wish to
      work (for example, age, sex, diagnosis)?
  6. a. Is it your policy to make a verbal or written contract that includes
         what patients can expect from you and what you can expect from
         them? yes _____ no _____
      b. If yes, is it verbal _____ or written _____ ?
      c. If yes, is this usually done at the end of the first session _____ second
         or third session _____ or later _____ ?
  7. Do you inform the patient about your prognostic conclusions? Routinely
      _____ ; only on the patient's request _____ ; other _____ .
  8. If your practice does include some drug therapy, what percentage of your
      case load is undergoing:
      a. acute drug therapy _____
      b. intermittent drug therapy _____
      c. ongoing drug therapy _____
  9. If you are a psychologist or a psychiatric social worker, do you have a
      collaborative relationship with a physician? yes _____ no _____
  10. If you are working with a married person, do you always have the spouse
      seen also? yes _____ no _____

    As is implied in the questions in Table 9–2, the Public Citizen
Health Research Group strongly recommended the contract as a useful consumer tool. The intent is not to be legalistic but rather to
"establish a mutual and routine accountability between patient and
therapist which has heretofore been unusual" (p. 35). The bulk of the
therapists who responded to the questionnaire reported that they did

make a verbal or written contract. But this was almost certainly a biased sample, and there is likely to be some resistance to the idea of a contract among many therapists. Nevertheless, there is a growing literature on the use of contracts, and behavior therapists have seemed especially favorable to the idea. Table 9–3 displays the sample contract suggested by the report.

Table 9–3. A Sample Consumer/Therapist Contract

---

(1)   I, *Mr. Client* agree to join with *Ms. Therapist* each Thursday
(2) afternoon from May 1, 1975, until June 5, 1975, at 3 P.M. until 3:50 P.M.
(3,4) During these six 50-minute sessions we will direct our mutual efforts toward three goals:

(5)   1. enabling me to fly in airplanes without fear
         2. explaining to my satisfaction why I always lose my temper when I visit my parents
         3. discussing whether it would be better for me to give up my full-time job and start working part-time.

(6)   I agree to pay $30 per session for the use of her resources, train-
(7) ing and experience as a psychotherapist. This amount is payable within 30 days of the session.

(8)   If I am not satisfied with the progress made on the goals here set forth, I may cancel any and all subsequent appointments for these sessions, provided that I give Ms. Therapist 3 days warning of my intention to cancel. In that event I am not required to pay for sessions not met. However, in the event that I miss a session without forewarning, I am financially responsible for that missed session. The one exception to this arrangement being unforeseen and unavoidable accident or illness.

(9) At the end of the six sessions Ms. Therapist and I agree to renegotiate
(10) this contract. We include the possibility that the stated goals will have
(11) changed during the six-week period. I understand that this agreement does not guarantee that I will have attained those goals; however, it does constitute an offer on my part to pay Ms. Therapist for access to her resources as a psychotherapist and her acceptance to apply all those resources as a psychotherapist in good faith.

(12)   I further stipulate that this agreement become a part of the medical record which is accessible to both parties at will, but to no other person without my written consent. The therapist will respect my right to maintain the confidentiality of any information communicated by me to the therapist during the course of therapy. In particular, the therapist will not publish, communicate or otherwise disclose, without my written consent, any such information which, if disclosed, would injure me in any way.

Date	Name of Client	Name of Professional

From *Through the Mental Health Maze: A Consumer's Guide to Finding a Psychotherapist, Including a Sample Consumer/Therapist Contract*, by S. Adams and M. Orgel. Copyright 1975 by The Public Citizen Health Research Group, 2000 P Street N.W., Washington, D.C. 20036. Reprinted by permission.

Although the language may seem a bit legalistic, it is important to emphasize that the issues covered are ones that routinely occur and that are handled implicitly or after the fact if not made explicit.

Through the Mental Health Maze provides useful advice on selecting a psychotherapist. Several other consumer guides have been published in recent years—for example, *A Consumer's Guide to Psychotherapy* (Wiener, 1975). One that I think is particularly comprehensive and useful is *You Are Not Alone* (Park & Shapiro, 1976), which is available in a Consumer's Union edition.

Advertising

Imagine that the following advertisement appeared in your local newspaper.

Do You Need a Psychotherapist?

Professional psychotherapy at reasonable fees. An initial 20-minute consultation to determine whether our services are appropriate for your problem is free. Therapy time costs $21 per 45 minutes, and 15- or 30-minute sessions are sometimes used. We are particularly qualified to deal with anxiety, phobias, insomnia, and parent/child problems.

Samuel Shrink, Ph.D.
Licensed Psychologist

Most of us have never seen such an ad. Before the recent actions by regulatory agencies and the courts, it would have been unethical for any member of the three major professions to so advertise and illegal for a state-licensed practitioner to do so. Restrictions against advertising have been motivated by a desire to maintain professional dignity and to protect the public from fraud and deceptive practices. Advertising restrictions are an important component of regulatory codes for both government and professional organizations. For example, "Ethical Standards for Psychologists" (American Psychological Association, 1977) describes appropriate and inappropriate means of representing services to the public.

If you examine the yellow pages of the telephone book under Physicians, Psychologists, and Marriage and Family Counselors, you will get a good idea of the range of acceptable listings for different professions. In general, the more established professions tend to be more discreet. Psychotherapists who are not members of the three major professions and who are not subject to statutory control can be much freer in advertising their services in the phone book or newspapers. Their advertising is subject to the same basic standards of accuracy and truthfulness that the Federal Trade Commission applies to any merchant or vendor. For example, one could not advertise a degree not actually earned.

In one sense, then, professional therapists are at a disadvantage in advertising their wares relative to their nonprofessional competitors. This is compensated for by their retaining professional good standing and sharing the privileges and prestige of their profession. But advertising can also be construed as information—as one way of providing consumers with data on services, fees, and other characteristics of psychotherapists. Prohibiting advertising can then be viewed as a disservice to consumers, in that it perpetuates the "veneer-of-uniformity" myth noted earlier—the assumption that all members of a profession are equivalent. "The Federal Trade Commission and the antitrust division of the U.S. Department of Justice have recently begun to critically examine the traditional bans on advertising set forth in many professional codes of ethics by so-called 'learned societies'" (Koocher, 1977, p. 149). Thus far, medicine and law have been the primary targets, but the principles emerging from court decisions would seem to apply to any profession.

In December 1975 the Federal Trade Commission unanimously issued a joint complaint

> "against the American Medical Association, the Connecticut State Medical Society, and the New Haven County Medical Association alleging that advertising prohibitions in their *Principles of Medical Ethics* (AMA, 1971) tended to restrict competition, fix prices, and otherwise deny consumers the opportunity to obtain information needed to select a physician" [Koocher, 1977, p. 150].

The Supreme Court recently struck down prohibitions against advertising that the State Bar of Arizona was attempting to enforce. Already there are instances of modest advertisements by young lawyers who are trying to provide low-cost legal services for routine matters, sometimes employing paraprofessional assistants to minimize professional time. The implications for psychotherapy are obvious. Admittedly, advertising is no panacea and could be abused. The central problem remains that of providing consumers with good information about psychotherapy and psychotherapists so that they can make intelligent decisions.

Choosing a Psychotherapist

Choosing a therapist can be a complex and difficult matter. The nature of the problem, the client's finances, and the client's attitudes and values are all critical issues. The personal qualities of the therapist and the client's confidence and comfort in talking to him or her are often important factors, but these are difficult to judge in advance. Following is a discussion of several of the issues that should be considered before approaching a prospective therapist. In this section, I will assume that you are the client seeking help.

Nature of the problem. For many problems it probably does not matter what kind of therapist you consult, but it can be quite important in some cases. For example, certain serious disorders such as manic/depressive reactions or marked confusion and thinking disturbance are likely to profit from drug therapy. A psychiatrist or nonmedical therapist who has a good collaborative relationship with a physician would be desirable. For certain specific kinds of problems such as sexual dysfunctions (premature ejaculation, frigidity) or bed-wetting, particular therapeutic techniques are likely to be most helpful, and finding a therapist who specializes in these procedures would be desirable. These suggestions are based on the assumption that certain kinds of treatment are best for certain kinds of problems. But many problems can be approached in several ways, and most psychotherapists are "general practitioners" and deal with a wide variety of problems.

Finances. You will need to consider your resources, including possible insurance coverage, and decide whether you want to go to a public agency or a private practitioner. If you are covered by insurance, the policy will probably restrict the kind of therapist the company will reimburse you for seeing. It will almost certainly have to be a professional therapist and quite possibly a psychiatrist. Community mental health clinics have sliding-fee schedules, under which you are charged according to your ability to pay. If you are a college student or spouse of a student, it is likely that you can receive free services at the college counseling center. Because agencies and practitioners vary in their charges, you may want to shop around. The number of sessions likely to be required is critical to any cost estimate. Whatever your choice, you should discuss the issue of fees and payments explicitly with the prospective therapist during the initial session.

Professional or paraprofessional? You may consider a professional therapist or a paraprofessional—someone without formal training in one of the core mental health disciplines. With professional therapists you have some basic knowledge about training and qualifications. They are also more *accountable.* If therapists are legally licensed, they are accountable to the state licensing board. Professionals are also accountable to their professional organizations and are subject to sanctions by them. Nonprofessionals are usually not accountable to any state or professional organization. This does not necessarily mean they are less *responsible* in their work than are professionals. Rather, it means that a dissatisfied customer has less recourse. Agency or institutional therapists are, of course, accountable to their work setting. Paraprofessional therapists may be less expensive, and this is often one attraction.

Treatment or education? You should consider your stated and implicit intent—what you want to purchase—and that of the prospective therapist—what is being offered. Most professional therapists offer treatment, and this implies a good deal of responsibility for the client and the outcome. But many programs are designated as educational or growth opportunities and are offered by both professional and paraprofessional workers. Such labeling, as we have noted, avoids certain legal constraints but also defines the givers' responsibility differently. If you are in "treatment" and you become sufficiently upset to need hospital care, your therapist is obliged to arrange it and remains responsible for your care until some other responsible party takes over. If you are in an educational or growth program and require hospitalization, your "trainer's" obligation is much less clear, and you may have to take care of yourself.

Such an extreme outcome is very unlikely. But both treatment and educational programs can be upsetting. Treatment is usually open-ended, and the therapist can stay with the client until termination is appropriate. Educational or growth programs usually have a fixed number of sessions. If a participant has unresolved problems or is upset at the end, there may not be any follow-up. Educational programs, however, do offer some advantages. They may be cheaper, they involve less stigma or social embarrassment, and they may offer experiences or training not otherwise available.

In smaller communities a client may have little choice, but in urban areas there may be a great many agencies and therapists. As I have noted, the yellow pages of the telephone book are a useful source of information about both private practitioners and agencies. Many communities publish directories of human-service agencies that provide information on public therapy offerings. But it is always nice to have some kind of personal recommendation. If you have friends who have received therapy, they may have some good suggestions. Your personal physician and clergyman are other referral resources. You must dig up whatever information you can and then make an appointment. Information about professional training and postdegree learning can often be obtained in advance (some therapists have simple brochures or statements describing their qualifications).

Your initial session with any therapist should be viewed as a mutual exploration of whether the two of you can profitably work together. It is best to indicate this at the outset and to be as candid as possible about yourself and about what information you feel you need from the prospective therapist. You should also recognize that in most cases you will be charged for this exploratory session whether or not you continue. You should realize that you will need to talk a good deal about yourself before the prospective therapist can determine whether he or she can help, what kind of therapy seems appropriate, and how long it may take. Your therapist should, however, be willing to describe his or her general approach, and the recommendations should make sense to you.

It may not take long for you to decide that you are comfortable with a particular therapist, but it may take longer for the two of you to agree on a treatment plan. And the plan may need to be revised as you go along. I do suggest the use of a written contract (or at least a verbal one). Nearly all therapy involves helping a client learn to be more explicit and direct, but not aggressive, in communicating with significant others, and so it is very useful to practice this with your therapist.

It is quite reasonable for a client to negotiate and deliberate at the outset. But once you have decided to go ahead, it is important to cooperate as fully as possible and make a genuine commitment to the therapeutic plan. Psychotherapy does not proceed in a smooth, linear fashion, and there will be disappointments, plateaus, and possible setbacks. Still, it needs to be given a fair trial. But if things do not go well over a period of time, you should raise the issue with your therapist and consider the possibility of getting another opinion or of calling off therapy. The original contract and treatment plan, with any subsequent revisions, should serve as a guideline for how things are going. The contract might specify a given number of sessions after which you and your therapist would review and renegotiate.

There are several good discussions of these issues in more detail than is possible to present here. *A Consumer's Guide to Psychotherapy* (Wiener, 1975), and *You Are Not Alone* (Park & Shapiro, 1976) contain readable and thorough discussions of the issues. *Through the Mental Health Maze* (Adams & Orgel, 1975), especially Chapters Five and Six, contains a compact and thoughtful statement.

Summary

Both society and the mental health professions have legitimate and important interests in the regulation of psychotherapy, and current regulatory practices reflect their joint concerns. Society's financial contributions, as well as the responsibility to protect the rights and welfare of citizens, justify legal regulatory activity. The professions' concerns for the public interest, the expert knowledge of professionals often needed in implementing regulation, and professional self-interest contribute to self-regulatory activity.

Government is particularly active in the regulation of institutional treatment. A person's right to refuse to be hospitalized is protected in most states by a requirement for some kind of judicial process. Dangerousness to oneself or others and the ability to care for oneself are becoming key criteria. The involuntary mental patient also has a right to treatment. The courts have reasoned that, if a person is involuntarily committed in a noncriminal proceeding, adequate treatment must be forthcoming lest the confinement really become indefinite punishment.

Government also plays a role in licensing the practice of psychotherapy. A psychiatrist must first be a licensed physician. Psychologists who hold out their services to the public for money must be licensed (or certified) by the state. Marriage and family counseling, which is practiced by both psychologists and psychiatric social workers, is also licensed in many states. Licensing for psychologists and social workers governs only private practice. Licensing procedures help maintain standards that protect the public and also serve to regulate the number of providers and control competition.

The licensing procedure in psychology typically has three stages. First, a required level of professional training, usually the Ph.D. plus a few years of supervised experience, is necessary. Second, there is a written examination, usually ranging broadly over psychology. And third, there is usually an oral examination focusing on professional, ethical, and clinical matters.

The confidentiality of client/therapist communication is not explicitly protected by law, but it is a key element in all the professions' ethical codes. A psychotherapist is obliged to break confidentiality under certain circumstances—for example, to protect either the client or someone who might be abused by the client.

All the psychotherapy professions are concerned with regulating the professional behavior of their members. Professional regulation includes selection of trainees, review of training programs to assure that they meet basic standards, and monitoring the progress of trainees through programs. Professions have established higher standards of competence that members may choose to attain after their formal training is completed. Psychiatry, psychology, and psychiatric social work all have such standards, with varying procedures for demonstrating competence.

Continuing education is another way the professions promote standards, because it provides the means for maintaining and upgrading skills. Most psychotherapists engage in one or more forms of continuing education. The forms include in-service training for the staff of agencies; workshops, which are intensive training programs lasting anywhere from half a day to two weeks; and institutes, which provide training in particular "schools" of psychotherapy. It is difficult, however, to monitor the quality or impact of continuing education.

All of the major professions have established ethical standards to guide the behavior of their members. These serve as an explicit guide for professional behavior toward clients, the public, and other professionals. Code standards include provisions for enforcement and sanctions if they are breached. The ultimate sanction is dismissal from the profession, but this is rarely imposed. Peer review is another mode of regulation and may be done formally or informally.

A final source of regulation is consumerism, which helps to heighten awareness of buyer and seller rights and obligations and helps the public obtain needed information. Several consumer guides are available to instruct potential clients on what issues they should consider. A written contract between client and therapist is also suggested. Advertising is a way of providing consumers with information that has previously been greatly restricted by professional associations. Recent court actions now prohibit restraint of certain kinds of advertising.

Suggested Readings

1. Park, C. C., & Shapiro, L. N. *You are not alone*. Boston: Little, Brown, 1976. A good, comprehensive consumer's guide.
2. The interested student should also consult each profession's ethical or professional standards. Some examples are noted below.
   a. The principles of medical ethics: With annotations especially applicable to psychiatry. Available from the American Psychiatric Association, 1700 18th Street NW, Washington, D.C. 20009.
   b. Standards for providers of psychological services. Available from the American Psychological Association, 1200 17th Street NW, Washington, D.C. 20036.
   c. Ethical standards of psychologists. Available from the address above.
3. Hogan, D. B. *The regulation of psychotherapists I: A study in the philosophy and practice of professional regulation*. Cambridge, Mass.: Ballinger, 1979. The author takes a strong stand against restrictive licensing.

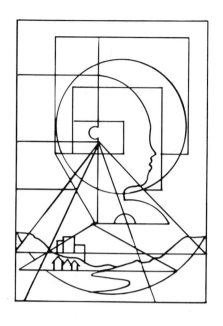

TEN

The Future of Psychotherapy: Problems and Prospects

London (1974) observed that psychology constituted one of the steadiest growth industries in the U.S. economy:

> No branch of psychology ... has grown so rapidly, done so well commercially or shown so little sign of slowing down as psychotherapy. If psychologists in general have been fruitful and multiplied, psychotherapists in particular have been fecund beyond belief [p. 63].

London's observations about psychology therapists also apply to psychiatrists and social workers as well as paraprofessionals. In the preceding chapters I have tried to describe psychotherapy as it is in the late 1970s and to convey a sense of the rapid growth and change that has been occurring for 25 years. This concluding chapter considers the future and discusses some of the key issues likely to affect psychotherapy, some of which have been touched on previously. A prime issue is who will benefit most from psychotherapy's growth and who will be neglected. The federal government's role in this process will also be examined. Next, strategies for increasing the supply of psychotherapy or reducing the demand will be discussed. The chapter's final section outlines ways that you can learn about the psychotherapy delivery system and possibly participate in planning or decision making.

A Boom for Whom?

It seems clear that the psychotherapy business will continue to flourish, at least in the short run. The large numbers of therapists who have recently graduated and who are in training will need and find jobs. But the public sector, especially in the urban areas, is now hard put to employ additional psychotherapists. Clinics, agencies, and mental hospitals are all feeling the budgetary pinch. Therefore, many more therapists, especially nonmedical ones—psychologists and social workers—are moving into private practice. Fortunately (or unfortunately, depending on your point of view) the marketplace appears capable of absorbing a great many practitioners. Health insurance coverage of psychotherapy has been an important factor in enabling the public to purchase private treatment.

Who Receives Psychotherapy?

The U.S. public is on a buying spree with respect to psychotherapy, and a wide variety of merchandise is being displayed (Gross, 1978). There appears to be an increasing willingness to construe difficulties in personal or psychological terms and a corresponding willingness to seek psychotherapeutic help. The great popularity of psychology courses in colleges and universities is probably both a cause and an effect of this phenomenon. Mental health professionals, aided by the media, have promoted the usefulness of therapeutic interventions in relieving distress and promoting personal growth.

The middle class seems particularly eager to pursue personal development. Therapy is often sought not so much to relieve misery but to enhance the quality of one's personal life. London (1974, p. 68) put it thusly: "Therapy serves the neuroses of its time. Hysteria was the neurosis of choice which opened the century. Anxiety was the symptom of its middle age. Boredom is the malaise of its ending." Boredom here refers to a phenomenon more profound than transient idleness: feelings of alienation and uncertainty about values and identity. Psychotherapy packaged as education and personal growth appeals to people concerned about such feelings, because it offers both pleasurable highs and value clarification, though not necessarily both during the same workshop or encounter group. To quote London again, "Men want to be healthy, wealthy, and wise in that order. As each is gained, the next gets wanted more" (1974, p. 68). Many modern therapies offer the promise of wisdom—increased self-knowledge—rather than relief of suffering. Psychoanalysis attempted to provide both but is now viewed as too long and cumbersome a path to wisdom. Today's pilgrims are more impatient.

Public settings are less likely to provide services for seekers of wisdom or personal growth. There is an implicit assumption that public money should support health services, including psychotherapy, for distressed people but should not be "frivolously" spent on the relief of boredom.

Who Doesn't Receive Psychotherapy?

To what degree is psychotherapy available to and utilized by suffering and distressed people? Available evidence indicates that only a minority of seriously distressed people seek out or receive therapy. Several kinds of evidence point to this conclusion. Survey studies find that a majority of people who report experiencing symptoms of mental illness either seeks no formal help whatsoever or instead seeks help and apparently finds some relief from professionals other than psychotherapists such as general physicians or clergymen (Gurin, Veroff, & Feld, 1960). These findings were touched on in Chapter Two. There is also evidence that members of the lower class are (1) more likely to experience serious mental disorder and (2) much less likely to receive any kind of psychotherapeutic help. Table 10–1, drawn from Heller and Monahan's (1977) summary of the "Midtown Manhattan" study (a survey of the incidence of mental disorders in New York City), illustrates the relationship between social class, mental disorder, and receiving psychotherapy. The finding that 28% of lower-class persons were judged seriously disturbed but only 1% were receiving psychotherapy is especially striking.

Table 10–1. Social Class, Judged Severity of Disturbance, and the Receiving of Psychotherapy in Midtown Manhattan

Social Class	Percentage Judged Severely Disturbed	Percentage Receiving Psychotherapy
Lower	28	1
Middle	18	4
Upper	9	20

Data from *Psychology and Community Change*, by K. Heller and J. Monahan. Copyright 1977 by Dorsey Press.

Such data have long been known to both mental health professionals and to responsible politicians. It is uncertain, however, what steps should be taken to remedy the situation. Expanding the federal program of community mental health centers might well increase the supply of psychotherapy and make it more available to those thus far not receiving any. National health insurance would reduce economic barriers to receiving therapeutic services. However, experience with previous health insurance programs that provide mental health coverage for blue-collar workers indicates that such people markedly underuse available psychotherapeutic services (Brown, 1976).

It does not appear that economic factors are the major barrier preventing distressed people from seeking psychotherapeutic services. Rather, the barriers seem to involve attitudinal and value issues. Many people still perceive a stigma attached to psychotherapy, because to receive it indicates that one is mentally ill, or "crazy." Many people also misperceive or misunderstand the nature of psychotherapy and may feel threatened by it. And there is also the real possibility that many distressed people who do not value psychotherapy may be better helped by some combination of drugs and other social services that more directly relieves their misery and distress.

The paradox remains that the greatest apparent increase in the consumption of psychotherapy is occurring in the affluent upper middle class. Also, there is increasing demand among antiestablishment but well-educated people who value increased awareness and understanding. Neither of these two kinds of client is the most needful; such people may best be able to purchase psychotherapy, often packaged as "education" or "growth enhancement," in the marketplace. Psychotherapy's essential reason for being, however, is to relieve the suffering of those who are distressed and dysfunctional. It is to provide relief for sufferers that the federal government gets into the business of training psychotherapists, building and financing hospitals, and perhaps paying the costs of psychotherapy via Medicare and national health insurance.

Federal Policy and the Future of Psychotherapy

Although the psychotherapy business seems certain to grow, the form and direction of its growth will be shaped by political and economic events. A key theme of this book has been the pervasive importance of federal policy and financing on the psychotherapy delivery system. Three important policy issues for psychotherapy are discussed here to illustrate the impact of government.

The President's Commission: Implications for Community Mental Health Centers

Early in his administration, President Jimmy Carter appointed a broad-based commission charged with reporting on the mental health needs of the nation. The commission was chaired by the president's wife, Rosalynn, and was composed of 20 distinguished persons from both the mental health professions and the public sector. The commission, in turn, appointed a number of task forces composed of members of the various mental health professions. The task forces provided specialized knowledge for the commission members to draw on in making recommendations. Task-force volunteers included both mental health professionals and former patients. The wide range of issues considered included costs, financing, and delivery of mental health services; research; prevention; legal and ethical issues; staffing; public attitudes and understanding; underserved populations; community support systems; families and mental health; life cycles and mental health; and barriers to care.

The commission's report included an assessment of the federal program of community mental health centers, along with suggestions for its future size and shape (President's Commission on Mental Health, 1978). Because the program was about at the halfway point in terms of implementation, the report may have a major impact on its future. As noted in Chapter Eight, a little less than 50% of American citizens are currently within reach of services provided by mental health centers. Although existing centers are now receiving sufficient funds to maintain themselves, relatively few new centers are being financed.

The commission recommended continued financing of new centers, including those that have been approved but not yet funded. But it recommended some important changes. One is that there be more flexibility in programming in order to meet local needs. Centers would no longer need to be "comprehensive," in the sense of providing an array of required services. They could offer only one or two services if this seemed appropriate to a particular community. Second, centers would be required to show that they are paying special attention to "underserved" populations. Particularly designated were the elderly, children, teenagers, racial minorities, and chronic mental patients. Third, the commission urged that mental health services be better coordinated with local health and social-service programs. If the commission's recommendations are adopted by the administration and Congress, there will be an expansion of centers and expanded job opportunities for both professional and paraprofessional therapists.

National Health Insurance

As noted in Chapter Eight, third-party payments are becoming increasingly prevalent for mental health services. Third parties include employers, insurance companies such as Blue Cross/Blue Shield, and the government. There are already two notable existing systems of government insurance for mental health services. One is Medicare. Certain mental health services are included within Medicare coverage, and it was noted earlier that the mental health professions are battling over who should be considered to qualify as legitimate independent providers of such coverage. The second is the Civilian Health and Medical Program of the Uniformed Services (CHAMPUS), which in 1975 covered nearly 8 million people and was the single largest group health insurance plan in the nation (Dorken, 1976). The CHAMPUS program provides health-care services, including psychotherapy, to members of the armed services and their dependents. Medicare and CHAMPUS are viewed as possible prototypes for national health insurance.

When national health insurance will begin is of great concern to mental health professionals as well as citizens and legislators. Its inevitability is assumed by most. When national health insurance arrives, it is likely that there will be at least minimal mental health coverage (Cummings, 1977). If initial experience is satisfactory—that is, not unduly costly—such coverage will probably be increased. Its implications for the psychotherapy professions are enormous. Cost barriers for services, at least of certain kinds, would be largely eliminated or greatly reduced. Government would support third-party payments to qualified psychotherapists. This would almost certainly lead to a marked expansion in the market or demand for psychotherapeutic services and would increase the need for qualified personnel. National health insurance might well be linked to community mental health centers as one way of financing their programs.

Psychologists have been lobbying actively to be considered as qualified independent providers of services under Medicare and are preparing the political groundwork needed to be qualified under national health insurance. Psychologists are already qualified providers under CHAMPUS and have pointed to the experience of that health-insurance plan as providing evidence supporting the cost-effectiveness of including nonmedical practitioners. An American Psychological Association task force has proposed principles and procedures for continuous evaluation of services under national health insurance (American Psychological Association Task Force on Continuing Evaluation in National Health Insurance, 1978). All the major psychotherapy professions are involved in lobbying over national health insurance. But medicine has traditionally been able to exert more political clout than psychology or social work.

Subsidized Training of Psychotherapists

Both an expanded program of community mental health centers and national health insurance would lead to a marked increase in the supply of psychotherapy and would require a continuing stream of qualified professionals to dispense it. These two developments would provide strong justification for the continuation of an important governmental policy and financing arrangement that is not well known to most laypersons. For 25 years the National Institute of Mental Health (NIMH) has heavily subsidized the training and education of the core mental health professions, and more recently it is subsidizing paraprofessional mental health training as well.

A major goal of the NIMH's training effort was to increase the supply of clinical specialists in psychiatry, psychiatric nursing, psychology, and social work. After World War II there was a clear shortage of qualified mental health personnel. In 1947 the total pool of the four core disciplines noted above numbered about 23,000. In 1977 it was estimated that there were over 121,000 psychiatrists, psychologists, psychiatric social workers, and psychiatric nurses (Brown, 1977). Psychiatrists increased from 4,700 to 28,000 during this same 30-year period. Although the NIMH was not solely responsible for this increase, it did make a major contribution. Training funds were allocated among the professions in the following way: 40% to psychiatry and 20% each to psychology, psychiatric social work, and psychiatric nursing. These basic proportions have remained, qualified by a slight reduction in psychiatry and the addition of training funds for paraprofessionals (Brown, 1977). The financing pattern reflects the relative dominance of psychiatry among the psychotherapeutic professions noted in Chapter Two.

It is important to note that psychiatry—and thereby the other core disciplines—is the only medical specialty to receive *direct* federal subsidies. Although much medical and health-related education is supported by federal money, the support is given to universities and medical schools rather than to a particular discipline or specialty. But psychiatry, social work, psychiatric nursing, and clinical psychology receive NIMH grants to support training programs. The training grants pay the salaries of faculty members and supporting clerical and technical employees and go to purchase needed equipment. Most importantly, NIMH funds have provided stipends to support the trainees in the various programs. The stipends have made careers in the core mental health disciplines attractive and attainable to many young people who could not afford to finance their own professional educations. Figure 10–1 presents the amounts of money the NIMH has spent on training over a 25-year period.

There are two striking features in the data depicted in Figure 10–1. First, there is the dramatic increase in training funds between 1950 and 1970, a jump of about $120 million. Second, there is a steady decline in training dollars after 1970, a $37-million reduction between 1970 and 1976. Because the reduction is in actual dollars and there has been considerable inflation, the decline in purchasing power of training dollars is estimated to be 52% (Brown, 1977).

The increase in training funds between 1950 and 1970 reflected a social policy decision to increase mental health personnel. The decrease in the last several years also reflects a social policy decision, but the executive and legislative branches of government have been in disagreement. In the late 1960s the administration judged that there was no longer any special need for preferential funding for psychiatry and the other core professions. The administration attempted to phase out training funds; Congress sought to restore them. The decline seen in Figure 10–1 was the result of this struggle (Brown, 1977).

The director of the NIMH from 1970 to 1977, Dr. Bertram Brown, has offered a cogent analysis of the motivations for ending preferential treatment for the mental health professions. One reason was a simple wish to balance the budget and cut back federal spending. The other reasons were more substantive. There was a belief on the part of both the public and their legislators that federal funds were being used to train practitioners who used their skills to make comfortable incomes in private practice while many who could not afford to pay for treatment remained unserved. This criticism was leveled primarily at psychiatry, but as the other professions—especially psychol-

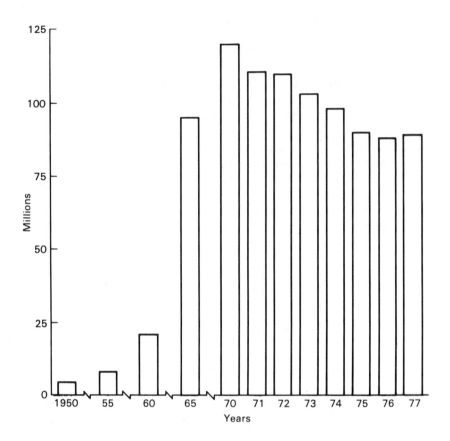

Figure 10–1. Annual NIMH Funds for Training Programs. (From "The Federal Government and Psychiatric Education: Progress, Problems and Prospects," by B. S. Brown. DHEW Publication No. (Adm) 77–511. Washington, D.C.: U.S. Government Printing Office, 1977.)

ogy—move more into independent private practice, they also become vulnerable.

Closely related to the issue of private practice is the maldistribution of therapists, which Brown viewed as the major issue.

New York, Massachusetts, and Washington, D.C. had more than double the national average of 11 psychiatrists per 100,000 population in 1974, while 11 states had fewer than 5 per 100,000. Computing in the differentials of rural, metropolitan, and central city areas, we are dealing with distribution ranges of 20- to 30-fold [Brown, 1977, p. 13].

Although his focus may have been on the maldistribution of psychiatrists, the problem affects the other psychotherapeutic disciplines as well (the distribution problem was noted in Chapter Two). Psychotherapists tend to cluster in large metropolitan areas. A recent study of the geographic distribution of psychologists found them concentrated in affluent urban states and in university towns, a pattern similar to that for other health providers (Richards & Gottfredson, 1978).

Many influential members of Congress represent the underserved areas of the United States, and they are most concerned about the maldistribution problem. Brown quoted the question of one influential congressman at an appropriations hearing: "Why should the people who live in these underserved areas have to pay taxes if they are not going to get any benefit out of this thing?" (Brown, 1977, p. 12).

A point not mentioned by Brown, but which I believe to be important, is that the mental health professions have grown sufficiently attractive—both economically and in terms of intrinsic interest—that subsidies are now less necessary to recruit competent persons. Graduate programs in clinical and counseling psychology are besieged by qualified applicants, many of whom are willing to finance their own education without NIMH stipends. The growth of professional schools of psychology is also contributing importantly to the supply of psychotherapists, because, by design, they train practitioners for public and private service. In psychology, at least, reduction or even withdrawal of NIMH training support would not greatly reduce the supply of psychotherapists.

Psychiatry and psychology are also vulnerable to congressional cutbacks, because their training programs are long and expensive. Partly because of this, Ph.D.'s and, especially, M.D.'s are more costly to agencies and institutions. As noted in Chapter Two, there is a growing acceptance of the idea that paraprofessionals, or at least people trained at the master's level, can deliver most psychotherapeutic services, especially in the supportive context of an agency or institution where professional supervision or consultation is available. In effect, there are two forces working against support of training in the core mental health disciplines, especially psychiatry and psychology. First, the professionals tend not to want to work in public settings, especially in rural or less affluent areas. Second, public agencies can stretch their limited staffing budgets further by employing subdoctoral and paraprofessional workers.

The President's Commission on Mental Health has also reviewed the maldistribution problem in relation to federal support of training programs. Their recommendation is to continue such support but with a "payback" provision, requiring graduates to work for a year (for every year of support) in an underserved community. A companion recommendation calls for continuation of training awards only to programs aimed at meeting major service-delivery priorities or the needs of underserved populations (President's Commission on Mental Health, 1978). Implementation of these recommendations could have profound implications for the psychotherapeutic professions.

Government's responsibility would appear to remain that of

identifying the truly distressed citizens and providing some kind of services for them. There are two major approaches to this problem, and they are not mutually exclusive. One is to increase the supply of psychotherapy, and the other is to decrease the demand. Government is giving some support to both.

Increasing the Supply of Psychotherapy

We have already discussed two major governmental alternatives for increasing supply. One is to expand the program of community mental health centers, thus making more public facilities and therapists available. If this is to be done, it will surely involve modifying the program to make the centers more responsive to the needs of distressed citizens. The Carter commission's report recommended increased emphasis on programs for children, the aged, the poor, and minorities, as evidence suggests that these are underserved but needful populations.

National health insurance covering psychotherapy would be a second way to stimulate supply, both in the public and private sectors. With more funds available to pay for therapy, there would be greater inducement for people to become practitioners.

Expanding the Role of Paraprofessional Therapists

As we have seen, however, professional psychotherapists are both expensive to produce and often tend to move into private practice, thereby serving the more affluent but less distressed clients. Increasing the supply of paraprofessional therapists is both economical and provides services for those who most need them. In 1975, "about 30% of direct community mental health services [were] provided by paraprofessional staff members, and in some agencies as much as 80% of services [came] from paraprofessionals" (Social Action Research Center, 1978, p. 5).

The use of indigenous paraprofessionals may have the further advantage of making services accessible to the poor and to minorities who would be less likely to approach middle-class professional workers. Current government policy seems to be fairly supportive of this strategy, and increased funds have been channeled toward training paraprofessional mental health workers. Human services, including psychotherapy, may be more effective and humane when provided to the poor by the poor, thus removing the status differential between helper and client (Heller & Monahan, 1977).

The New Careers programs are probably the best-known institutionalized implementation of this strategy (Heller & Monahan, 1977). The federal government has provided funds for a number of such programs, which typically involve cooperation between university training programs and community agencies. A federal grant provides stipends for the trainees and also provides money for faculty salaries. The agencies agree to provide field supervision and make available career opportunities for the trainees commensurate with their developing skills and competencies. Such a program has a number of interesting side effects. It is politically very attractive, because it increases the supply of psychotherapists while simultaneously providing jobs for the poor, most of whom are marginally employed or unemployed. These economic benefits are very significant, and the New Careers program is certainly good for the paraprofessional givers, whatever their impact upon their clients.

There is, however, another side effect, which may have both a positive and negative effect. The impact of paraprofessional mental health workers from the lower social classes on professional human-service agencies is considerable. There are likely to be tensions and pressures for institutional change as the economically disadvantaged and their indigenous paraprofessional representatives press for more responsiveness on the part of the agencies. Constructive change in this direction has been an important goal of the New Careers movement, but it must be acknowledged that such changes sometimes arouse resistance on the part of the establishment mental health professionals. There is also the question of the durability of changes engendered by the New Careers program after the federal financing—which is intended to be a short-term incentive—is removed. The hope is that agencies will have experienced the economic and performance advantages of paraprofessional workers and will continue to utilize them. It is possible, however, that trainees may acquire skills and expectations of employment but be unable to find jobs once federal financing expires.

Quasi-Therapeutic Programs

Psychotherapy attempts to relieve distress or to promote growth and constructive personality change. But there are other programs or procedures that citizens can use to attain these goals. I will now discuss three of them: transformational groups, self-help groups, and self-help books. All three contain some of the key elements of psychotherapy, but they also have important differences. All can be viewed as increasing the supply of therapylike services because they can, and do, reach large numbers of people, and all are largely sponsored by the private sector, rather than government.

Transformational Groups

Transformational groups offer short-term experiences, usually presented as educational or growth enhancing, that aim at bringing about rapid and marked changes in the participants. *Est* (Erhard

Seminars Training) is probably the best known. It works with as many as 250 people at a time, meeting together for several long evening and weekend sessions. Former clients assist the group leaders on a volunteer basis, also contributing to efficiency and economy. Most other transformational-group programs work with smaller numbers.

Much of the group movement does not deal with seriously distressed individuals. Rather, the various programs attempt to provide educational, growth, or awareness-expanding experiences for people who are already functioning reasonably well but who feel overly inhibited, lacking in purpose, or lacking in satisfaction in their lives. Relatively little is known yet about how well such programs' goals are accomplished, and systematic research and evaluation of these enterprises is scant. But the main point is that the seriously dysfunctional individual is either not served or is poorly served by them. They do provide additional choice and opportunity for many middle-class people and seem to be able to compete well and thrive in the marketplace.

Self-Help Books

Self-reliance is highly valued in U.S. society, and most people would like to be able to solve their own problems. This is probably an important factor in the recent surge of do-it-yourself therapy. Self-help books have always been with us, typically packaging whatever therapeutic concepts and procedures are in vogue. As the number of different kinds of psychotherapies has dramatically increased over the last several years, so have their corresponding self-help-book versions.

Virtually nothing is known about who buys self-help books, and to what effect. Although some suggestions have been offered concerning professional quality control of "over-the-counter" self-help books (Rosen, 1976), there seems no way to accomplish this without infringing on freedom of the press. Some self-help programs are based on a good deal of clinical and research information; others are more speculative. Ideally, a treatment ought to have well-documented clinical effectiveness when administered by a therapist before being disseminated in a self-help book. This is rarely the case, however (Glasgow & Rosen, 1978). Further, clinically effective treatment may not work at all when self-administered. In a study of self-administered treatment for premature ejaculation, clients who received short weekly telephone calls providing guidance and support were quite successful. However, clients left completely on their own—as with a self-help book—failed to complete the program and were not helped (Zeiss, 1978).

Self-help books may have a positive indirect effect in helping to educate readers about the nature and source of their difficulties. Conversely, they may sensitize readers to psychological issues and stresses and produce a greater demand for therapy. Those who are concerned that the public frequently fails to distinguish between natural, inherent problems in living and psychological dysfunctions requiring professional treatment would worry about this possibility.

Self-Help Groups

Self-help groups are "usually formed by peers who have come together for mutual assistance in satisfying a common need, overcoming a common handicap or life-disrupting problem, and bringing about desired social and/or personal change" (Katz & Bender, 1976, p. 278). The self-help-group movement is both gaining momentum and attracting the attention of social scientists. Such groups offer inexpensive service in a context that minimizes or eliminates stigma. Because they are peer run, they offer most of the same advantages as the indigenous paraprofessional—for example, ease of communication with persons with similar problems and from the same social background.

Alcoholics Anonymous is probably the most well-known group and has the largest clientele. Addiction-like problems seem especially likely to give rise to self-help programs. Take Off Pounds Sensibly (TOPS), and Synanon, a program for heroin addicts, are other examples. Women's consciousness-raising groups are a still more recent example of the self-help approach. Over 50% of 1700 participants in these groups were found to have previously received psychotherapy, suggesting that such groups are joined for many of the same reasons that lead women to enter therapy (Lieberman & Bond, 1976). Recovery, Inc., is a self-help organization for former mental patients. Members may also be under the care of a professional therapist. In fact, self-help groups such as Alcoholics Anonymous are frequently used as resources by professional therapists.

Reducing Demand: Prevention

It appears that the major thrust of mental health education has been to increase the public's demand for services. The public has been instructed that mental health is a natural phenomenon akin to physical health and can therefore be restored by treatment. It has also been persuaded that an increasing number of feelings, behaviors, and "symptoms" indicate potential mental illness and should be brought to the attention of a qualified professional. And more recently, the public is hearing that improved communication, assertiveness, sexual enjoyment, and sense of well-being are also obtainable if one will but make the effort. And pay the price. The result is an increase in the demand for services and the psychotherapy boom described above.

What can be done to decrease demand? Some years ago,

Schofield (1964) urged that educational programs be mounted to help citizens distinguish between normal "problems in living" and mental illness requiring professional help. This suggestion appears to have gone unheeded. The difficulties involved in where to draw the line between problems in living and serious mental illness may have been a major reason, as well as the reluctance of therapists to discourage business.

A more fundamental strategy for decreasing demand is to reduce the prevalence and incidence of mental illness—that is, to prevent serious dysfunction from occurring or developing. This is a similar strategy to that adopted for many physical diseases and is made attractive by some dramatic successes in the area of physical illness such as with yellow fever and polio. Prevention, then, looms as a potentially powerful alternative to psychotherapy, and this is partly reflected in current NIMH financing priorities.

How does one prevent serious dysfunction? Must one have precise knowledge of causes? How would the effectiveness of prevention programs be determined? These are important but difficult questions. Here I will briefly touch on some of the issues; they are more fully discussed in some recent textbooks in community psychology (for example, see Heller & Monahan, 1977; Bloom, 1975).

Primary, Secondary, and Tertiary Prevention

Gerald Caplan, a psychiatrist, has been the most influential theoretician of the prevention of mental disorder. Caplan distinguishes three types of prevention: primary, secondary, and tertiary.

> The term preventive psychiatry refers to the body of professional knowledge, both theoretical and practical, which may be utilized to plan and carry out programs for reducing (1) the incidence of mental disorders of all types in a community (primary prevention), (2) the duration of a significant number of those disorders which do occur (secondary prevention), and (3) the impairment which may result from those disorders (tertiary prevention) [Caplan, 1964, pp. 16–17].

In essence, primary prevention attempts to prevent disorders from occurring and involves interventions prior to the onset of dysfunction. Secondary prevention attempts to identify and treat dysfunction as early as possible in order to reduce duration and severity. Tertiary prevention is an attempt to minimize the degree of handicap or impairment resulting from dysfunction that has already occurred; it is synonymous with psychotherapy and probably is best not construed as prevention at all. This typology has been influential and useful. But, as with all typologies, there are situations or programs that are hard to classify. Programs for chronic former hospital patients aim at promoting community adjustment and preventing relapse and a return to the hospital. Is this tertiary or secondary prevention?

Community-Wide, Milestone, and High-Risk Approaches

A useful way of categorizing preventive programs has been proposed by Bloom (1975). In *community-wide* programs all the residents are recipients. Water purification and fluoridation are examples in the health field. A mental health example might involve a community-wide effort to improve basic child-care facilities. In the *milestone* approach, citizens are exposed to programs at specified periods in their lives. Vaccinations for disease shortly after birth or just before entering school are examples from the health field. Psychological milestones are identified as being, on the basis of both theory and data, stressful stages in normal life. Psychological milestones might include initial school attendance, marriage, birth of a first child, divorce, or widowhood. In the *high-risk* approach, the focus is on vulnerable populations or individuals, who are known to be at risk for specific disorders. This would include those who are identified as showing early onset of some emotional or behavioral problem. Children of alcoholic parents, children of single-parent households, children about to undergo major surgery, or survivors of natural or manmade disasters are examples of high-risk populations.

As Heller and Monahan (1977) pointed out, the three types of programs have both strengths and liabilities. High-risk programs can be better focused and tailored to meet the needs of specific populations but run the ethical risk of labeling or stereotyping individuals, with resultant negative consequences. This risk is compounded by the professional tendency to overpredict disturbance and risk noted in Chapter Nine. Community-wide and milestone interventions avoid problems of labeling but are most costly, because many more people get the program than actually need it.

Person-Focused and Environment-Focused Prevention Efforts

Both for physical and mental health there are two major possible strategies for preventive activities. One approach attempts to modify the stressfulness of the environment or to make it more supportive of healthy functioning. Improving the quality of the water supply or changing the school or home environment are examples. The other approach is to strengthen the coping capacities of individuals by such means as vaccinations, stress training, enhancing their sense of participation and control in their lives, and facilitating their use of naturally existing resources outside the mental health system. These two approaches are not mutually exclusive and sometimes can be integrated. For example, promotion of neighborhood organizations to deal with local problems can be construed both as a means of reducing the stressfulness of the environment and as a means of expanding the social-support network of participating individuals and giving them increased sense of mastery over their local environment.

Some Brief Examples of Prevention Programs

The concept of prevention can be made more concrete by briefly describing some examples.

Prevention of Cultural/Familial Mental Retardation

Low intelligence scores of mothers are associated with low intelligence scores of their children. Cultural/familial mental retardation refers to low measured intelligence without identifiable pathology of the central nervous system and is almost exclusively found in the economically deprived. The Milwaukee Project (Heber & Garber, 1972) sought out children of low-intelligence mothers, and 20 newborns each were assigned to control and preventive programs. The prevention program involved intensive perceptual/motor, cognitive, language, and social/emotional development programs for the children, in addition to intensive work with the mothers to upgrade their homemaking and child-rearing skills.

Although the results of this study are not yet completely in, measures of intellectual learning and language clearly favor the experimental children by a wide margin. This is an example of primary prevention with a high-risk group.

Adjusting to College Life

Entering college is a stressful milestone event. Freshmen are overrepresented among clients in university mental health clinics, and dropping out of school appears to be most frequent in the freshman year. Bloom (1975) developed a program in which questionnaires were periodically administered concerning problems of adjusting to college life. Participants received written information about how their entire group responded to the questionnaire items, thus permitting them to compare their reactions to those of the group. In addition, articles and other information concerning adjustments to college life were made available.

The program appeared to be favorably received by participants, and enrollment data for the sophomore year indicated fewer dropouts among the experimentals. However, this was mostly a function of different transfer rates; fewer experimentals transferred to other schools. This program was relatively economical, in the sense that it did not require any professional time with individual students.

Early Intervention with Problem Drinkers

Alcoholism and other excessive drinking are a major health and mental health problem. One manifestation is driving while drinking, a practice dangerous to both the drinker and other citizens. People with a first conviction for driving under the influence of alcohol constitute a naturally identified high-risk group. Evidence indicates that the repeat rate for such people is relatively high. A program that attempts to intervene with first-offender drunken drivers nicely illustrates the secondary prevention approach and avoids the pitfalls of labeling, because identification occurs by the natural process of the legal system.

One program in my community aims at training first offenders to manage their drinking more effectively and also includes the option of not drinking at all. A major focus is on helping participants monitor their alcohol consumption, estimate blood-alcohol levels, and recognize the early signs of loss of control. The participants are also trained and encouraged to avoid driving when blood-alcohol levels exceed acceptable levels.

Economic and Political Obstacles to Prevention

"An ounce of prevention is worth a pound of cure" is a trite but nevertheless appealing axiom. But it will take many years for even successful prevention programs to have any noticeable impact on the incidence of mental disorder and the demands for psychotherapeutic services. The federal government appears willing to devote some resources to exploring the potential of this approach for mental disorder. At the state and local levels it is more difficult to divert resources away from direct treatment services toward prevention. The benefits of preventive services are difficult to document, both conceptually and practically. This is partly because it is difficult to specify outcomes in any measurable way and also because the outcomes—in the sense of reduced incidence—may be much delayed in time. Citizens do not actively seek preventive services in the same way that they seek treatment for their current distresses. If voters are unable to obtain direct social services, politicians will hear about it. Moreover, delivery of direct services can be readily documented in terms of counting how many clients were seen (and presumably helped).

Many mental health professionals are persuaded by the logic of the argument for devoting more resources to preventive programs. Politicians appear to be becoming more aware of the persuasiveness of this point of view. But citizen awareness appears to lag considerably behind. Coupled with scarce resources and citizen demand for direct treatment services, this lag appears to limit the applicability of prevention as a strategy for reducing demand for psychotherapeutic services.

Suggestions for Citizen Inquiry and Involvement

This book hopes to provide a conceptual framework that will help you understand the different forms of psychotherapy and to increase your knowledge of the political and economic factors that affect the delivery system. Beyond informing you, I hope that some will become engaged with the psychotherapeutic enterprise as concerned citizens. There are at least two bases for citizen concern. One is humanitarian, because psychotherapy is an effort to relieve misery and improve functioning for people who are experiencing great distress or living less-than-fulfilling lives. The second is economic or political. As has been stressed, psychotherapeutic services directly or indirectly consume considerable tax dollars, and we all have a legitimate concern with how well this money is being spent.

Most of you are college students or members of a university community. I will first consider some issues related to the college environment. But at the same time, most of you are also part of a larger community, either the one in which your college or university is situated or the one where you plan to live. The possibilities for engagement in towns and cities is also considered.

The College Community

Virtually every college or university provides counseling or mental health services for troubled or distressed students. These are typically provided by counseling centers and through a student health center. Larger institutions may have other facilities as well, such as a psychology or psychoeducational clinic operated for the purpose of complementing a training program in education or psychology. You could survey the resources available at your school. This would include consideration of the kinds of services provided, eligibility for services, the number and background of employees providing services, the costs (if any) to clients, and the ways in which the different services are financed or supported. Often, your student fees contribute to the support of services at counseling centers or student health centers.

I also suggest that you collect data, either informally or even formally, on the utilization of services. Do your friends, for example, know where to go for counseling? I am constantly surprised about students' ignorance of the availability of free counseling services as well as other mental health services on my campus. Other interesting questions might include whether there are important segments of the student community who apparently could use services but are not getting them or whether the existing counseling and student health settings might provide new or different services that would better meet the needs of the university community.

You might want to consider the old problem of outcome and

accountability. How do the various agencies on your campus evaluate their efforts? What kinds of information do they collect and report to whomever they are responsible to? Can you make any inferences about the cost-effectiveness of these services? For example, many counseling centers must deal with the issue of whether to offer long-term counseling to a relatively few students or to provide crisis-intervention services to many. Finally, in line with the theme of this last chapter, you might think about how paraprofessionals or peer-group support could complement available services and whether there are possibilities for prevention by reducing the stress in the campus environment. The transition from high school and one's hometown to a college or university and a new community involves many stresses. Most colleges are well aware of this problem and have programs designed to ease the transition for new students. Can you identify these programs on your campus? And can you think of ways that they might be improved and extended?

Your Town or City: The Real World

The complexity of the mental health system in your community will depend on its size. But the issues for you to consider and possibilities for engagement are basically similar to those outlined for the campus setting: What are the various services, what do they provide, who offers them, how much do they cost, and who receives them? A major difference between town and gown is that the community is likely to have a number of private practitioners. You may be curious about their professional training and the range of their fees. I would also suggest that you keep an eye out for paraprofessional private practitioners—that is, people without formal training in psychiatry, psychology, or social work who are catering to the private sector. Often, as has been noted, these services are packaged as educational or growth opportunities rather than therapy. A finger-led browse through the yellow pages under Physicians, Psychologists, Counselors, and Marriage and Family Counseling can be informative.

It is the public sector where you have a legitimate concern as taxpayer and citizen as well as concerned humanist. As a first step, survey the available tax-supported services in your community. This includes mental health clinics and state hospitals but also covers services for juveniles. The usual questions noted above would apply. I especially urge you to determine the nature of the financing of these institutions and where in the political process decisions are made about staffing, programs, and level of support. As a citizen, you have a right and possibly an opportunity to participate in such political decisions. Some public agencies employ citizens' advisory boards. Advisory boards serve as a liaison with the community, informing the public about what the agency is doing and informing the agency about public sentiment, needs, and perception of the agency. It may be possible for you to get yourself appointed to such an advisory board, because they are often short of interested citizens who are willing to put some time into the program.

I suggest that you find out whether your community has a Mental Health Association chapter. The association is a nationally organized citizens' group whose purpose is to help educate the public about issues of mental health and mental illness and to improve services for the mentally ill. It is the mental health equivalent of organizations such as the Lung Association or American Cancer Society. Consider joining and supporting your local Mental Health Association. Membership can be a way of learning about your community's mental health resources and problems and can provide a base for raising money, serving on advisory boards, surveying community needs, and developing needed resources.

In most communities, the state government is a major contributor to public facilities. Therefore, your involvement may have to expand beyond your local community, and you may need to become familiar with the workings of the state mental health system and its relations to the state political process. Your state will have a Department of Mental Hygiene, Mental Health Division, or Department of Human Resources (the names vary). You can inquire about the financing and organization of this state agency and how it relates to individual communities and cities. Many states have a state master plan for the development of mental health facilities in all counties and major cities. The plan often includes information about the demographic characteristics of each community, its mental health needs, its available resources, and its plans for the future. Find out whether your state has a plan and what the plan says about your own community. In fact, there may be more than one plan, in that some states have separate programs for those with mental and emotional disturbances, those with alcohol and drug problems, and perhaps retarded and handicapped individuals.

Your Mental Health Association, if there is one, can be a valuable source of information about the state mental health system. Remember that such information is public and that your elected and appointed state officials have some obligation to help you become informed. So do not be afraid to ask questions or request information.

One last suggestion. Where possible, try to visit some of the facilities, especially the large institutions, for the mentally ill, retarded, or aged. The mental hospital is often a sensitive indicator of the commitment that your state or local government has for dealing with the less fortunate among us. The chronic mental patient, as I have noted, is the most vexing problem for the mental health professions and for society. The quality of institutional and community care for the chronic mental patient, therefore, provides important information about what your state and community are willing to do. Go and see for yourself.

Summary

There is a discernible boom in psychotherapy, in that the number of psychotherapists is rapidly increasing and they do not lack for clients. Many current psychotherapy consumers seek an escape from boredom, feelings of alienation, and uncertainty about values and personal identity. Increased wisdom rather than relief of distress seems a goal of many clients.

There are several key social policy considerations that will determine the future character and strength of the psychotherapeutic enterprise. One concerns the federal government stand on community mental health centers. Increased support of the centers will increase the availability of services and provide more jobs for psychotherapists. Second is the possibility of national health insurance, including coverage for mental health services. The federal government would become a much more active third-party payer for services, and this would be a major stimulus to the psychotherapy industry. The third consideration involves government subsidization of the training of psychotherapists. The federal government has been a major contributor to the support of trainees in the major psychotherapy professions but has begun to decrease its contribution in recent years. On the one hand, a more vigorous program of mental health centers or national health insurance or both would provide an important justification for continuing or even increasing this support. On the other hand, the willingness of many young people to finance their own professional education together with the marketability of psychotherapeutic skills may argue for decreased government subsidies.

Psychotherapy has received considerable governmental support primarily because of its value in relieving the suffering of those who are seriously dysfunctional. But there is a good deal of evidence that psychotherapy is limited in its capacity to meet this need. Research indicates that the less seriously disturbed are the ones more likely to seek out or receive psychotherapy.

Increasing the supply of psychotherapy and decreasing demand for it are two major strategies that are supported in varying degrees by government. Expanding the role of paraprofessional therapists is one means of increasing the supply. Quasi-therapeutic programs such as transformational groups, self-help books, and self-help groups also serve to stretch the supply.

Decreasing demand is best accomplished by preventing the onset of mental disorder (primary prevention) or minimizing its seriousness (secondary prevention). Prevention programs may reach all residents of a given community; may reach citizens at certain milestones in their lives such as the beginning of grade school or college, marriage, divorce, or widowhood; or may deal with individuals known to be at high risk. Prevention may focus either on individuals and attempt to increase their competence in coping with stress or may attempt to reduce stressful factors in the environment. Although the rationale for prevention is plausible and great strides have been made in physical health, economic and political obstacles to the prevention of psychological dysfunction are strong. It is difficult to demonstrate tangible results, and already-distressed individuals constitute salient and politically potent constituencies.

Some possibilities for citizen involvement in both academic and community mental health settings were described. There are opportunities for involvement in the planning, delivery, and evaluation of mental health services.

Suggested Readings

1. London, P. The psychotherapy boom: From the long couch for the sick to the push button for the bored. *Psychology Today,* 1974, pp. 63–68. A short, lively account of psychotherapy—its past, present, and possible future.
2. The President's Commission on Mental Health, *Report to the President, 1978* (Vol. 1). U.S. Government Printing Office, June 1978. This report touches on most of the issues—personnel and professional training, economics, prevention—covered in Chapter Ten as well as topics considered in Chapters Eight and Nine.
3. Heller, K., & Monahan, J. *Psychology and community change.* Homewood, Ill.: Dorsey, 1977. A good account of prevention strategies and issues.

APPENDIX

Selected Psychotherapeutic Methods

This appendix provides brief, non-evaluative descriptions of several therapeutic methods not covered in the text. Key references for each approach are also provided to guide you to more information. Where possible, I have tried to list both a primary and a secondary reference.

The first section considers multiple-client psychotherapy—that dealing with couples, families, and groups. Then, various therapies are presented and are related, where possible, to the three major approaches described in Chapters Five through Seven.

Treating Larger Social Systems: Couples, Families, and Groups

This text has emphasized individual therapy. But in practice much psychotherapy is administered to larger and more complex social units. This section describes some of the important reasons for working with larger units and considers some of the key issues involved.

It is fundamental to recognize that couples, families, and groups can all be approached from each of the three major perspectives that this book has considered. Psychoanalytic, humanistic, and behavioral psychotherapists all deal with these larger units and have no difficulty in extrapolating theory and technique to them. The three approaches share key assumptions about the advantages of treating larger social units, and all must deal with the major problems that arise.

Couples: Therapy for Distressed Relationships

Many couples seek psychotherapeutic help because they are experiencing intense unhappiness and distress with each other. Sometimes couples are urged to seek help before resorting to legal action. Other couples simply want to better their relationship by improving their ability to solve problems, their communication, or their sexual relations. These basic reasons that couples seek help—to reduce pain or for self-improvement—exactly parallel the therapy-seeking motives of individuals.

Therapists vary considerably in their format for dealing with distressed couples. Probably the most common approach is to see the couple together, to try to deal with all of the issues as shared, and to avoid or minimize individual contact with one or the other partner. Some therapists, however, prefer a mixture of individual talks and joint sessions, and a few therapists may concentrate most of their time with the individual partners. Decisions about this issue reflect a therapist's view of the nature of troubled relationships. Many view the distress as inherently residing in the interaction or the dyad;

others give more weight to the conflicts, motives, and needs of the individuals involved.

Couple therapists who operate from a psychoanalytic framework tend to focus on the interplay of each partner's defense mechanisms and other unconscious processes as they affect the relationship. The ways in which the partners may be "transferring" to the relationship the needs, expectations, and ways of relating of prior important relationships are considered very important. Because couple therapy tends to be short and focused on reality, psychoanalytically oriented therapists do not delve heavily into historical origins but are alert for current manifestations. Interpretations and perhaps some direct suggestions are offered to help couples alter what appear to be dysfunctional ways of relating.

Humanistic therapists dealing with couples are more variable but tend to focus on improving communication and on encouraging direct expressions of needs and wants. Their goal is to foster greater sharing and intimacy between partners. The focus is very much on the "here and now," and role playing or other Gestalt techniques may well be employed.

Behaviorally oriented couple therapists tend to be the most directive of those discussed. The emphasis is on helping couples learn relationship skills they are believed to be deficient in. These abilities include pinpointing or specifying the behaviors in one's partner that are pleasing or displeasing, negotiating contracts to bring about desired changes in each other's behavior, and improving communication. Enhancing communication skills—in the sense of learning to listen to one's partner, to reflect back a partner's meaning and feelings, and to clearly express one's own meanings and feelings—appears to be a common goal shared by couple therapists of all theoretical persuasions.

Suggested Reading

Paolino, T. J., & McCrady, B. S. *Marriage and marital therapy: Psychoanalytic, behavioral and systems theory perspectives.* New York: Brunner/Mazel, 1978. Contributed chapters describe the different approaches to psychotherapy with couples.

Families

Family therapy was touched on in Chapter Seven in the section on behavioral approaches to children. It was noted that behavioral therapy focuses on training parents to more effectively manage their children, whereas the psychoanalytic approach often stresses the intrapsychic feelings and conflicts of the child. Many therapists view a child's or adolescent's problems as symptomatic of faulty family relationships and therefore choose to deal with entire families. Family therapy is becoming a more popular strategy as interactional views of human problems gain ascendance. The therapist typically tries to see all members of the family together. Sometimes a cotherapist is employed to help keep track of things, because there are many possible interactions that can occur at the same time. Consistent with the assumption that the target client's problems are a manifestation of faulty family communication, interaction, or expectations, the aim is to achieve changes in the *family system*, not just to relieve symptoms or change the target client. Family therapists believe that, unless a change in the system is brought about, individuals within it will continue to experience difficulty.

As with couples, families can be approached from a variety of ideological perspectives, from psychoanalytic to behavioristic. Family therapists tend to be active and directive, however, even when operating from a psychoanalytic perspective. A therapist might, for example, rearrange where family members are seated as a way of introducing a change in family alliances or communication. Or one member might be asked to react to the direct or indirect communication of another family member.

Suggested Readings

Foley, V. Family therapy. In R. J. Corsini (Ed.), *Current psychotherapies* (2nd ed.). Itasca, Ill.: Peacock, 1979. Pp. 460–499. A good introductory overview.

Lieberman, R. Behavioral approaches to family and couple therapy. In G. Erickson & T. Hogan (Eds.), *Family therapy, an introduction to theory and technique.* New York: Jason Aronson, 1976. A useful description of the behavioral approach to family work.

Minuchin, S. *Families and family therapy.* Cambridge, Mass.: Harvard University Press, 1974. An influential description of the structural position by a major exponent.

Groups

Group therapy is also practiced from all theoretical perspectives. It is sometimes recommended and utilized as an adjunct or complement to individual therapy; often it is the only treatment that a client receives. Group size also varies considerably. Therapy groups tend to consist of six to eight clients. Encounter or growth-enhancing groups are usually larger in size, ranging up to the 250 or so seen in *est* programs. Often, especially in agency or institutional settings, two therapists lead a group. Cotherapists are useful for several reasons: they can better track the group's interactions; they can exchange ideas or feelings with each other and thus, for example, model certain behaviors for clients; and they provide an additional person— particularly, for example, if one is a male and the other a female—for group members to identify with.

Groups have some important advantages. Clients experience similarities with other members, which counteracts feelings of isolation and deviance. Group members can offer support and encouragement. Perhaps most importantly, the group provides opportunities for learning about one's stimulus value and ways of relating with others in a setting that much more closely approximates real life than does individual therapy.

Groups can also be characterized as open (or ongoing) or closed. The closed group is one formed by a particular set of clients and continues for either a fixed number of sessions or until the clients decide to dissolve it; no additional clients are invited or permitted to join. An open-ended group permits new clients to enter, and there is no fixed number of sessions or any clear ending point. Open groups are common in institutional settings, where the residents of a given ward or area of a hospital constitute the group, and membership changes with admissions and discharges.

Another issue concerns the heterogeneity or homogeneity of the group's clients with respect to sex, age, and type of problem. Particular kinds of clients may be more comfortable with others who share similar situations and problems. For example, a group of adolescent boys or girls might deal with the issues unique to this age group. Women's consciousness-raising groups are another obvious example. Alcoholics, drug addicts, obese people trying to lose weight, or even groups of married couples are other somewhat homogeneous groups. The argument for heterogeneous groups is that they more nearly reflect the real world and provide participants with a better opportunity to learn to deal with various issues and persons.

A final distinction, noted before, concerns the avowed function of the group. There has been a phenomenal growth of groups aimed at fostering awareness, enrichment, and growth. Many of these growth groups are run by paraprofessionals; many operate outside of the conventional mental health system. They typically disavow therapeutic intent and try to warn away those who may be seriously disturbed. But, as I have repeatedly emphasized, in terms of their actual operations, processes, and functions, they are not distinguishable from psychotherapy.

Suggested Readings

Frank, J. D. *Persuasion and healing* (Rev. ed.). Baltimore: Johns Hopkins University Press, 1973. Chapter Ten is a good overview of group therapy.

Shaffer, J. B. P., & Galinsky, M. D. *Models of group therapy and sensitivity training.* Englewood Cliffs, N.J.: Prentice-Hall, 1974. Contains chapters on 12 different approaches to group therapy, including those covered in Chapters Five through Seven of this book.

Psychoanalytic Therapies

There are numerous psychoanalytic therapies, some of them derivatives of Freudian thought and others alternative conceptions. The older or more traditional variants of psychoanalytic thought and therapy are associated with specific individuals. These were the great theorists and practitioners who either themselves or with their followers developed "schools." A partial listing here would include Carl Jung, Otto Rank, Alfred Adler, Karen Horney, and Harry Stack Sullivan. They still have their adherents and, often, their unique training settings (institutes, usually set in large urban centers). Some of their ideas continue to be actively taught in academic settings, especially medical schools.

Two of Freud's earliest and closest associates, Alfred Adler and Carl Jung, split off and moved in opposite directions. Jungian therapy retains a small group of committed followers but is not as prominent on the contemporary scene as are the views of Adler. Through the work of his disciple Rudolph Dreikurs, Adler's ideas are now quite influential in the realm of parent/child relationships, child guidance, and school counseling as well as still providing a base for therapy with adults.

Jungian Psychotherapy

Jung shared Freud's basic belief that insight into the unconscious is the key to psychotherapeutic change. Jung broadened the concept of the unconscious, however, viewing it as a reservoir of creative tendencies in addition to primitive impulses. Further, Jung's unconscious included fantasies and symbols that are universal in the sense of reflecting eternal themes and issues prevalent in all past and present cultures. Because the unconscious cannot be known directly, but only through symbolic communication, much of Jungian analysis concerns interpreting symbols, particularly as expressed in dreams. Jungians emphasize phenomenological aspects of dreams, focusing more on the manifest content than on the presumed latent content, as do Freudian dream interpreters.

Jungians also give more weight, relative to orthodox Freudians, to the present meanings of conflicts and the future goals of the patient. Different age levels are viewed as requiring different solutions to problems, and Jung was among the first to emphasize self-realization and spirituality as issues to be dealt with in middle and later life. In a sense, he anticipated some of the more recent work on adult stages in human life discussed both in the technical literature and in popular books such as *The Seasons of a Man's Life* (Levinson, 1978).

Procedurally, Jungian therapists tend to be more active than orthodox psychoanalysts, especially in discussions of symbols and dreams. They rarely use a couch, preferring face-to-face interactions. Jungian therapy also tends to be shorter, patients being seen both less frequently and for fewer sessions. The following quotation conveys the flexibility of the Jungian method:

> The analyst may teach, suggest, cajole, give advice, reflect feelings, or give support. The main emphasis is on the conscious assimilation of the immediate experience, using as well techniques that have now become the stock in trade of the Gestalt therapy and the encounter movement [Kaufman, 1979, p. 112].

Interpretation remains the major specific intervention of the therapist:

> The main thrust of the analytical process may be summarized as an attempt to make conscious as much as possible what has been unconscious; thereby a behavioral change becomes possible. After the reality situation and patient's phenomenological world have been established, dream interpretation is undertaken. Dream work is the core of Jungian therapy [Kaufman, 1979, p. 112–113].

Suggested Readings

Kaufman, Y. Analytic psychotherapy. In R. J. Corsini (Ed.), *Current psychotherapies* (2nd ed.). Itasca, Ill.: Peacock, 1979. Pp. 95–130. A readable overview of Jungian therapy. Contains references to Jung's original writings, which are voluminous.

Adlerian Psychotherapy

While Jung was moving toward greater emphasis on the unconscious, Adler was turning toward a greater concern with conscious intentions, adaptive behavior, life-style, and, in general, the importance of social forces in shaping personality and neurosis. Specifically, Adlerians focus on the family, the child's position in it, and, especially, the way in which the child deals with the inherent powerlessness of childhood. A key construct is the notion of life-style, which includes the aspirations, long-range goals, and necessary conditions for one's social well-being that the individual develops within the family system.

Adlerian therapy has been described as having four major aims: "(1) establishing and maintaining a 'good' relationship; (2) uncovering the dynamics of the patient, his life style, his goals and how they affect his life movement; (3) interpretation, culminating in insight; and (4) reorientation" (Mozak, 1979, p. 64). The reorientation goal implies a more active educative component in Adlerian therapy, a factor involved in the popularity of this approach in educational circles.

Adlerians work in a face-to-face relationship with clients, often without a desk, as a way of implying a cooperative, nonauthoritarian relationship. The establishment of a good relationship is accomplished by standard means. The therapist conveys an interested, respectful, accepting, and honest attitude toward the client. The analysis, or what might be thought of as the diagnostic phase of treatment, may be accomplished formally or informally. The therapist is alert for cues to the client's life-style and the resulting "script" that the client has constructed. Scripts are similar to the "games" of transactional analysis (discussed in the next section) and refer to habitual expectations or interaction patterns between the client and significant others.

The *life-style investigation* is the major formal assessment procedure used by Adlerian therapists. It typically begins with an exploration of the client's family constellation that seeks clues concerning the formation of the life-style. Another part of the assessment consists of interpreting the client's early recollections. The client is asked to verbalize a memory from very early childhood, and this is then treated as a projective set of data and interpreted. Data about the family constellation and early recollections then permit the therapist to infer the client's "basic mistakes," which are essentially faulty assumptions about one's self, others, and the interactions between the two. Basic mistakes include impossible goals of security—for example, "I have to please everybody"—and minimization or denial of one's worth—"I'm *just* a housewife." A description of the client's assets are also included—a commendable addition, because many therapeutic assessments overemphasize problems and pathology.

Over the course of therapy, Adlerians appear to be relatively eclectic in procedure and technique. Interpretation is a major tool within the Adlerian framework and is used with ordinary communications, dreams, fantasies, and the therapeutic relationship. The emphasis of interpretation is on "purpose rather than cause." By this is apparently meant that Adlerians emphasize the payoff function—the rewards or benefits—that various behaviors or scripts provide for the client. Advice and encouragement are also acceptable practices, as are role playing and related action procedures. Adlerians also give suggestions and homework assignments in a manner similar to that of behavior therapists. For example, if a client continually makes "if-only-I-could" statements, the therapist may request that the client act during the next week "as if" he or she could be or act in the way desired. Adlerians also give specific tasks, such as recommending that a depressed individual engage in pleasant activities or try to give pleasure to another person.

The reorientation phase overlaps with the analytic and interpretative phase of therapy. The therapist attempts to persuade or encourage the client to make active use in everyday life of what he or she is learning in treatment. Reorientation involves persuading the client "gently or forcefully that change is in his best interest" (Mozak, 1979, p. 69).

The eclecticism and concreteness of the Adlerian approach relative to other psychodynamic therapies have undoubtedly contributed to its popularity.

Suggested Readings

Ansbacher, H. H., & Ansbacher, R. (Eds.). *The individual psychology of Alfred Adler*. New York: Basic Books, 1956. Selections from Adler's writings, with commentary by the editors.

Mozak, H. H. Adlerian psychotherapy. In R. J. Corsini (Ed.), *Current psychotherapies* (2nd ed.). Itasca, Ill.: Peacock, 1979. Pp. 44–94.

Transactional Analysis

A much more recent and currently very popular derivative of psychoanalysis is transactional analysis (TA), which reconceptualizes id, ego, and superego constructs in terms of three interacting ego states: Parent, Child, and Adult. The Parent corresponds to the Freudian superego and consists of countless experiences, events, roles, and admonitions taken in "straight" without "editing," primarily within the first five years of life. The Parent, in effect, represents internalized roles for living imparted by the main socializing agents, the parents, during early life. The Child roughly corresponds to the Freudian id. It is also largely formed during the first five years of life and is primarily composed of a set of *feelings*, because it develops during a period when the child has limited verbal or cognitive capacity. The Child is that helpless, vulnerable, and dependent part of us, but it is also the storehouse of creativity, curiosity, and the urge to explore. The Adult corresponds to the Freudian ego and has been described as a "data processing computer, which grinds out decisions after computing the information from three sources: the Parent, the Child, and the data which the Adult has gathered and is gathering" (Harris, 1969, p. 53).

Based on experiences during the first five years of life, each person arrives at a fundamental life position, of which there are four possible variations:

1. I'm not OK—you're OK.
2. I'm not OK—you're not OK.
3. I'm OK—you're not OK.
4. I'm OK—you're OK.

Of these, only the fourth—basic acceptance of both self and others—is considered to be a mature and healthy state of affairs.

Like many derivatives of Freudian thought, TA emphasizes social needs and motives more than Freud, who stressed sex and aggression. We are all assumed to need certain basic "strokes" for our well-being. The TA basic list of needs includes stroke hunger, structure hunger, excitement hunger, recognition hunger, and leadership hunger.

The basic life positions lead to the formation of certain scripts and games, by which we play out the positions in our interactions with others. The essence of TA therapy is analyzing the current interactions of Parent, Child, and Adult and their manifestations in scripts and games and then teaching people how to change their basic life position and thereby change the scripts and games engaged in. The intent is to increase clients' awareness of when they are operating in Parent, Child, or Adult states and of how interpersonal interactions and communications can become muddied when transactions between two persons involve differing ego states. That is, we communicate best with another person when our Adult speaks to his or hers or our Child speaks to his or her Child. Difficulties arise when an Adult communication is met by a Parental rejoinder, as in "Where are my cuff links?"—an Adult request for information—which is met by "Probably where you left them, sloppy!"—a Parent-to-Child response (Holland, 1975).

Transactional analysis is commonly conducted in groups, making it potentially a very efficient treatment. Background reading is usually recommended to familiarize participants with the basic structural concepts. The typical TA group has eight members and meets once a week for 2 hours. A blackboard and a tape recorder are often available (Holland, 1975).

The group then proceeds to interact, with the intent that each participant learn to track which ego states he or she is operating in at any given moment or in any given transaction. Reaction from the group and occasional playback by means of the tape recorder are used to increase awareness and better tracking of ego states. An "empty-chair" technique, in which the client role-plays with one of his or her own troublesome ego states, is also used. This procedure is similar to one used in Gestalt therapy. Clients also learn the consequences of different ego states for themselves and for others. Much of the therapeutic interaction involves transactional and script analysis, especially learning to spot crossed transactions—for example, when a "Parent" response is given to an "Adult" communication.

Games and scripts become the focus of extended therapy. A game is a "recurring set of transactions, often repetitious, superficially plausible with a concealed motivation" (Harris, 1969, p. 146). For example, a young woman who believes that men are basically seeking to take advantage of her sexually may interact with a young man whose script involves the assumption that women are rejecting and ungiving. Much of the interaction may be plausible and rational, but they play out their scripts: she may act in a sexually provocative way without being fully aware she is doing so, enticing him into making a move that is clumsy and then rejecting him. Thus, both can fulfill their scripts, or expectations.

Because of its relatively simple set of concepts, its utility in groups, and the availability of much literature on the subject, TA has been quite influential. Many people who find Freudian ideas objectionable or murky readily accept TA, often without being aware of its Freudian roots.

Suggested Readings

Berne, E. *Games people play.* New York: Grove Press, 1964. A readable, influential book by the founder of TA.

Harris, T. A. *I'm OK—You're OK.* New York: Harper & Row, 1969. Written for the lay public by another influential figure in the development of TA.

Holland, G. A. Transactional analysis. In R. J. Corsini (Ed.), *Current psychotherapies*, Itasca, Ill.: Peacock, 1975. Pp. 353–400. A useful overview.

Humanistic Therapies

This section covers several kinds of humanistic psychotherapies. The first part deals with body therapies, some of which have psychoanalytic derivatives (for example, bioenergetics). Treating them under a humanistic heading is somewhat arbitrary.

Body Therapies

It has been emphasized that psychotherapy is an inherently verbal endeavor. By definition it characteristically excludes intrusive procedures such as medication or electric shock. At least this has been the traditional view of things. But in recent years this previously important distinction has been blurring. A number of therapeutic or quasi-therapeutic approaches have evolved that deemphasize verbal communication and instead emphasize body manipulation or body language. Some body therapies are clearly Freudian or psychoanalytic derivatives; some owe their heritage to humanistic approaches; and for some the roots are obscure. In this section I first outline several key characteristics shared by all the body therapies and then briefly describe the principal features of some of the more influential ones.

There are at least two dozen body therapies, but all share several key features. First, all involve attempts to produce direct changes in a client's physical functioning and sensing. Changes in musculature, posture, breathing, and even seeing are the focus of treatment. Increasing the individual's awareness of the kinesthetic structural and sensory aspects of one's own body—getting "in touch"—is the major focus. Second, there is an assumption of the inherent "goodness" of bodily experiencing and expressiveness. It is a belief in the "wisdom" of the body, an assumption that an individual's bodily reactions provide a true measure of emotional reaction. As do client-centered and Gestalt therapists, body therapists believe that many people have lost the ability to become aware of the messages that their bodies are trying to send them and have thus become insensitive to their own feelings and emotions. Third, there is the idea that the natural flow of physical energy can be blocked. Blocking has come about because of emotional conflicts and impedes the individual's further emotional development. Much of body therapy is devoted to detecting blockages in physical energy—for example, finding in what parts of the person's body the blocking is taking place—and then removing the blockage. Fourth, there is reliance on body diagnosis—using bodily signs such as carriage and muscle tightness as a means of diagnosing, or *inferring*, emotional conflicts. The use of body diagnosis follows directly from the third assumption that blocking is keyed by emotional conflicts.[1]

Given these basic assumptions, body therapists believe that it is necessary and often sufficient to directly manipulate the body. Purely verbal means of treatment are believed to be ineffective in altering bodily processes that have become habitual and highly overlearned. In a sense, body therapies share the assumption with behavior therapists that attitude change follows behavior more readily than behavior follows attitude change.

In practice, body therapies range from those such as rolfing that are almost exclusively nonverbal to those such as bioenergetics or even Gestalt therapy that emphasize a mixture of words and actions. In some approaches the therapist directly lays hands on the client; in fact, there may be vigorous manipulation of muscles and limbs. In other body therapies the client moves through directed exercises with only minimal direct contact by the therapist.

Suggested Reading

Harper, R. A. *The new psychotherapies.* Englewood Cliffs, N.J.: Prentice-Hall, 1975. Pages 125–138 contain short summaries of the major body therapies.

Bioenergetics

Bioenergetic therapy appears to be gaining influence and illustrates a number of the basic principles involved in body therapies. The approach descends from Wilhelm Reich, originally a disciple of Freud's, who called attention to the role of muscular tension in defending against repressed impulses. Reich's views were significantly modified and expanded by one of his students, Alexander Lowen. Lowen assumes that there is one fundamental energy in the human body that underlies both psychic and somatic phenomena, and this is

[1] I am grateful to Susan Phillips and Freda McEwan for their analysis of these commonalities.

termed bioenergy. All neurotic problems are viewed as rooted in the deflection or blocking of the basic bioenergy. The normally function-ing individual naturally regulates bioenergy flow, holding the energy when appropriate and then discharging it when needed in action—say, for example, in sexual expression. The neurotic, on the other hand, may be unable to hold energy, acting or discharging it im-pulsively, or may be blocked and suppress its natural flow when action is appropriate.

Bioenergetic therapy involves talking, exercises carried out largely by the client, and occasional therapist probing or manipula-tion of the client's body. In this way the bioenergetic therapist analyzes both the psychological and physical aspects of the problem. Diagnosis, which takes place at the beginning of therapy and also occasionally throughout it as a means of gauging progress, relies in good part on carriage and muscle tension, both in the free-standing individual and especially while the client carries out several standard exercises. Clients' physical and psychological reactions to the exer-cises provide important cues for the therapist. To facilitate the read-ing of these bodily cues, bioenergetic clients typically work in their underwear.

Therapy consists of an interplay of exercises and talk. The exer-cises help the client and therapist locate the source of tension and blocking. The talk helps the client to integrate bodily feelings and emotions with cognitive understanding. One emphasis is on gaining greater sensory awareness of one's bodily feelings and the emotional meanings of these feelings. A combination of the client's exposed position and the simultaneous work on both bodily and verbal ex-pression sometimes leads to very strong emotional expression, which the therapist must be prepared to accept and deal with.

Bioenergetic principles and techniques are being disseminated through workshops and demonstrations in numerous settings. How-ever, formal training is limited to several institutes and requires 5 years of seminars and supervised experience, albeit on a part-time basis.

Suggested Reading

Lowen, A. *Bioenergetics*. New York: Penguin, 1976.

Primal Therapy

Primal therapy is a recent innovation developed by Arthur Janov. It has some similarities to psychoanalytic treatment but is probably closer to body therapy. Janov believes that neurosis has its roots in early childhood. The child experiences primal pain when his or her primal needs such as food, comfort, and so forth are not met. These pains remain stored in the body and produce layers of tension, which is inadequately discharged. At some fateful day, the child splits off part of the self, and the primal pain becomes disconnected from awareness and instead is expressed in various neurotic systems. The job of primal therapy is to help the client relive critical experiences of primal pain so that the pain is reexperienced and the heretofore split person is once more integrated. The means by which this is accomplished are often quite dramatic and are in large part responsible for the fairly widespread publicity enjoyed by primal therapy. The therapy is not practiced very widely, however, and because of its expense and the intense expressions of emotionality that occur is not to be undertaken lightly.

Primal therapy begins with an intense 3-week period during which the client is instructed to abstain from usual activities and responsibilities. The client goes to a place arranged by the therapist and engages in daily individual treatments punctuated by rest and exercises. The procedure involves early memory associations, breathing exercises, verbal confrontation, and the like. Therapist and client are together for much of the 3 weeks. The culmination of this process is the "primal scream," or an intense abreactive or cathartic experience. The client is then seen in group therapy for 6 to 9 months for a continuation of the abreactive experiences, a kind of working-through process. The therapy is very expensive—the 3-week period was estimated in 1976 to cost about $5,000.

Suggested Reading

Janov, A. *The primal scream.* New York: Dell, 1970. The founder of primal therapy describes and defends his approach.

Existential Psychotherapy

Existential therapy is one of the important and influential humanistic psychotherapies. I did not elect to include it in Chapter Six for two major reasons. First, I believe that the client-centered and Gestalt approaches have greater current influence. And second, the existential approach is really a set of approaches, none of which is easily summarized.

Existential therapy shares the key assumptions of the humanistic approach that were described at the beginning of Chapter Six: the importance of choice and freedom, the uniqueness of the human experience, a phenomenological emphasis, the "realness" of the therapeutic relationship, and an emphasis on present experience.

Existential therapy is rooted in European existential philosophy, and the first existential therapists also had European roots. Existentialism disavows the distinction between subject and object. The meaning of any fact depends on a person's relationship to it. The term *being* is used to designate a state similar to client-centered *con-*

gruence or Gestalt *awareness*. It is an awareness and acceptance of both one's inner experiencing and one's relatedness to the environment. A major strategy in existential therapy is for the therapist to engage the client in a real, or "authentic," interpersonal encounter in an effort to heighten the client's sense of "being."

Being is constantly changing and developing. But there is also a strong realization of the inevitability of nonbeing, of death. *Existential anxiety* is a term for this "normal" concern about nonbeing. Existential anxiety is also related to or triggered by choices or options. Each choice presents the possibility of failing to fulfill one's potential or giving up opportunities.

It is especially difficult to describe the methods of existential therapy, because they vary greatly and because some therapists disavow systematizing the approach, arguing that this tends to get in the way of a genuine interpersonal encounter. Some existential therapists use many psychoanalytic concepts and methods but construe them within the metaphors of existentialism. Rollo May, the most influential American existential therapist, appears to operate this way. Others tend toward an encounterlike format involving a good deal of confrontation and therapist self-disclosure.

An existential therapist with a distinctive style and discernible technique is Victor Frankl, originator of logotherapy. Logotherapy emphasizes the spiritual dimension of man, which Frankl believes is neglected by other approaches. Logotherapy aims at helping clients accept responsibility for themselves and move toward their ultimate possibility. Philosophical discussion and suggestion are used toward this end. The client's attitudes toward a symptom, rather than the symptom itself, are often the focus of discussion.

Frankl has also developed a specific technique—paradoxical intention—to deal with certain anxieties and phobic reactions. He believes that a key factor in anxiety reaction and phobias is anticipatory anxiety, which serves to produce the condition that is feared. In paradoxical intention, the client is told to no longer fight or flee from the symptom but to "join" it, produce it, and exaggerate it. For example, a client troubled by extreme blinking in social situations would be told to blink often and intensively. This procedure short-circuits the anticipatory anxiety and serves to "distance" the client from the symptom. Clients find that after a while they have trouble producing the symptom and that it no longer occurs unexpectedly.

Suggested Readings

Frankl, V. E. *Man's search for meaning* (Rev. ed.). New York: Washington Square Press, 1963. A readable description by the originator of logotherapy.

Shaffer, J. B. P. *Humanistic psychology*. Englewood Cliffs, N.J.:

Prentice-Hall, 1978. Chapters Two and Four contain broad summaries of basic existential concepts and their application in psychotherapy.

Directive Therapies

No additional behavior-therapy methods are considered here, because several of the major kinds were described in Chapter Seven. The final two approaches described stand somewhat close to behavior therapy, in that the therapist tends to be more directive and to help the client focus on specific, often behavioral, treatment goals.

Reality Therapy

Reality therapy was developed by psychiatrist William Glasser during the 1950s. Like many other new approaches, it initially emphasized its divergence from the psychoanalytic perspective. Essential to the approach is the conviction that each person is responsible and accountable for his or her own behavior. The term *irresponsible* is used to describe inappropriate, manipulative, or self-defeating behavior that other approaches would label neurotic or dysfunctional. The client's past, no matter how cruel, is not to be used as an excuse for irresponsible behavior; "until an individual accepts the fact that he is responsible for what he does, there can be no treatment" (Glasser & Zunin, 1979, p. 302).

Reality therapy is based on the premise that people have a common basic need for identity, a feeling of separateness and distinctness. A successful identity, in turn, is viewed as depending on a person's giving and receiving love and worth. People whose identity is compromised by deficits in love or worth are regarded as being in need of therapy. They are behaving irresponsibly in order to try to satisfy their needs.

Reality therapy stresses the involvement of the therapist in the client's life. The therapist shows interest and concern but focuses on present behavior rather than feelings. Reality therapy shares with behavior therapy the assumption that good feelings follow effective behavior rather than vice versa.

After demonstrating involvement, the reality therapist begins to *reject irresponsible behavior* and encourages the client to do likewise by prompting the client to make value judgments about his or her behavior. Then the therapist actively encourages the learning of responsible ways to fulfill the client's needs. This is often done by prompting the client to make concrete plans for the future (that is, tomorrow) and make a commitment to the plan. If the plan is not followed, excuses are not discussed or accepted, nor is the client punished or reprimanded. Instead, the therapist might say: "The plan didn't work. Let's make a new one together." At other times the therapist might say: "You said you would do it. When will you do it?" There is a persistent focus on helping clients commit themselves to specific courses of action for which they take responsibility.

Reality therapy has been used with a wide variety of clients and settings. It is reported to be particularly effective with chronic mental patients and with juveniles exhibiting behavior problems. Both groups tend to deny and avoid responsibility. Chronic mental patients become dependent and shape the environment to care for them. Juveniles with behavioral problems blame their parents, the schools, the police, or their friends. Reality therapy can be useful in helping such people take responsibility for themselves and develop and carry out plans for satisfying their needs without depending on or hurting others.

Suggested Readings

Glasser, W. *Reality therapy: A new approach to psychiatry.* New York: Harper & Row, 1965. A description by the originator of this approach.
Glasser, W., & Zunin, L. M. Reality therapy. In R. J. Corsini (Ed.), *Current psychotherapies* (2nd ed.). Itasca, Ill.: Peacock, 1979. Pp. 302–339. A clear overview of reality therapy.

Hypnosis

Hypnosis arouses considerable curiosity and misunderstanding among the public. Even within the professional community there is a fair amount of controversy. These reactions stem in part from uncertainty over the nature of the hypnotic phenomenon. Some experts believe that hypnosis represents a qualitatively different state of consciousness, within which mental and physical accomplishments are possible that cannot otherwise be performed. Other experts contend that hypnosis is not qualitatively different from other situations that combine strong suggestion and motivation. Whichever of these views is correct, the use of hypnosis in psychotherapy seems clearly to be increasing—in good part, I believe, because hypnosis lends itself readily to directive short-term interventions, which are becoming more the mode in contemporary psychotherapy.

A basic fact for you to keep in mind is that hypnosis is not a form of psychotherapy per se; hypnosis is a *tool* utilized by therapists of varying theoretical approaches. Further, it is rare that hypnosis is the only, or even the major, psychotherapeutic procedure used. Rather, it is mostly employed as an adjunct in the context of whatever other procedures the therapist characteristically uses.

Prior to the use of hypnosis, the therapist discusses the procedure with the client, explains what the client might experience, relieves any fears the client might have about being "controlled," and indicates how the procedure could be useful in treatment. There are many induction techniques; most therapists have a few standard ones. The use of hypnosis in therapy depends on the therapist's approach and the client's problem. Psychodynamic therapists may employ it to help explore fantasies or repressed material that seems otherwise difficult for the client to confront. Sometimes the information gained is largely for the therapist's use, and the client may be instructed to remember only as much on awakening as he or she is comfortable with. Therapists who are more directive may use hypnosis to promote the development of certain attitudes or behaviors. For example, a client may want to strengthen his or her ability to avoid certain foods or substances such as cigarettes or alcohol. A therapist may use hypnosis to induce vivid imagery within which the client—again in imagination—imagines intensely uncomfortable feelings in association with the substances he or she would like to avoid. A general strategy used by many hypnotherapists is to ascertain, with the help of hypnosis, what their clients really want to achieve and then to use hypnotic suggestion to encourage them in this direction.

Many prospective clients look on hypnosis as a kind of magic pill or panacea, something that can be administered to help them change behavior or overcome a problem immediately and with little conscious effort. Experts in the therapeutic use of hypnosis agree that it does not work this way.

References

Adams, S., & Orgel, M. *Through the mental health maze: A consumer's guide to finding a psychotherapist, including a sample consumer/therapist contract.* Washington, D.C.: Public Citizen's Health Research Group, 1975.

Albee, G. W. Conceptual models and manpower requirements in psychology. *American Psychologist,* 1968, *23,* 317–320.

Albee, G. W., & Kessler, M. Evaluating individual deliverers: Private practice and professional standards review organizations. *Professional Psychology,* 1977, *8,* 502–515.

Alexander, F., & French, T. M. *Psychoanalytic therapy: Principles and application.* New York: Wiley, 1946.

Allen, K. E., Hart, B. M., Buell, J. S., Harris, F. Q., & Wolf, M. W. Effects of social reinforcement on isolate behavior of a nursery school child. *Child Development,* 1964, *35,* 511–518.

American Medical Association. *Directory of residency training programs 1978–1979.* Chicago: Author, 1978.

American Psychiatric Association. *The principles of medical ethics: With annotations especially applicable to psychiatry.* Washington, D.C.: Author, 1973.

American Psychological Association. Standards for providers of psychological services. *American Psychologist,* 1977, *32,* 495–505.

American Psychological Association. APA-approved doctoral programs in clinical, counseling, and school psychology: 1978. *American Psychologist,* 1978, *33,* 1127–1128.

American Psychological Association. Task Force on Continuing Evaluation in National Health Insurance. Continuing evaluation and accountability controls for a national health insurance program. *American Psychologist,* 1978, *33,* 305–310.

Anthony, W. A., & Carkhuff, R. R. The functional professional therapeutic agent. In A. S. Gurman & A. M. Razin (Eds.), *Effective psychotherapy.* Oxford: Pergamon Press, 1977, 103–114.

Axline, V. M. *Play therapy.* Boston: Houghton Mifflin, 1947.

Ayllon, T., & Azrin, N. H. *The token economy: A motivational system for therapy and rehabilitation.* New York: Appleton-Century-Crofts, 1968.

Azrin, N. H. A strategy for applied research: Learning based but outcome oriented. *American Psychologist,* 1977, *32,* 140–149.

Bandura, A. *Principles of behavior modification.* New York: Holt, Rinehart & Winston, 1969.

Bandura, A. *Social learning theory.* Englewood Cliffs, N.J.: Prentice-Hall, 1977.

Bandura, A., Blanchard, E. B., & Ritter, B. The relative efficacy of desensitization and modeling approaches for inducing behavioral, affective, and attitudinal changes. *Journal of Personality and Social Psychology,* 1969, *13,* 173–199.

Barton, E. S., Guess, D., Garcia, E., & Baer, D. M. Improvement of retardates' mealtime behavior by timeout procedure using multiple baseline techniques. *Journal of Applied Behavior Analysis,* 1970, *3,* 77–84.

Beck, A., & Greenberg, R. L. Cognitive therapy with women. In V. Franks & V. Burtle (Eds.), *Women in therapy: New psychotherapies for a changing society.* New York: Brunner/Mazel, 1974.

Bent, R. Impact of peer review on future health practice. In H. Dorken and Associates, *The professional psychologist today.* San Francisco: Jossey-Bass, 1976, 233–252.

Bergin, A. E. The evaluation of therapeutic outcomes. In A. E. Bergin & S. L. Garfield (Eds.), *Handbook of psychotherapy and behavior change: An empirical analysis* (1st ed.). New York: Wiley, 1971.

Bergin, A. E., & Lambert, M. J. The evaluation of therapeutic outcomes. In S. L. Garfield & A. E. Bergin (Eds.), *Handbook of psychotherapy and behavior change: An empirical analysis* (2nd ed.). New York: Wiley, 1978.

Bergin, A. E., & Strupp, H. H. *Changing frontiers in the science of psychotherapy.* Chicago: Aldine-Atherton, 1972.

Bernard, L. D. Education for social work. In J. B. Turner (Ed.), *Encyclopedia of Social Work* (Vol. 1). New York: National Association of Social Workers, 1977. Pp. 290–300.

Bernstein, D. A. Behavioral fear assessment: Anxiety or artifact? In H. Adams & P. Unikel (Eds.), *Issues and trends in behavior therapy.* Springfield, Ill.: Charles C Thomas, 1973.

Bloom, B. L. *Community mental health: A general introduction.* Monterey, Calif.: Brooks/Cole, 1975.

Bockoven, J. S. *Moral treatment in community mental health.* New York: Springer, 1972.

Bordin, E. S. Inside the therapeutic hour. In E. A. Rubenstein & M. B.

Parloff (Eds.), *Research in psychotherapy.* Washington, D.C.: American Psychological Association, 1959.

Brown, B. S. Obstacles to treatment for blue-collar workers. In *New dimensions in mental health.* Washington, D.C.: U.S. Department of Health, Education and Welfare, 1976.

Brown, B. S. *The federal government and psychiatric education: Progress, problems and prospects.* Washington, D.C.: U.S. Government Printing Office, 1977. (DHEW Publication No. [Adm] 77-511.)

Butcher, J. N., & Koss, M. P. Research on brief and crisis oriented psychotherapies. In S. L. Garfield & A. E. Bergin (Eds.), *Handbook of psychotherapy and behavior change: An empirical analysis* (2nd ed.). New York: Wiley, 1978.

Campbell, D. T., & Stanley, J. C. *Experimental and quasi-experimental designs for research.* Chicago: Rand McNally, 1966.

Caplan, G. *Principles of preventive psychiatry.* New York: Basic Books, 1964.

Caplan, G. *The theory and practice of mental health consultation.* New York: Basic Books, 1970.

Carek, D. J. *Principles of child psychotherapy.* Springfield, Ill.: Charles C Thomas, 1972.

Carkhuff, R. R., & Alexik, M. Effect of client depth of self-exploration upon high and low functioning counselors. *Journal of Counseling Psychology,* 1967, *14,* 350–355.

Carkhuff, R. R., & Berenson, B. G. *Beyond counseling and therapy* (2nd ed.). New York: Holt, Rinehart & Winston, 1977.

Carkhuff, R. R., Kratochvil, D., & Friel, T. Effects of professional training: Communication and dissemination of facilitative conditions. *Journal of Counseling Psychology,* 1968, *15,* 68–71.

Chinsky, J. M., & Rappaport, J. Brief critique of meaning and reliability of "accurate empathy" ratings. *Psychological Bulletin,* 1971, *73,* 379–382.

Ciminero, A. R., Calhoun, K. S., & Adams, H. E. (Eds.), *Handbook for behavioral assessment.* New York: Wiley, 1977.

Colby, K. M. *A primer for psychotherapists.* New York: Ronald, 1951.

Craighead, E. W., Kazdin, A. E., & Mahoney, M. J. *Behavior modification: Principles, issues and applications.* Boston: Houghton Mifflin, 1976.

Cummings, N. A. The anatomy of psychotherapy under national health insurance. *American Psychologist,* 1977, *32,* 711–718.

DiLoreto, A. *Comparative psychotherapy: An experimental analysis.* Chicago: Aldine-Atherton, 1971.

Dollard, J., & Miller, N. E. *Personality and psychotherapy.* New York: McGraw-Hill, 1950.

Dorken, H. CHAMPUS ten-state claim experience for mental disorders. In H. Dorken and Associates, *The professional psychologist today.* San Francisco: Jossey-Bass, 1976, 145–164.

Dorken, H., and Associates. *The professional psychologist today.* San

Francisco: Jossey-Bass, 1976.

Dorken, H., & Cummings, N. A. A school of psychology as innovation in professional education: The California School of Professional Psychology. *Professional Psychology*, 1977, *8*, 129–148.

Ellis, A. *Reason and emotion in psychotherapy.* New York: Lyle Stuart, 1962.

Ellis A. Rational-emotive therapy. In V. Binder, A. Binder, & B. Rimland (Eds.), *Modern therapies.* Englewood Cliffs, N.J.: Prentice-Hall, 1976.

Ellsworth, R. B. *Nonprofessionals in psychiatric rehabilitation: The psychiatric aide and the schizophrenic patient.* New York: Appleton-Century-Crofts, 1968.

Ennis, B., & Siegel, L. *The rights of mental patients: An American Civil Liberties Union handbook.* New York: Richard W. Baron, 1973.

Eysenck, H. J. The effects of psychotherapy: An evaluation, *Journal of Consulting Psychology*, 1952, *16*, 319–354.

Fenichel, O. *Problems of psychoanalytic technique.* Albany, N.Y.: *Psychoanalytic Quarterly*, 1941.

Fine, R. Psychoanalysis. In R. Corsini (Ed.), *Current psychotherapies.* Itasca, Ill.: Peacock, 1973, 1–33.

Fisher, E. B., Jr., & Winkler, R. C. Case study: Self-control over intrusive experiences. *Journal of Consulting and Clinical Psychology*, 1975, *43*, 911–916.

Fisher, S., & Greenberg, R. P. *The scientific credibility of Freud's theories and therapy.* New York: Basic Books, 1977.

Ford, D. H., & Urban, H. B. *Systems of psychotherapy.* New York: Wiley, 1963.

Frank, J. D. *Persuasion and healing: A comparative study of psychotherapy.* Baltimore: Johns Hopkins University Press, 1973.

Freud, S. *Therapy and technique.* New York: Collier Books, 1963.

Garfield, S. L. Research on client variables in psychotherapy. In S. L. Garfield & A. E. Bergin (Eds.), *Handbook of psychotherapy and behavior change: An empirical analysis* (2nd ed.). New York: Wiley, 1978.

Garfield, S. L., & Kurtz, R. A study of eclectic views. *Journal of Consulting and Clinical Psychology*, 1977, *45*, 78–83.

Geer, J. A. The development of a scale to measure fear. *Behavior Research and Therapy*, 1965, *3*, 45–53.

Gelder, M. G., Bancroft, J. H. J., Gath, D. H., Johnston, D. W., Matthews, A. M., & Shaw, P. M. Specific and non-specific factors in behavior therapy. *British Journal of Psychiatry*, 1973, *123*, 445–462.

Gendlin, E. T. Experiential psychotherapy. In R. J. Corsini (Ed.), *Current psychotherapies* (2nd ed.). Itasca, Ill.: Peacock, 1979, 340–373.

Glasgow, R. E., & Rosen, G. M. Behavioral bibliotherapy: A review of self-help behavior therapy manuals. *Psychological Bulletin*, 1978, *85*, 1–23.

Goldfried, M. R., & Davison, G. C. *Clinical behavior therapy.* New York: Holt, Rinehart & Winston, 1976.

Goldstein, A. P. *Structured learning therapy.* New York: Academic Press, 1973.

Goldstein, A. P., Heller, K., & Sechrest, L. B. *Psychotherapy and the psychology of behavior change.* New York: Wiley, 1966.

Gordon, T. *PET: Parent effectiveness training.* New York: New American Library, 1975.

Green, H. *I never promised you a rose garden.* New York: Holt, Rinehart & Winston, 1964.

Gross, M. L. *The psychological society.* New York: Random House, 1978.

Gurin, G., Veroff, J., & Feld, S. *Americans view their mental health: A nationwide survey.* New York: Basic Books, 1960.

Hallam, R. S., & Rachman, S. Current status of aversion therapy. In M. Hersen, R. M. Eisler, & P. Miller (Eds.), *Progress in behavior modification* (Vol. 2). New York: Academic Press, 1976.

Hand, I., Lamontagne, Y., & Marks, I. M. Group exposure (flooding) in vivo for agoraphobics. *British Journal of Psychiatry,* 1974, *124,* 588–602.

Harper, R. A. *Psychoanalysis and psychotherapy: 36 systems.* New York: Prentice-Hall, 1959.

Hart, J. T., & Tomlinson, T. M. *New directions in client-centered therapy.* Boston: Houghton Mifflin, 1970.

Harway, N. I., Dittmann, A. T., Rausch, H. L., Bordin, E. S., & Rigler, D. The measurement of depth of interpretation. *Journal of Consulting Psychology,* 1955, *19,* 247–253.

Heber, R., & Garber, H. An experiment in the prevention of cultural-familial mental retardates. In E. Richardson (chairman), *The president's committee on mental retardation.* Washington, D.C.: U.S. Government Printing Office, 1972, 10–13.

Heller, K., & Monahan, J. Psychology and community change. Homewood, Ill.: Dorsey Press, 1977.

Henry, W. E. Personal and social identities of psychotherapists. In A. S. Gurman & A. M. Razin (Eds.), *Effective psychotherapy.* Oxford: Pergamon Press, 1977, 47–62.

Henry, W. E., Sims, J. H., & Spray, S. L. *The fifth profession.* San Francisco: Jossey-Bass, 1971.

Hersen, M., & Barlow, D. H. *Single case experimental designs.* New York: Pergamon Press, 1976.

Hersen, M., & Bellak, A. S. (Eds.). *Behavioral assessment: A practical handbook.* New York: Pergamon Press, 1977.

Holden, C. Nader on mental health centers: A movement that got bogged down. *Science,* 1972, *177,* 413–415.

Holland, G. A. Transactional analysis. In R. J. Corsini (Ed.), *Current psychotherapies.* Itasca, Ill.: Peacock, 1975, 353–400.

Hollingshead, A. G., & Redlich, F. C. *Social class and mental illness: A community study.* New York: Wiley, 1958.

Howard, K. I., & Orlinsky, D. E. Psychotherapeutic processes. In P. Mussen & M. Rosenzweig (Eds.), *Annual Review of Psychology* (Vol. 23). Palo Alto, Calif.: Annual Review, 1972, 615–668.

Hunter, M., Schooler, C., & Spohn, H. E. The measurement of characteristic patterns of ward behavior in chronic schizophrenics. *Journal of Consulting Psychology,* 1962, *26,* 69–73.

Jacobson, E. *Progressive relaxation.* Chicago: University of Chicago Press, 1938.

Johnson, S. M., & Bolstad, O. D. Methodological issues in naturalistic observation: Some problems and solutions for field research. In L. A. Hamerlynck, L. C. Handy, & E. J. Mash (Eds.), *Behavior change: Methodology, concepts and practice.* Champaign, Ill.: Research Press, 1973.

Jones, M. C. The elimination of children's fears. *Journal of Experimental Psychology,* 1924, *7,* 382–390.

Kadushin, C. *Why people go to psychiatrists.* New York: Atherton, 1969.

Katz, A. H., & Bender, E. I. Self-help groups in western society: History and prospects. *Journal of Applied Behavioral Science,* 1976, *12,* 265–282.

Kaufman, Y. Analytic psychotherapy. In R. J. Corsini (Ed.), *Current psychotherapies* (2nd ed.). Itasca, Ill.: Peacock, 1979, 95–130.

Kazdin, A. E. Evaluating the generalizability of findings in analogue therapy research. *Journal of Consulting and Clinical Psychology,* 1978, *46,* 673–686.

Kazdin, A. E., & Wilson, G. T. *Evaluation of behavior therapy: Issues, evidence, and research strategies.* Cambridge, Mass.: Ballinger, 1978.

Kernberg, O. F., Burstein, E. D., Coyne, L., Appelbaum, A., Horowitz, L., & Voth, H. Psychotherapy and psychoanalysis: Final report of the Menninger Foundation Psychotherapy Research Project. *Bulletin of the Menninger Clinic,* 1972, *36,* 1–275.

Kiesler, D. J. *The process of psychotherapy.* Chicago: Aldine, 1973.

Kiesler, D. J., Mathieu, P. L., & Klein, M. H. Sampling from the recorded therapy interview: A comparative study of different segment lengths. *Journal of Consulting Psychology,* 1964, *28,* 349–357.

Kirkpatrick, L. Oregon's new mental commitment statute: The expanded responsibilities of courts and counsel. *Oregon Law Review,* 1974, *53,* 245–272.

Klein, M. H., Mathieu, P. L., Gendlin, E. T., & Kiesler, D. J. *The experiencing scale* (Vol. 2). Madison: Wisconsin Psychiatric Institute, 1970.

Knight, R. P. Evaluation of the results of psychoanalytic therapy. *American Journal of Psychiatry,* 1941, *98,* 434–446.

Koocher, G. P. Advertising for psychologists: Pride and prejudice or sense and sensibility? *Professional Psychology,* 1977, *8,* 149–160.

Kopel, S. A., & Arkowitz, H. The role of attribution and self-perception in behavior change: Implications for behavior therapy. *Genetic Psychology Monographs*, 1975, *92*, 175–212.

Korchin, S. J. *Modern clinical psychology: Principles of intervention in the clinic and community.* New York: Basic Books, 1976.

Lazarus, A. A. *Behavior therapy and beyond.* New York: McGraw-Hill, 1971.

Lehman, H. E. The placebo response and the double-blind study. In P. Hoch & J. Zubin (Eds.), *Evaluation of psychiatric treatment.* New York: Grume & Stratton, 1964.

Leitenberg, H. The use of single-case methodology in psychotherapy research. *Journal of Abnormal Psychology*, 1973, *82*, 87–101.

Leitenberg, H. Behavioral approaches to treatment of neuroses. In H. Leitenberg (Ed.), *Handbook of behavior modification and behavior therapy.* Englewood Cliffs, N.J.: Prentice-Hall, 1976.

Levinson, D. J. *The seasons of a man's life.* New York: Knopf, 1978.

Levitsky, A., & Perls, F. S. The rules and games of Gestalt therapy. In J. Fagan & I. L. Shepherd (Eds.), *Gestalt therapy now.* New York: Harper & Row, 1970, 140–149.

Lewin, K. K. *Brief psychotherapy.* St. Louis: Warren H. Green, 1970.

Lichtenstein, E. Techniques for assessing outcomes of psychotherapy. In P. McReynolds (Ed.), *Advances in psychological assessment* (Vol. 2). Palo Alto, Calif.: Science and Behavior Books, 1971.

Lichtenstein, E., & Danaher, B. G. Modification of smoking behavior: A critical analysis of theory, research, and practice. In M. Hersen, R. M. Eisler, & P. M. Miller (Eds.), *Progress in behavior modification* (Vol. 3). New York: Academic Press, 1976, 79–132.

Lieberman, M. A., & Bond, G. A. The problem of being a woman: A survey of 1,700 women in consciousness-raising groups. *Journal of Applied Behavioral Science*, 1976, *12*, 363–380.

Lindemann, E. Symptomatology and management of acute grief. *American Journal of Psychiatry*, 1944, *101*, 141–148.

London, P. The end of ideology in behavior modification. *American Psychologist*, 1972, *27*, 913–920.

London, P. The psychotherapy boom: From the long couch for the sick to the push button for the bored. *Psychology Today*, June 1974, 63–68.

Lovaas, O. I., & Newsom, C. D. Behavior modification with psychotic children. In H. Leitenberg (Ed.), *Handbook of behavior modification and behavior therapy.* Englewood Cliffs, N.J.: Prentice-Hall, 1976, 303–360.

Lowen, A. *Bioenergetics.* New York: Penguin, 1976.

Luborsky, L. L., Graff, H., Pulver, S., & Curtis, H. A. Clinical-quantative examination of consensus on the concept of transference. *Archives of General Psychiatry*, 1973, *29*, 69–75.

Luborsky, L., Singer, B., & Luborsky, L. Comparative studies of psychotherapies: Is it true that everyone has won and all must have prizes? *Archives of General Psychiatry,* 1975, *32,* 995–1008.

Luborsky, L. L., & Spence, D. P. Quantitative research on psychoanalytic therapy. In S. L. Garfield & A. E. Bergin (Eds.), *Handbook of psychotherapy and behavior change: An empirical analysis.* New York: Wiley, 1978.

Mahoney, M. J. *Cognition and behavior modification.* Cambridge, Mass.: Ballinger, 1974.

Mahoney, M. J. Reflections on the cognitive-learning trend in psychotherapy. *American Psychologist,* 1977, *32,* 5–9.

Mahoney, M. J., Kazdin, A. E., & Lesswing, N. J. Behavior modification: Delusion or deliverance? In C. M. Franks & G. T. Wilson (Eds.), *Annual Review of Behavior Therapy* (Vol. 2). New York: Brunner/Mazel, 1974, 11–40.

Mahoney, M. J., & Thoresen, C. E. *Self-control: Power to the person.* Monterey, Calif.: Brooks/Cole, 1974.

Marks, I. M. *Fears and phobias.* New York: Academic Press, 1969.

Marks, I. M. Management of sexual disorders. In H. Leitenberg (Ed.), *Handbook of behavior modification and behavior therapy.* Englewood Cliffs, N.J.: Prentice-Hall, 1976.

Marks, I. M. Behavioral psychotherapy of adult neuroses. In S. L. Garfield & A. E. Bergin (Eds.), *Handbook of psychotherapy and behavior change: An empirical analysis.* New York: Wiley, 1978.

Marks, I. M., & Gelder, M. G. Transvestism and fetishism: A clinical and psychological change during faradic aversion. *British Journal of Psychiatry,* 1967, *113,* 711–739.

Marmor, J. *Psychiatrists and their patients.* Washington, D.C.: American Psychiatric Association, 1975.

Martin, D. G. *Introduction to psychotherapy.* Monterey, Calif.: Brooks/Cole, 1971.

Masters, W. H., & Johnson, V. *Human sexual inadequacy.* Boston: Little, Brown, 1970.

May, P. R. A. Research in psychotherapy and psychoanalysis. *International Journal of Psychiatry,* 1973, *11,* 78–86.

Meichenbaum, D. *Cognitive-behavior modification.* New York: Plenum, 1977.

Menninger, K. *Theory of psychoanalytic technique.* New York: Basic Books, 1958.

Minuchin, S. *Families and family therapy.* Cambridge, Mass.: Harvard University Press, 1974.

Mischel, W. *Personality and assessment.* New York: Wiley, 1968.

Moore, D. L. The Veterans Administration as a training resource. *The Clinical Psychologist,* 1979, *32,* 4–8.

Moos, R. H. *Evaluating treatment environments.* New York: Wiley, 1974.

Mozak, H. H. Adlerian psychotherapy. In R. J. Corsini (Ed.), *Current psychotherapies* (2nd ed.). Itasca, Ill.: Peacock, 1979, 64–94.

Munroe, R. L. *Schools of psychoanalytic thought.* New York: Dryden Press, 1955.

Nathan, P. E. *Alcoholism.* In H. Leitenberg (Ed.), *Handbook of behavior modification and behavior therapy.* Englewood Cliffs, N.J.: Prentice-Hall, 1976.

National Center for Health Statistics. *Characteristics of patients of selected types of medical specialists and practitioners: United States July 1963–June 1964.* (Public Health Service Publication No. 1000, Series 10, No. 28.) Washington, D.C.: U.S. Government Printing Office, 1966.

O'Leary, K. D., & Borkovec, T. D. Conceptual, methodological and ethical problems of placebo groups in psychotherapy research. *American Psychologist,* 1978, *33,* 821–830.

O'Leary, K. D., & O'Leary, S. G. Behavior modification in the school. In H. Leitenberg (Ed.), *Handbook of behavior modification and behavior therapy.* Englewood Cliffs, N.J.: Prentice-Hall, 1976.

Ozarin, L. D., Redick, R. W., & Taube, C. A. A quarter century of psychiatric care, 1950–1974: A statistical review. *Hospital and Community Psychiatry,* 1976, *27*(7), 515–519.

Park, C. C., & Shapiro, L. N. *You are not alone.* Boston: Little, Brown, in association with Atlantic Monthly Press, 1976.

Parloff, M. B., Waskow, I. E., & Wolfe, B. E. Research on client variables in psychotherapy. In S. L. Garfield & A. E. Bergin (Eds.), *Handbook of psychotherapy and behavior change: An empirical analysis.* New York: Wiley, 1978, 233–282.

Patterson, G. R. Interventions for boys with conduct problems: Multiple settings, treatments, and criteria. *Journal of Consulting and Clinical Psychology,* 1974, *42,* 471–481.

Patterson, G. R., & Reid, J. B. Intervention for families of aggressive boys: A replication study. *Behavior Therapy and Research,* 1973, *11,* 383–394.

Paul, G. L. *Insight vs. desensitization in psychotherapy: An experiment in anxiety reduction.* Stanford, Calif.: Stanford University Press, 1966.

Paul, G. L. The strategy of outcome research in psychotherapy. *Journal of Consulting Psychology,* 1967, *31,* 109–118.

Paul, G. L., & Lentz, R. J. *Psychosocial treatment of chronic mental patients: Milieu versus social-learning programs.* Cambridge, Mass.: Harvard University Press, 1977.

Perls, F. S. *Gestalt therapy verbatim.* Lafayette, Calif.: Real People Press, 1969.

Perls, F. S. Four lectures. In J. Fagan & I. L. Shepherd (Eds.), *Gestalt therapy now.* New York: Harper & Row, 1971.

Perls, F. S. *The Gestalt approach and eyewitness to therapy.* Palo Alto, Calif.: Science and Behavior Books, 1973.

Polster, E., & Polster, M. *Gestalt therapy integrated.* New York: Random House, 1973.

President's Commission on Mental Health. *Report to the President.* Washington, D.C.: U.S. Government Printing Office, 1978.

Reinehr, R. C. *The machine that oils itself.* Chicago: Nelson-Hall, 1975.

Richards, J. A., & Gottfredson, G. D. Geographic distribution of U.S. psychologists: A human ecological analysis. *American Psychologist,* 1978, *33,* 1–9.

Rioch, M. J. Pilot projects in training mental health counselors. In E. L. Cowen, E. A. Gardner, & M. Zax (Eds.), *Emergent approaches to mental health problems.* New York: Appleton-Century-Crofts, 1967.

Robbins, L. L., & Wallerstein, R. S. The research strategy and tactics of the psychotherapy research project of the Menninger Foundation and the problem of controls. In E. A. Rubinstein & M. B. Parloff (Eds.), *Research in psychotherapy.* Washington, D.C.: American Psychological Association, 1959.

Rogers, C. R. *Counseling and psychotherapy.* Boston: Houghton Mifflin, 1942.

Rogers, C. R. *Client centered therapy.* Boston: Houghton Mifflin, 1951.

Rogers, C. R. A theory of therapy, personality and interpersonal relationships as developed in the client-centered framework. In S. Koch (Ed.), *Psychology: A study of a science* (Vol. 3). New York: McGraw-Hill, 1959, 184–256.

Rogers, C. R. *On becoming a person.* Boston: Houghton Mifflin, 1961.

Rogers, C. R. Psychotherapy today or where do we go from here? In G. E. Stollak, B. G. Guerney, & M. Rothberg (Eds.), *Psychotherapy research: Selected readings.* Chicago: Rand McNally, 1966.

Rogers, C. R., & Dymond, R. F. *Psychotherapy and personality change.* Chicago: University of Chicago Press, 1954.

Rogers, C. R., Gendlin, E. T., Kiesler, D. J., & Truax, C B. (Eds.), *The therapeutic relationship and its impact: A study of psychotherapy with schizophrenics.* Madison: University of Wisconsin Press, 1967.

Rosen, G. M. The development and use of nonprescription behavior therapies. *American Psychologist,* 1976, *31,* 139–141.

Rosenhan, D. L. On being sane in insane places. *Science,* 1973, *179,* 250–258.

Rosenthal, T., & Bandura, A. Psychological modeling: Theory and practice. In S. L. Garfield & A. E. Bergin (Eds.), *Handbook of psychotherapy and behavior change: An empirical analysis.* New York: Wiley, 1978.

Ryan, W. (Ed.). *Distress in the city.* Cleveland: Case Western Reserve University Press, 1969.

Schaffer, J. B. P., & Galinsky, M. D. *Models of group therapy and sensitivity training.* Englewood Cliffs, N.J.: Prentice-Hall, 1974.

Schofield, W. *Psychotherapy: The purchase of friendship.* Englewood Cliffs, N.J.: Prentice-Hall, 1964.

Shah, S. A. Dangerousness: A paradigm for exploring some issues in law and psychology. *American Psychologist,* 1978, *33,* 224–238.

Shapiro, A. K., & Morris, L. A. Placebo effects in medical and psychological therapies. In. S. L. Garfield & A. E. Bergin (Eds.), *Handbook of psychotherapy and behavior change: An empirical analysis* (2nd ed.). New York: Wiley, 1978.

Shepherd, I. L. Limitations and cautions in the Gestalt approach. In J. Fagan & I. L. Shepherd (Eds.), *Gestalt therapy now.* New York: Harper & Row, 1970, 234–238.

Shlien, J. M. Comparison of results with different forms of psychotherapy. *American Journal of Psychotherapy,* 1964, *18* Suppl. 1, 15–22.

Skinner, B. F. *Science and human behavior.* New York: Macmillan, 1953.

Sloane, R. B., Staples, F. R., Cristol, A. H., Yorkston, N. J., & Whipple, K. *Psychotherapy versus behavior therapy.* Cambridge, Mass.: Harvard University Press, 1975.

Smith, M. L., & Glass, G. V. Meta-analysis of psychotherapy outcome studies. *American Psychologist,* 1977, *32,* 752–760.

Social Action Research Center. *Paraprofessionals in mental health.* Berkeley, Calif.: Author, 1978.

Solomon, R. L., Kamin, L. J., & Wynne, L. C. Traumatic avoidance learning: The outcomes of several extinction procedures with dogs. *Journal of Abnormal and Social Psychology,* 1953, *48,* 291–302.

Speisman, J. Depth of interpretation and verbal resistance in psychotherapy. *Journal of Consulting Psychology,* 1959, *23,* 93–99.

Stahl, J. R., & Leitenberg, H. Behavioral treatment of the chronic mental patient. In H. Leitenberg (Ed.), *Handbook of behavior modification and behavior therapy.* Englewood Cliffs, N.J.: Prentice-Hall, 1976, 211–241.

Stampfl, T. G., & Levis, D. J. Essentials of implosive therapy: A learning-theory-based psychodynamic behavioral therapy. *Journal of Abnormal Psychology,* 1967, *72,* 495–503.

Storms, L. H. Implosive therapy: An alternative to systematic desensitization. In V. Binder, A. Binder, & B. Rimland (Eds.), *Modern therapies.* Englewood Cliffs, N.J.: Prentice-Hall, 1976.

Stuart, R. B. Behavioral control of overeating. *Behavior Research and Therapy,* 1967, *5,* 357–365.

Stunkard, A. J., & Mahoney, M. J. Behavioral treatment of the eating disorders. In H. Leitenberg (Ed.), *Handbook of behavior modification and behavior therapy.* Englewood Cliffs, N.J.: Prentice-Hall, 1976.

Swoboda, J. S., Elwork, A., Sales, B. D., & Levine, D. Knowledge of and compliance with privileged communication and child-abuse reporting laws. *Professional Psychology,* 1978, *9,* 448–457.

Tarasoff vs. *Regents of University of California,* 529 P.2d 553.118 Cal. Reptr. 129 (1974).

Taylor, B. J., & Wagner, N. N. Sex between therapists and clients: A review and analysis. *Professional Psychology*, 1976, 7, 593–601.

Tharpe, R. G., & Wetzel, R. J. *Behavior modification in the natural environment.* New York: Academic Press, 1969.

Thoresen, C. E., & Mahoney, M. J. *Behavioral self-control.* New York: Holt, Rinehart & Winston, 1974.

Torrey, E. F. *The mind game: Witchdoctors and psychiatrists.* New York: Bantam Books, 1972.

Truax, C. B. Reinforcement and nonreinforcement in Rogerian psychotherapy. *Journal of Abnormal Psychology*, 1966, 71, 1–9.

Truax, C. B., & Carkhuff, R. R. The experimental manipulation of therapeutic conditions. *Journal of Consulting Psychology*, 1965, 29, 119–124.

Truax, C. B., & Mitchell, K. M. Research on certain therapist interpersonal skills in relation to process and outcome. In A. E. Bergin & S. L. Garfield (Eds.), *Handbook of psychotherapy and behavior change: An empirical analysis.* New York: Wiley, 1971.

Ullmann, L. P. *Institution and outcome: A comparative study of psychiatric hospitals.* New York: Pergamon Press, 1967.

U.S. Department of Commerce. *Statistical abstract of the United States.* Washington, D.C.: Author, 1976.

U.S. Veterans Administration. *Annual report—Administrator of Veterans' Affairs.* Washington, D.C.: U.S. Government Printing Office, 1976.

Wahler, R. G. Deviant child behavior within the family: Developmental speculation and behavior change strategies. In H. Leitenberg (Ed.), *Handbook of behavior modification and behavior therapy.* Englewood Cliffs, N.J.: Prentice-Hall, 1976, 516–546.

Wallach, S. A constitutional right to treatment: Past, present, and future. *Professional Psychology*, 1976, 7, 453–467.

Wallen, R. Gestalt therapy and Gestalt psychology. In J. Fagan & I. L. Shepherd (Eds.), *Gestalt therapy now.* New York: Harper & Row, 1970, 8–13.

Walters, H., & Gilmore, S. K. Placebo versus social learning effects in parent training procedures designed to alter the behaviors of aggressive boys. *Behavior Research and Therapy*, 1973, 4, 361–377.

Wanderer, Z. W. Existential depression treated by desensitization of phobias: Strategies and transcript. *Journal of Behavior Therapy and Experimental Psychiatry*, 1972, 3, 111–116.

Watson, J. B., & Raynor, R. Conditioned emotional reactions. *Journal of Experimental Psychology*, 1920, 3, 1–14.

Watson, J. P., Gaind, R., & Marks, I. M. Prolonged exposure: A rapid treatment for phobias. *British Medical Journal*, 1971, 1, 13–15.

Werry, J., & Quay, H. Observing the classroom behavior of elementary school children. *Exceptional Children*, 1969, 35, 461–470.

Wexler, D. B. Token and taboo: Behavior modification, token economies and the law. *California Law Review*, 1973, 61, 81–109.

Wiener, D. N. *A consumer's guide to psychotherapy.* New York: Hawthorn Books, 1975.

Wiggins, J. S. *Personality and prediction: Principles of personality assessment.* Reading, Mass.: Addison-Wesley, 1973.

Wiltz, N. A., Jr., & Patterson, G. R. An evaluation of parent training procedures designed to alter inappropriate aggressive behavior of boys. *Behavior Therapy,* 1974, *5,* 515–521.

Wolf, S. Effects of suggestion and conditioning on the action of chemical agents in human subjects—The pharmacology of placebos. *Journal of Clinical Investigation,* 1950, *29,* 100–109.

Wolpe, J. *Psychotherapy by reciprocal inhibition.* Stanford, Calif.: Stanford University Press, 1958.

Wolpe, J., & Lazarus, A. A. *Behavior therapy techniques.* New York: Pergamon Press, 1966.

Wyatt vs. Stickney, 344 F.Supp.373 387 (M.D.Ala.1972) Aff'd in part, modified in part sub. nom. *Wyatt vs. Aderholt,* 505 F.2d 1305 (5th Cir. 1974).

Yontef, G. M. Gestalt therapy: Clinical phenomenology. In V. Binder, A. Binder, & B. Rimland (Eds.), *Modern therapies.* Englewood Cliffs, N.J.: Prentice-Hall, 1976.

Zeiss, R. A. Self-treatment for premature ejaculation. *Journal of Consulting and Clinical Psychology,* 1978, *46,* 1234–1241.

Name Index

Adams, H. E., 186
Adams, S., 239, 297–299
Adler, A., 158, 334, 337
Albee, G. W., 26, 289
Alexander, F., 116, 121, 234
Alexik, M., 155
Allen, K. E., 87
Ansbacher, H. H., 337
Ansbacher, R., 337
Anthony, W. A., 26
Applebaum, A., 126
Arkowitz, H., 197, 183
Axline, B. M., 204
Ayllon, T., 201–202
Azrin, N. H., 201–202

Baer, D. M., 89
Bancroft, J. H. S., 199
Bandura, A., 157, 179, 183, 188,
    197–199, 212, 233
Barlow, D. H., 86, 97
Barton, E. S., 89
Beck, A., 31
Bender, E. I., 319
Bent, R., 295
Berenson, B. G., 138, 159
Bergin, A. E., 8, 61, 66, 80, 130,
    227–229, 271
Bernard, L. D., 17
Berne, R., 339
Bernstein, D. A., 72
Blanchard, E. B., 197, 198
Bloom, B. L., 30, 262–264, 269,
    320–321

Bockoven, J. S., 6, 253, 261
Bolstad, O. D., 72
Bond, G. A., 319
Bordin, E. S., 124–125
Borkovec, T. D., 84
Brown, B. S., 13, 33, 309, 313–315,
    349
Buell, J. S., 87
Burstein, E. D., 126
Butcher, J. N., 246

Calhous, K. S., 186
Campbell, D. T., 75, 94, 97
Caplan, G., 115, 320
Carek, D. J., 204
Carkhuff, R. R., 26, 138, 154–155, 159
Chinsky, J. M., 65, 156
Ciminero, A. R., 186
Colby, K. M., 108, 110–111, 114, 134
Coyne, L., 126
Cozby, P. C., 97
Craighead, W. E., 179
Cristol, A. H., 131, 222
Cummings, N. A., 266, 311
Curtis, H. A., 65, 130

Danaher, B. G., 211, 222
Davison, G. C., 186–187, 233
DiLoreto, A., 215
Dittmann, A. T., 124
Dollard, J., 178
Dorken, H., 16, 266, 281
Dreikurs, R., 334
Dymond, R. F., 149, 151

Ellis, A., 176, 212, 214, 291
Ellsworth, R. B., 252
Ennis, B., 273
Eysenck, H. J., 67, 80, 130

Feld, S., 24, 81, 309
Fisher, E. B., 216, 219
Fisher, S., 65, 130–131
Foley, V., 332
Frank, J. D., 5, 10, 20, 33, 42, 53, 56,
    60–61, 66, 92, 157, 252, 254, 333
Frankl, V. E., 343
French, T. M., 116, 121
Freud, S., 6, 66, 108, 112–113, 116,
    122–123, 132, 134
Friel, T., 159

Gaind, R., 196
Galinsky, M. D., 47, 333
Garber, H., 322
Garcia, E., 89
Garfield, S. L., 22, 61, 100, 246
Gath, D. H., 199
Geer, J. A., 186
Gelder, M. G., 199, 210
Gendlin, E. T., 69, 138, 142, 147–148,
    159, 176
Gilmore, S. K., 208
Glasgow, R., 318
Glass, G. V., 229
Glasser, W., 344–345
Goldfried, M. R., 186–187, 213, 233
Goldstein, A. P., 34
Gordon, T., 159
Graff, H., 65, 130
Green, H., 250, 254
Greenberg, R. P., 31, 65, 130–131
Gross, M. L., 10, 19, 29, 308
Guess, D., 89
Gurin, G., 24, 33, 81, 309

Hallam, R. S., 210
Hand, I., 196
Harper, R. A., 41, 340
Harris, F. Q., 87
Harris, T. A., 337, 339
Hart, J. T., 87, 138
Harway, N. I., 124
Heber, R., 322
Heller, K., 30, 309, 316, 320–321, 328
Henry, W. E., 11, 22–23
Hersen, M., 86, 97
Hogan, D. B., 306
Holden, C., 34
Holland, G. A., 339
Horney, K., 334

Horwitz, L., 126
Howard, K. I., 22, 31, 34
Hunter, M., 201

Jacobson, E., 191
Janov, A., 341–342
Johnson, S. M., 72
Johnson, V., 91–93, 97, 194
Johnston, D. W., 199
Jones, M. C., 178, 190
Jung, C., 334–335

Kadushin, C., 33
Kamin, L. J., 195
Katz, A. H., 319
Kaufman, Y., 335
Kazdin, A. E., 94, 179, 220, 230
Kernberg, O. F., 126–128
Kessler, M., 289
Kiesler, D. J., 69, 93, 138, 142,
    147–148, 152, 176
Kirkpatrick, L., 276–277
Klein, M. H., 147–148, 152
Knight, R., 130
Koocher, G. P., 297, 301
Kopel, S. A., 179, 183
Korchin, S. J., 136, 137, 223, 226, 287
Koss, M. P., 246
Kratochvil, D., 159
Kurtz, R. A., 22, 100

Lambert, J. J., 66, 80, 130, 228, 271
Lamontagne, Y., 196
Lazarus, A. A., 191, 193, 233
Lehman, H. E., 57
Leitenberg, H., 86, 88, 193, 201,
    203, 233
Lentz, R. J., 202–203, 253, 259, 260
Lesswing, N. J., 220
Levinson, D. J., 334
Levis, D. J., 196
Levitsky, A., 163, 167
Lewin, K. K., 105, 115
Lichtenstein, E., 70–71, 97, 211, 222
Lieberman, M. A., 319
Lieberman, R., 332
Lindemann, E., 115
London, P., 307–308, 328
Lovaas, O. I., 210
Lowen, A., 65, 340, 341
Luborsky, Lester, 65, 122–123, 130,
    134, 228–229
Luborsky, Lise, 228–229

Mahoney, M. J., 179, 211, 215–216,
    220, 222

Marks, I., 31, 93, 196, 210
Marmor, J., 245–246
Martin, D. G., 156
Masters, W., 91–93, 97, 194
Mathieu, P. L., 147–148, 152
Matthews, D. W., 199
McCrady, B. S., 331
Meichenbaum, D., 212, 215, 222
Menninger, K., 107, 114–115
Miller, N. E., 178
Minuchin, S., 204, 332
Mischel, W., 21
Mitchell, K. M., 141–142, 157, 159
Monahan, J., 30, 309, 316, 320–321, 328
Moore, D. L., 247
Moos, R. H., 255, 257, 259
Morris, L. A., 57, 61
Mozak, H. H., 335–337
Munroe, R. L., 9

Nathan, P. E., 211, 222
Newsom, C. D., 210

O'Leary, K. D., 84, 206
O'Leary, S. G., 206
Orgel, M., 239, 297–299
Orlinsky, D. E., 22, 31, 34
Ozarin, L. D., 29

Paolino, T. J., 331
Park, C. C., 254, 265–266, 273–275, 277, 300, 304, 306
Parloff, M. B., 94, 158
Patterson, G. R., 206–208, 233
Paul, G. L., 68, 86, 193, 202, 259–260
Perls, F. S., 65, 137, 160, 162–165, 167–170, 176
Polster, E., 137, 171
Polster, M., 137, 171
Pulver, S., 65, 130

Quay, H., 31

Rachman, S., 210
Rank, O., 334
Rappaport, J., 65, 156
Rausch, H. L., 124
Rayner, R., 188
Redick, R. W., 29
Redlich, F. C., 30
Reich, W., 340
Reid, J. B., 206
Reinehr, R. C., 253, 270
Rigler, D., 124
Rioch, M. J., 132

Ritter, B., 197–198
Robbins, L. L., 101
Rogers, C. R., 41, 65, 69, 73, 138–146, 149, 151–152, 156–158, 176
Rosen, G. M., 318
Rosenhan, D. L., 255–256, 270
Rosenthal, T., 197–198
Ryan, W., 30–31

Schofield, W., 21, 23, 320
Schooler, C., 201
Shaffer, J. B. P., 47, 333, 343
Shah, S. A., 274
Shapiro, A. K., 57, 61
Shapiro, L. N., 254, 265–266, 273–275, 277, 300, 304, 306
Shaw, P. M., 199
Shepherd, I. L., 173
Shlien, J. M., 158
Siegel, L., 273
Simpkins, J., 176
Sims, J. H., 11
Singer, B., 229
Skinner, B. F., 178, 199
Sloane, R. B., 131, 222
Smith, M. L., 229
Solomon, R. L., 195
Speisman, J., 123–125, 126, 127
Spence, D. P., 122–123, 134
Spohn, H. E., 201
Spray, S. L., 11
Stahl, J. R., 201, 203
Stampfl, T. G., 196
Stanley, J. C., 75, 94, 97
Staples, F. R., 131, 222
Storms, L. H., 196
Strupp, H. H., 8
Stuart, R. B., 216
Stunkard, A. J., 206, 222
Sullivan, H. S., 334

Taube, C. A., 29
Taylor, B. J., 271
Tharpe, R. G., 221
Thoresen, C. E., 212, 215
Tomlinson, T. M., 138
Torrey, E. F., 52, 62
Truax, C. B., 69, 89, 123, 138, 141–142, 154–155, 157, 159, 176

Ullman, L. P., 251

Veroff, J., 24, 81, 309
Voth, H., 126

Wagner, N. N., 271
Wahler, R. G., 205–206, 211

Wallach, S. A., 203, 279
Wallen, R., 160
Wallerstein, R. S., 101
Walters, H., 208
Wanderer, Z., 50
Waskow, I. E., 94, 158
Watson, J. P., 196
Werry, J., 31
Wetzel, R. J., 221
Wexler, D. B., 203
Whipple, K., 131, 222
Wiener, D. N., 300, 304
Wiggins, J. S., 21

Wilson, G. T., 230
Winkler, R. C., 216, 219
Wolf, M. W., 87
Wolfe, B. E., 94, 158
Wolpe, J., 47, 178, 188–189, 191, 217
Wynne, L. C., 195

Yontef, G. M., 162
Yorkston, N. J., 131, 222

Zeiss, R. A., 318
Zunin, L. M., 344–345

Subject Index

ABPP, 286–287
Adlerian therapy, 335–337
Advertising, 300–301
American Medical Association, 284, 293
American Psychological Association, 17, 37, 293–294
Analogue research, 94

Behavior therapy:
  anxiety treatment, 47–50, 188–199
  assessment, 183–187
  assumptions, 179–182
  aversion, 208–211
  case illustration, 47–50, 216–220
  with children, 203–208
  with chronic mental patients, 200–203
  cognitive, 211, 215
  comparative analysis, 223–226
  desensitization, 47–50, 189–194, 199
  evaluation, 220–231
  flooding, 194–197, 199
  goals, 183
  implosion (see flooding)
  modeling, 197–199
  operant methods, 199–208
  relaxation training, 47–50, 191–192
  research, 192–193, 196–199, 201–202, 206–208
  self-control, 215–216, 219
  time out, 205

Behavior therapy (continued)
  token economy, 201–203
Bioenergetics, 340–341
Body therapies, 339–340
Box-score evaluation, 226–230

Certification, 280–283
Choosing a therapist, 301–304
Citizen involvement, 324–326
Clergy as therapist, 24–25
Client-centered therapy:
  case example, 149–151
  congruence (see genuineness)
  empathy, 144–151
  evaluation, 155–159
  experiencing, 145–148
  genuineness, 140–142
  personality theory, 138–140
  process (see experiencing)
  regard, unconditional positive, 142–143
  research, 152–155
Clients:
  age and sex, 30–31
  in community, 28–29
  compatibility with therapists, 34–35
  growth seeking, 29–30
  in hospital, 28
  paths to becoming, 32–34
  social class, 30, 308–310
Commitment, involuntary, 273–277
Common processes, 52–60, 92–93, 171–172, 222–223

Common processes *(continued)*
   and placebos, 56–60
   and specific processes, 52–53
Community mental health centers,
   262–265, 310–311
Confidentiality, 284–285
Consumerism, 296–301
Continuing education, 288–292
Contracts, 298–300
Control groups *(see* Rival
   hypotheses)
Counseling, 4 *(see also*
   Psychotherapy)

Demoralization, 33
Dream interpretation, 44, 112–114,
   165, 168–169
Duration of therapy, 245–246

Ethics, 292–294
Evaluative criteria of therapy:
   cost-effectiveness, 66–67, 131–132,
      158, 172, 220–221, 230
   outcome, 67–89, 130–131, 157–158,
      171–172, 221–223, 226–231
   quality of theory, 64–66, 129–130,
      155–157, 170–171, 220, 230
Existential therapy, 342–344
External validity, 94–95

Family therapy, 203–204, 331–332
Fees, 239, 241, 265–266

Gestalt therapy:
   assumptions and definitions,
      160–162
   case example, 168–170
   dream work, 165, 168–169
   evaluation, 170–173
   games and exercises, 166–167
   ground rules, 166
   strategies, 162–166
Group designs *(see* Rival hypotheses)
Group therapy, 167–168, 332–333

Health insurance, 265–266, 311–312
Health-Sickness Rating Scale, 129
Humanistic therapy:
   assumptions, 136–138
   case illustration, 45–47
   comparative analysis, 223–226
Hypnosis, 345–346

Institutes, 20, 291–292
Internal validity, 94–95 *(see also*
   Rival hypotheses)

Jungian therapy, 334–335

Licensing, 280–283

Marital therapy, 330–331
Masters and Johnson sexual therapy
   (see Sexual therapy)
Mendota Project, 152–154
Menninger psychotherapy research
   projects, 125–129
Mental health system, state, 260–262
Mental hospitals, 200–201, 251–260
   (see also Psychotherapy settings)
Milieu therapy, 253
Multiple-baseline design, 89

NIMH, 262–263
Nonprofessional *(see*
   Paraprofessionals)
Nonspecific processes *(see* Common
   processes)

Outcome research *(see also* Rival
   hypotheses):
   box-score approach, 226–230
   complexities, 68–74
   dependent variable, 70–74
   independent variable, 68–69
   meta-analysis, 229–230
   subjects, 69–70

Paraprofessionals, 25–28, 316–317
Patient rights, 202–203, 273–280
Patients *(see* Clients)
Peer review, 295–296
Placebos, 56–60 *(see also* Common
   processes)
President's Commission on Mental
   Health, 265, 310, 315, 328
Prevention of disorder, 319–323
Primal therapy, 341–342
Private practice *(see* Psychotherapy
   settings)
Privileged communication, 284–285
Process research, 93–94, 123–125
Professional rivalry, 267
Psychiatric social work, 7, 17–18, 37
Psychiatry, 6–7, 11–14
Psychoanalysis, 18–20
Psychoanalytic psychotherapy:
   case example, 42–45, 116–122
   comparative analysis, 223–226
   dream interpretation, 112–114
   evaluation, 129–132
   free association, 105–106
   insight, 114–115

Psychoanalytic psychotherapy
      (continued)
   interpretation, 109–112
   and psychoanalysis, 103–104, 115
   regression, 107
   research, 122–129
   resistance, 106
   transference, 107–108
   working through, 114
Psychology, profession, 14–17
Psychotherapists:
   compatibility with clients, 34–35
   invisible, 23–25
   maldistribution, 314–315
   paraprofessional, 25–28
   personal qualities, 22–23
   professional differentiation and
      overlap, 20–22
   training, 11–20
   training subsidies, 312–316
Psychotherapy:
   and counseling, 4
   definition, 5
   history of, 5–10
Psychotherapy settings:
   private hospitals, 249–251
   private practice, 239–241
   public agencies, 241–245
   state hospitals, 248–249

Psychotherapy settings *(continued)*
   VA hospitals, 247–248

Rational-emotive therapy, 212–215
Reactivity, 79
Reality therapy, 344–345
Reversal design, 86–88
Rival hypotheses, 74–82
   and clinical trials, 90
   and group designs, 82–86
   and single-case designs, 86–89

Self-help books, 318–319
Self-help groups, 319
Sexual therapy, 91–93
Social Action Research Center, 316
Spontaneous remission, 80–81
Statistical regression, 77

Third-party payment, 265–266 *(see
   also* Health insurance)
Transactional analysis (TA), 337–339
Transformational groups, 317–318

Ward Atmosphere Scales, 257–259
Witchdoctor, as psychotherapist,
   51–52

YAVIS, 31, 34